D0985195

Listen At Home
With
Octopus Pie

Meredith Gran

Copyright © 2011 by Meredith Gran.

Printed in Canada

ISBN 978-0-9818600-4-6

www.octopuspie.com

Designed by Meredith Gran and Richard Stevens

This book is dedicated, none too smirkingly, to the fans of Octopus Pie who financed its publication through pre-orders. The comic has seen a lot of changes over the years, yet the fans endure. Thanks so much for making these books possible.

As with all of my books, thanks are due to Rich Stevens, who keeps me sane and makes sure the pages are laid out and designed coherently, and not just a mashed-together booklet full of butts. He is very good at it.

Exile On Jericho Turnpike

I grew up in a commuter town on Long Island where this story takes place, and I hold diner culture particularly close to my heart. They were a staple for my family at birthdays and holidays, particularly with grandparents. The place Eve goes with her family is called the Triple Crown Diner in Bellerose, NY, off of Jericho Turnpike. I remember the pot roast being pretty good.

Some readers have said that Eve's father looks surprisingly old in this story. I drew him as somewhat of a projection of Eve's fears, that her loved ones are ailing and supposedly neglected. She notices every limp in her father's step, every weakness in his mind and body, and I attempted to show that in his appearance.

Eve's inability to have a lasting impact on her family is, in a way, a tribute to my own. With each passing year away from home, the plight of loved ones seems more urgent. Giving up on family feels reckless; persisting can seem cruel and futile. It's difficult to face that reality without feeling a bit numb.

Eve's friend Bert first appeared in "Renaissance Unfair" as Will's nemesis. He was a spoiled jerk, and now he's just a jerk.

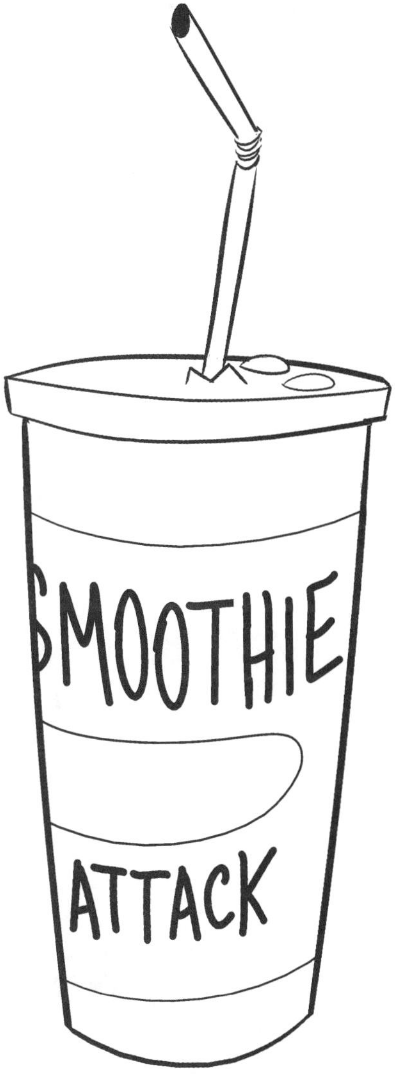
SMOOTHIE
ATTACK

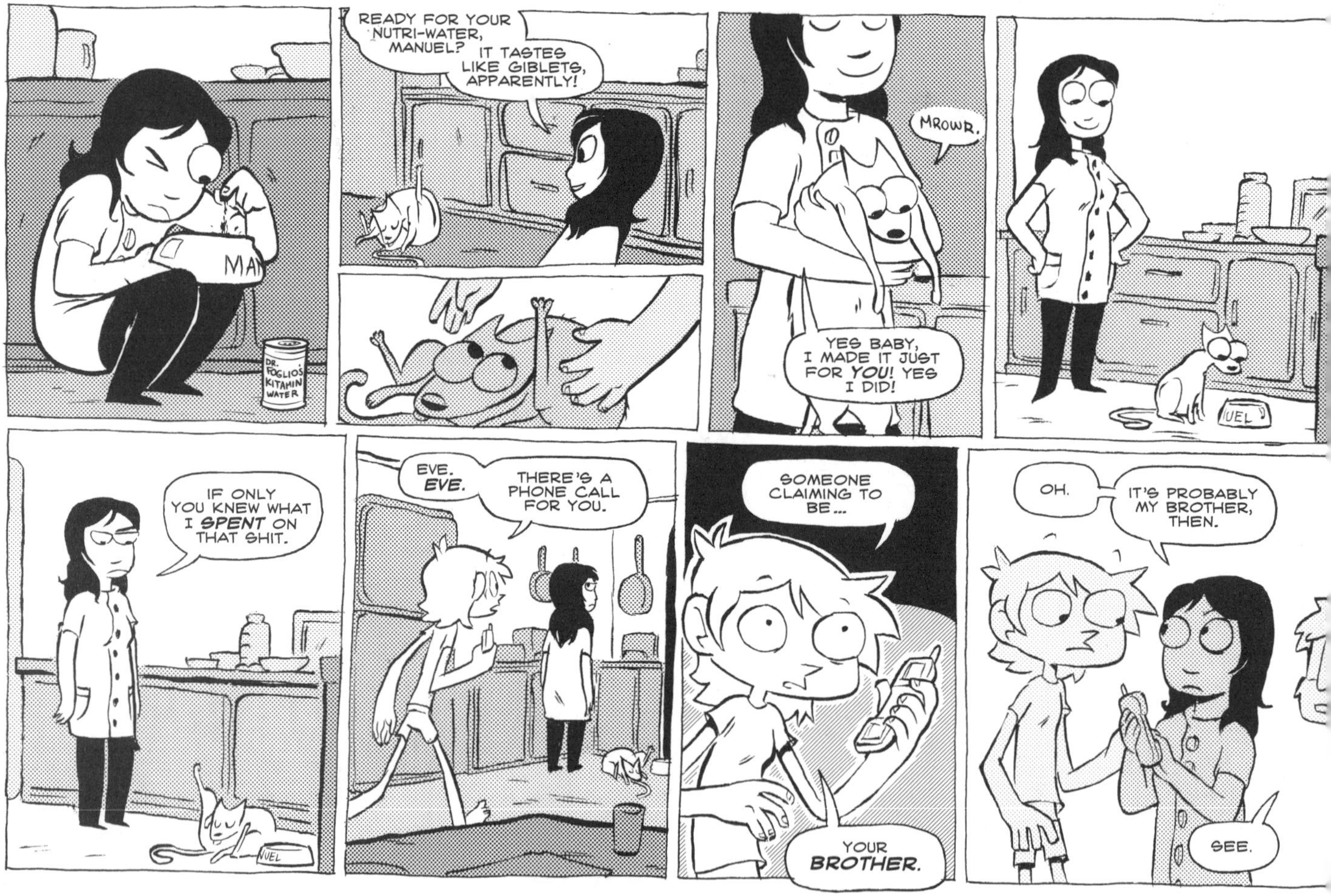
MA
DR. FOGLIO'S KITAMIN WATER
READY FOR YOUR NUTRI-WATER, MANUEL?
IT TASTES LIKE GIBLETS, APPARENTLY!
MROWR.
YES BABY, I MADE IT JUST FOR *YOU*! YES I DID!
UEL
IF ONLY YOU KNEW WHAT I *SPENT* ON THAT SHIT.
NUEL
EVE. ***EVE.***
THERE'S A PHONE CALL FOR YOU.
SOMEONE CLAIMING TO BE...
YOUR **BROTHER.**
OH.
IT'S PROBABLY MY BROTHER, THEN.
SEE.

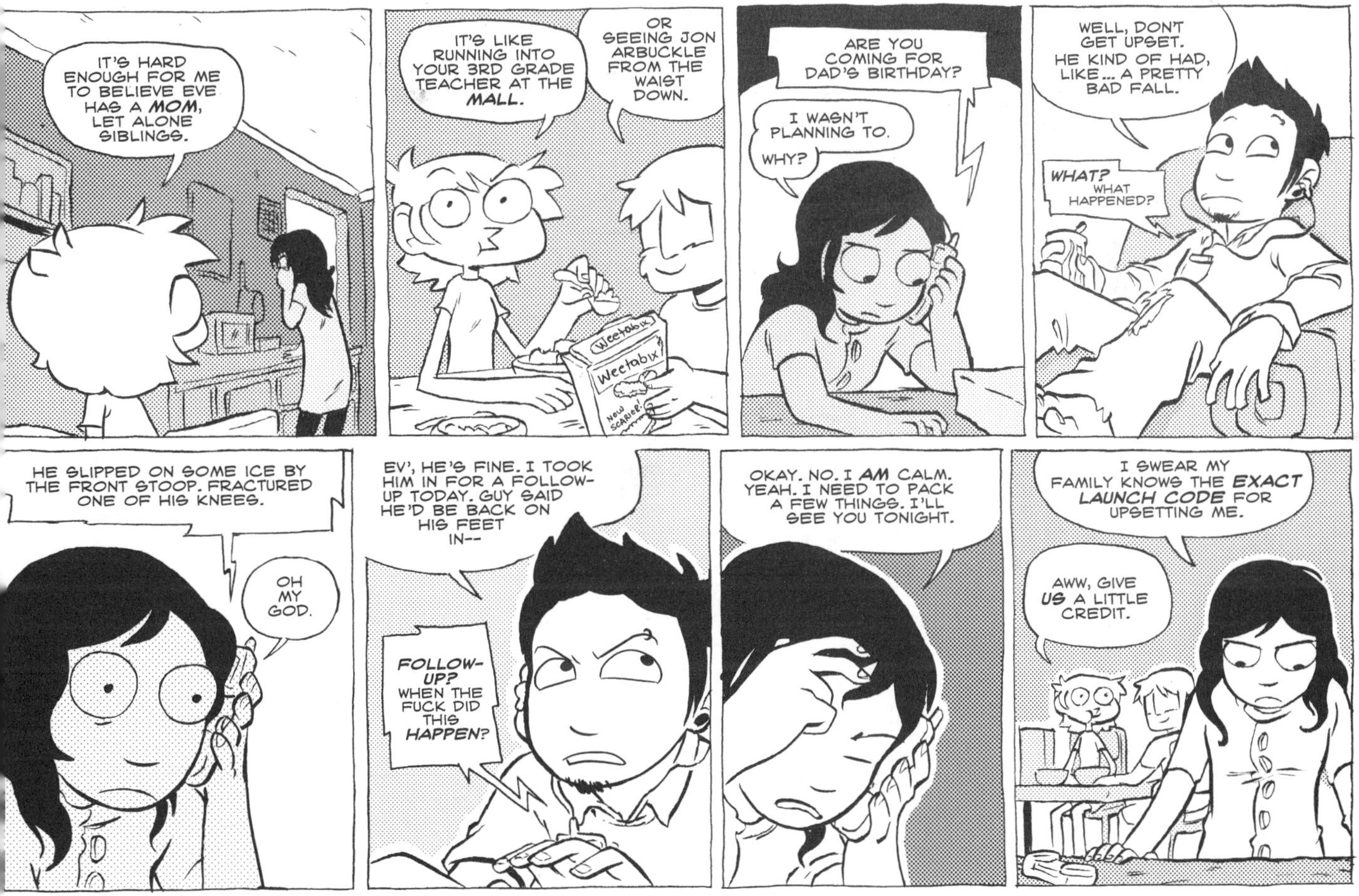
IT'S HARD ENOUGH FOR ME TO BELIEVE EVE HAS A MOM, LET ALONE SIBLINGS.
IT'S LIKE RUNNING INTO YOUR 3RD GRADE TEACHER AT THE MALL.
OR SEEING JON ARBUCKLE FROM THE WAIST DOWN.
Weetabix
Weetabix
NEW SCARIER!
ARE YOU COMING FOR DAD'S BIRTHDAY?
I WASN'T PLANNING TO.
WHY?
WELL, DON'T GET UPSET. HE KIND OF HAD, LIKE... A PRETTY BAD FALL.
WHAT? WHAT HAPPENED?
HE SLIPPED ON SOME ICE BY THE FRONT STOOP. FRACTURED ONE OF HIS KNEES.
OH MY GOD.
EV', HE'S FINE. I TOOK HIM IN FOR A FOLLOW-UP TODAY. GUY SAID HE'D BE BACK ON HIS FEET IN--
FOLLOW-UP? WHEN THE FUCK DID THIS HAPPEN?
OKAY. NO. I AM CALM. YEAH. I NEED TO PACK A FEW THINGS. I'LL SEE YOU TONIGHT.
I SWEAR MY FAMILY KNOWS THE EXACT LAUNCH CODE FOR UPSETTING ME.
AWW, GIVE US A LITTLE CREDIT.

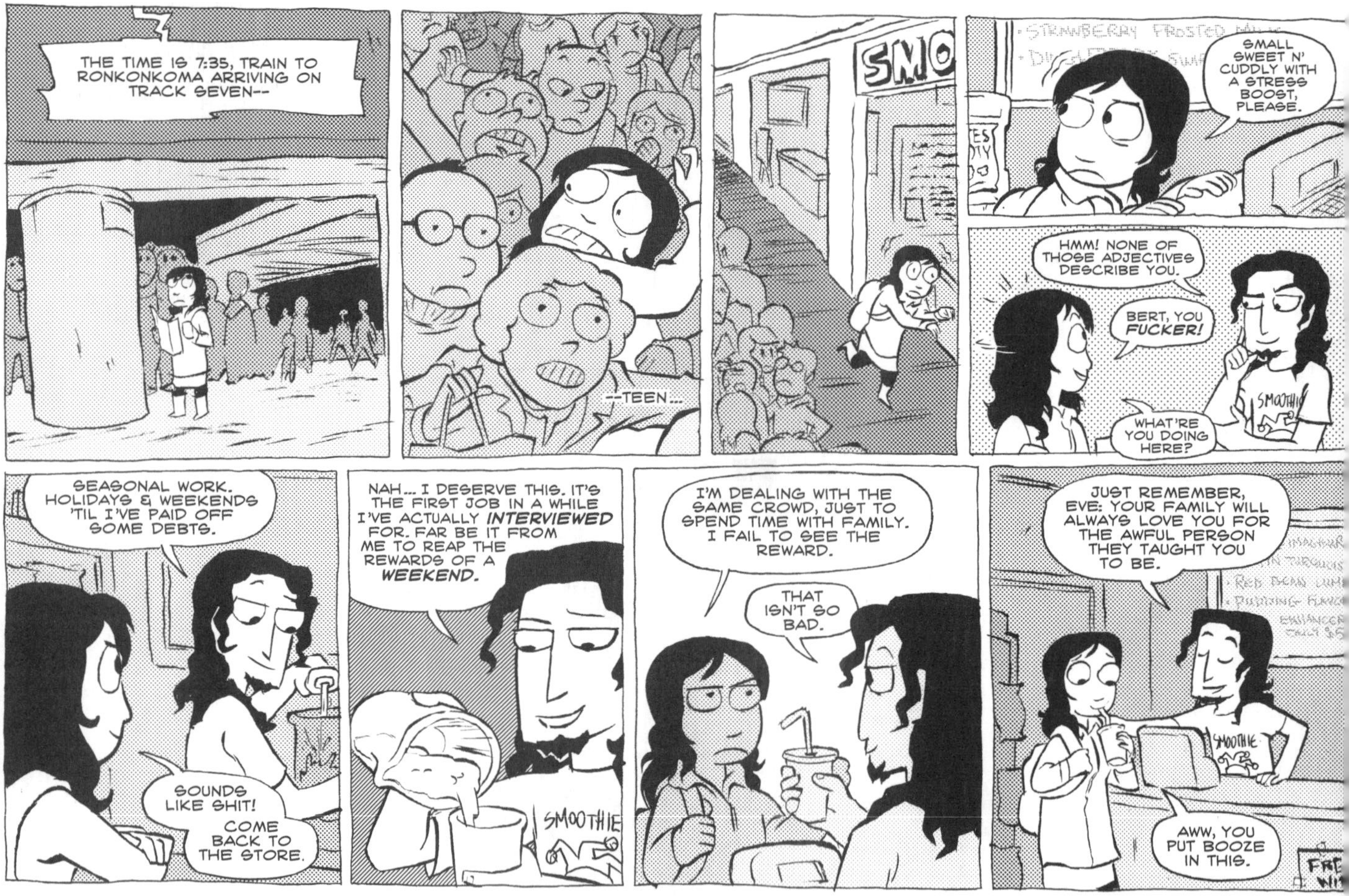
THE TIME IS 7:35, TRAIN TO RONKONKOMA ARRIVING ON TRACK SEVEN--
--TEEN...
SMALL SWEET N' CUDDLY WITH A STRESS BOOST, PLEASE.
HMM! NONE OF THOSE ADJECTIVES DESCRIBE YOU.
BERT, YOU FUCKER!
WHAT'RE YOU DOING HERE?
SMOOTHIE
SEASONAL WORK. HOLIDAYS & WEEKENDS 'TIL I'VE PAID OFF SOME DEBTS.
SOUNDS LIKE SHIT!
COME BACK TO THE STORE.
NAH... I DESERVE THIS. IT'S THE FIRST JOB IN A WHILE I'VE ACTUALLY INTERVIEWED FOR. FAR BE IT FROM ME TO REAP THE REWARDS OF A WEEKEND.
SMOOTHIE
I'M DEALING WITH THE SAME CROWD, JUST TO SPEND TIME WITH FAMILY. I FAIL TO SEE THE REWARD.
THAT ISN'T SO BAD.
JUST REMEMBER, EVE: YOUR FAMILY WILL ALWAYS LOVE YOU FOR THE AWFUL PERSON THEY TAUGHT YOU TO BE.
SMOOTHIE
AWW, YOU PUT BOOZE IN THIS.

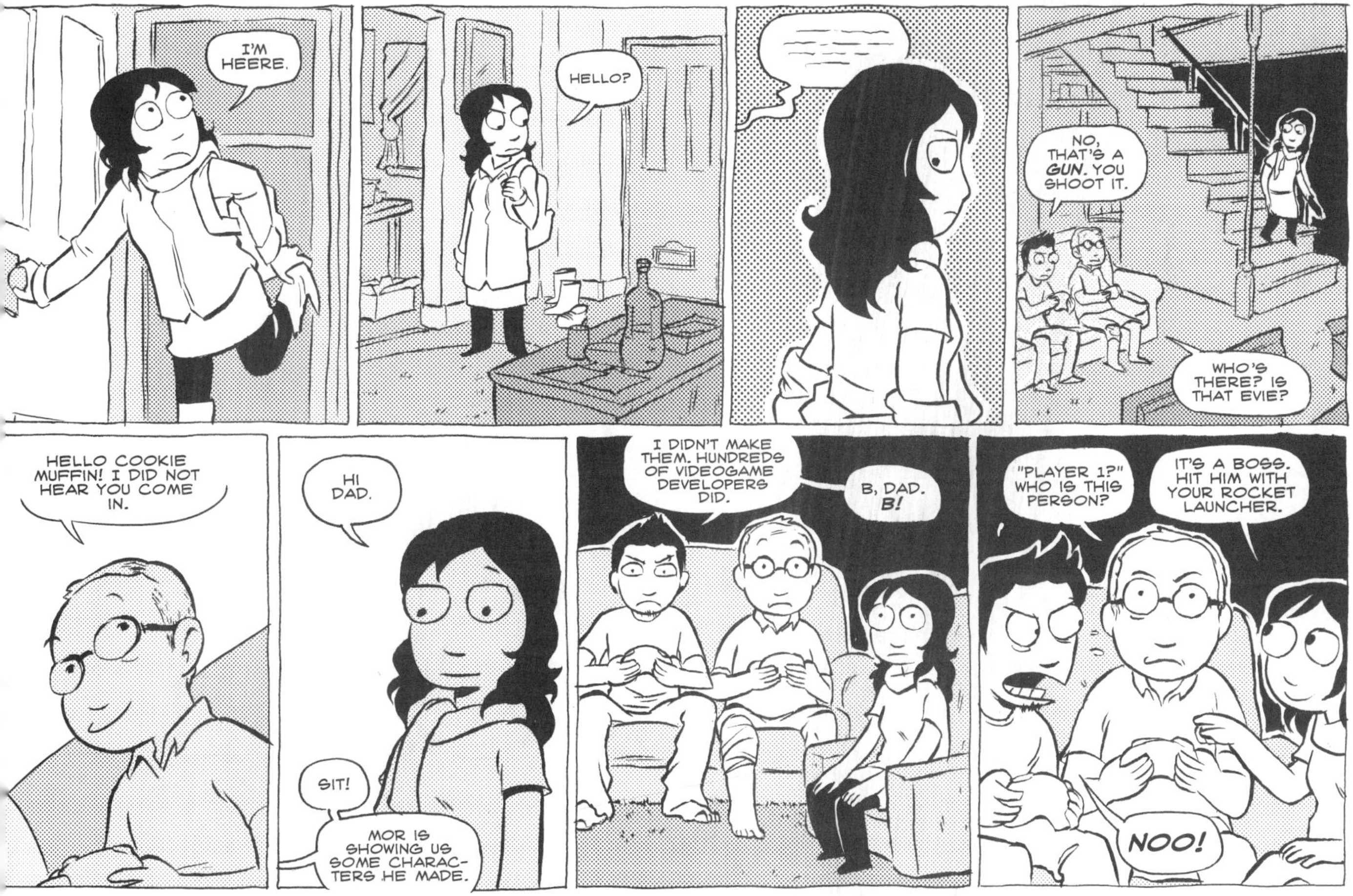
I'M HEERE.
HELLO?
NO, THAT'S A **GUN**. YOU SHOOT IT.
WHO'S THERE? IS THAT EVIE?
HELLO COOKIE MUFFIN! I DID NOT HEAR YOU COME IN.
HI DAD.
SIT!
MOR IS SHOWING US SOME CHARACTERS HE MADE.
I DIDN'T MAKE THEM. HUNDREDS OF VIDEOGAME DEVELOPERS DID.
B, DAD. **B!**
"PLAYER 1?" WHO IS THIS PERSON?
IT'S A BOSS. HIT HIM WITH YOUR ROCKET LAUNCHER.
NOO!

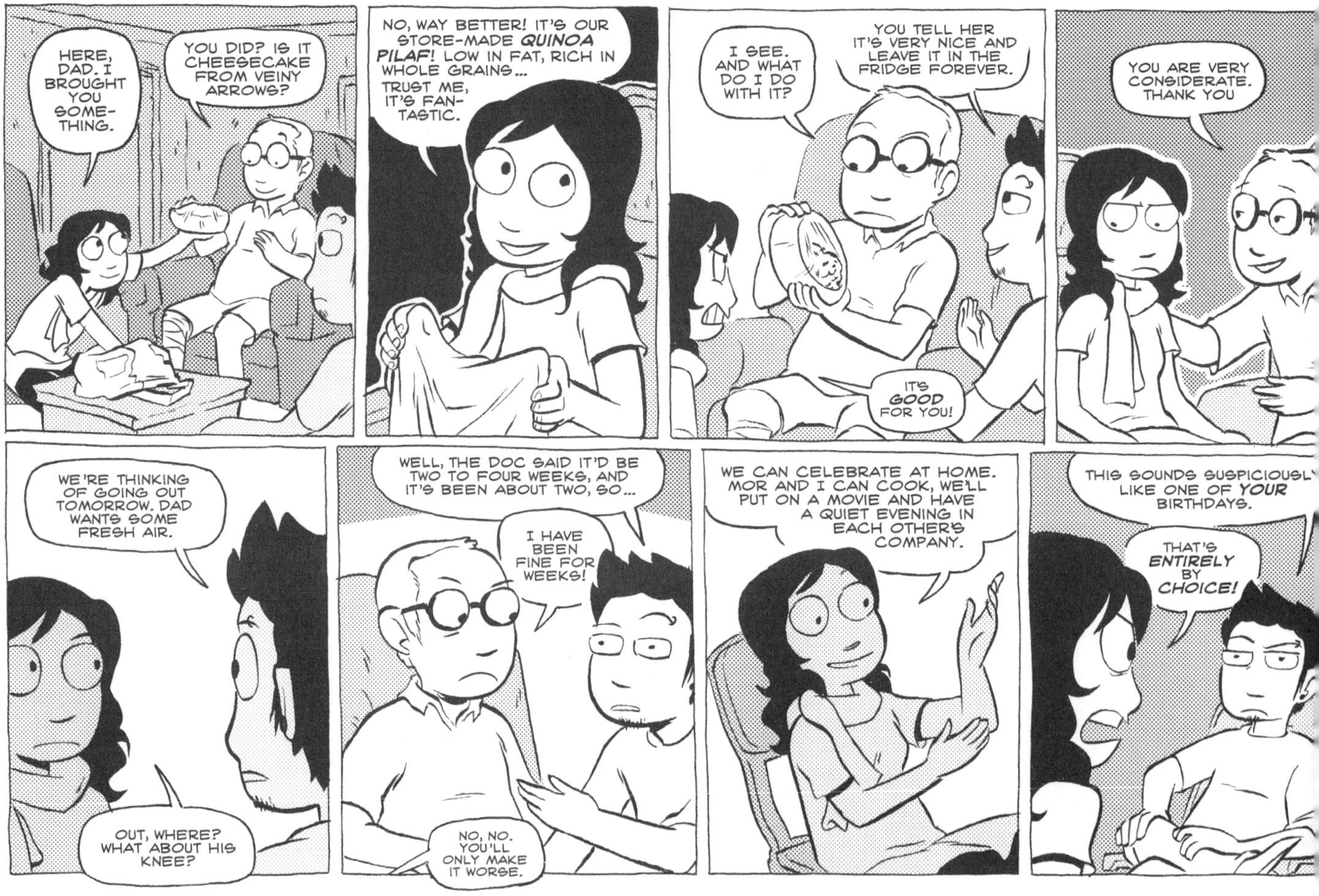
HERE, DAD. I BROUGHT YOU SOME-THING.
YOU DID? IS IT CHEESECAKE FROM VEINY ARROWS?
NO, WAY BETTER! IT'S OUR STORE-MADE QUINOA PILAF! LOW IN FAT, RICH IN WHOLE GRAINS... TRUST ME, IT'S FAN-TASTIC.
I SEE. AND WHAT DO I DO WITH IT?
YOU TELL HER IT'S VERY NICE AND LEAVE IT IN THE FRIDGE FOREVER.
IT'S GOOD FOR YOU!
YOU ARE VERY CONSIDERATE. THANK YOU
WE'RE THINKING OF GOING OUT TOMORROW. DAD WANTS SOME FRESH AIR.
OUT, WHERE? WHAT ABOUT HIS KNEE?
WELL, THE DOC SAID IT'D BE TWO TO FOUR WEEKS, AND IT'S BEEN ABOUT TWO, SO...
I HAVE BEEN FINE FOR WEEKS!
NO, NO. YOU'LL ONLY MAKE IT WORSE.
WE CAN CELEBRATE AT HOME. MOR AND I CAN COOK, WE'LL PUT ON A MOVIE AND HAVE A QUIET EVENING IN EACH OTHER'S COMPANY.
THIS SOUNDS SUSPICIOUSLY LIKE ONE OF YOUR BIRTHDAYS.
THAT'S ENTIRELY BY CHOICE!

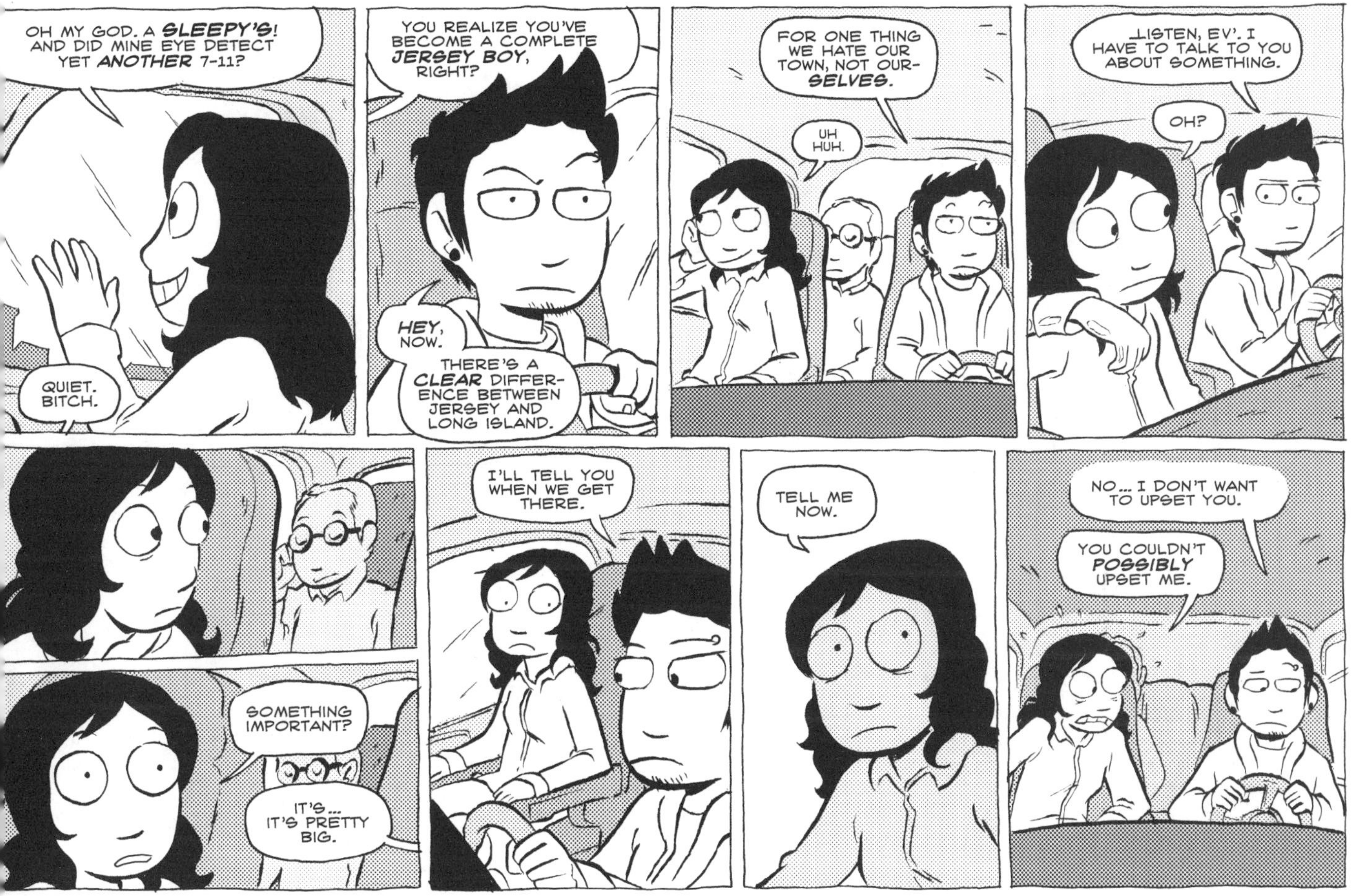
OH MY GOD. A SLEEPY'S! AND DID MINE EYE DETECT YET ANOTHER 7-11?
QUIET. BITCH.
YOU REALIZE YOU'VE BECOME A COMPLETE JERSEY BOY, RIGHT?
HEY, NOW.
THERE'S A CLEAR DIFFERENCE BETWEEN JERSEY AND LONG ISLAND.
FOR ONE THING WE HATE OUR TOWN, NOT OURSELVES.
UH HUH.
LISTEN, EV'. I HAVE TO TALK TO YOU ABOUT SOMETHING.
OH?
SOMETHING IMPORTANT?
IT'S... IT'S PRETTY BIG.
I'LL TELL YOU WHEN WE GET THERE.
TELL ME NOW.
NO... I DON'T WANT TO UPSET YOU.
YOU COULDN'T POSSIBLY UPSET ME.

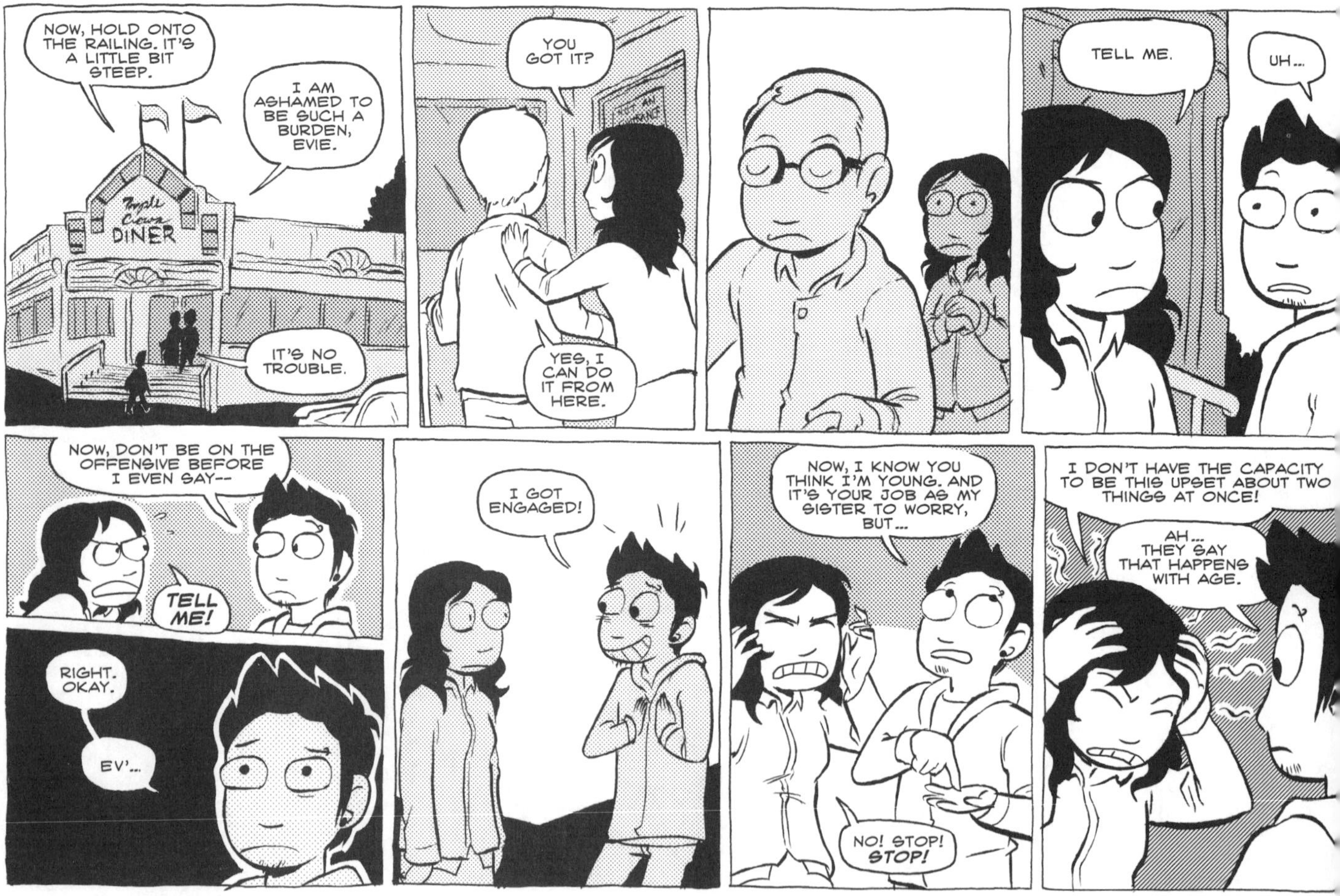

NOW, HOLD ONTO THE RAILING. IT'S A LITTLE BIT STEEP.
I AM ASHAMED TO BE SUCH A BURDEN, EVIE.
DINER
IT'S NO TROUBLE.
YOU GOT IT?
YES, I CAN DO IT FROM HERE.
TELL ME.
UH...
NOW, DON'T BE ON THE OFFENSIVE BEFORE I EVEN SAY--
TELL ME!
RIGHT. OKAY.
EV'...
I GOT ENGAGED!
NOW, I KNOW YOU THINK I'M YOUNG. AND IT'S YOUR JOB AS MY SISTER TO WORRY, BUT...
NO! STOP! STOP!
I DON'T HAVE THE CAPACITY TO BE THIS UPSET ABOUT TWO THINGS AT ONCE!
AH... THEY SAY THAT HAPPENS WITH AGE.

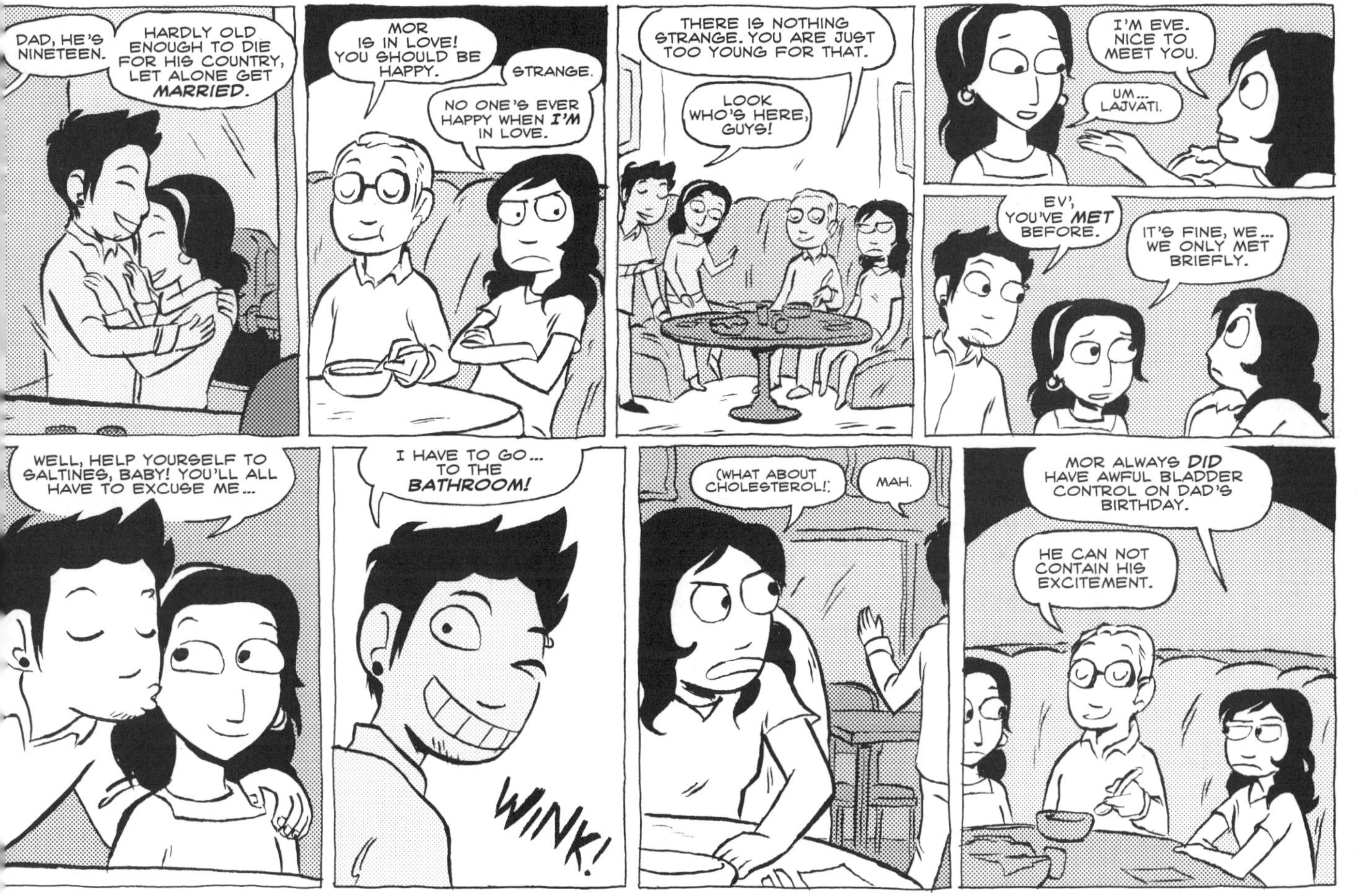
DAD, HE'S NINETEEN.
HARDLY OLD ENOUGH TO DIE FOR HIS COUNTRY, LET ALONE GET MARRIED.
MOR IS IN LOVE! YOU SHOULD BE HAPPY.
STRANGE.
NO ONE'S EVER HAPPY WHEN I'M IN LOVE.
THERE IS NOTHING STRANGE. YOU ARE JUST TOO YOUNG FOR THAT.
LOOK WHO'S HERE, GUYS!
I'M EVE. NICE TO MEET YOU.
UM... LAJVATI.
EV', YOU'VE MET BEFORE.
IT'S FINE, WE... WE ONLY MET BRIEFLY.
WELL, HELP YOURSELF TO SALTINES, BABY! YOU'LL ALL HAVE TO EXCUSE ME...
I HAVE TO GO... TO THE BATHROOM!
WINK!
(WHAT ABOUT CHOLESTEROL!)
MAH.
MOR ALWAYS DID HAVE AWFUL BLADDER CONTROL ON DAD'S BIRTHDAY.
HE CAN NOT CONTAIN HIS EXCITEMENT.

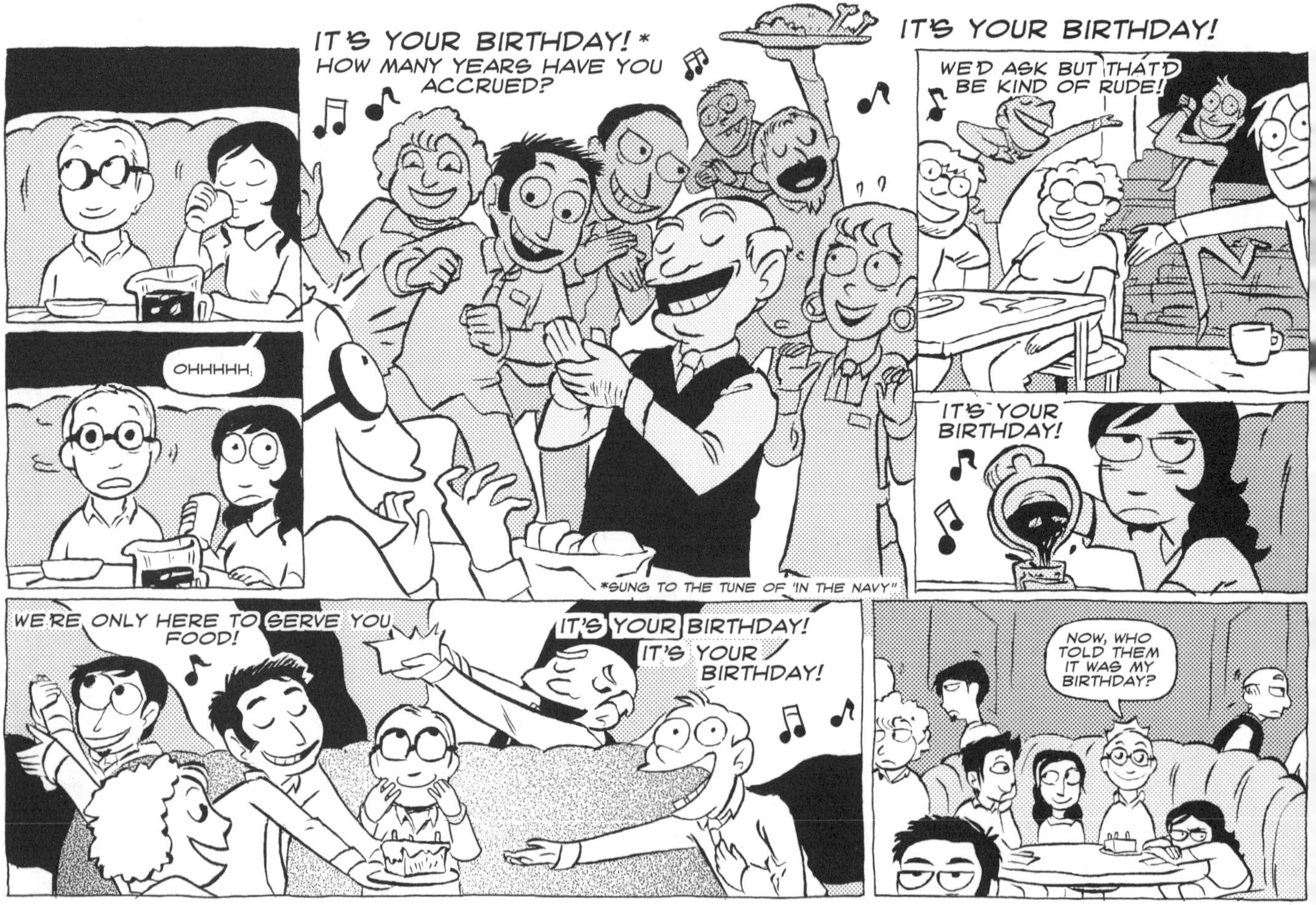
OHHHHH.
IT'S YOUR BIRTHDAY! *
HOW MANY YEARS HAVE YOU ACCRUED?
IT'S YOUR BIRTHDAY!
WE'D ASK BUT THAT'D BE KIND OF RUDE!
IT'S YOUR BIRTHDAY!
*SUNG TO THE TUNE OF "IN THE NAVY"
WE'RE ONLY HERE TO SERVE YOU FOOD!
IT'S YOUR BIRTHDAY!
IT'S YOUR BIRTHDAY!
NOW, WHO TOLD THEM IT WAS MY BIRTHDAY?

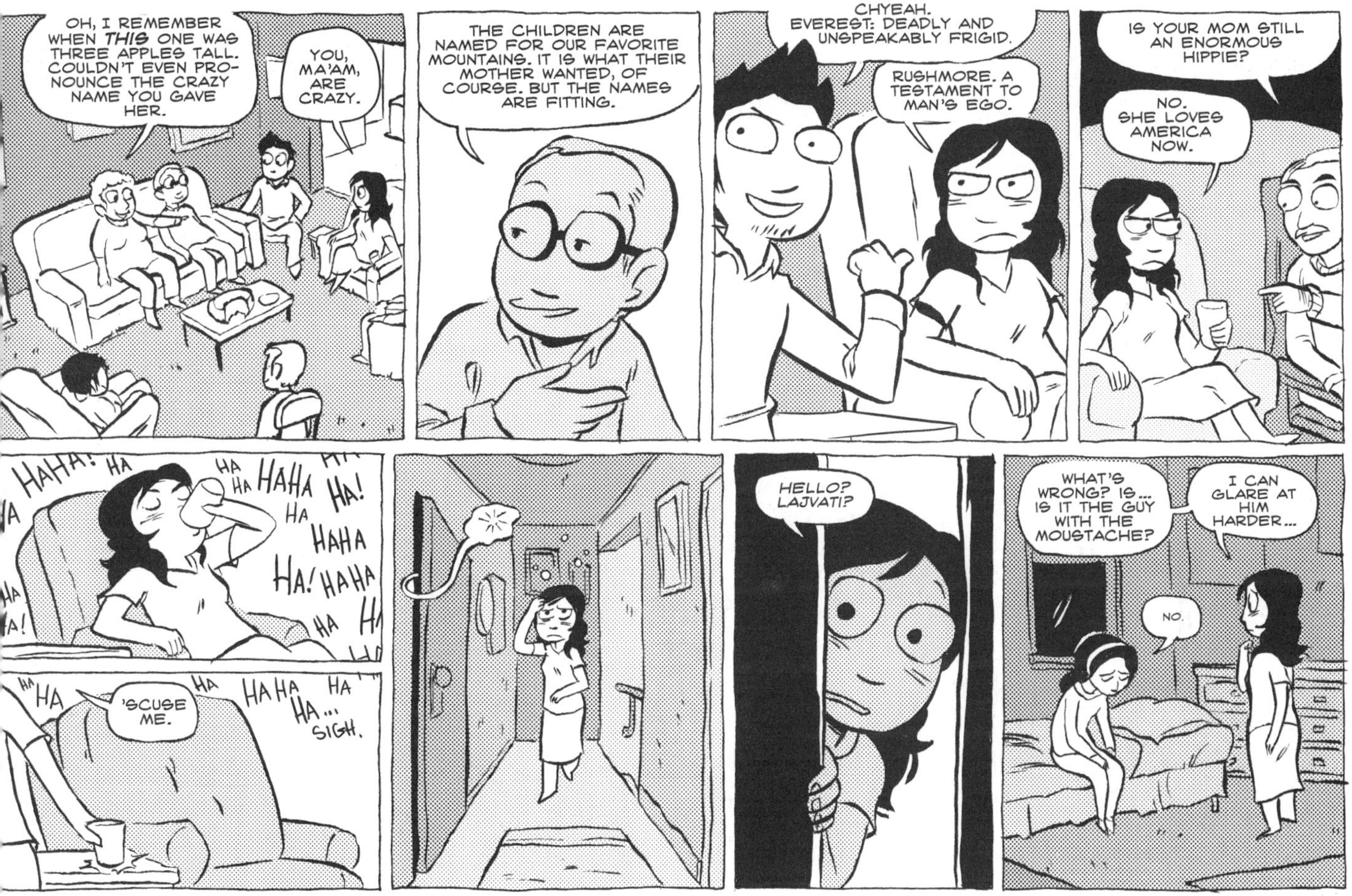
OH, I REMEMBER WHEN THIS ONE WAS THREE APPLES TALL. COULDN'T EVEN PRONOUNCE THE CRAZY NAME YOU GAVE HER.
YOU, MA'AM, ARE CRAZY.
THE CHILDREN ARE NAMED FOR OUR FAVORITE MOUNTAINS. IT IS WHAT THEIR MOTHER WANTED, OF COURSE. BUT THE NAMES ARE FITTING.
CHYEAH. EVEREST: DEADLY AND UNSPEAKABLY FRIGID.
RUSHMORE. A TESTAMENT TO MAN'S EGO.
IS YOUR MOM STILL AN ENORMOUS HIPPIE?
NO. SHE LOVES AMERICA NOW.
HAHA! HA HA HA HAHA HA! HA HAHA HA! HAHA HA
HA HA 'SCUSE ME. HA HAHA HA HA... SIGH.
HELLO? LAJVATI?
WHAT'S WRONG? IS... IS IT THE GUY WITH THE MOUSTACHE?
I CAN GLARE AT HIM HARDER...
NO.

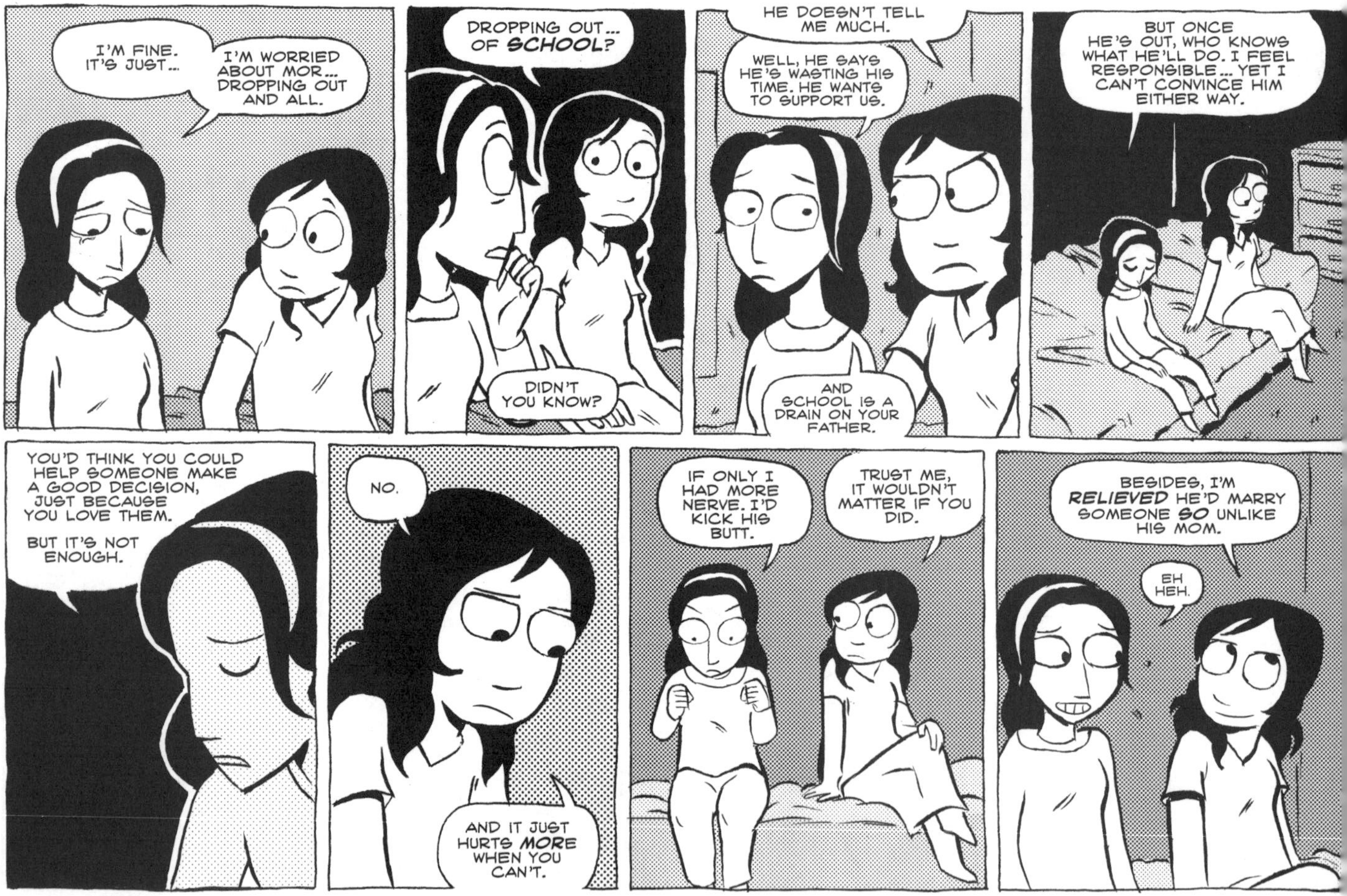
I'M FINE. IT'S JUST...
I'M WORRIED ABOUT MOR... DROPPING OUT AND ALL.
DROPPING OUT... OF SCHOOL?
DIDN'T YOU KNOW?
HE DOESN'T TELL ME MUCH.
WELL, HE SAYS HE'S WASTING HIS TIME. HE WANTS TO SUPPORT US.
AND SCHOOL IS A DRAIN ON YOUR FATHER.
BUT ONCE HE'S OUT, WHO KNOWS WHAT HE'LL DO. I FEEL RESPONSIBLE... YET I CAN'T CONVINCE HIM EITHER WAY.
YOU'D THINK YOU COULD HELP SOMEONE MAKE A GOOD DECISION, JUST BECAUSE YOU LOVE THEM.
BUT IT'S NOT ENOUGH.
NO.
AND IT JUST HURTS MORE WHEN YOU CAN'T.
IF ONLY I HAD MORE NERVE. I'D KICK HIS BUTT.
TRUST ME, IT WOULDN'T MATTER IF YOU DID.
BESIDES, I'M RELIEVED HE'D MARRY SOMEONE SO UNLIKE HIS MOM.
EH HEH.

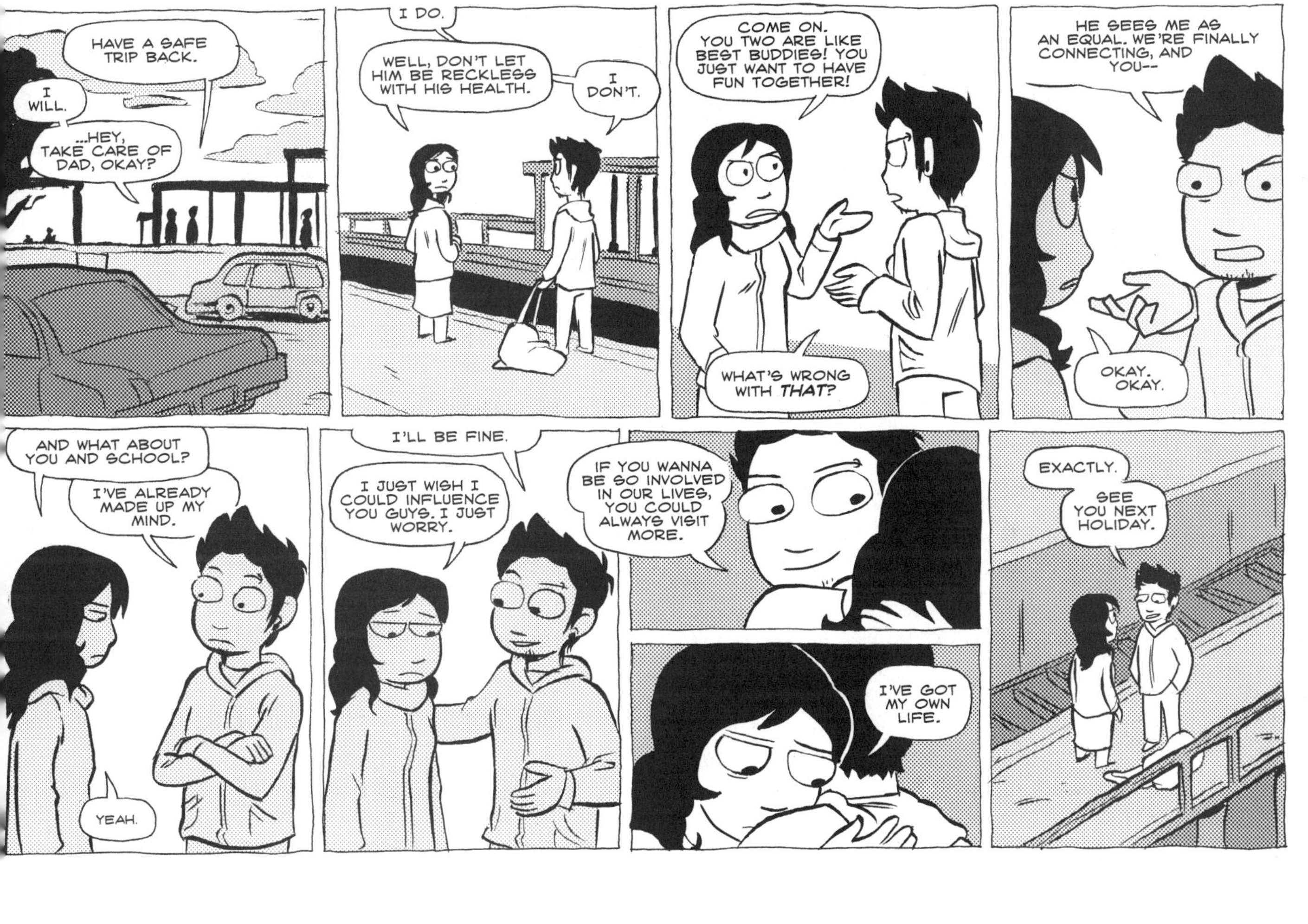
HAVE A SAFE TRIP BACK.
I WILL.
...HEY, TAKE CARE OF DAD, OKAY?
I DO.
WELL, DON'T LET HIM BE RECKLESS WITH HIS HEALTH.
I DON'T.
COME ON. YOU TWO ARE LIKE BEST BUDDIES! YOU JUST WANT TO HAVE FUN TOGETHER!
WHAT'S WRONG WITH *THAT*?
HE SEES ME AS AN EQUAL. WE'RE FINALLY CONNECTING, AND YOU--
OKAY. OKAY.
AND WHAT ABOUT YOU AND SCHOOL?
I'VE ALREADY MADE UP MY MIND.
YEAH.
I'LL BE FINE.
I JUST WISH I COULD INFLUENCE YOU GUYS. I JUST WORRY.
IF YOU WANNA BE SO INVOLVED IN OUR LIVES, YOU COULD ALWAYS VISIT MORE.
I'VE GOT MY OWN LIFE.
EXACTLY.
SEE YOU NEXT HOLIDAY.

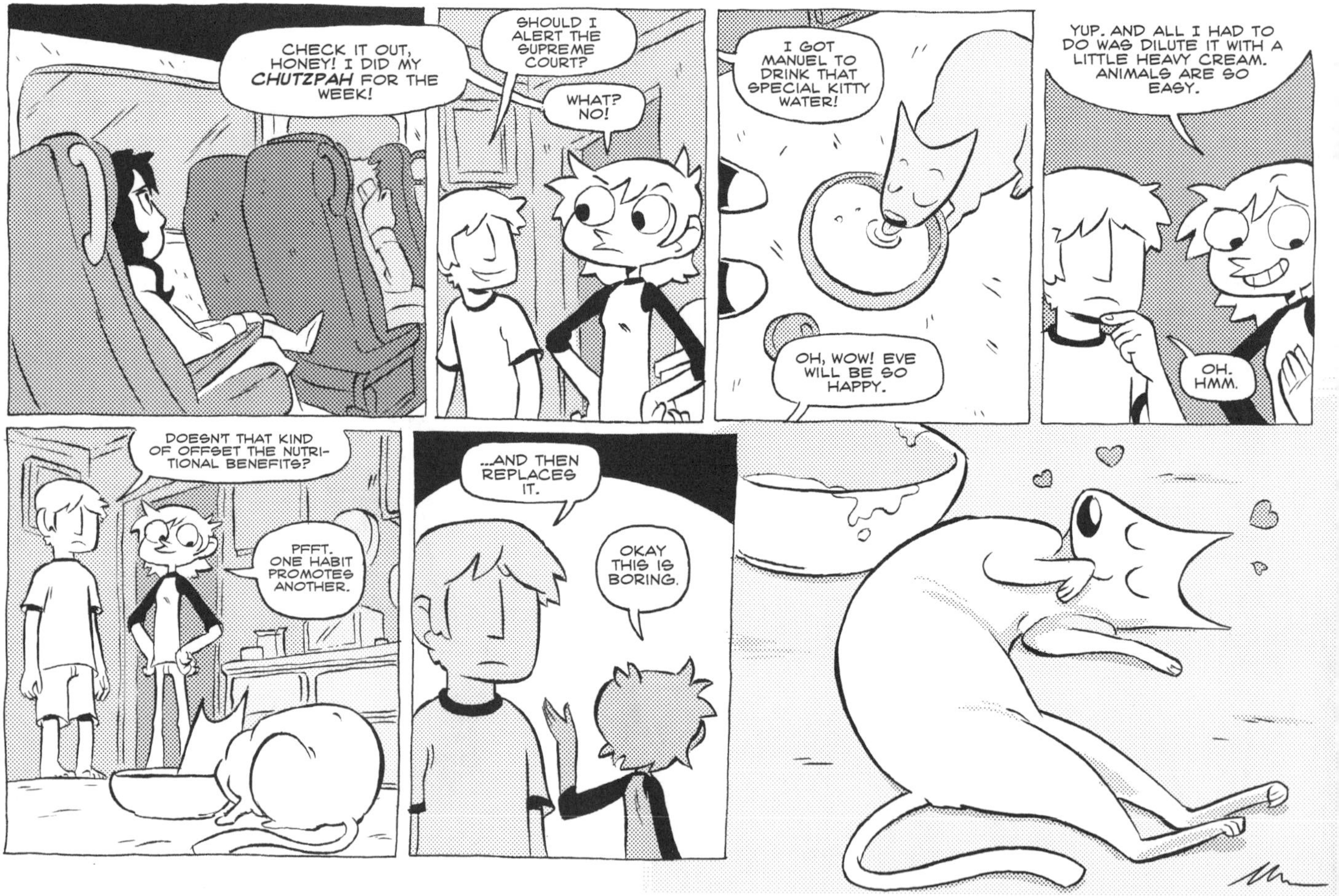
CHECK IT OUT, HONEY! I DID MY *CHUTZPAH* FOR THE WEEK!
SHOULD I ALERT THE SUPREME COURT?
WHAT? NO!
I GOT MANUEL TO DRINK THAT SPECIAL KITTY WATER!
OH, WOW! EVE WILL BE SO HAPPY.
YUP. AND ALL I HAD TO DO WAS DILUTE IT WITH A LITTLE HEAVY CREAM. ANIMALS ARE SO EASY.
OH. HMM.
DOESN'T THAT KIND OF OFFSET THE NUTRI-TIONAL BENEFITS?
PFFT. ONE HABIT PROMOTES ANOTHER.
...AND THEN REPLACES IT.
OKAY THIS IS BORING.

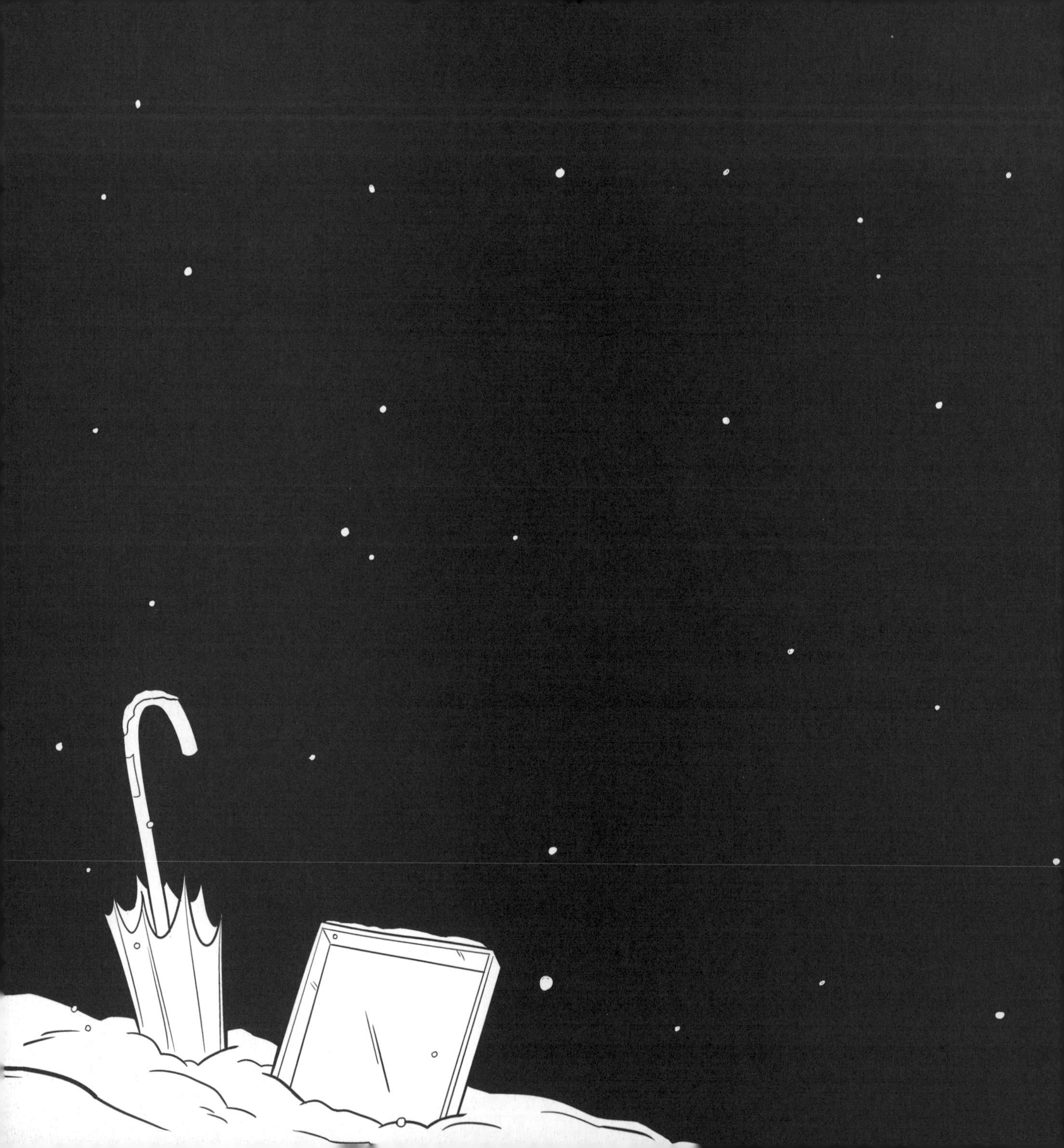

Love Anxiously

Upon rereading this story, I'm surprised at just how manic the pacing is. Full of gags, romantic intrigue and startling realizations, it's a dense story, but very loosely held together by its theme of jealousy. And for all the plot action, the characters talk too much. In hindsight I wish I'd taken my time with Eve and Will's exchanges; their chemistry seems to build around empty witticisms from the chapter's start. It's not until they're trying to mend their mistakes at the diner that any sort of honest characterization comes through.

I had a lot of small things to say in very little time during the Valentine's Day season. This is a big challenge when posting an ongoing webcomic: timing things for the days and weeks they're posted, but preserving them in a more permanent archive. I'd like to think I've gotten better at including/omitting plot elements as they're needed, and writing out entire chapters in advance, as opposed to the loose outline used for this story. I'm still fond of love anxiously though, for Hanna and Marek's bubbling arc, the glimpse into Park's day job, and the sheer number of embarrassments Eve faces.

A former boyfriend once wrestled a knife from a hysterical woman*; his story was a fairly direct source for Will's phobia. Though Will may be a bit more of a cad.

*not me.

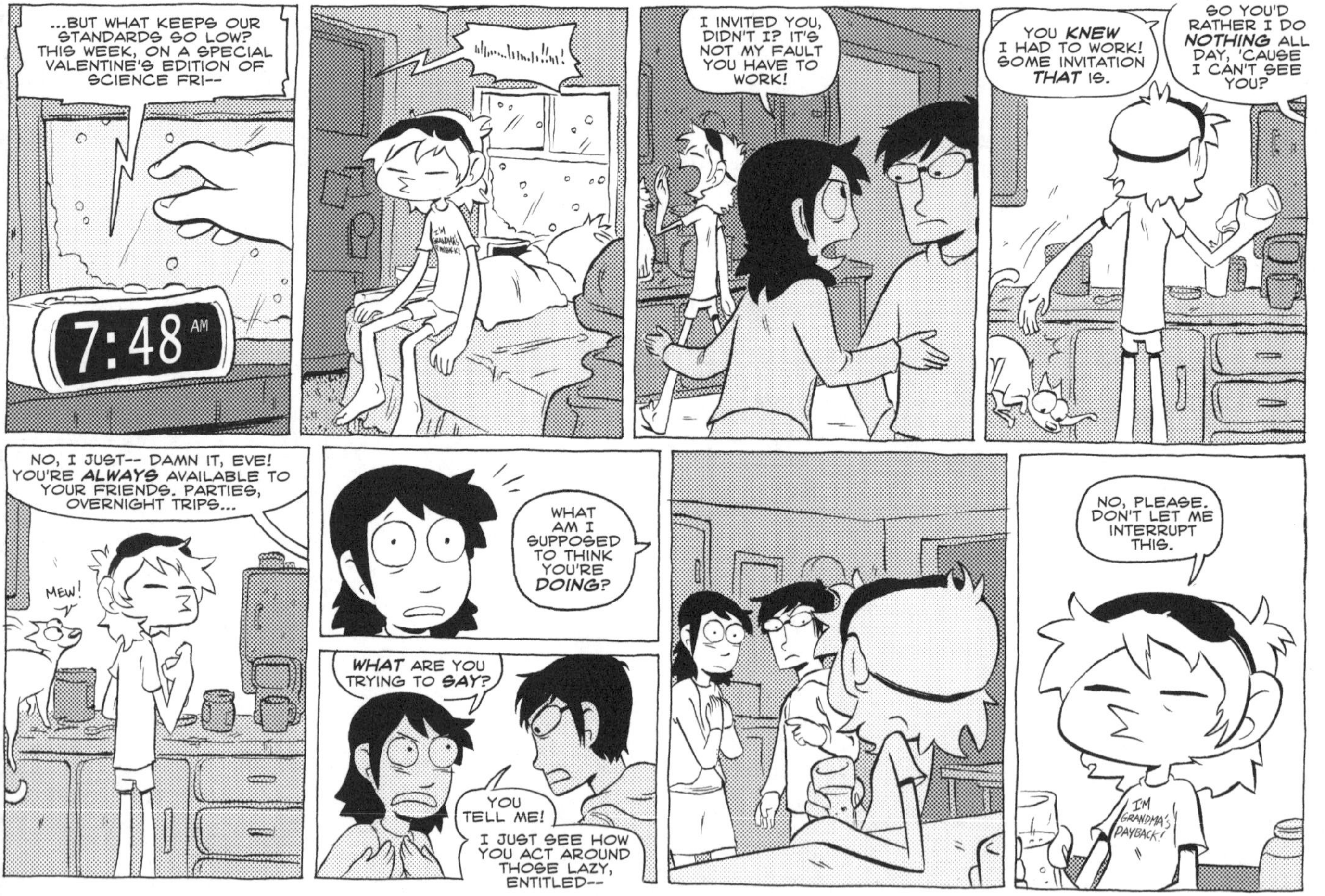

...BUT WHAT KEEPS OUR STANDARDS SO LOW? THIS WEEK, ON A SPECIAL VALENTINE'S EDITION OF SCIENCE FRI--
7:48 AM
I INVITED YOU, DIDN'T I? IT'S NOT MY FAULT YOU HAVE TO WORK!
YOU KNEW I HAD TO WORK! SOME INVITATION THAT IS.
SO YOU'D RATHER I DO NOTHING ALL DAY, 'CAUSE I CAN'T SEE YOU?
NO, I JUST-- DAMN IT, EVE! YOU'RE ALWAYS AVAILABLE TO YOUR FRIENDS. PARTIES, OVERNIGHT TRIPS...
MEW!
WHAT AM I SUPPOSED TO THINK YOU'RE DOING?
WHAT ARE YOU TRYING TO SAY?
YOU TELL ME!
I JUST SEE HOW YOU ACT AROUND THOSE LAZY, ENTITLED--
NO, PLEASE. DON'T LET ME INTERRUPT THIS.
I'M GRANDMA'S PAYBACK!

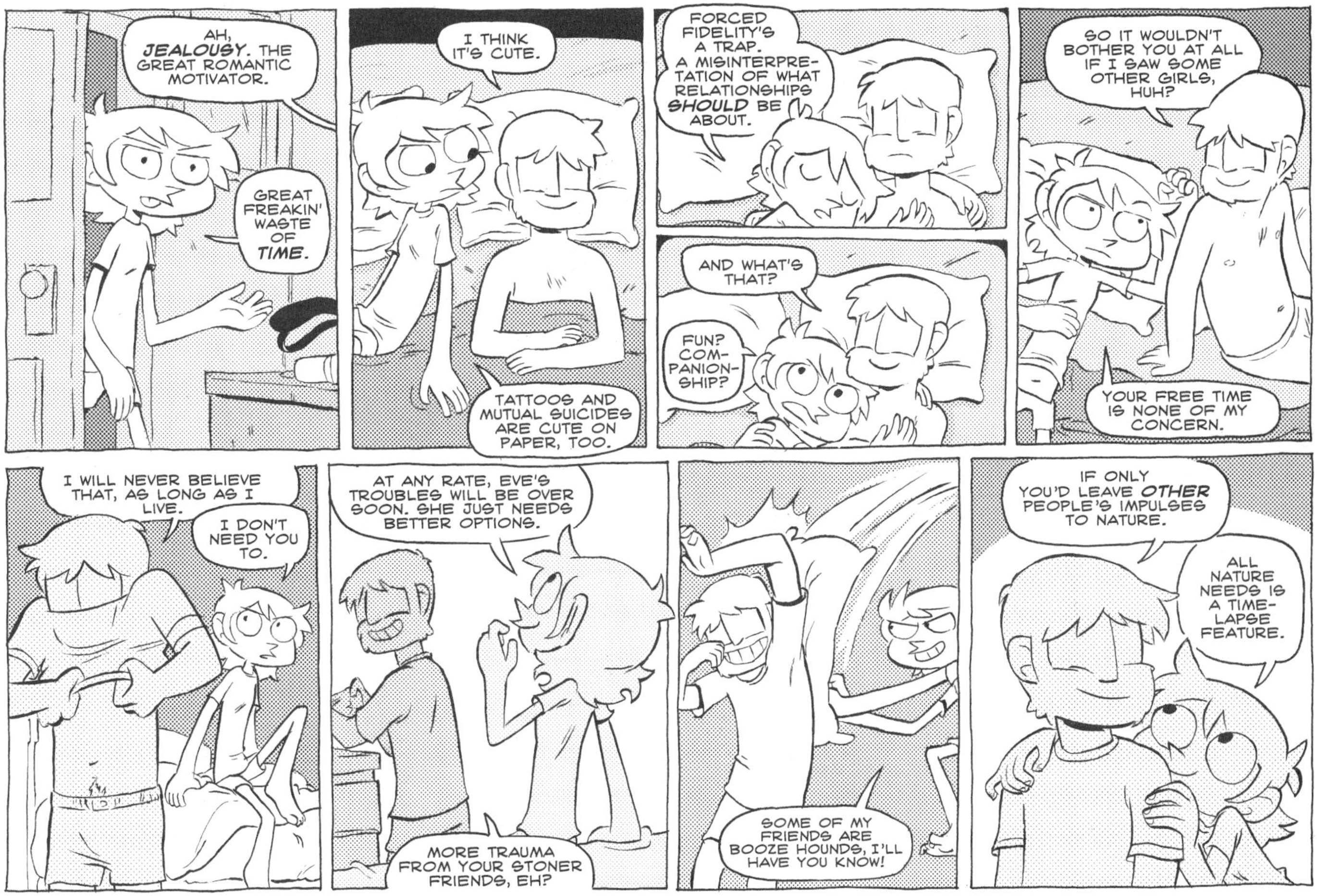
AH, JEALOUSY. THE GREAT ROMANTIC MOTIVATOR.
GREAT FREAKIN' WASTE OF TIME.
I THINK IT'S CUTE.
TATTOOS AND MUTUAL SUICIDES ARE CUTE ON PAPER, TOO.
FORCED FIDELITY'S A TRAP. A MISINTERPRETATION OF WHAT RELATIONSHIPS SHOULD BE ABOUT.
AND WHAT'S THAT?
FUN? COMPANIONSHIP?
SO IT WOULDN'T BOTHER YOU AT ALL IF I SAW SOME OTHER GIRLS, HUH?
YOUR FREE TIME IS NONE OF MY CONCERN.
I WILL NEVER BELIEVE THAT, AS LONG AS I LIVE.
I DON'T NEED YOU TO.
AT ANY RATE, EVE'S TROUBLES WILL BE OVER SOON. SHE JUST NEEDS BETTER OPTIONS.
MORE TRAUMA FROM YOUR STONER FRIENDS, EH?
SOME OF MY FRIENDS ARE BOOZE HOUNDS, I'LL HAVE YOU KNOW!
IF ONLY YOU'D LEAVE OTHER PEOPLE'S IMPULSES TO NATURE.
ALL NATURE NEEDS IS A TIME-LAPSE FEATURE.

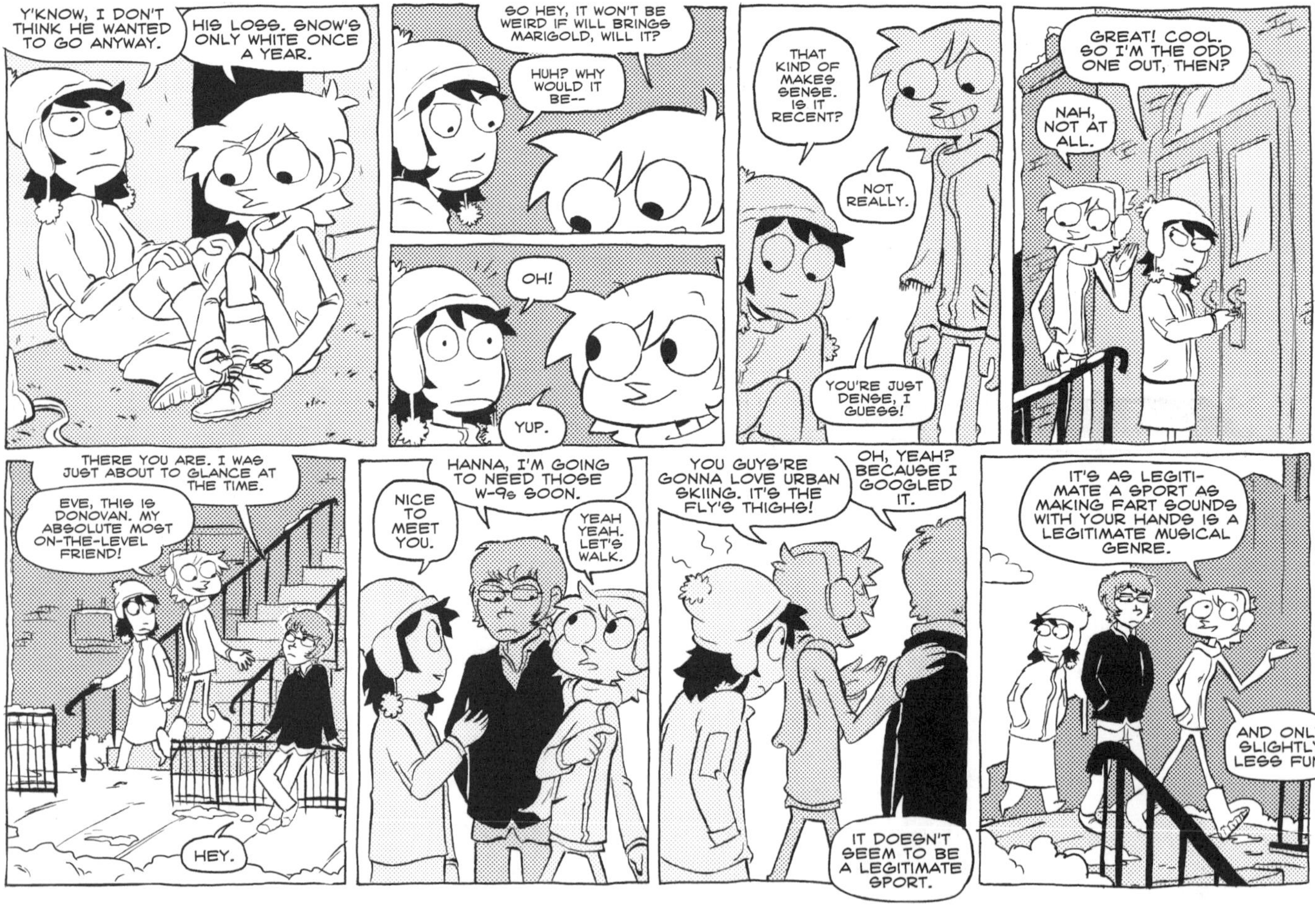
Y'KNOW, I DON'T THINK HE WANTED TO GO ANYWAY.
HIS LOSS. SNOW'S ONLY WHITE ONCE A YEAR.
SO HEY, IT WON'T BE WEIRD IF WILL BRINGS MARIGOLD, WILL IT?
HUH? WHY WOULD IT BE--
OH!
YUP.
THAT KIND OF MAKES SENSE. IS IT RECENT?
NOT REALLY.
YOU'RE JUST DENSE, I GUESS!
GREAT! COOL. SO I'M THE ODD ONE OUT, THEN?
NAH, NOT AT ALL.
THERE YOU ARE. I WAS JUST ABOUT TO GLANCE AT THE TIME.
EVE, THIS IS DONOVAN. MY ABSOLUTE MOST ON-THE-LEVEL FRIEND!
HEY.
NICE TO MEET YOU.
HANNA, I'M GOING TO NEED THOSE W-9s SOON.
YEAH YEAH. LET'S WALK.
YOU GUYS'RE GONNA LOVE URBAN SKIING. IT'S THE FLY'S THIGHS!
OH, YEAH? BECAUSE I GOOGLED IT.
IT DOESN'T SEEM TO BE A LEGITIMATE SPORT.
IT'S AS LEGITI-MATE A SPORT AS MAKING FART SOUNDS WITH YOUR HANDS IS A LEGITIMATE MUSICAL GENRE.
AND ONLY SLIGHTLY LESS FUN.

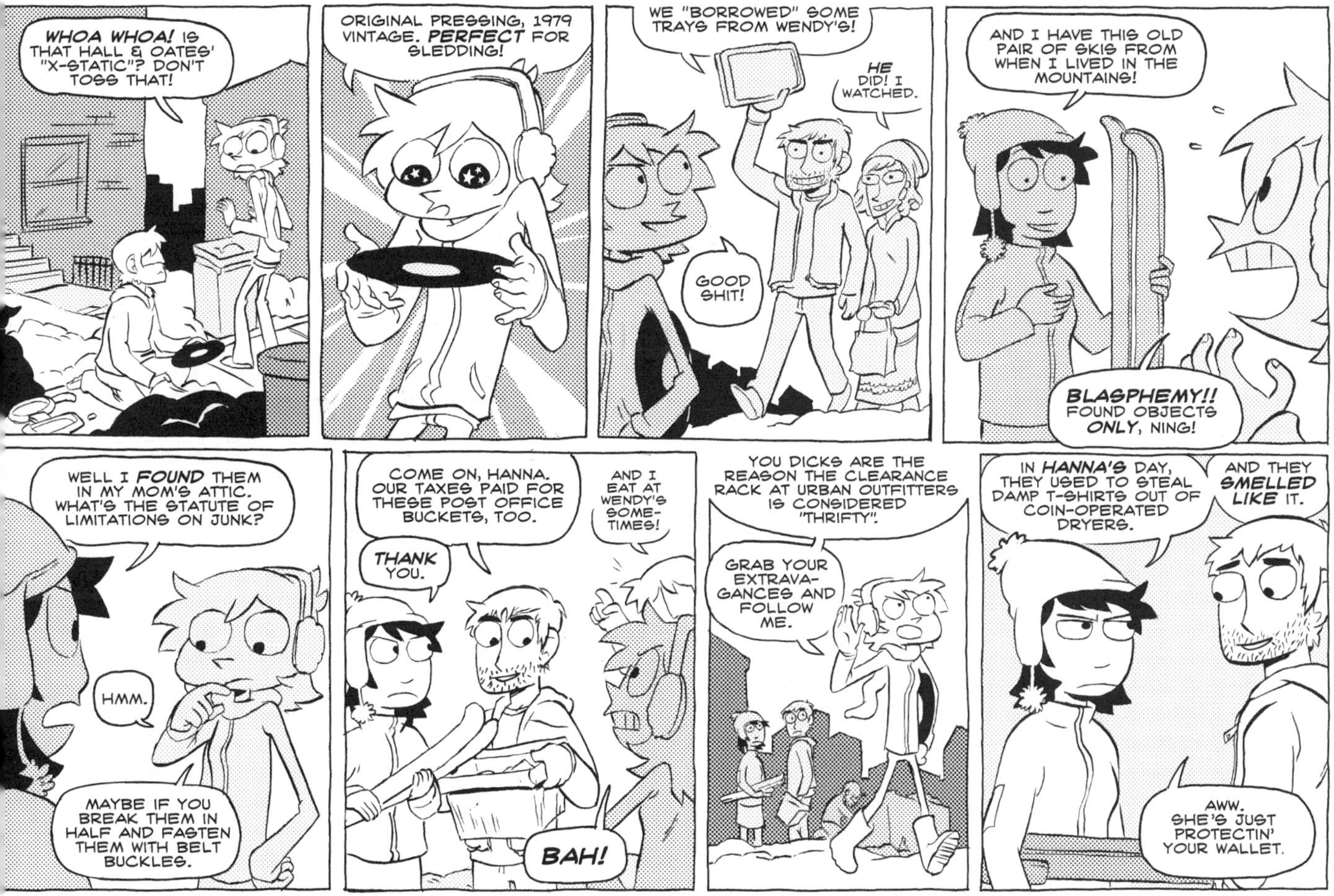
WHOA WHOA! IS THAT HALL & OATES' "X-STATIC"? DON'T TOSS THAT!
ORIGINAL PRESSING, 1979 VINTAGE. PERFECT FOR SLEDDING!
WE "BORROWED" SOME TRAYS FROM WENDY'S!
HE DID! I WATCHED.
GOOD SHIT!
AND I HAVE THIS OLD PAIR OF SKIS FROM WHEN I LIVED IN THE MOUNTAINS!
BLASPHEMY!! FOUND OBJECTS ONLY, NING!
WELL I FOUND THEM IN MY MOM'S ATTIC. WHAT'S THE STATUTE OF LIMITATIONS ON JUNK?
HMM.
MAYBE IF YOU BREAK THEM IN HALF AND FASTEN THEM WITH BELT BUCKLES.
COME ON, HANNA. OUR TAXES PAID FOR THESE POST OFFICE BUCKETS, TOO.
AND I EAT AT WENDY'S SOME-TIMES!
THANK YOU.
BAH!
YOU DICKS ARE THE REASON THE CLEARANCE RACK AT URBAN OUTFITTERS IS CONSIDERED "THRIFTY".
GRAB YOUR EXTRAVA-GANCES AND FOLLOW ME.
IN HANNA'S DAY, THEY USED TO STEAL DAMP T-SHIRTS OUT OF COIN-OPERATED DRYERS.
AND THEY SMELLED LIKE IT.
AWW. SHE'S JUST PROTECTIN' YOUR WALLET.

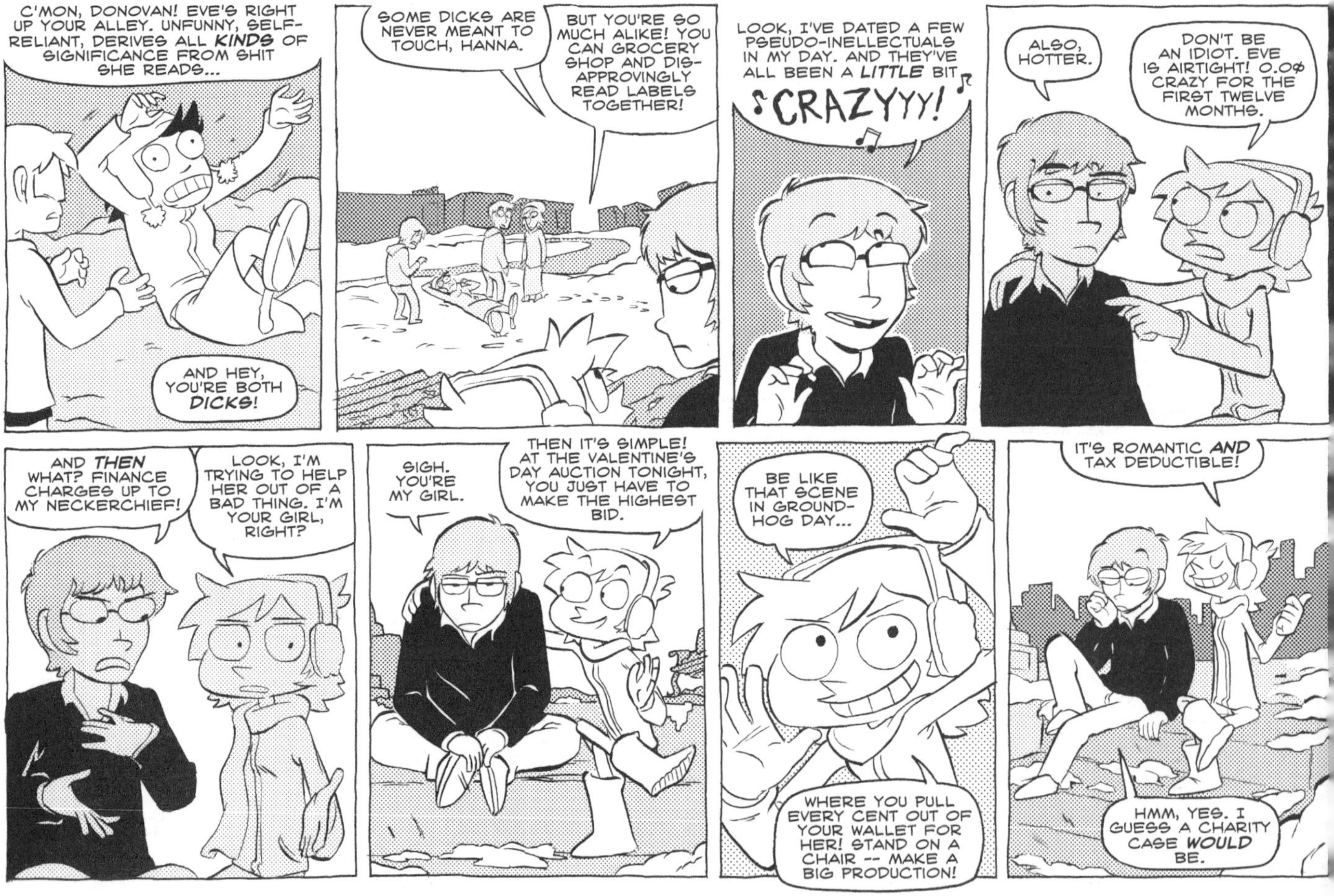
C'MON, DONOVAN! EVE'S RIGHT UP YOUR ALLEY. UNFUNNY, SELF-RELIANT, DERIVES ALL KINDS OF SIGNIFICANCE FROM SHIT SHE READS...
AND HEY, YOU'RE BOTH DICKS!
SOME DICKS ARE NEVER MEANT TO TOUCH, HANNA.
BUT YOU'RE SO MUCH ALIKE! YOU CAN GROCERY SHOP AND DIS-APPROVINGLY READ LABELS TOGETHER!
LOOK, I'VE DATED A FEW PSEUDO-INELLECTUALS IN MY DAY. AND THEY'VE ALL BEEN A LITTLE BIT
CRAZYYYY!
ALSO, HOTTER.
DON'T BE AN IDIOT. EVE IS AIRTIGHT! 0.0¢ CRAZY FOR THE FIRST TWELVE MONTHS.
AND THEN WHAT? FINANCE CHARGES UP TO MY NECKERCHIEF!
LOOK, I'M TRYING TO HELP HER OUT OF A BAD THING. I'M YOUR GIRL, RIGHT?
SIGH. YOU'RE MY GIRL.
THEN IT'S SIMPLE! AT THE VALENTINE'S DAY AUCTION TONIGHT, YOU JUST HAVE TO MAKE THE HIGHEST BID.
BE LIKE THAT SCENE IN GROUND-HOG DAY...
WHERE YOU PULL EVERY CENT OUT OF YOUR WALLET FOR HER! STAND ON A CHAIR -- MAKE A BIG PRODUCTION!
IT'S ROMANTIC AND TAX DEDUCTIBLE!
HMM, YES. I GUESS A CHARITY CASE WOULD BE.

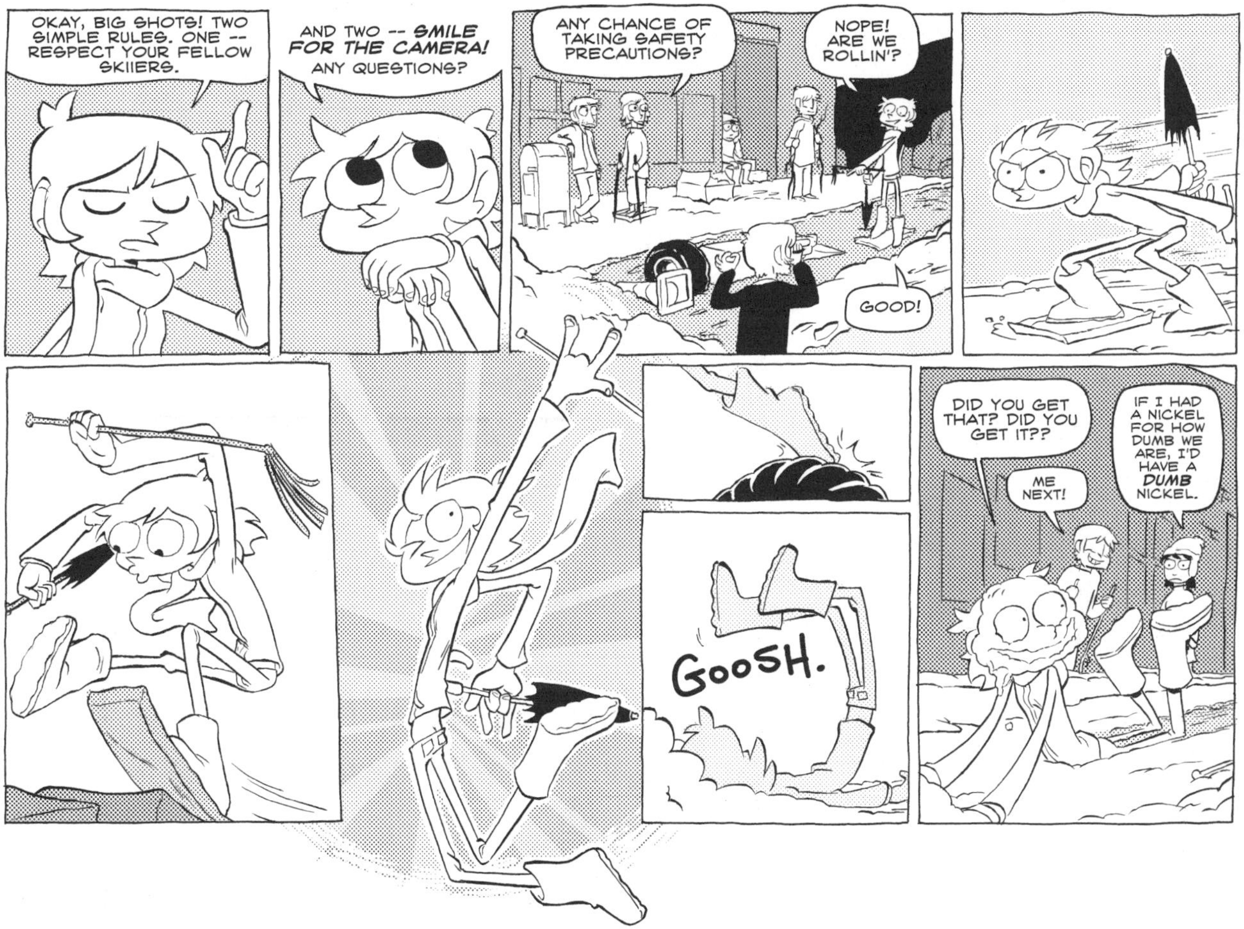
OKAY, BIG SHOTS! TWO SIMPLE RULES. ONE -- RESPECT YOUR FELLOW SKIIERS.
AND TWO -- SMILE FOR THE CAMERA! ANY QUESTIONS?
ANY CHANCE OF TAKING SAFETY PRECAUTIONS?
NOPE! ARE WE ROLLIN'?
GOOD!
GOOSH.
DID YOU GET THAT? DID YOU GET IT??
ME NEXT!
IF I HAD A NICKEL FOR HOW DUMB WE ARE, I'D HAVE A DUMB NICKEL.

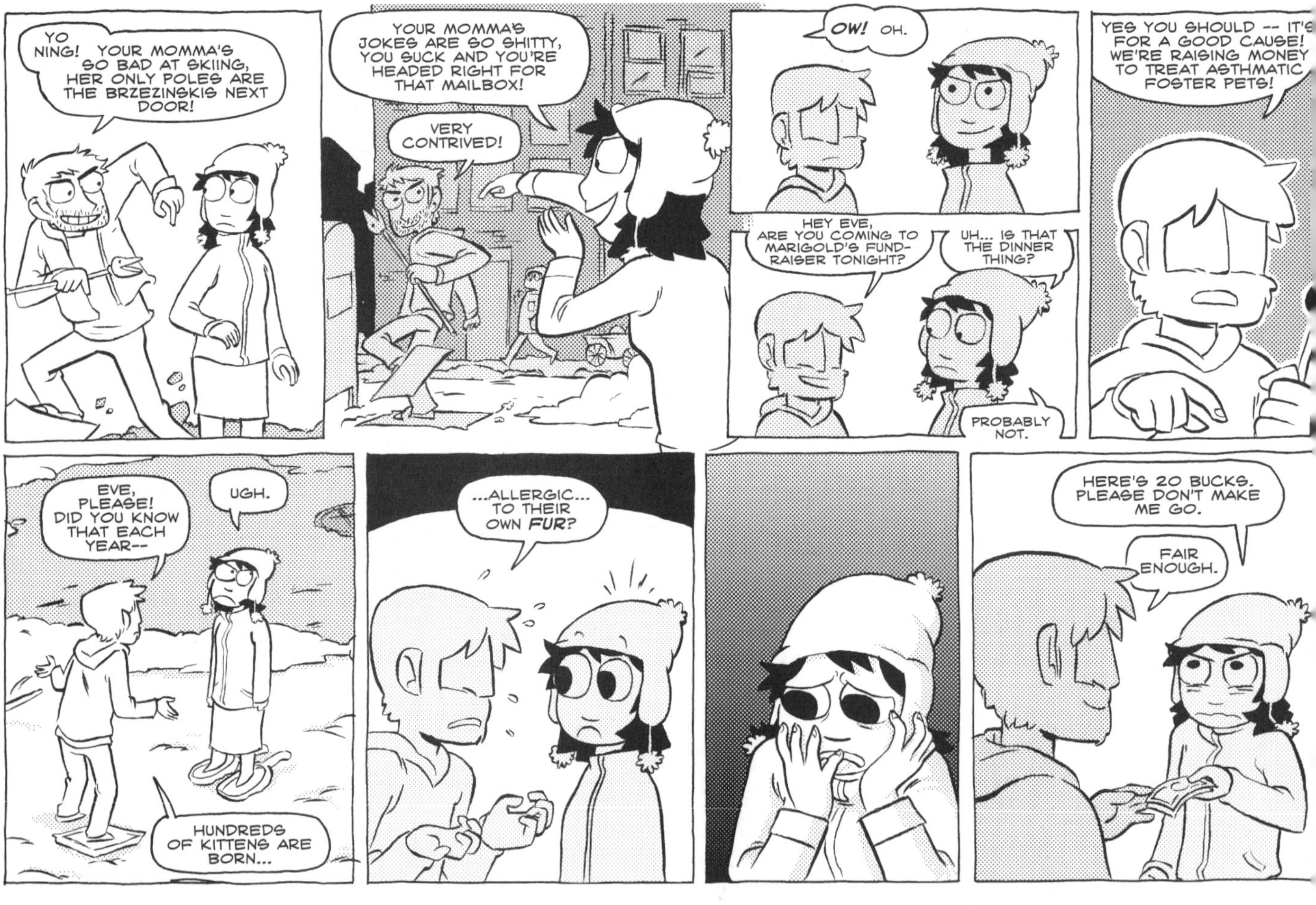
YO NING! YOUR MOMMA'S SO BAD AT SKIING, HER ONLY POLES ARE THE BRZEZINSKIS NEXT DOOR!
YOUR MOMMA'S JOKES ARE SO SHITTY, YOU SUCK AND YOU'RE HEADED RIGHT FOR THAT MAILBOX!
VERY CONTRIVED!
OW! OH.
HEY EVE, ARE YOU COMING TO MARIGOLD'S FUND-RAISER TONIGHT?
UH... IS THAT THE DINNER THING?
PROBABLY NOT.
YES YOU SHOULD -- IT'S FOR A GOOD CAUSE! WE'RE RAISING MONEY TO TREAT ASTHMATIC FOSTER PETS!
EVE, PLEASE! DID YOU KNOW THAT EACH YEAR--
UGH.
HUNDREDS OF KITTENS ARE BORN...
...ALLERGIC... TO THEIR OWN FUR?
HERE'S 20 BUCKS. PLEASE DON'T MAKE ME GO.
FAIR ENOUGH.

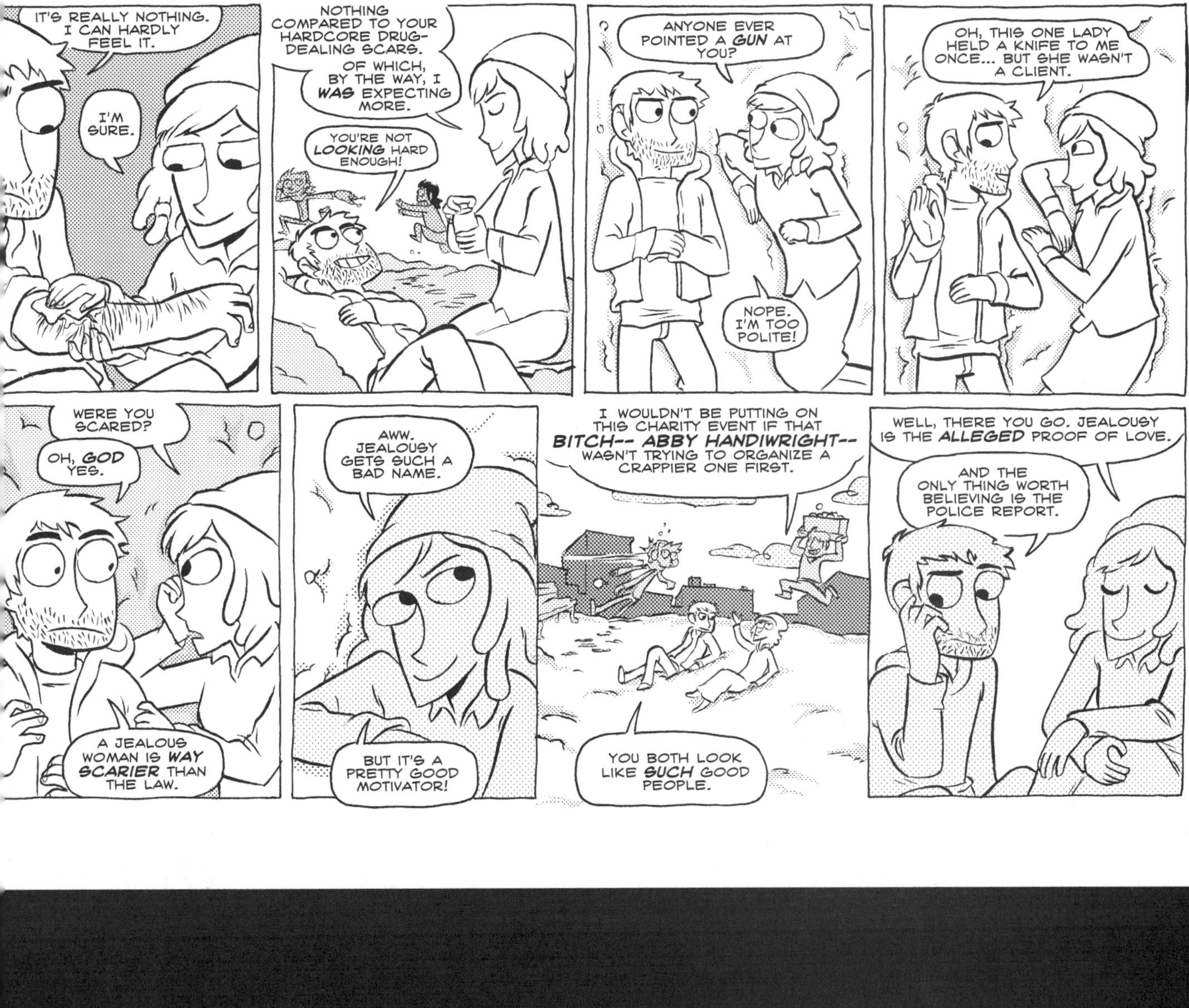
IT'S REALLY NOTHING. I CAN HARDLY FEEL IT.
I'M SURE.
NOTHING COMPARED TO YOUR HARDCORE DRUG-DEALING SCARS.
OF WHICH, BY THE WAY, I WAS EXPECTING MORE.
YOU'RE NOT LOOKING HARD ENOUGH!
ANYONE EVER POINTED A GUN AT YOU?
NOPE. I'M TOO POLITE!
OH, THIS ONE LADY HELD A KNIFE TO ME ONCE... BUT SHE WASN'T A CLIENT.
WERE YOU SCARED?
OH, GOD YES.
A JEALOUS WOMAN IS WAY SCARIER THAN THE LAW.
AWW. JEALOUSY GETS SUCH A BAD NAME.
BUT IT'S A PRETTY GOOD MOTIVATOR!
I WOULDN'T BE PUTTING ON THIS CHARITY EVENT IF THAT BITCH-- ABBY HANDIWRIGHT-- WASN'T TRYING TO ORGANIZE A CRAPPIER ONE FIRST.
YOU BOTH LOOK LIKE SUCH GOOD PEOPLE.
WELL, THERE YOU GO. JEALOUSY IS THE ALLEGED PROOF OF LOVE.
AND THE ONLY THING WORTH BELIEVING IS THE POLICE REPORT.

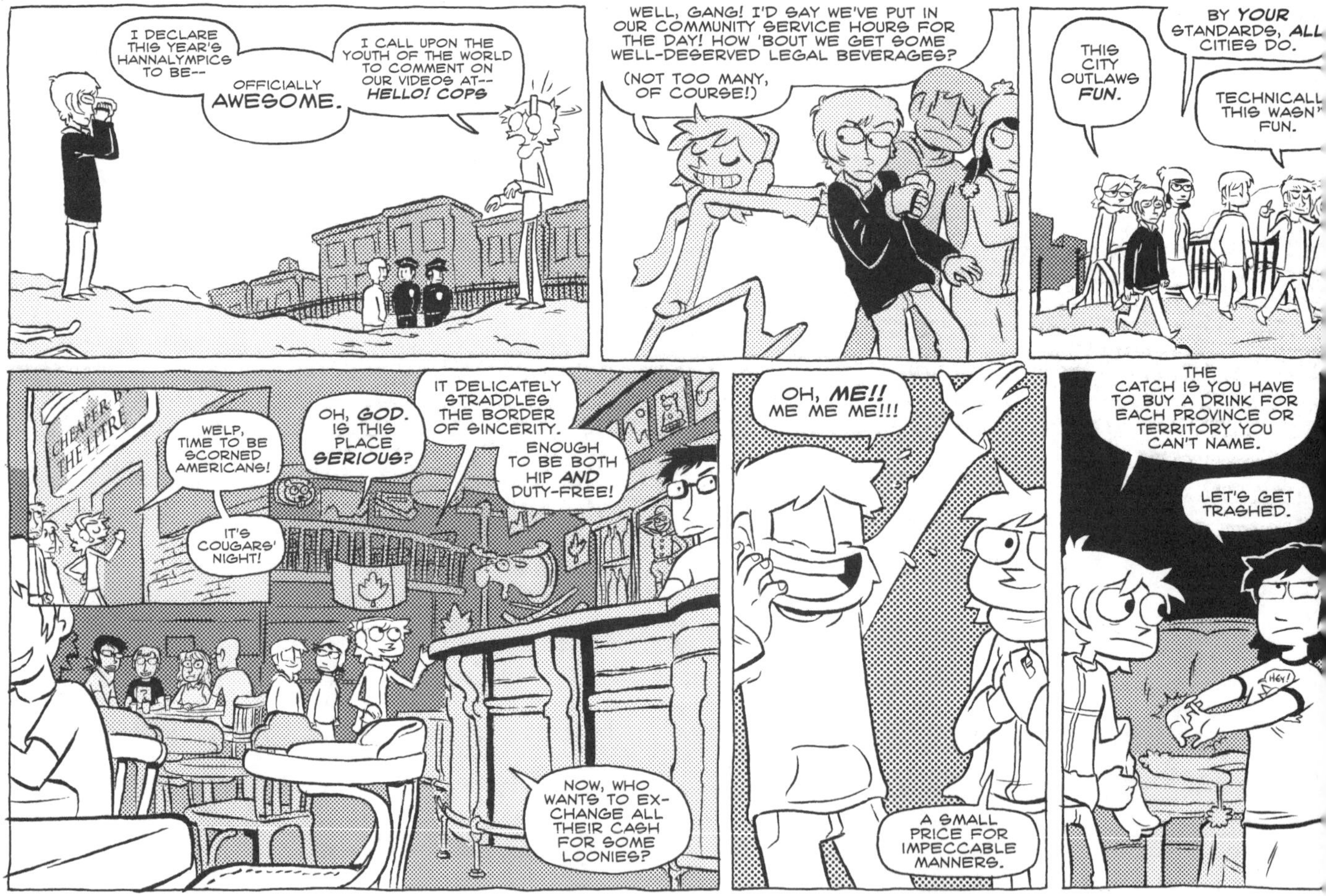
I DECLARE THIS YEAR'S HANNALYMPICS TO BE--
OFFICIALLY AWESOME.
I CALL UPON THE YOUTH OF THE WORLD TO COMMENT ON OUR VIDEOS AT-- HELLO! COPS
WELL, GANG! I'D SAY WE'VE PUT IN OUR COMMUNITY SERVICE HOURS FOR THE DAY! HOW 'BOUT WE GET SOME WELL-DESERVED LEGAL BEVERAGES?
(NOT TOO MANY, OF COURSE!)
THIS CITY OUTLAWS FUN.
BY YOUR STANDARDS, ALL CITIES DO.
TECHNICALL THIS WASN' FUN.
CHEAPER B
THE LITRE
WELP, TIME TO BE SCORNED AMERICANS!
IT'S COUGARS' NIGHT!
OH, GOD. IS THIS PLACE SERIOUS?
IT DELICATELY STRADDLES THE BORDER OF SINCERITY.
ENOUGH TO BE BOTH HIP AND DUTY-FREE!
NOW, WHO WANTS TO EX-CHANGE ALL THEIR CASH FOR SOME LOONIES?
OH, ME!! ME ME ME!!!
A SMALL PRICE FOR IMPECCABLE MANNERS.
THE CATCH IS YOU HAVE TO BUY A DRINK FOR EACH PROVINCE OR TERRITORY YOU CAN'T NAME.
LET'S GET TRASHED.
HEY!

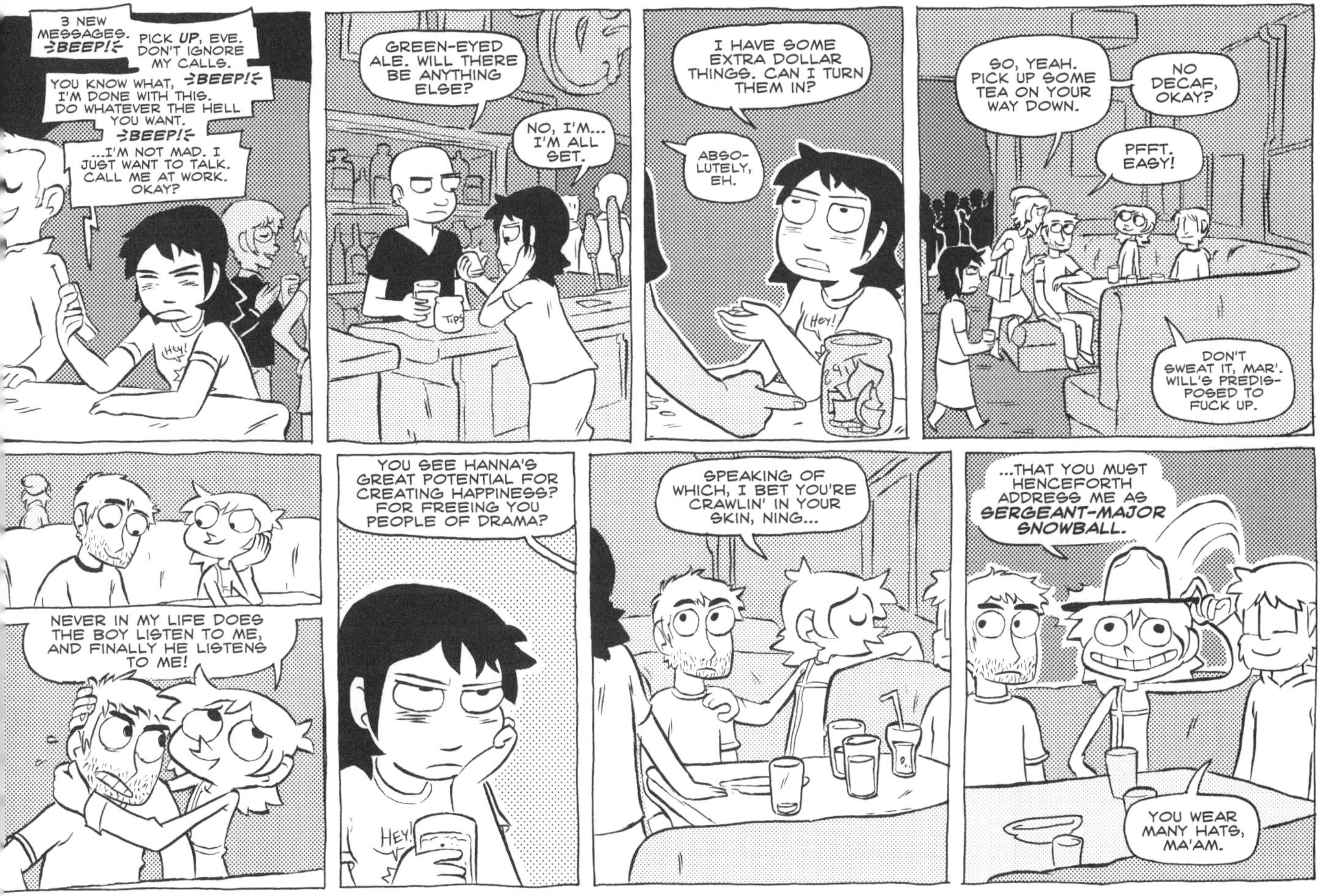
3 NEW MESSAGES. BEEP!
PICK UP, EVE. DON'T IGNORE MY CALLS.
YOU KNOW WHAT, BEEP! I'M DONE WITH THIS. DO WHATEVER THE HELL YOU WANT.
BEEP! ...I'M NOT MAD. I JUST WANT TO TALK. CALL ME AT WORK. OKAY?
HEY!
GREEN-EYED ALE. WILL THERE BE ANYTHING ELSE?
NO, I'M... I'M ALL SET.
TIPS
I HAVE SOME EXTRA DOLLAR THINGS. CAN I TURN THEM IN?
ABSO-LUTELY, EH.
HEY!
SO, YEAH. PICK UP SOME TEA ON YOUR WAY DOWN.
NO DECAF, OKAY?
PFFT. EASY!
DON'T SWEAT IT, MAR'. WILL'S PREDIS-POSED TO FUCK UP.
NEVER IN MY LIFE DOES THE BOY LISTEN TO ME, AND FINALLY HE LISTENS TO ME!
YOU SEE HANNA'S GREAT POTENTIAL FOR CREATING HAPPINESS? FOR FREEING YOU PEOPLE OF DRAMA?
HEY!
SPEAKING OF WHICH, I BET YOU'RE CRAWLIN' IN YOUR SKIN, NING...
...THAT YOU MUST HENCEFORTH ADDRESS ME AS SERGEANT-MAJOR SNOWBALL.
YOU WEAR MANY HATS, MA'AM.

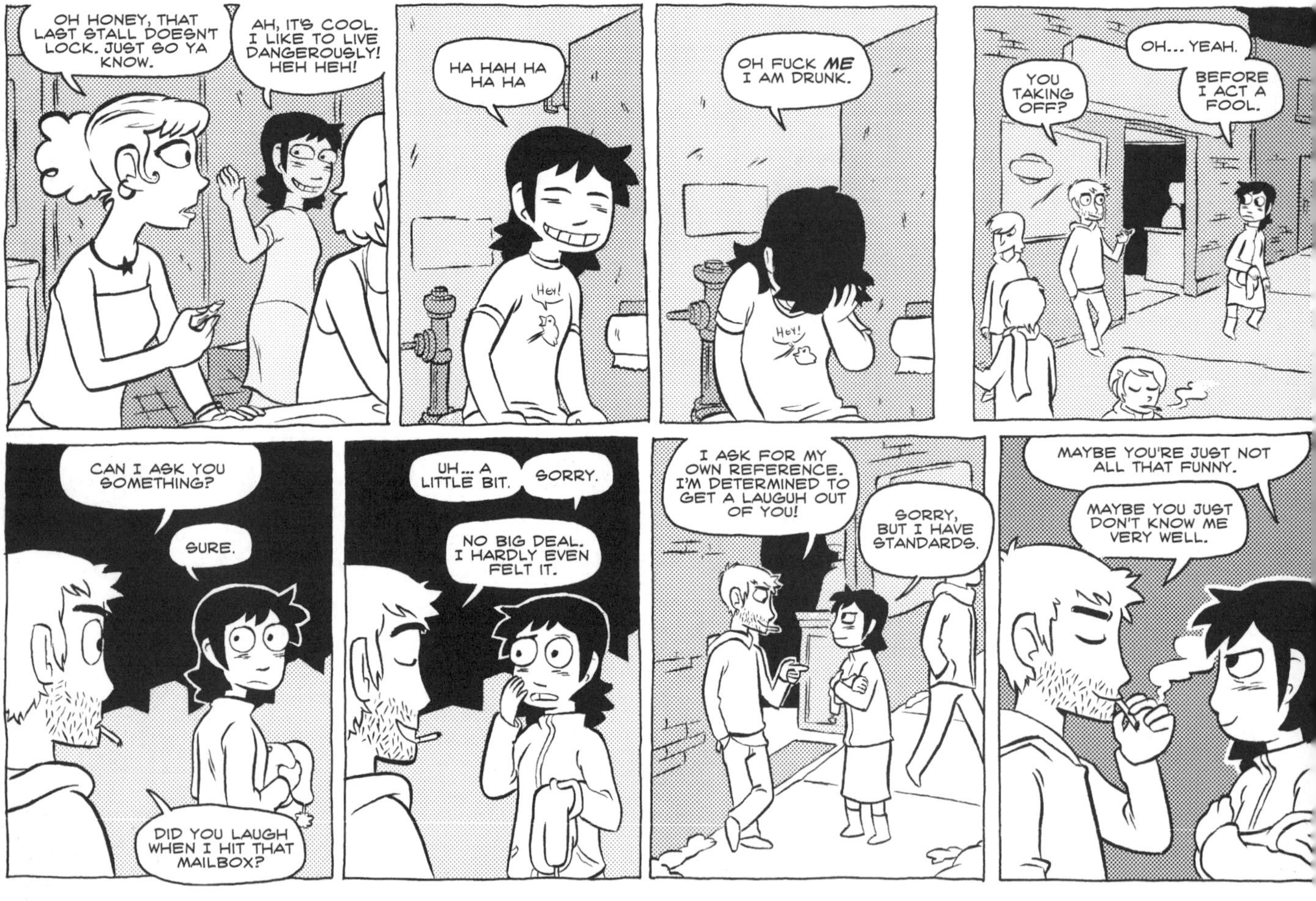
OH HONEY, THAT LAST STALL DOESN'T LOCK. JUST SO YA KNOW.
AH, IT'S COOL. I LIKE TO LIVE DANGEROUSLY! HEH HEH!
HA HAH HA HA HA
Hey!
OH FUCK ME I AM DRUNK.
Hey!
YOU TAKING OFF?
OH... YEAH.
BEFORE I ACT A FOOL.
CAN I ASK YOU SOMETHING?
SURE.
DID YOU LAUGH WHEN I HIT THAT MAILBOX?
UH... A LITTLE BIT.
SORRY.
NO BIG DEAL. I HARDLY EVEN FELT IT.
I ASK FOR MY OWN REFERENCE. I'M DETERMINED TO GET A LAUGUH OUT OF YOU!
SORRY, BUT I HAVE STANDARDS.
MAYBE YOU'RE JUST NOT ALL THAT FUNNY.
MAYBE YOU JUST DON'T KNOW ME VERY WELL.

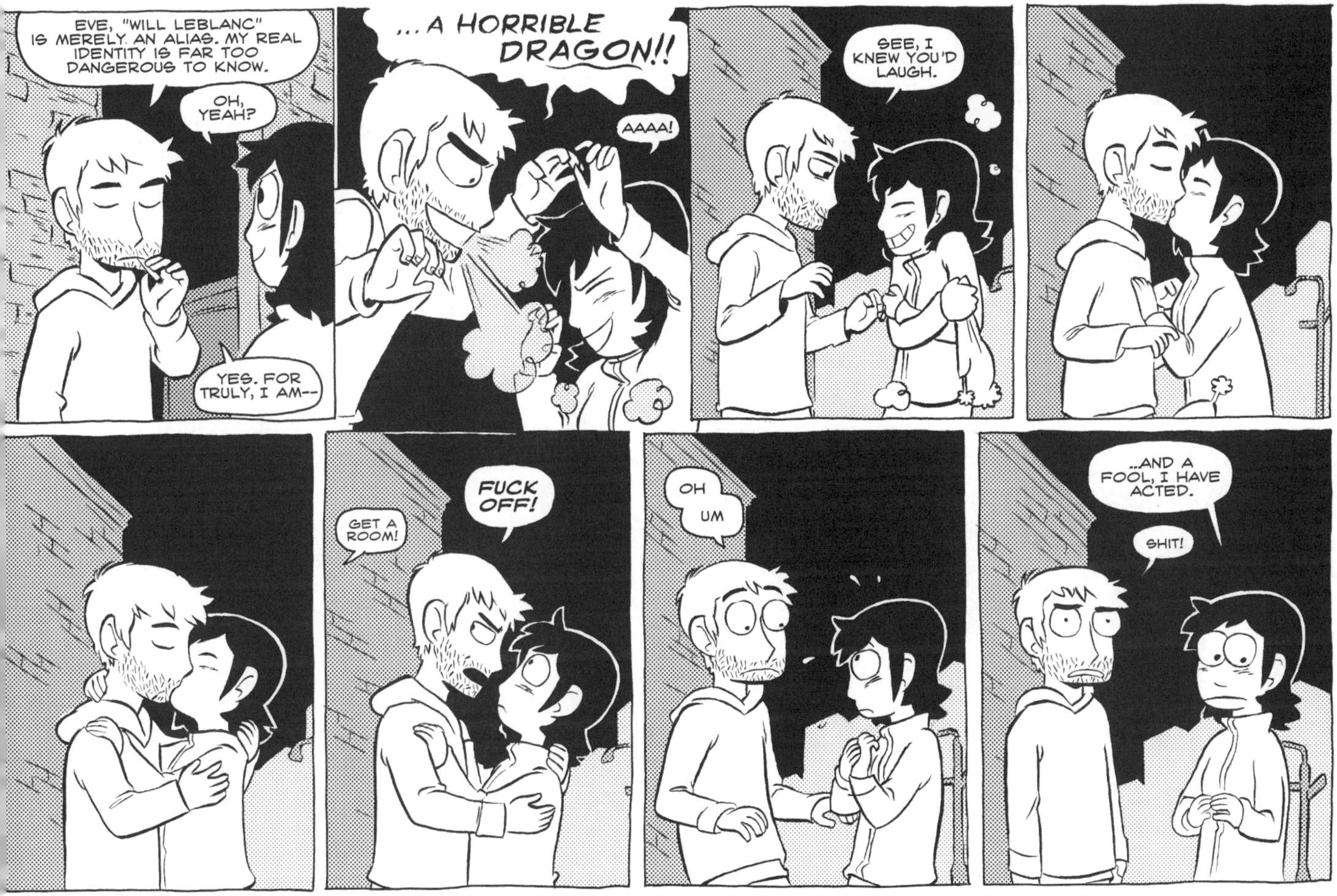
EVE, "WILL LEBLANC" IS MERELY AN ALIAS. MY REAL IDENTITY IS FAR TOO DANGEROUS TO KNOW.
OH, YEAH?
YES. FOR TRULY, I AM--
...A HORRIBLE DRAGON!!
AAAA!
SEE, I KNEW YOU'D LAUGH.
GET A ROOM!
FUCK OFF!
OH
UM
..AND A FOOL, I HAVE ACTED.
SHIT!

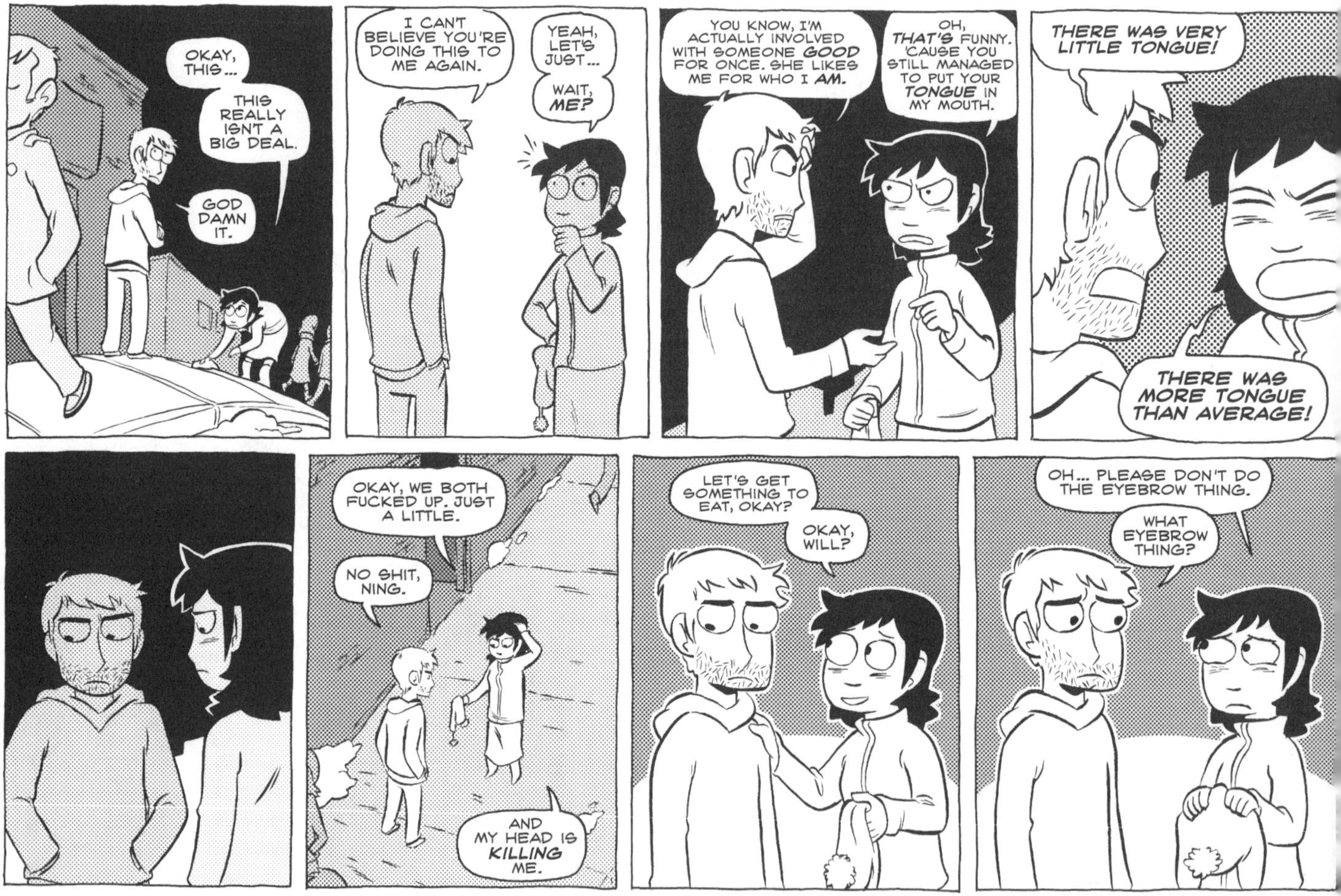
OKAY, THIS...
THIS REALLY ISN'T A BIG DEAL.
GOD DAMN IT.
I CAN'T BELIEVE YOU'RE DOING THIS TO ME AGAIN.
YEAH, LET'S JUST...
WAIT, ME?
YOU KNOW, I'M ACTUALLY INVOLVED WITH SOMEONE GOOD FOR ONCE. SHE LIKES ME FOR WHO I AM.
OH, THAT'S FUNNY. 'CAUSE YOU STILL MANAGED TO PUT YOUR TONGUE IN MY MOUTH.
THERE WAS VERY LITTLE TONGUE!
THERE WAS MORE TONGUE THAN AVERAGE!
OKAY, WE BOTH FUCKED UP. JUST A LITTLE.
NO SHIT, NING.
AND MY HEAD IS KILLING ME.
LET'S GET SOMETHING TO EAT, OKAY?
OKAY, WILL?
OH... PLEASE DON'T DO THE EYEBROW THING.
WHAT EYEBROW THING?

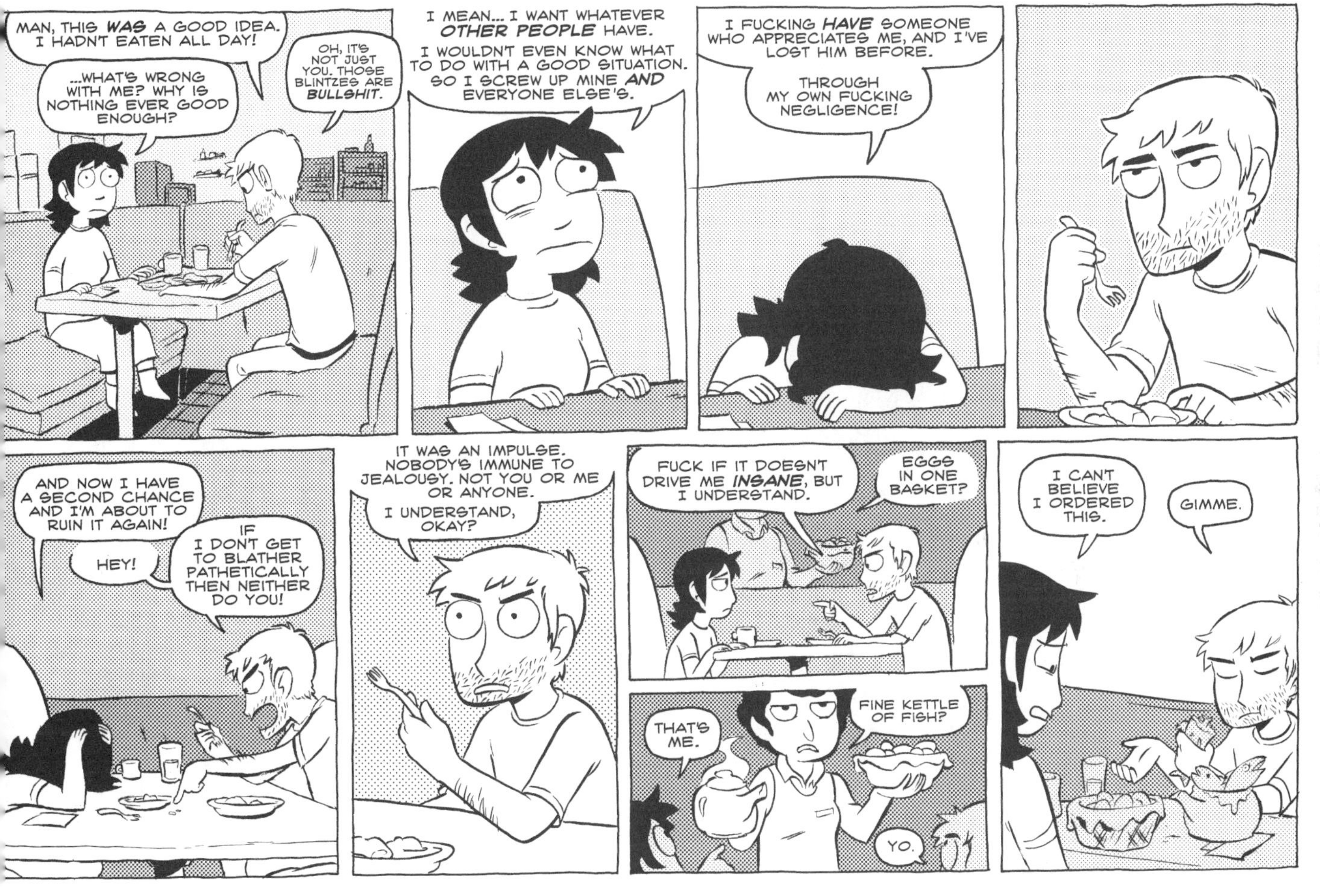
MAN, THIS **WAS** A GOOD IDEA. I HADN'T EATEN ALL DAY!
...WHAT'S WRONG WITH ME? WHY IS NOTHING EVER GOOD ENOUGH?
OH, IT'S NOT JUST YOU. THOSE BLINTZES ARE **BULLSHIT**.
I MEAN... I WANT WHATEVER **OTHER PEOPLE** HAVE.
I WOULDN'T EVEN KNOW WHAT TO DO WITH A GOOD SITUATION. SO I SCREW UP MINE **AND** EVERYONE ELSE'S.
I FUCKING **HAVE** SOMEONE WHO APPRECIATES ME, AND I'VE LOST HIM BEFORE.
THROUGH MY OWN FUCKING NEGLIGENCE!
AND NOW I HAVE A SECOND CHANCE AND I'M ABOUT TO RUIN IT AGAIN!
HEY!
IF I DON'T GET TO BLATHER PATHETICALLY THEN NEITHER DO YOU!
IT WAS AN IMPULSE. NOBODY'S IMMUNE TO JEALOUSY. NOT YOU OR ME OR ANYONE.
I UNDERSTAND, OKAY?
FUCK IF IT DOESN'T DRIVE ME **INSANE**, BUT I UNDERSTAND.
EGGS IN ONE BASKET?
THAT'S ME.
FINE KETTLE OF FISH?
YO.
I CAN'T BELIEVE I ORDERED THIS.
GIMME.

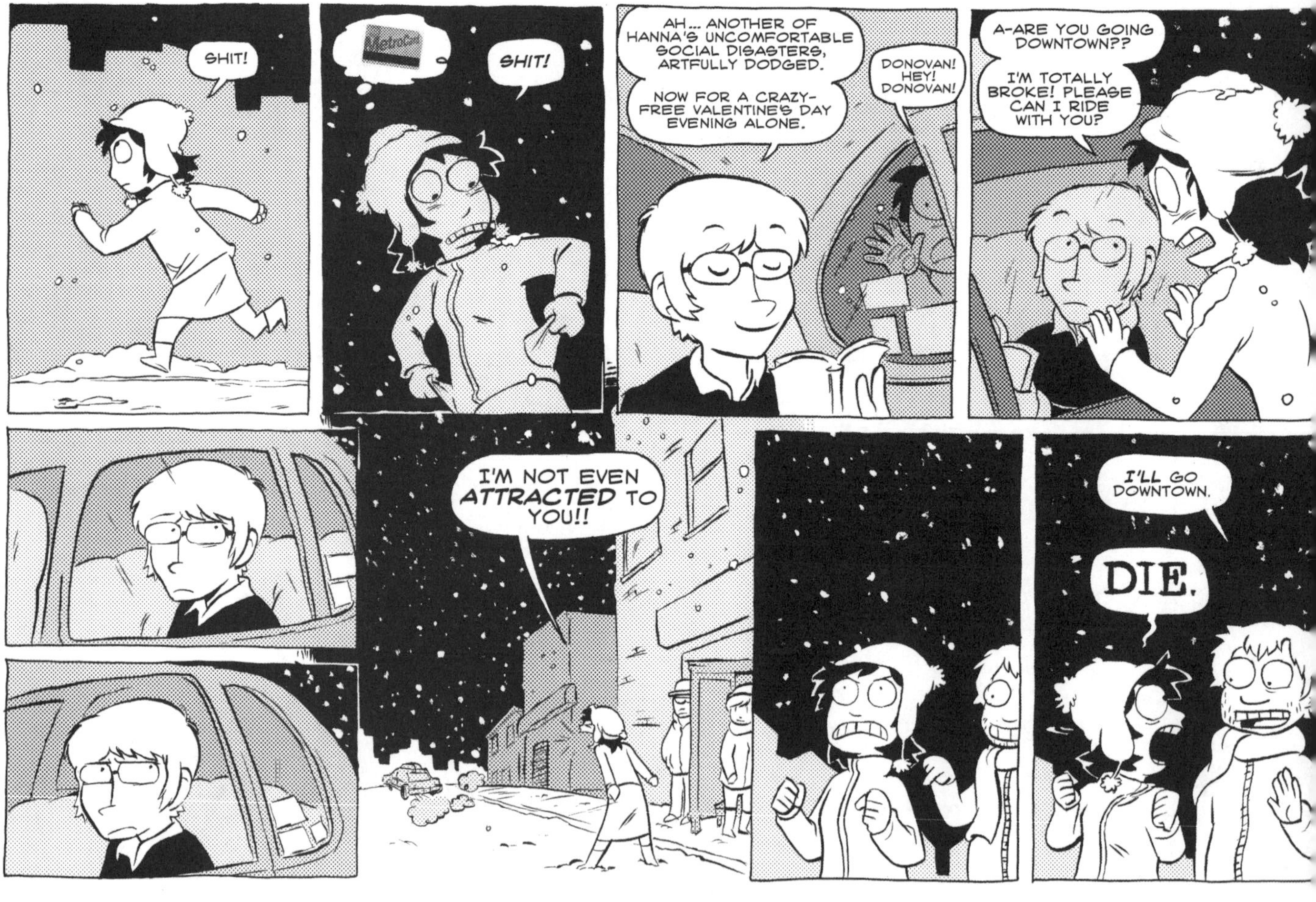
SHIT!
MetroCard
SHIT!
AH... ANOTHER OF HANNA'S UNCOMFORTABLE SOCIAL DISASTERS, ARTFULLY DODGED.
NOW FOR A CRAZY-FREE VALENTINE'S DAY EVENING ALONE.
DONOVAN! HEY! DONOVAN!
A-ARE YOU GOING DOWNTOWN??
I'M TOTALLY BROKE! PLEASE CAN I RIDE WITH YOU?
I'M NOT EVEN ATTRACTED TO YOU!!
I'LL GO DOWNTOWN.
DIE.

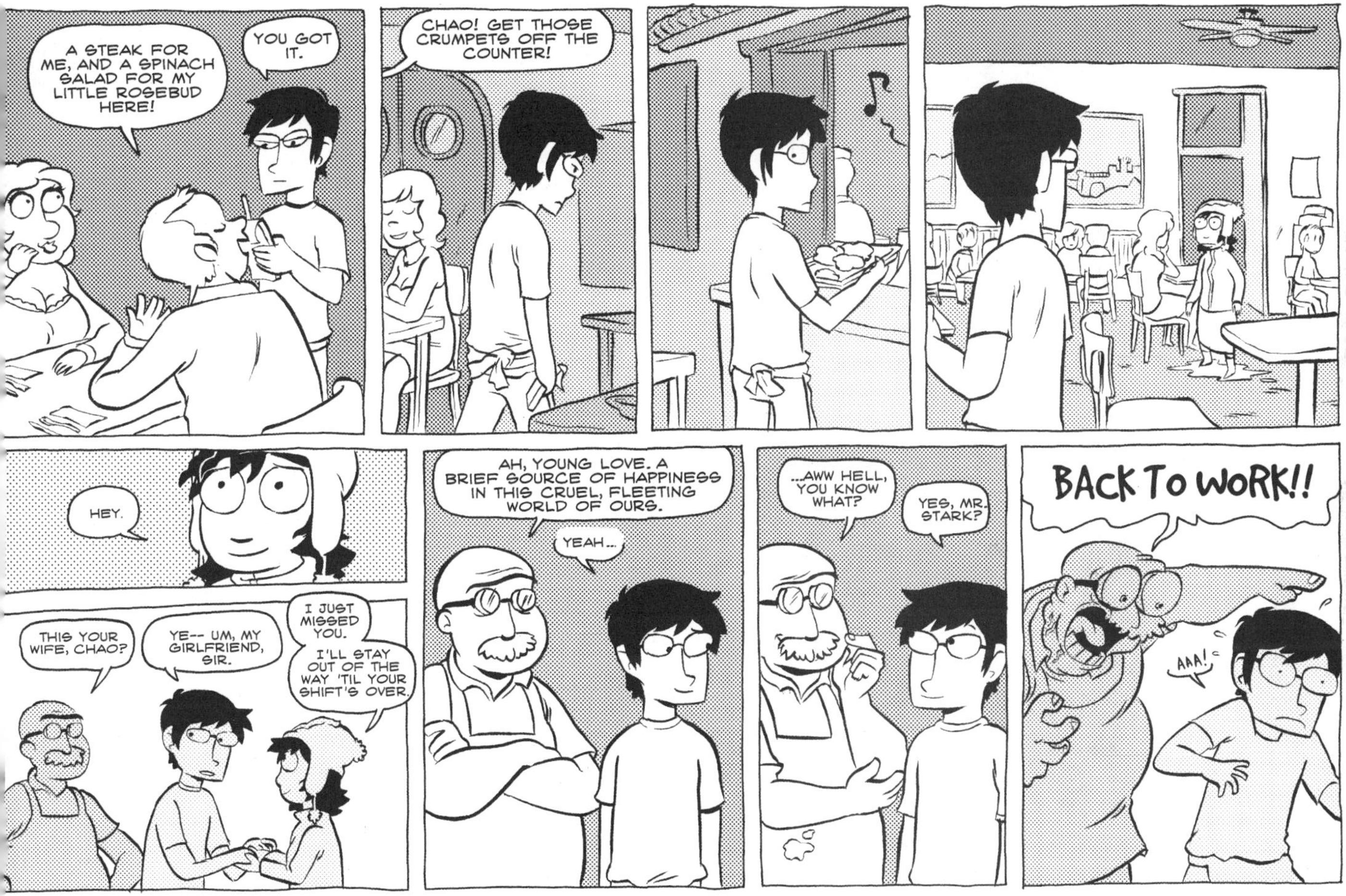
A STEAK FOR ME, AND A SPINACH SALAD FOR MY LITTLE ROSEBUD HERE!
YOU GOT IT.
CHAO! GET THOSE CRUMPETS OFF THE COUNTER!
HEY.
THIS YOUR WIFE, CHAO?
YE-- UM, MY GIRLFRIEND, SIR.
I JUST MISSED YOU.
I'LL STAY OUT OF THE WAY 'TIL YOUR SHIFT'S OVER.
AH, YOUNG LOVE. A BRIEF SOURCE OF HAPPINESS IN THIS CRUEL, FLEETING WORLD OF OURS.
YEAH...
...AWW HELL, YOU KNOW WHAT?
YES, MR. STARK?
BACK TO WORK!!
AAA!

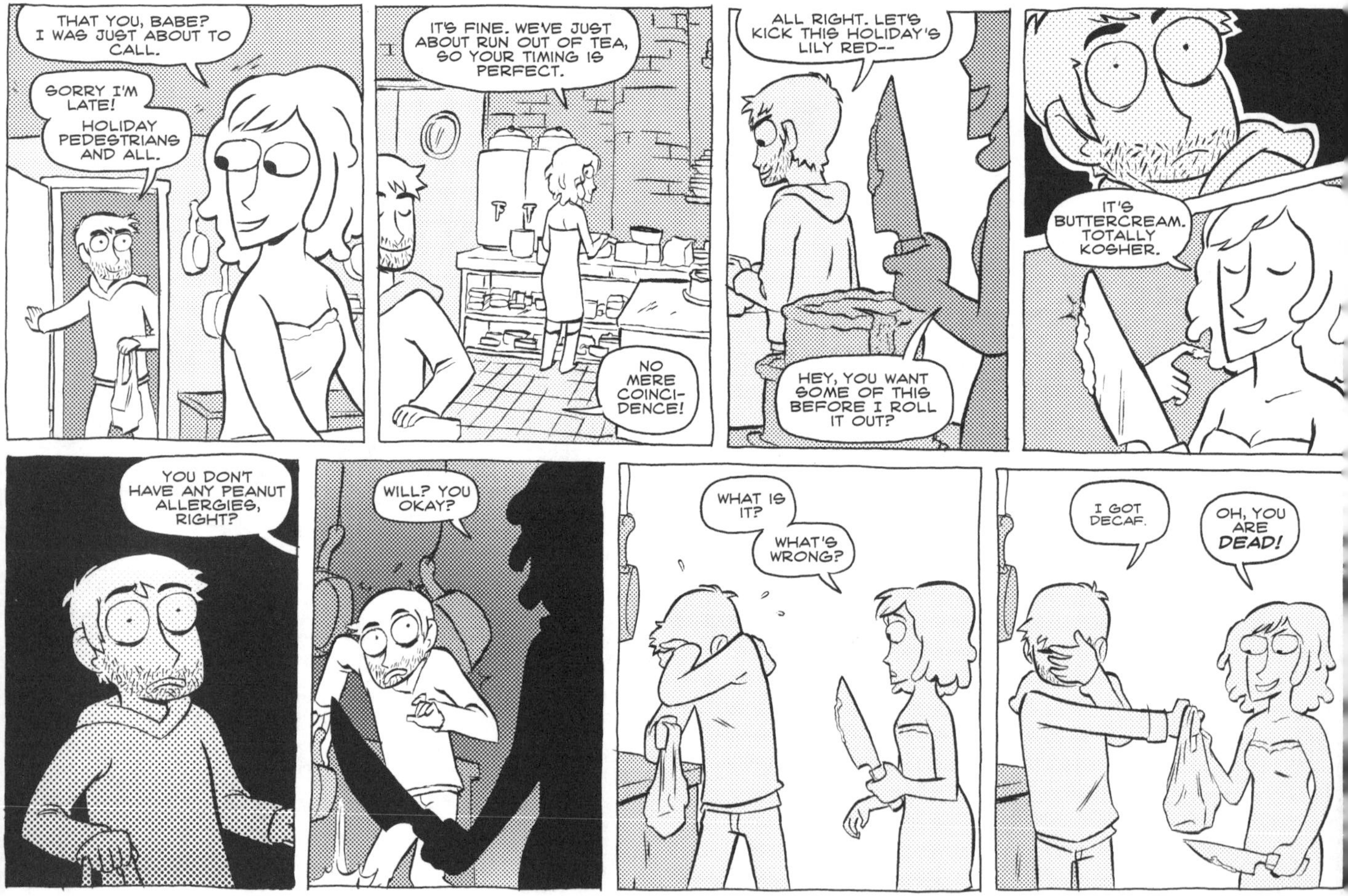
THAT YOU, BABE? I WAS JUST ABOUT TO CALL.
SORRY I'M LATE!
HOLIDAY PEDESTRIANS AND ALL.
IT'S FINE. WE'VE JUST ABOUT RUN OUT OF TEA, SO YOUR TIMING IS PERFECT.
NO MERE COINCI-DENCE!
ALL RIGHT. LET'S KICK THIS HOLIDAY'S LILY RED--
HEY, YOU WANT SOME OF THIS BEFORE I ROLL IT OUT?
IT'S BUTTERCREAM. TOTALLY KOSHER.
YOU DON'T HAVE ANY PEANUT ALLERGIES, RIGHT?
WILL? YOU OKAY?
WHAT IS IT?
WHAT'S WRONG?
I GOT DECAF.
OH, YOU ARE DEAD!

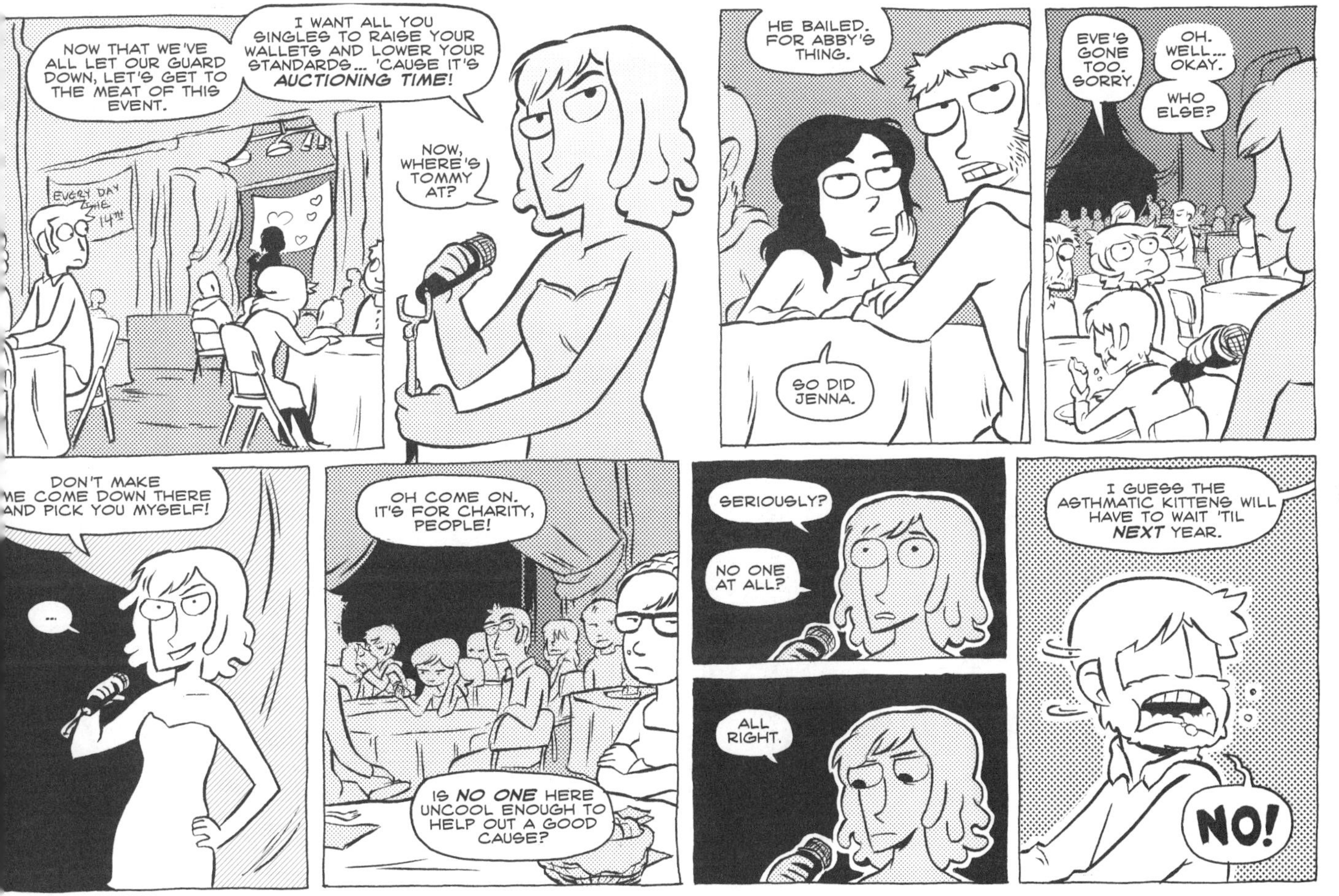
NOW THAT WE'VE ALL LET OUR GUARD DOWN, LET'S GET TO THE MEAT OF THIS EVENT.
I WANT ALL YOU SINGLES TO RAISE YOUR WALLETS AND LOWER YOUR STANDARDS... 'CAUSE IT'S AUCTIONING TIME!
EVERY DAY THE 14TH
NOW, WHERE'S TOMMY AT?
HE BAILED. FOR ABBY'S THING.
SO DID JENNA.
EVE'S GONE TOO. SORRY.
OH. WELL... OKAY.
WHO ELSE?
DON'T MAKE ME COME DOWN THERE AND PICK YOU MYSELF!
...
OH COME ON. IT'S FOR CHARITY, PEOPLE!
IS NO ONE HERE UNCOOL ENOUGH TO HELP OUT A GOOD CAUSE?
SERIOUSLY?
NO ONE AT ALL?
ALL RIGHT.
I GUESS THE ASTHMATIC KITTENS WILL HAVE TO WAIT 'TIL NEXT YEAR.
NO!

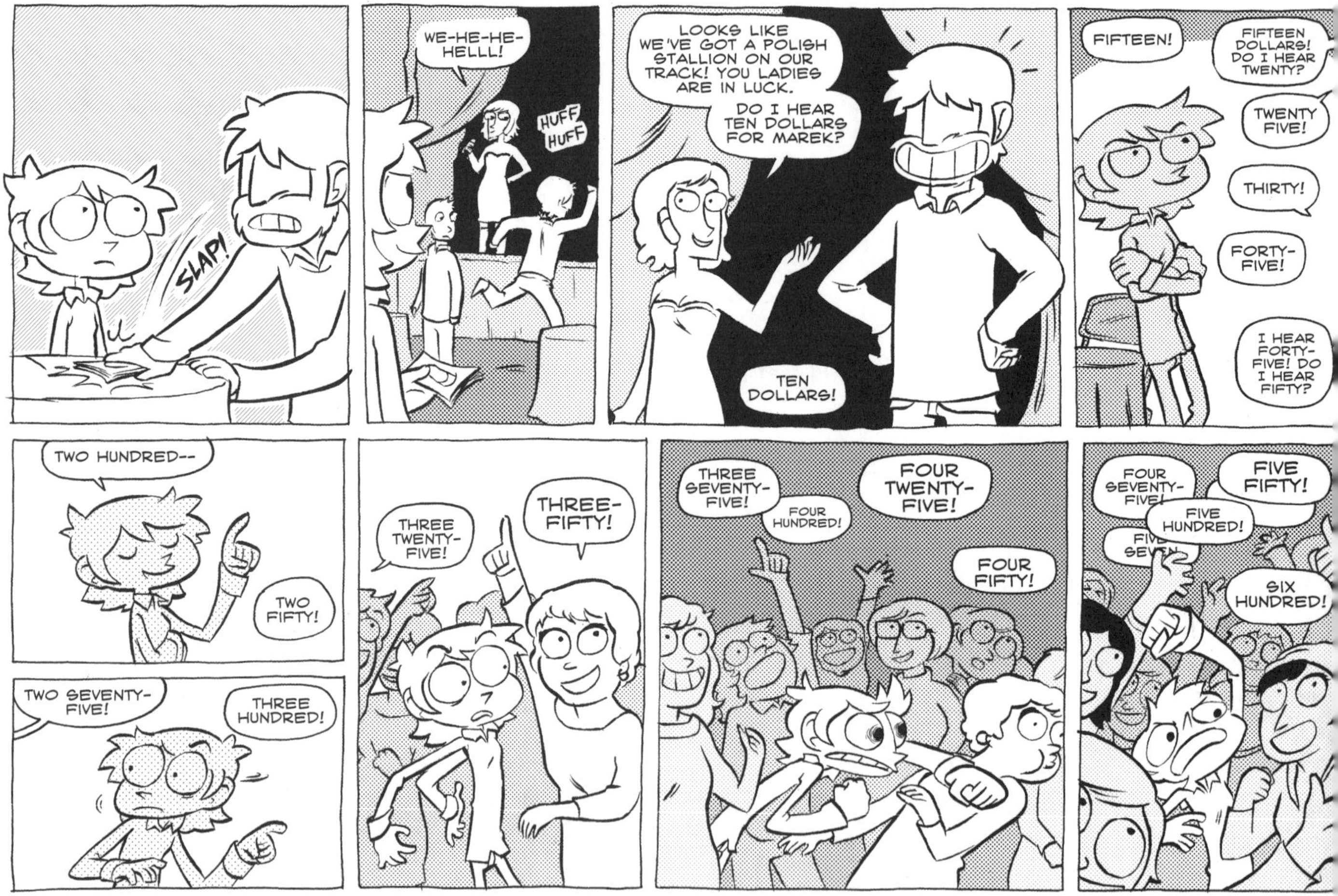
SLAP!
WE-HE-HE-HELLL!
HUFF HUFF
LOOKS LIKE WE'VE GOT A POLISH STALLION ON OUR TRACK! YOU LADIES ARE IN LUCK.
DO I HEAR TEN DOLLARS FOR MAREK?
TEN DOLLARS!
FIFTEEN!
FIFTEEN DOLLARS! DO I HEAR TWENTY?
TWENTY FIVE!
THIRTY!
FORTY-FIVE!
I HEAR FORTY-FIVE! DO I HEAR FIFTY?
TWO HUNDRED--
TWO FIFTY!
TWO SEVENTY-FIVE!
THREE HUNDRED!
THREE TWENTY-FIVE!
THREE-FIFTY!
THREE SEVENTY-FIVE!
FOUR HUNDRED!
FOUR TWENTY-FIVE!
FOUR FIFTY!
FOUR SEVENTY-FIVE!
FIVE FIFTY!
FIVE HUNDRED!
SIX HUNDRED!

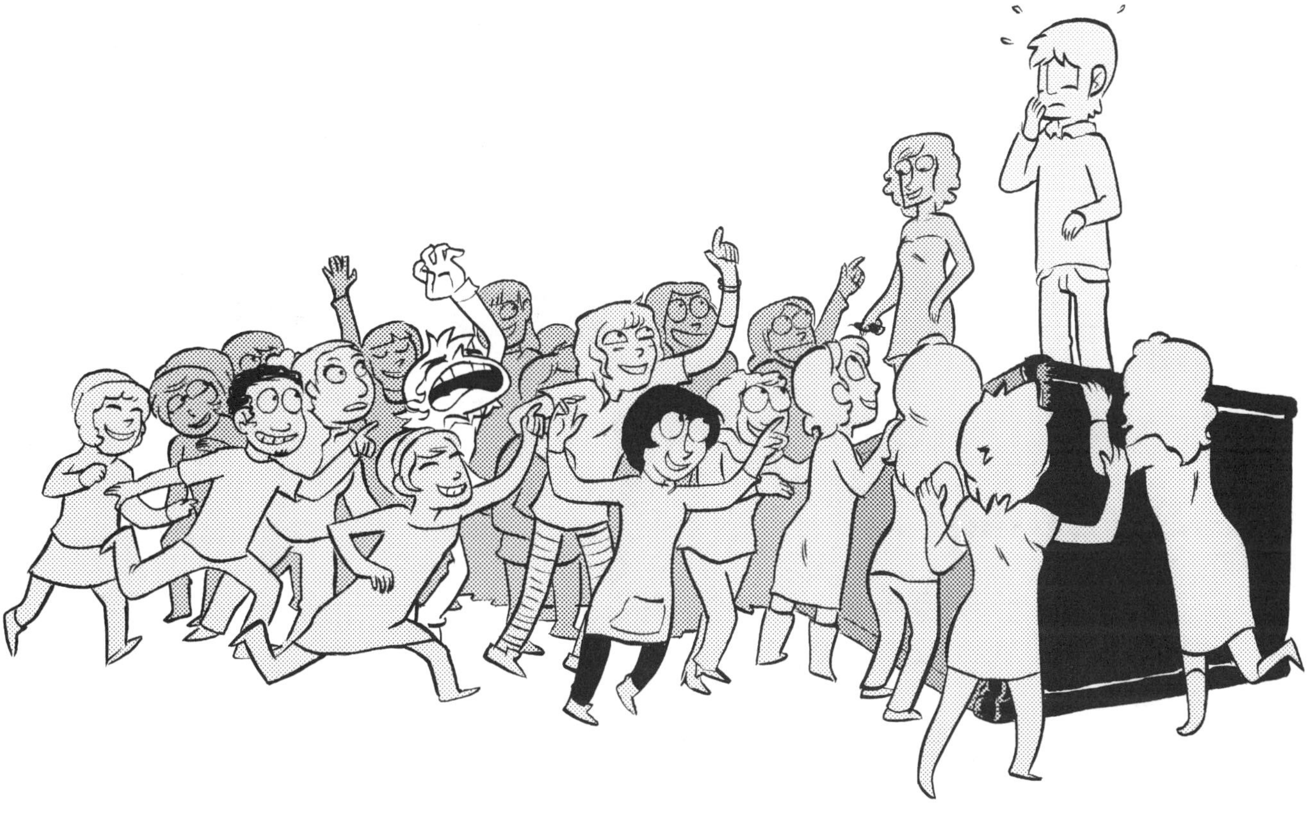

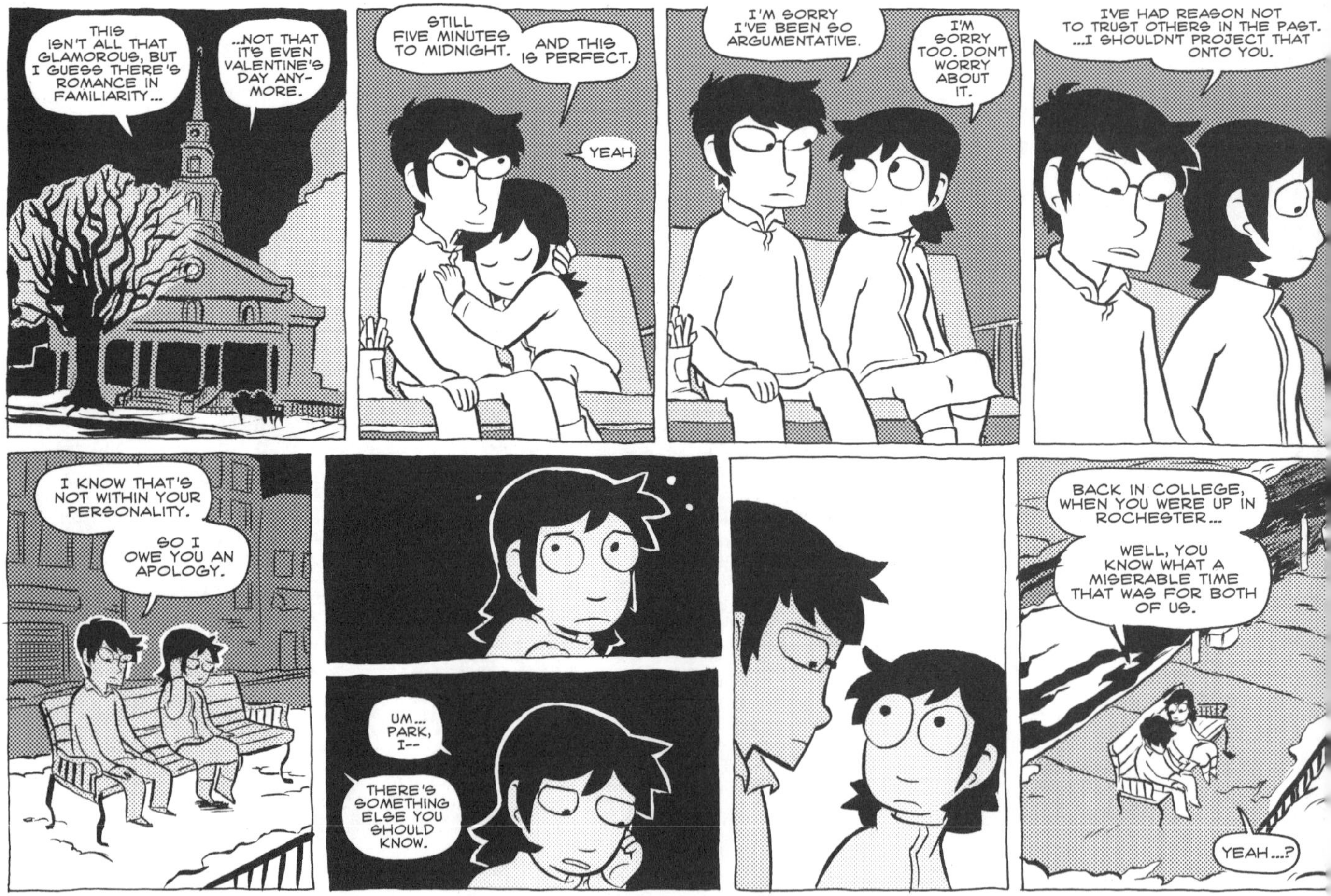
THIS ISN'T ALL THAT GLAMOROUS, BUT I GUESS THERE'S ROMANCE IN FAMILIARITY...
...NOT THAT IT'S EVEN VALENTINE'S DAY ANY-MORE.
STILL FIVE MINUTES TO MIDNIGHT.
AND THIS IS PERFECT.
YEAH.
I'M SORRY I'VE BEEN SO ARGUMENTATIVE.
I'M SORRY TOO. DON'T WORRY ABOUT IT.
I'VE HAD REASON NOT TO TRUST OTHERS IN THE PAST. ...I SHOULDN'T PROJECT THAT ONTO YOU.
I KNOW THAT'S NOT WITHIN YOUR PERSONALITY.
SO I OWE YOU AN APOLOGY.
UM... PARK, I--
THERE'S SOMETHING ELSE YOU SHOULD KNOW.
BACK IN COLLEGE, WHEN YOU WERE UP IN ROCHESTER...
WELL, YOU KNOW WHAT A MISERABLE TIME THAT WAS FOR BOTH OF US.
YEAH...?

BEFORE WE BROKE UP, I WAS ALREADY SEEING SOMEONE ELSE.
FOR QUITE A WHILE.
I THOUGHT THAT MIGHT'VE BEEN THE CASE.

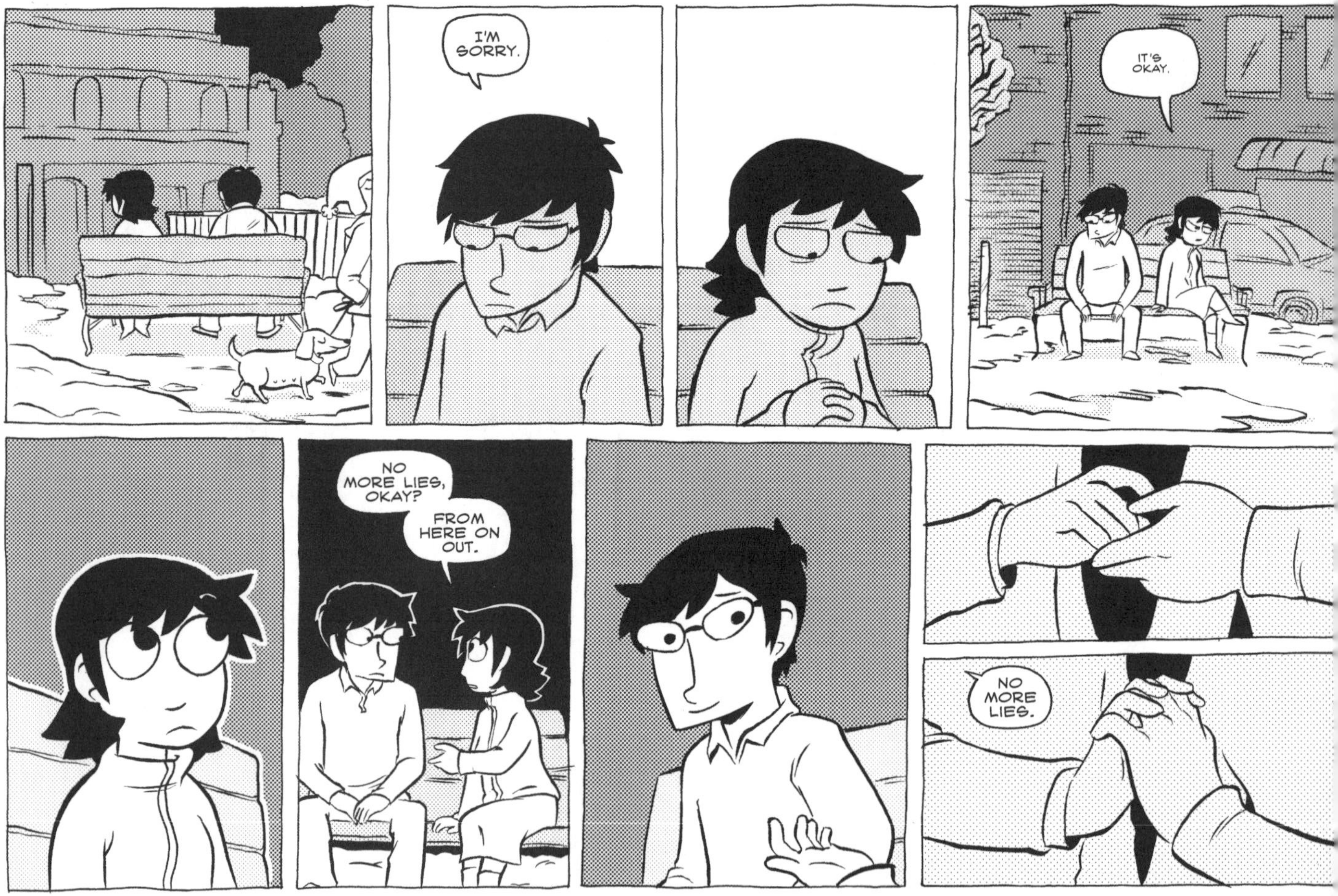
I'M SORRY.
IT'S OKAY.
NO MORE LIES, OKAY?
FROM HERE ON OUT.
NO MORE LIES.

OH YEAH, HANNA'S TAUGHT ME ALL KINDS OF TECHNIQUES WITH FRENCH DESSERTS.

THERE'S *NOTHING* SHE CAN'T MAKE.

OH MAN, LAST WEEK? SHE MADE THIS CHERRY CLAFOUTIS? IT WAS SO GOOD I WAS VISIBLY CRYING.

SWEET TEARS WITH EVERY BITE!

SHE'S SUCH A GENIUS.

I'M SORRY. YOU PAID FOR THIS DATE, AND ALL I CAN TALK ABOUT IS BAKING!

UH... YEAH, IT'S FINE.

SO... WHAT MUSIC DO YOU LIKE?

OH, CLASSIC DISCO, MOSTLY. HANNA HATES IT, THOUGH.

SHE'LL COME HOME AND BE LIKE, *"WHAT IS THAT INCESSANT STEREOPHONIC DIARRHEA??"*

PORTABLE RADIO!

VI-VI-VI-VIVA LA

PORTABLE RADIO!

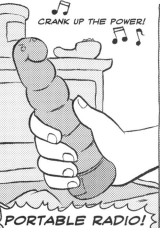

CRANK UP THE POWER!

PORTABLE RADIO!

TURN UP THE POWER ALL *NIGHT.*

Lifetime TV

Supermarket Sweep was a TV game show my siblings and I were fully confident we could win. We spent a large part of our week at the grocery store with our mom, which made us experts. We shouted at the TV, and lamented regularly that kids weren't allowed on the show. So I guess this is your standard issue wish fulfillment story.

I used this story to air one of Eve's (and my) least endearing roles: the bossy big sister. I still catch myself treating my younger brother like less than an adult, even though he's out of college and about five feet taller than me. It's fun to see how ineffectively a bossy sibling's behavior translates to the adult world. Eve is beaten down at work and ridiculed by her friends, but still feels like she has some remnants of authority at home.

Mor's kindness to Eve is all but overshadowed by the supermarket action, but to me it's the heart of this story. He has the power to be his own person and stand up for himself, but ultimately lets Eve push him around. I wonder how often I've done this to my own brother, only for it to go unacknowledged or be quietly forgiven.

As a side note, I'd really like to use Eve's Good & Evil sides some more. They're the people she could've been if she'd been turned 2 degrees in either direction, and I find that as interesting a part of her character as anything.

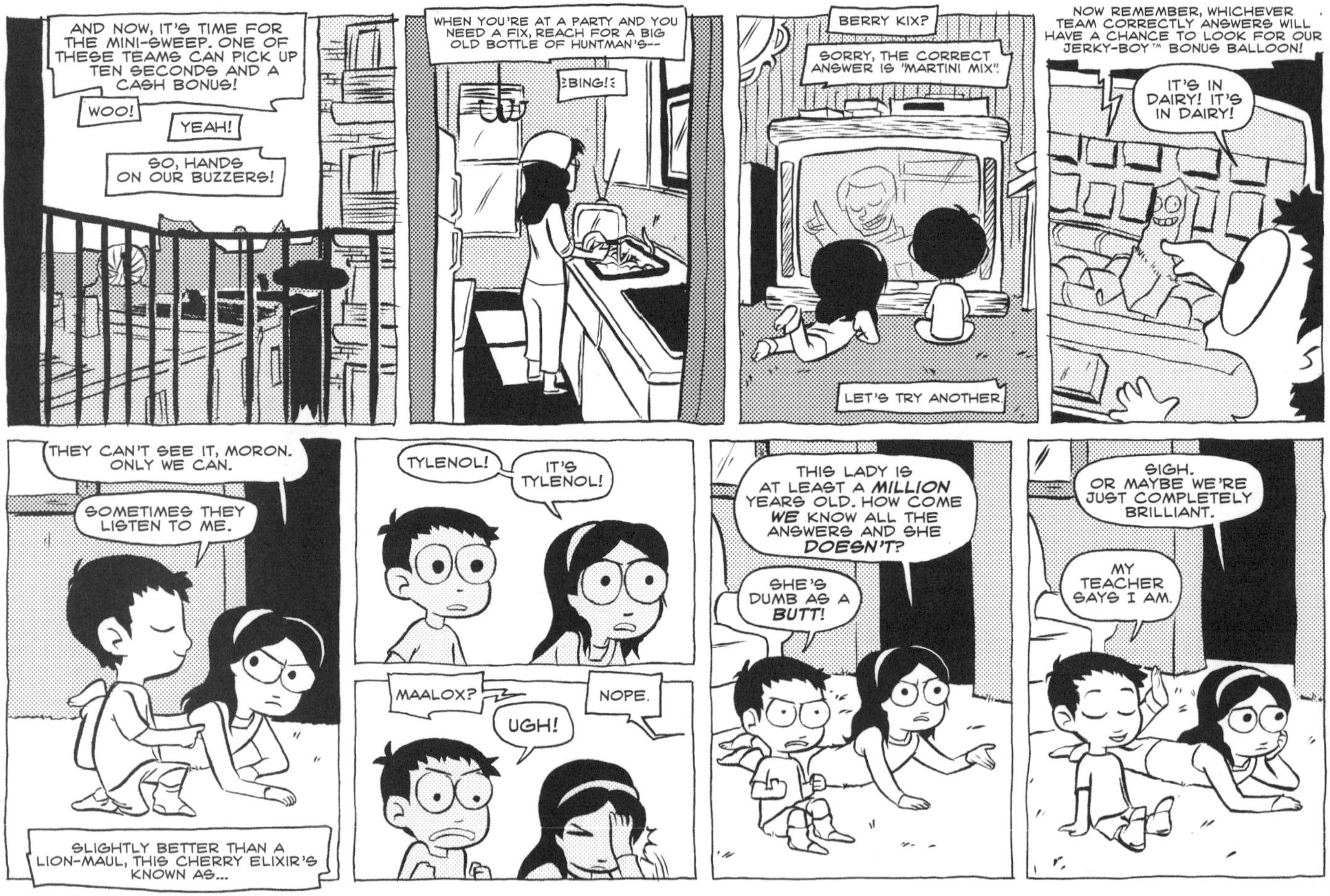

AND NOW, IT'S TIME FOR THE MINI-SWEEP. ONE OF THESE TEAMS CAN PICK UP TEN SECONDS AND A CASH BONUS!
WOO!
YEAH!
SO, HANDS ON OUR BUZZERS!
WHEN YOU'RE AT A PARTY AND YOU NEED A FIX, REACH FOR A BIG OLD BOTTLE OF HUNTMAN'S--
BING!
BERRY KIX?
SORRY, THE CORRECT ANSWER IS "MARTINI MIX".
LET'S TRY ANOTHER.
NOW REMEMBER, WHICHEVER TEAM CORRECTLY ANSWERS WILL HAVE A CHANCE TO LOOK FOR OUR JERKY-BOY™ BONUS BALLOON!
IT'S IN DAIRY! IT'S IN DAIRY!
THEY CAN'T SEE IT, MORON. ONLY WE CAN.
SOMETIMES THEY LISTEN TO ME.
SLIGHTLY BETTER THAN A LION-MAUL, THIS CHERRY ELIXIR'S KNOWN AS...
TYLENOL!
IT'S TYLENOL!
MAALOX?
NOPE.
UGH!
THIS LADY IS AT LEAST A *MILLION* YEARS OLD. HOW COME *WE* KNOW ALL THE ANSWERS AND SHE *DOESN'T*?
SHE'S DUMB AS A *BUTT*!
SIGH. OR MAYBE WE'RE JUST COMPLETELY BRILLIANT.
MY TEACHER SAYS I AM.

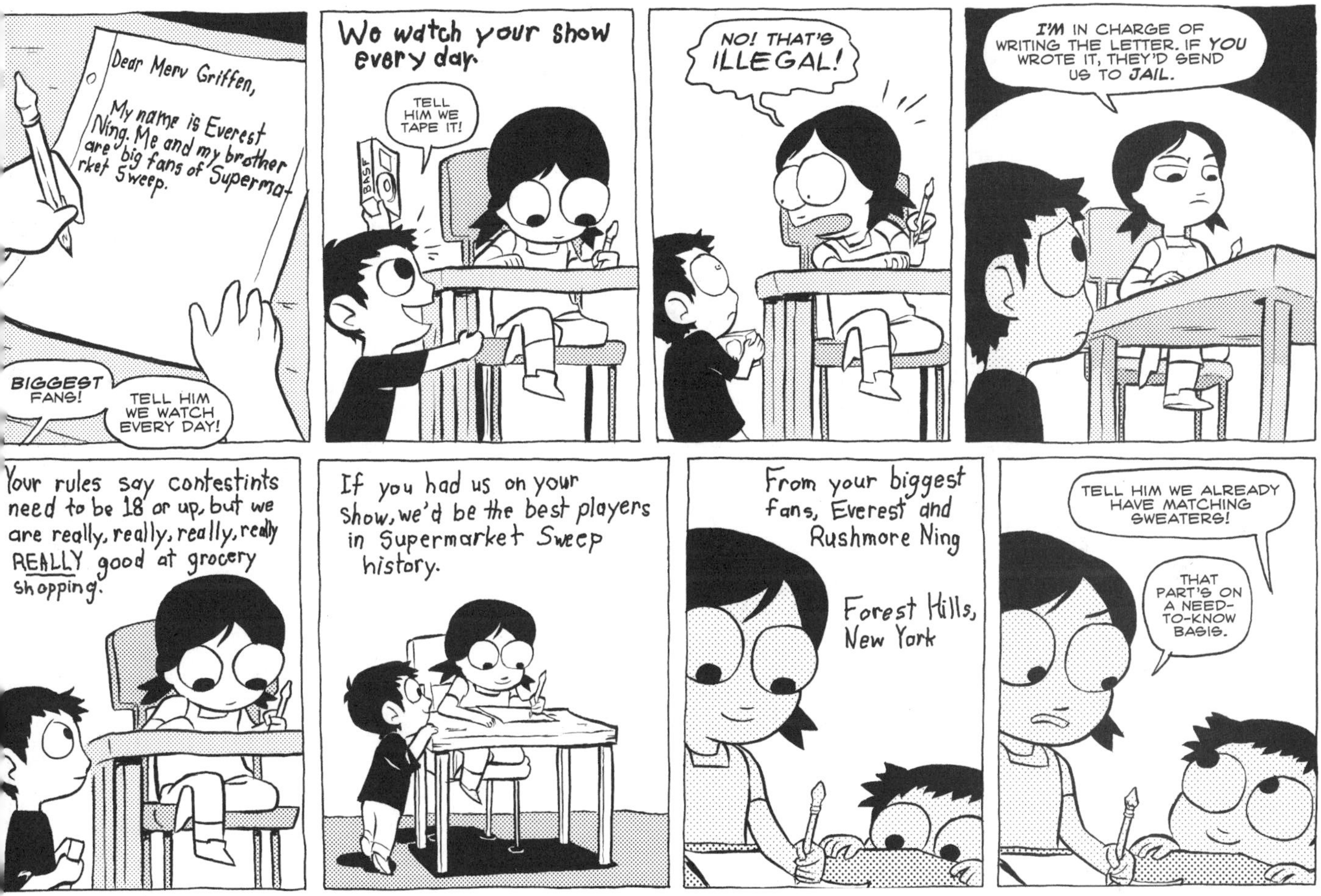
Dear Merv Griffen,
My name is Everest Ning. Me and my brother are big fans of Supermarket Sweep.
BIGGEST FANS!
TELL HIM WE WATCH EVERY DAY!
We watch your show every day.
TELL HIM WE TAPE IT!
BASF
NO! THAT'S ILLEGAL!
I'M IN CHARGE OF WRITING THE LETTER. IF YOU WROTE IT, THEY'D SEND US TO JAIL.
Your rules say contestints need to be 18 or up, but we are really, really, really, really REALLY good at grocery shopping.
If you had us on your show, we'd be the best players in Supermarket Sweep history.
From your biggest fans, Everest and Rushmore Ning
Forest Hills, New York
TELL HIM WE ALREADY HAVE MATCHING SWEATERS!
THAT PART'S ON A NEED-TO-KNOW BASIS.

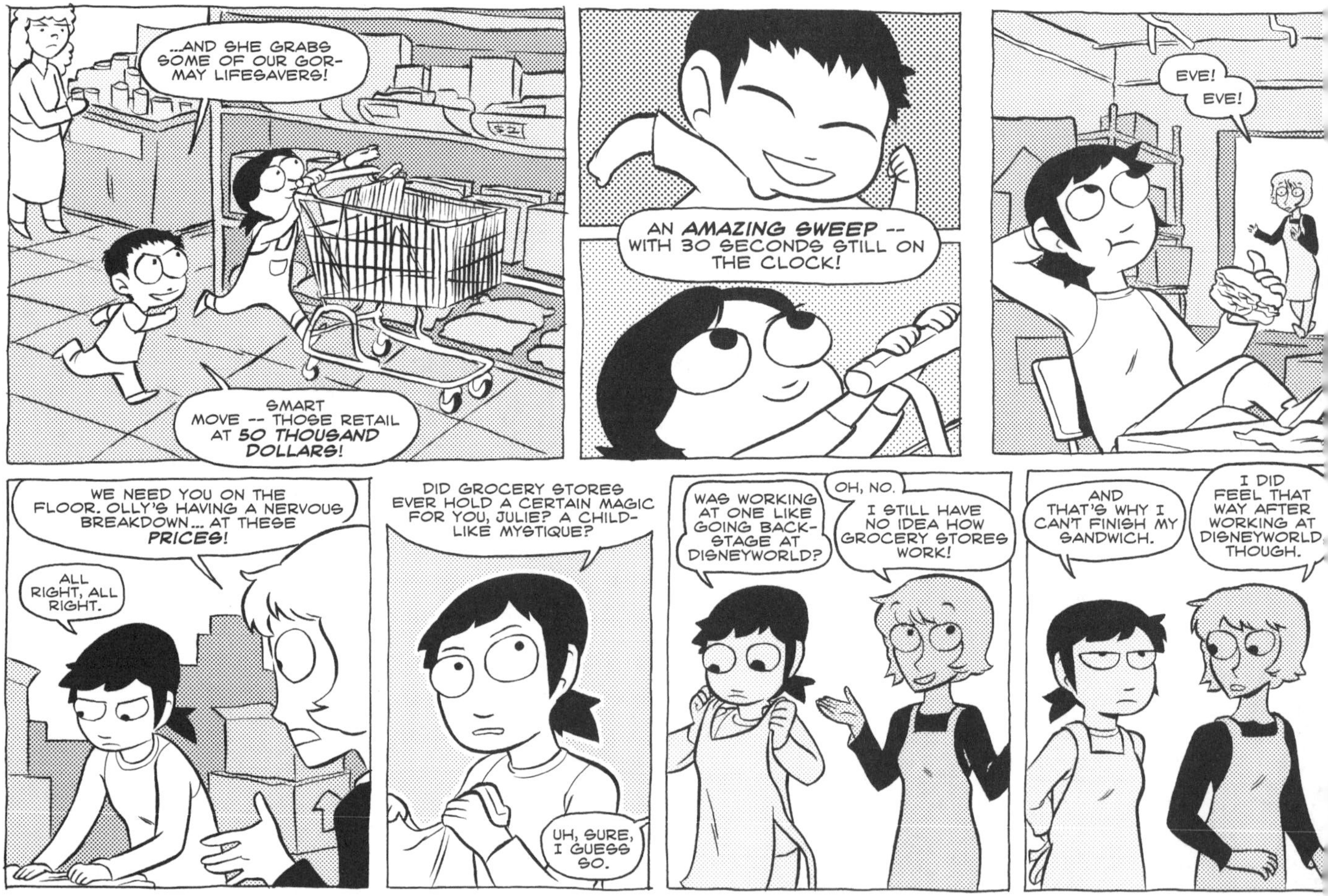
...AND SHE GRABS SOME OF OUR GOR-MAY LIFESAVERS!
SMART MOVE -- THOSE RETAIL AT 50 THOUSAND DOLLARS!
AN AMAZING SWEEP -- WITH 30 SECONDS STILL ON THE CLOCK!
EVE!
EVE!
WE NEED YOU ON THE FLOOR. OLLY'S HAVING A NERVOUS BREAKDOWN... AT THESE PRICES!
ALL RIGHT, ALL RIGHT.
DID GROCERY STORES EVER HOLD A CERTAIN MAGIC FOR YOU, JULIE? A CHILD-LIKE MYSTIQUE?
UH, SURE, I GUESS SO.
WAS WORKING AT ONE LIKE GOING BACK-STAGE AT DISNEYWORLD?
OH, NO.
I STILL HAVE NO IDEA HOW GROCERY STORES WORK!
AND THAT'S WHY I CAN'T FINISH MY SANDWICH.
I DID FEEL THAT WAY AFTER WORKING AT DISNEYWORLD THOUGH.

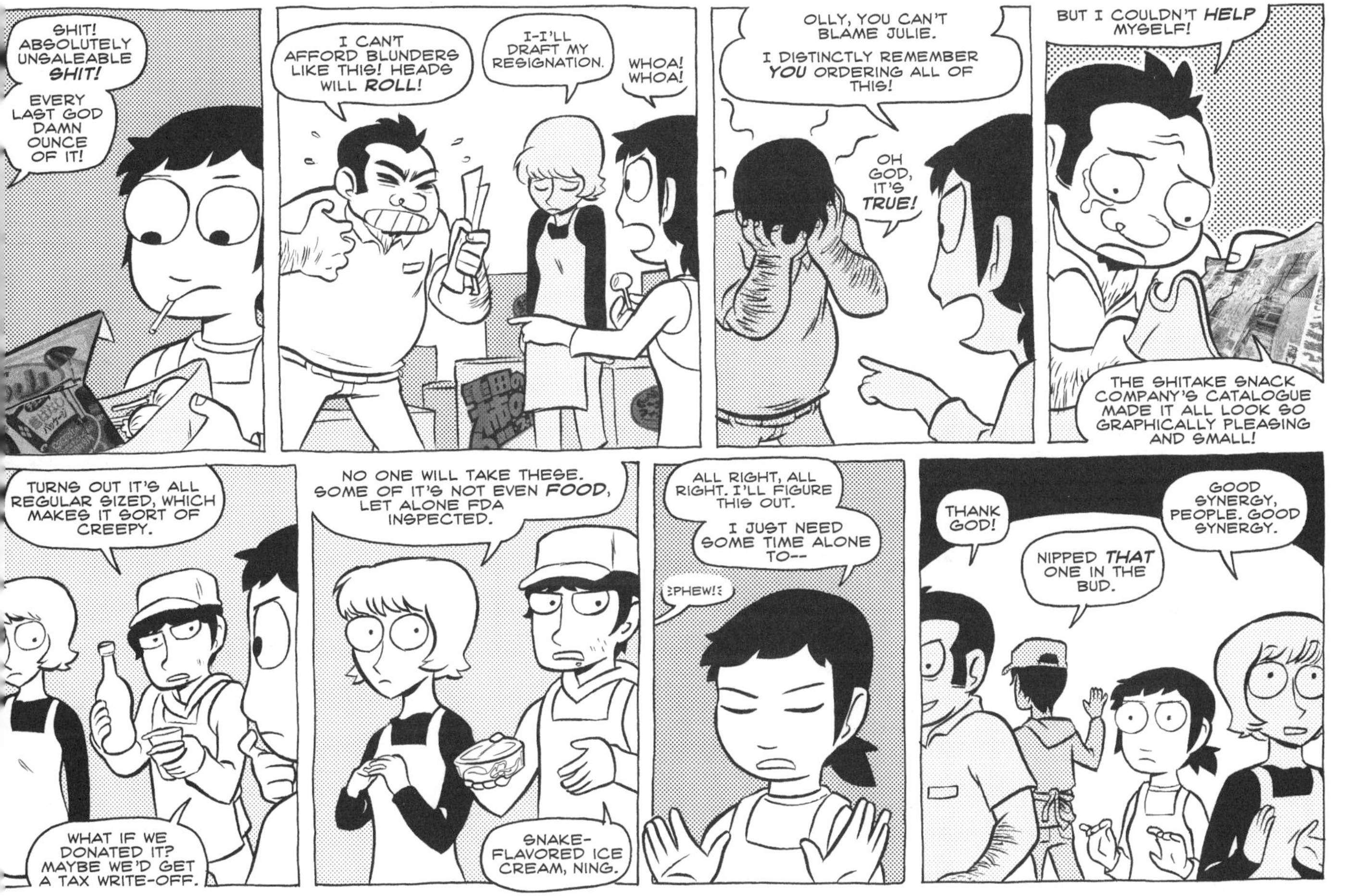
SHIT! ABSOLUTELY UNSALEABLE SHIT!
EVERY LAST GOD DAMN OUNCE OF IT!
I CAN'T AFFORD BLUNDERS LIKE THIS! HEADS WILL ROLL!
I-I'LL DRAFT MY RESIGNATION.
WHOA! WHOA!
OLLY, YOU CAN'T BLAME JULIE.
I DISTINCTLY REMEMBER YOU ORDERING ALL OF THIS!
OH GOD, IT'S TRUE!
BUT I COULDN'T HELP MYSELF!
THE SHITAKE SNACK COMPANY'S CATALOGUE MADE IT ALL LOOK SO GRAPHICALLY PLEASING AND SMALL!
TURNS OUT IT'S ALL REGULAR SIZED, WHICH MAKES IT SORT OF CREEPY.
WHAT IF WE DONATED IT? MAYBE WE'D GET A TAX WRITE-OFF.
NO ONE WILL TAKE THESE. SOME OF IT'S NOT EVEN FOOD, LET ALONE FDA INSPECTED.
SNAKE-FLAVORED ICE CREAM, NING.
ALL RIGHT, ALL RIGHT. I'LL FIGURE THIS OUT.
I JUST NEED SOME TIME ALONE TO--
PHEW!
THANK GOD!
NIPPED THAT ONE IN THE BUD.
GOOD SYNERGY, PEOPLE. GOOD SYNERGY.

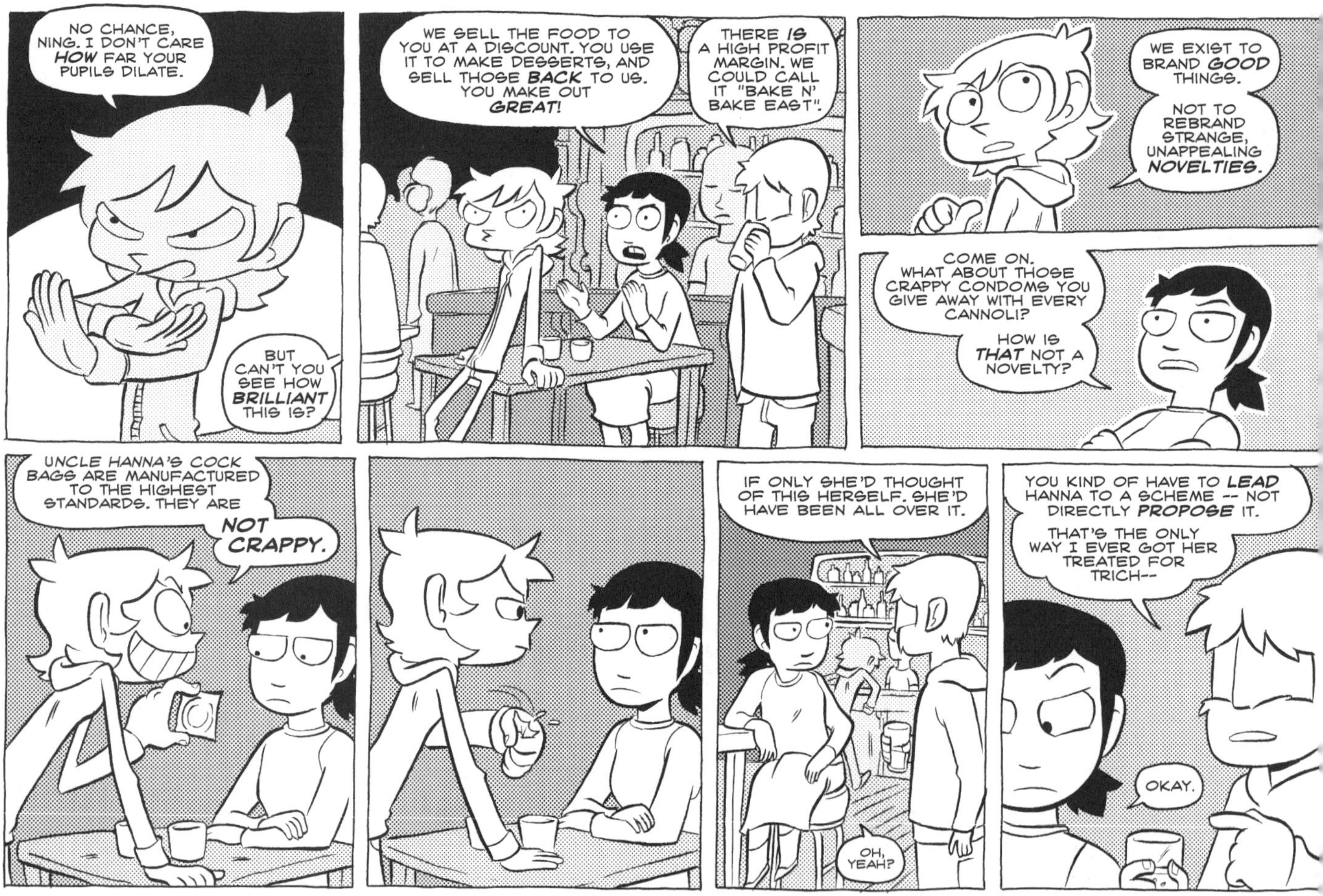
NO CHANCE, NING. I DON'T CARE HOW FAR YOUR PUPILS DILATE.
BUT CAN'T YOU SEE HOW BRILLIANT THIS IS?
WE SELL THE FOOD TO YOU AT A DISCOUNT. YOU USE IT TO MAKE DESSERTS, AND SELL THOSE BACK TO US. YOU MAKE OUT GREAT!
THERE IS A HIGH PROFIT MARGIN. WE COULD CALL IT "BAKE N' BAKE EAST".
WE EXIST TO BRAND GOOD THINGS.
NOT TO REBRAND STRANGE, UNAPPEALING NOVELTIES.
COME ON. WHAT ABOUT THOSE CRAPPY CONDOMS YOU GIVE AWAY WITH EVERY CANNOLI?
HOW IS THAT NOT A NOVELTY?
UNCLE HANNA'S COCK BAGS ARE MANUFACTURED TO THE HIGHEST STANDARDS. THEY ARE
NOT CRAPPY.
IF ONLY SHE'D THOUGHT OF THIS HERSELF. SHE'D HAVE BEEN ALL OVER IT.
OH, YEAH?
YOU KIND OF HAVE TO LEAD HANNA TO A SCHEME -- NOT DIRECTLY PROPOSE IT.
THAT'S THE ONLY WAY I EVER GOT HER TREATED FOR TRICH--
OKAY.

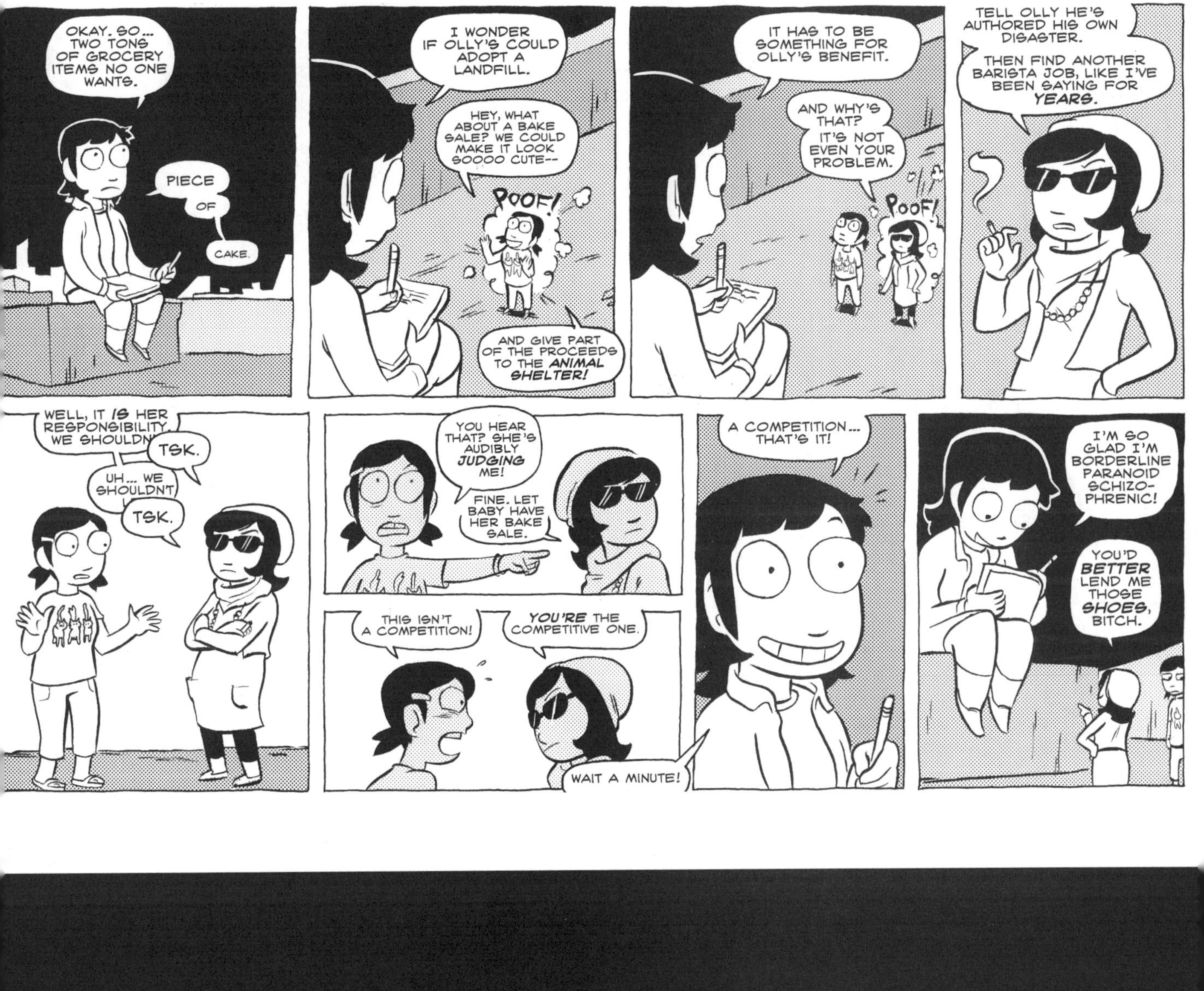
OKAY. SO... TWO TONS OF GROCERY ITEMS NO ONE WANTS.
PIECE
OF
CAKE.
I WONDER IF OLLY'S COULD ADOPT A LANDFILL.
HEY, WHAT ABOUT A BAKE SALE? WE COULD MAKE IT LOOK SOOOO CUTE--
POOF!
AND GIVE PART OF THE PROCEEDS TO THE ANIMAL SHELTER!
IT HAS TO BE SOMETHING FOR OLLY'S BENEFIT.
AND WHY'S THAT?
IT'S NOT EVEN YOUR PROBLEM.
POOF!
TELL OLLY HE'S AUTHORED HIS OWN DISASTER.
THEN FIND ANOTHER BARISTA JOB, LIKE I'VE BEEN SAYING FOR YEARS.
WELL, IT IS HER RESPONSIBILITY. WE SHOULDN'
TSK.
UH... WE SHOULDN'T
TSK.
YOU HEAR THAT? SHE'S AUDIBLY JUDGING ME!
FINE. LET BABY HAVE HER BAKE SALE.
THIS ISN'T A COMPETITION!
YOU'RE THE COMPETITIVE ONE.
WAIT A MINUTE!
A COMPETITION... THAT'S IT!
I'M SO GLAD I'M BORDERLINE PARANOID SCHIZO-PHRENIC!
YOU'D BETTER LEND ME THOSE SHOES, BITCH.

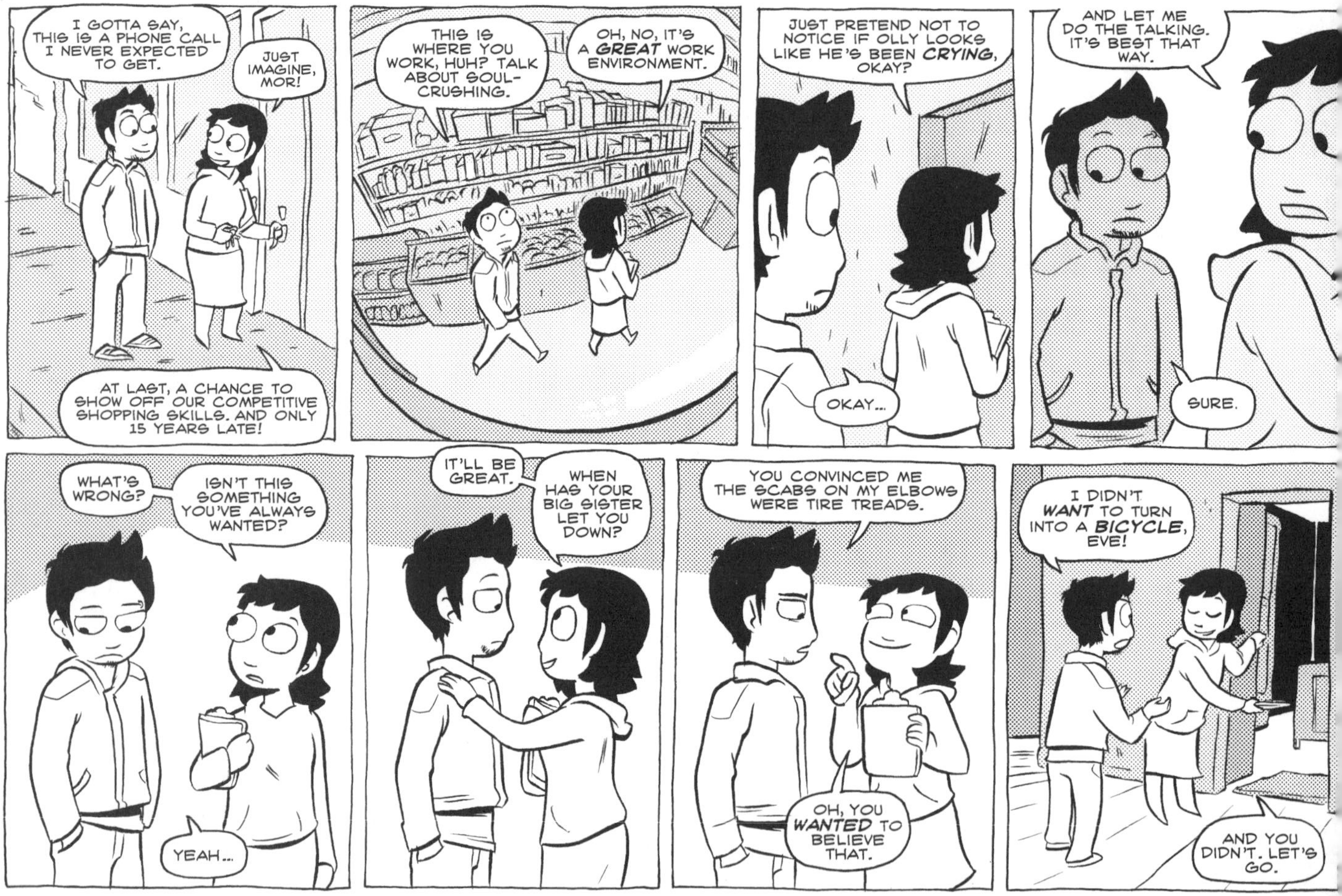

I GOTTA SAY, THIS IS A PHONE CALL I NEVER EXPECTED TO GET.
JUST IMAGINE, MOR!
AT LAST, A CHANCE TO SHOW OFF OUR COMPETITIVE SHOPPING SKILLS. AND ONLY 15 YEARS LATE!
THIS IS WHERE YOU WORK, HUH? TALK ABOUT SOUL-CRUSHING.
OH, NO, IT'S A GREAT WORK ENVIRONMENT.
JUST PRETEND NOT TO NOTICE IF OLLY LOOKS LIKE HE'S BEEN CRYING, OKAY?
OKAY...
AND LET ME DO THE TALKING. IT'S BEST THAT WAY.
SURE.
WHAT'S WRONG?
ISN'T THIS SOMETHING YOU'VE ALWAYS WANTED?
YEAH...
IT'LL BE GREAT.
WHEN HAS YOUR BIG SISTER LET YOU DOWN?
YOU CONVINCED ME THE SCABS ON MY ELBOWS WERE TIRE TREADS.
OH, YOU WANTED TO BELIEVE THAT.
I DIDN'T WANT TO TURN INTO A BICYCLE, EVE!
AND YOU DIDN'T. LET'S GO.

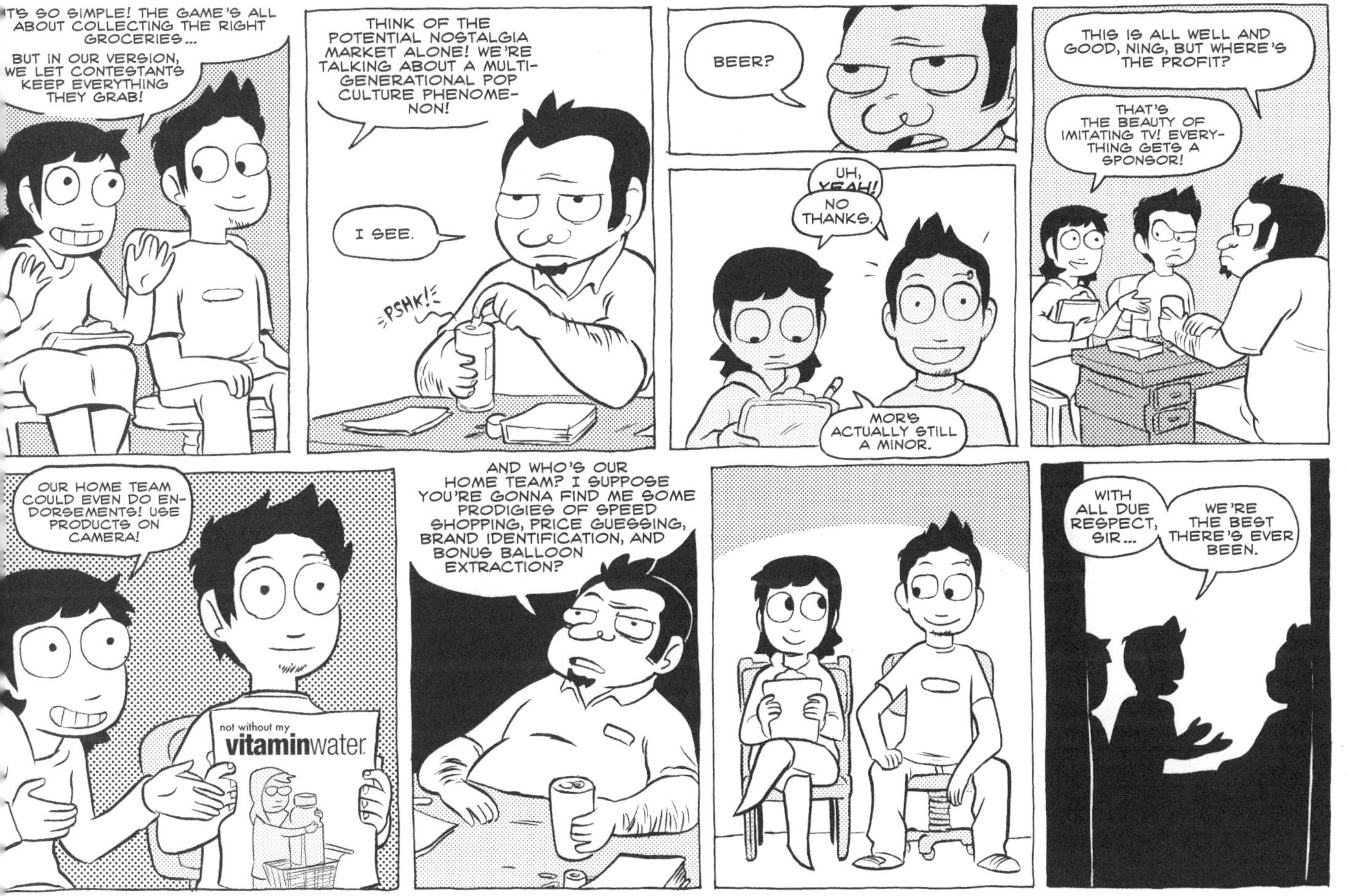
IT'S SO SIMPLE! THE GAME'S ALL ABOUT COLLECTING THE RIGHT GROCERIES...
BUT IN OUR VERSION, WE LET CONTESTANTS KEEP EVERYTHING THEY GRAB!
THINK OF THE POTENTIAL NOSTALGIA MARKET ALONE! WE'RE TALKING ABOUT A MULTI-GENERATIONAL POP CULTURE PHENOMENON!
I SEE.
PSHK!
BEER?
UH, YEAH!
NO THANKS.
MOR'S ACTUALLY STILL A MINOR.
THIS IS ALL WELL AND GOOD, NING, BUT WHERE'S THE PROFIT?
THAT'S THE BEAUTY OF IMITATING TV! EVERYTHING GETS A SPONSOR!
OUR HOME TEAM COULD EVEN DO ENDORSEMENTS! USE PRODUCTS ON CAMERA!
not without my
vitaminwater
AND WHO'S OUR HOME TEAM? I SUPPOSE YOU'RE GONNA FIND ME SOME PRODIGIES OF SPEED SHOPPING, PRICE GUESSING, BRAND IDENTIFICATION, AND BONUS BALLOON EXTRACTION?
WITH ALL DUE RESPECT, SIR...
WE'RE THE BEST THERE'S EVER BEEN.

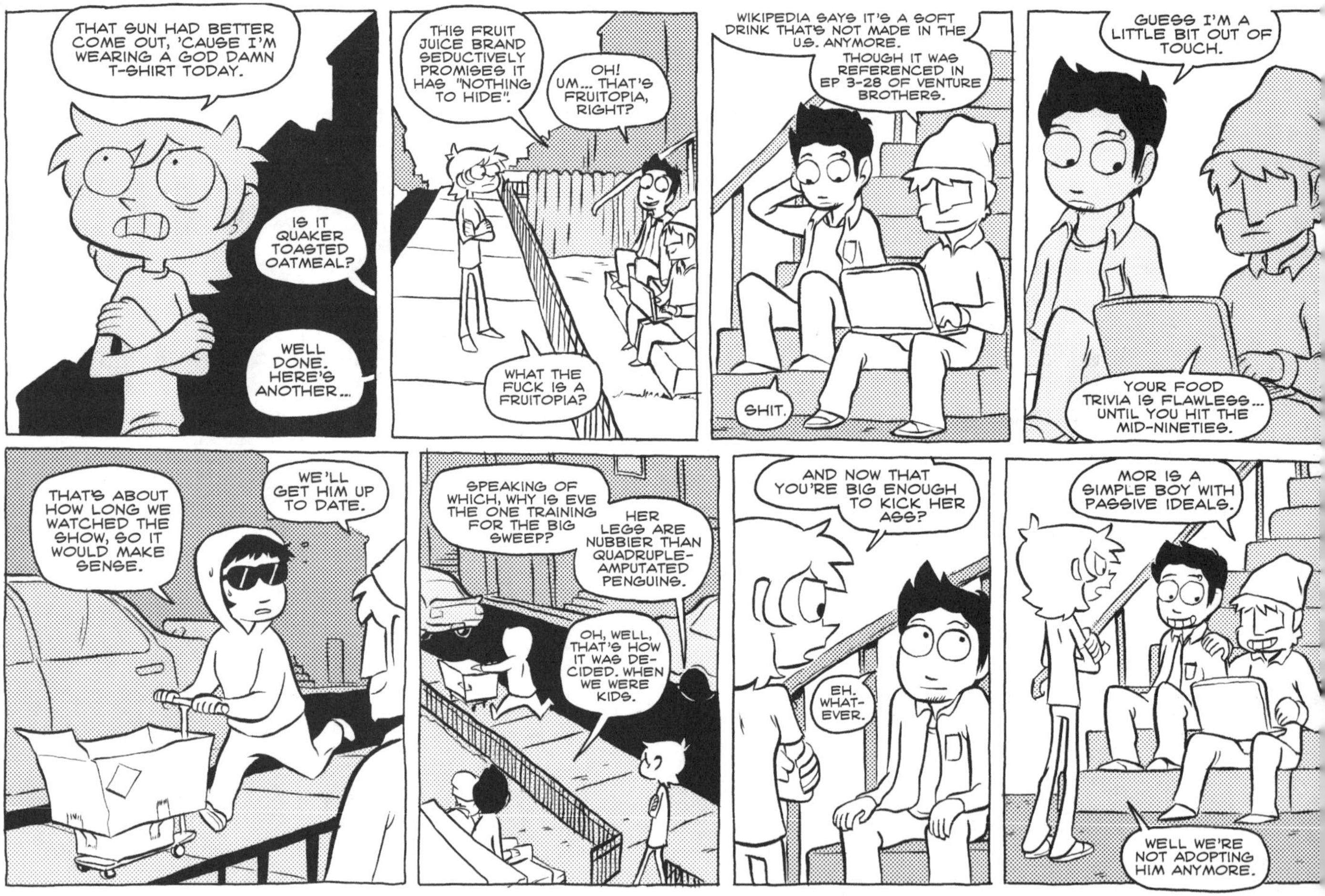

THAT SUN HAD BETTER COME OUT, 'CAUSE I'M WEARING A GOD DAMN T-SHIRT TODAY.
IS IT QUAKER TOASTED OATMEAL?
WELL DONE. HERE'S ANOTHER...
THIS FRUIT JUICE BRAND SEDUCTIVELY PROMISES IT HAS "NOTHING TO HIDE".
OH! UM... THAT'S FRUITOPIA, RIGHT?
WHAT THE FUCK IS A FRUITOPIA?
WIKIPEDIA SAYS IT'S A SOFT DRINK THAT'S NOT MADE IN THE U.S. ANYMORE.
THOUGH IT WAS REFERENCED IN EP 3-28 OF VENTURE BROTHERS.
SHIT.
GUESS I'M A LITTLE BIT OUT OF TOUCH.
YOUR FOOD TRIVIA IS FLAWLESS... UNTIL YOU HIT THE MID-NINETIES.
THAT'S ABOUT HOW LONG WE WATCHED THE SHOW, SO IT WOULD MAKE SENSE.
WE'LL GET HIM UP TO DATE.
SPEAKING OF WHICH, WHY IS EVE THE ONE TRAINING FOR THE BIG SWEEP?
HER LEGS ARE NUBBIER THAN QUADRUPLE-AMPUTATED PENGUINS.
OH, WELL, THAT'S HOW IT WAS DE-CIDED. WHEN WE WERE KIDS.
AND NOW THAT YOU'RE BIG ENOUGH TO KICK HER ASS?
EH. WHAT-EVER.
MOR IS A SIMPLE BOY WITH PASSIVE IDEALS.
WELL WE'RE NOT ADOPTING HIM ANYMORE.

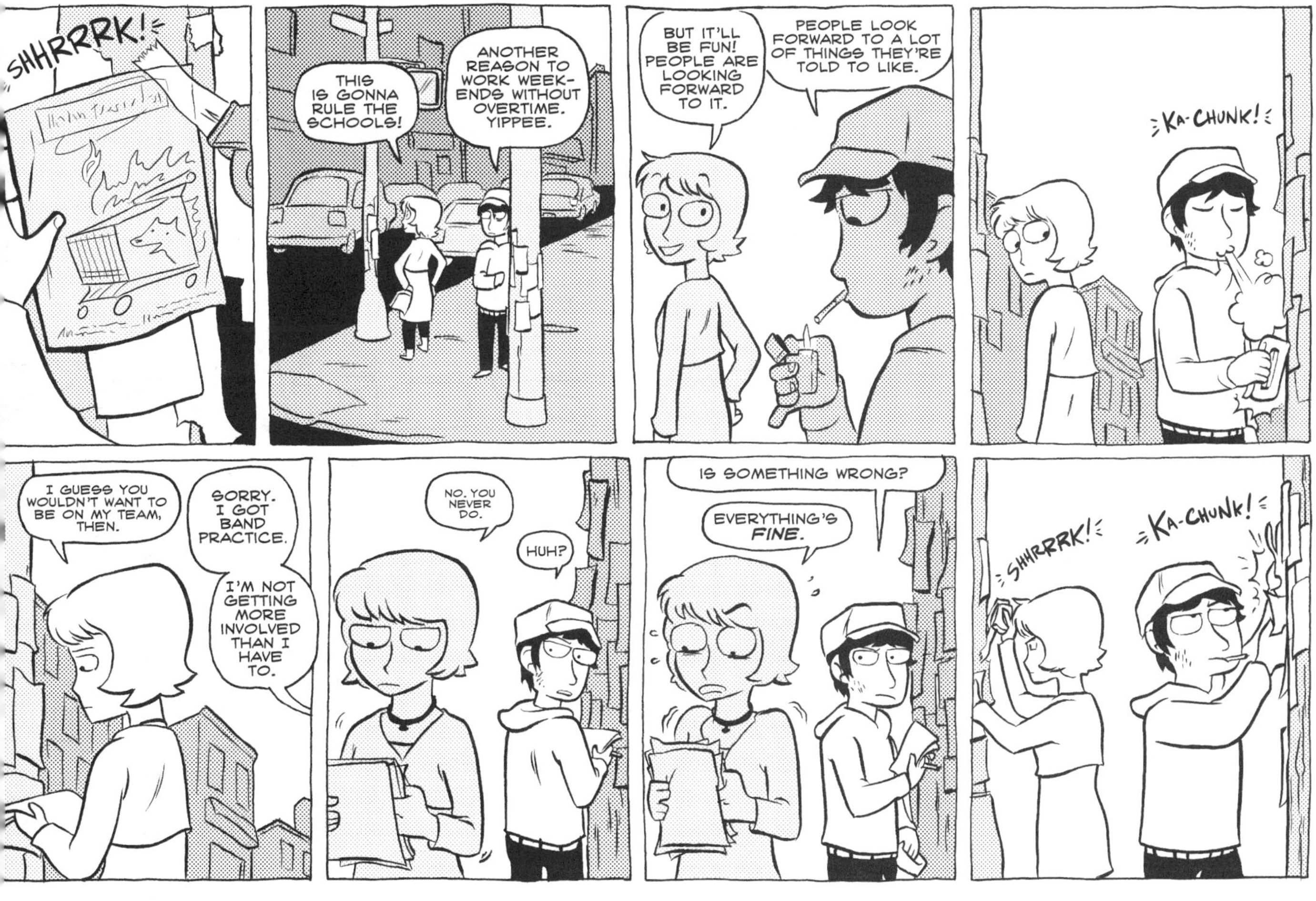
SHHRRRK!
THIS IS GONNA RULE THE SCHOOLS!
ANOTHER REASON TO WORK WEEK-ENDS WITHOUT OVERTIME. YIPPEE.
BUT IT'LL BE FUN! PEOPLE ARE LOOKING FORWARD TO IT.
PEOPLE LOOK FORWARD TO A LOT OF THINGS THEY'RE TOLD TO LIKE.
KA-CHUNK!
I GUESS YOU WOULDN'T WANT TO BE ON MY TEAM, THEN.
SORRY. I GOT BAND PRACTICE.
I'M NOT GETTING MORE INVOLVED THAN I HAVE TO.
NO. YOU NEVER DO.
HUH?
IS SOMETHING WRONG?
EVERYTHING'S FINE.
SHHRRRK!
KA-CHUNK!

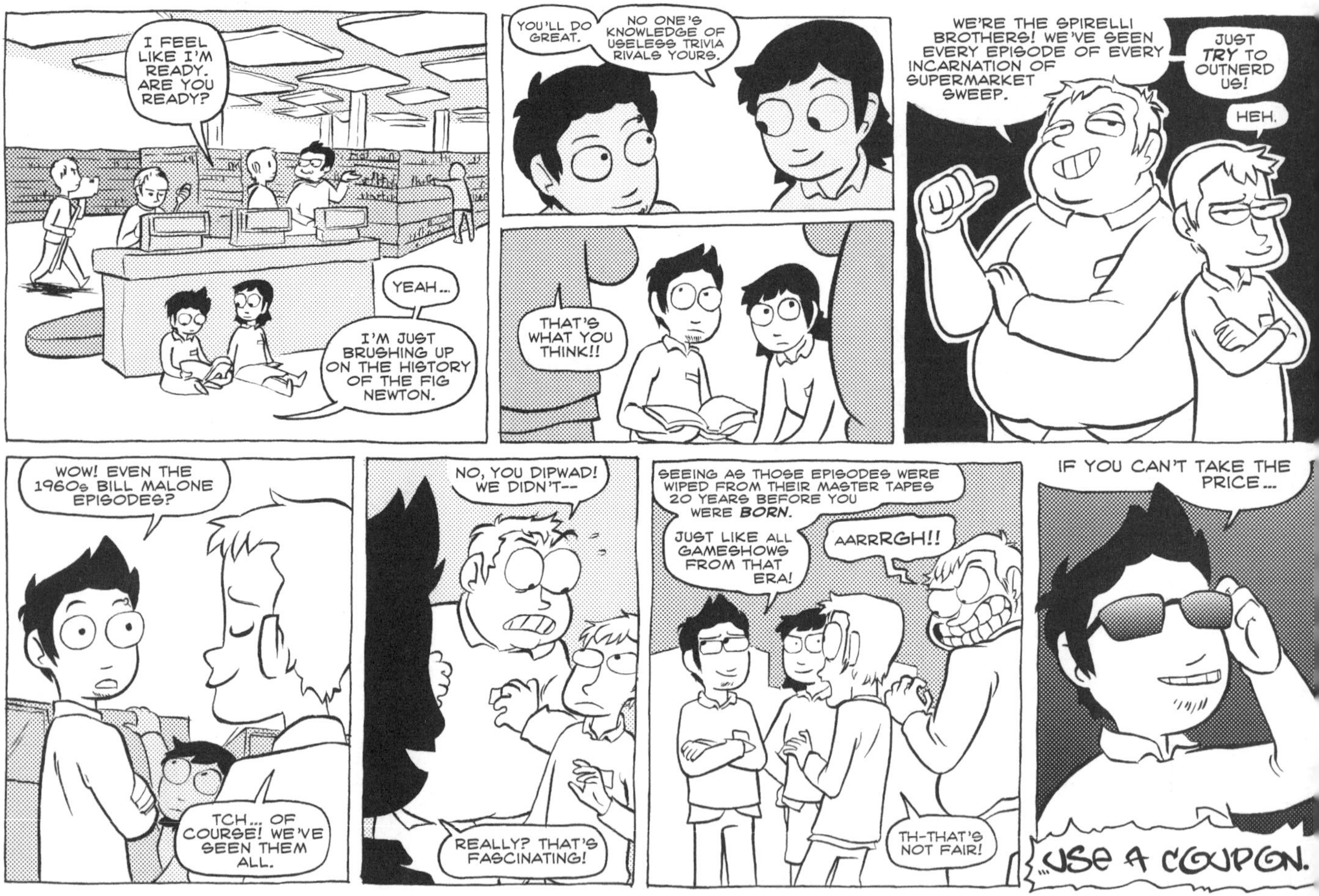
I FEEL LIKE I'M READY. ARE YOU READY?
YEAH...
I'M JUST BRUSHING UP ON THE HISTORY OF THE FIG NEWTON.
YOU'LL DO GREAT.
NO ONE'S KNOWLEDGE OF USELESS TRIVIA RIVALS YOURS.
THAT'S WHAT YOU THINK!!
WE'RE THE SPIRELLI BROTHERS! WE'VE SEEN EVERY EPISODE OF EVERY INCARNATION OF SUPERMARKET SWEEP.
JUST TRY TO OUTNERD US!
HEH.
WOW! EVEN THE 1960s BILL MALONE EPISODES?
TCH... OF COURSE! WE'VE SEEN THEM ALL.
NO, YOU DIPWAD! WE DIDN'T--
REALLY? THAT'S FASCINATING!
SEEING AS THOSE EPISODES WERE WIPED FROM THEIR MASTER TAPES 20 YEARS BEFORE YOU WERE BORN.
JUST LIKE ALL GAMESHOWS FROM THAT ERA!
AARRRGH!!
TH-THAT'S NOT FAIR!
IF YOU CAN'T TAKE THE PRICE...
...USE A COUPON.

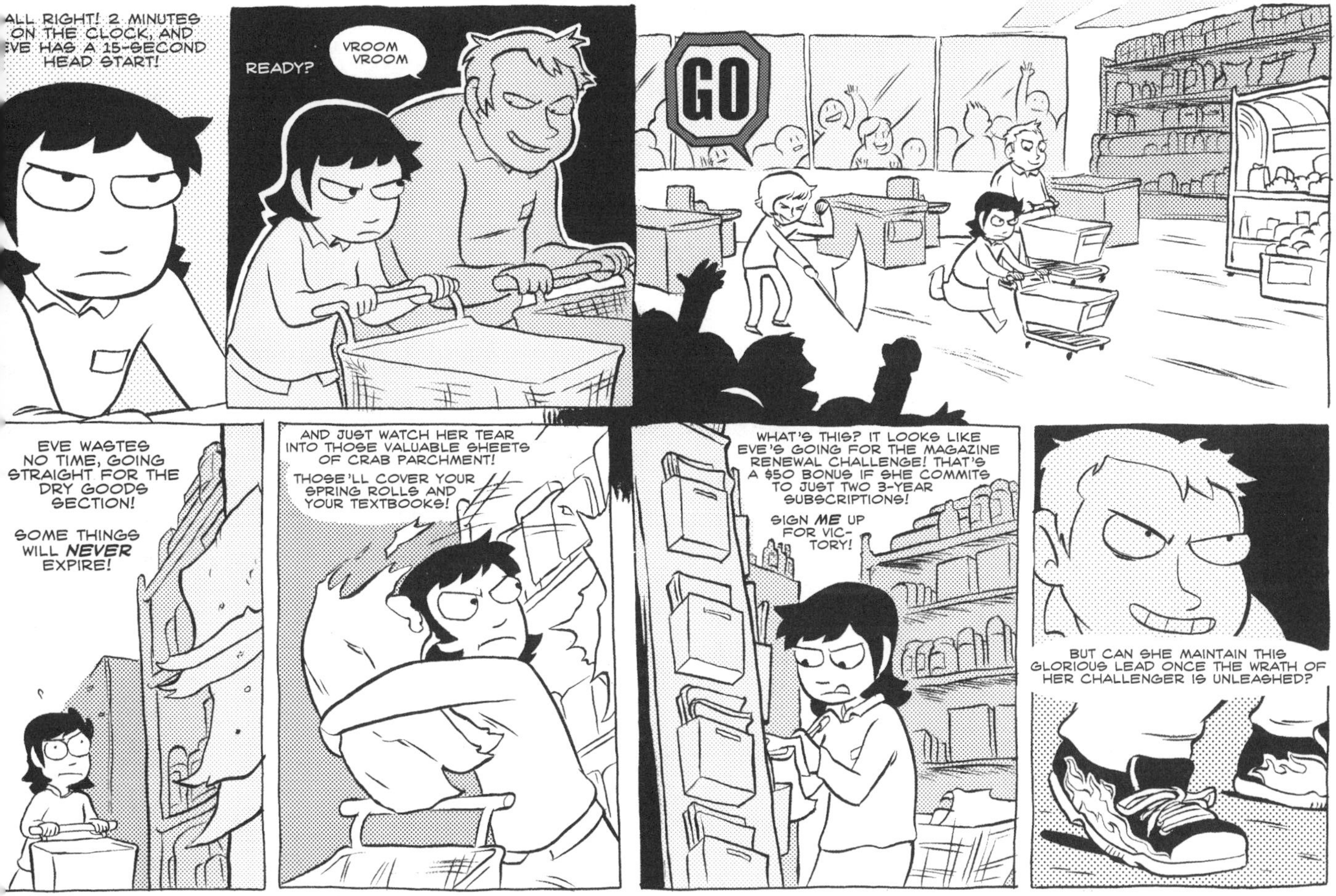
ALL RIGHT! 2 MINUTES ON THE CLOCK, AND EVE HAS A 15-SECOND HEAD START!
READY?
VROOM VROOM
GO
EVE WASTES NO TIME, GOING STRAIGHT FOR THE DRY GOODS SECTION!
SOME THINGS WILL NEVER EXPIRE!
AND JUST WATCH HER TEAR INTO THOSE VALUABLE SHEETS OF CRAB PARCHMENT!
THOSE'LL COVER YOUR SPRING ROLLS AND YOUR TEXTBOOKS!
WHAT'S THIS? IT LOOKS LIKE EVE'S GOING FOR THE MAGAZINE RENEWAL CHALLENGE! THAT'S A $50 BONUS IF SHE COMMITS TO JUST TWO 3-YEAR SUBSCRIPTIONS!
SIGN ME UP FOR VIC-TORY!
BUT CAN SHE MAINTAIN THIS GLORIOUS LEAD ONCE THE WRATH OF HER CHALLENGER IS UNLEASHED?

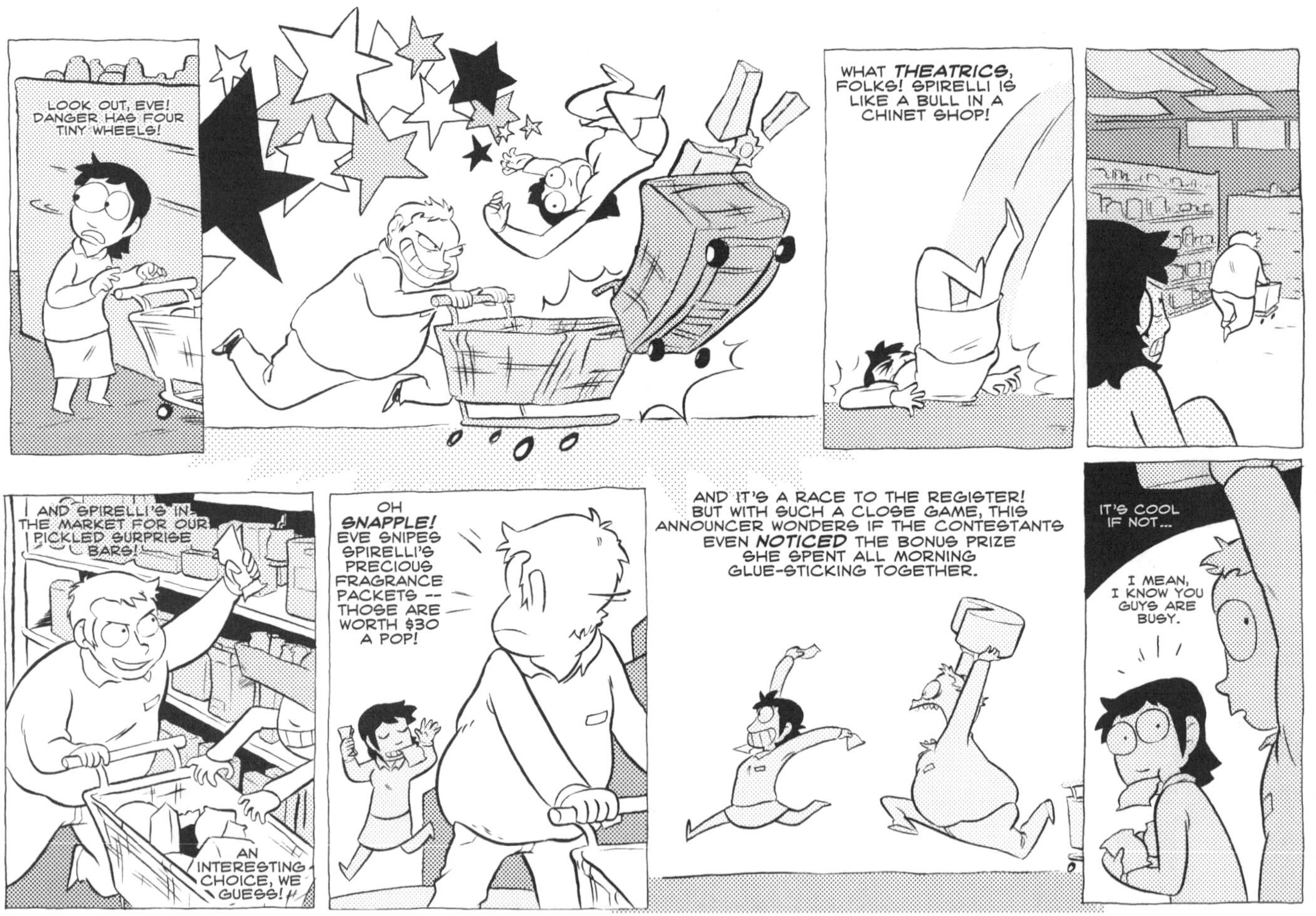
LOOK OUT, EVE! DANGER HAS FOUR TINY WHEELS!
WHAT *THEATRICS*, FOLKS! SPIRELLI IS LIKE A BULL IN A CHINET SHOP!
AND SPIRELLI'S IN THE MARKET FOR OUR PICKLED SURPRISE BARS!
AN INTERESTING CHOICE, WE GUESS!
OH *SNAPPLE!* EVE SNIPES SPIRELLI'S PRECIOUS FRAGRANCE PACKETS -- THOSE ARE WORTH $30 A POP!
AND IT'S A RACE TO THE REGISTER! BUT WITH SUCH A CLOSE GAME, THIS ANNOUNCER WONDERS IF THE CONTESTANTS EVEN *NOTICED* THE BONUS PRIZE SHE SPENT ALL MORNING GLUE-STICKING TOGETHER.
IT'S COOL IF NOT...
I MEAN, I KNOW YOU GUYS ARE BUSY.

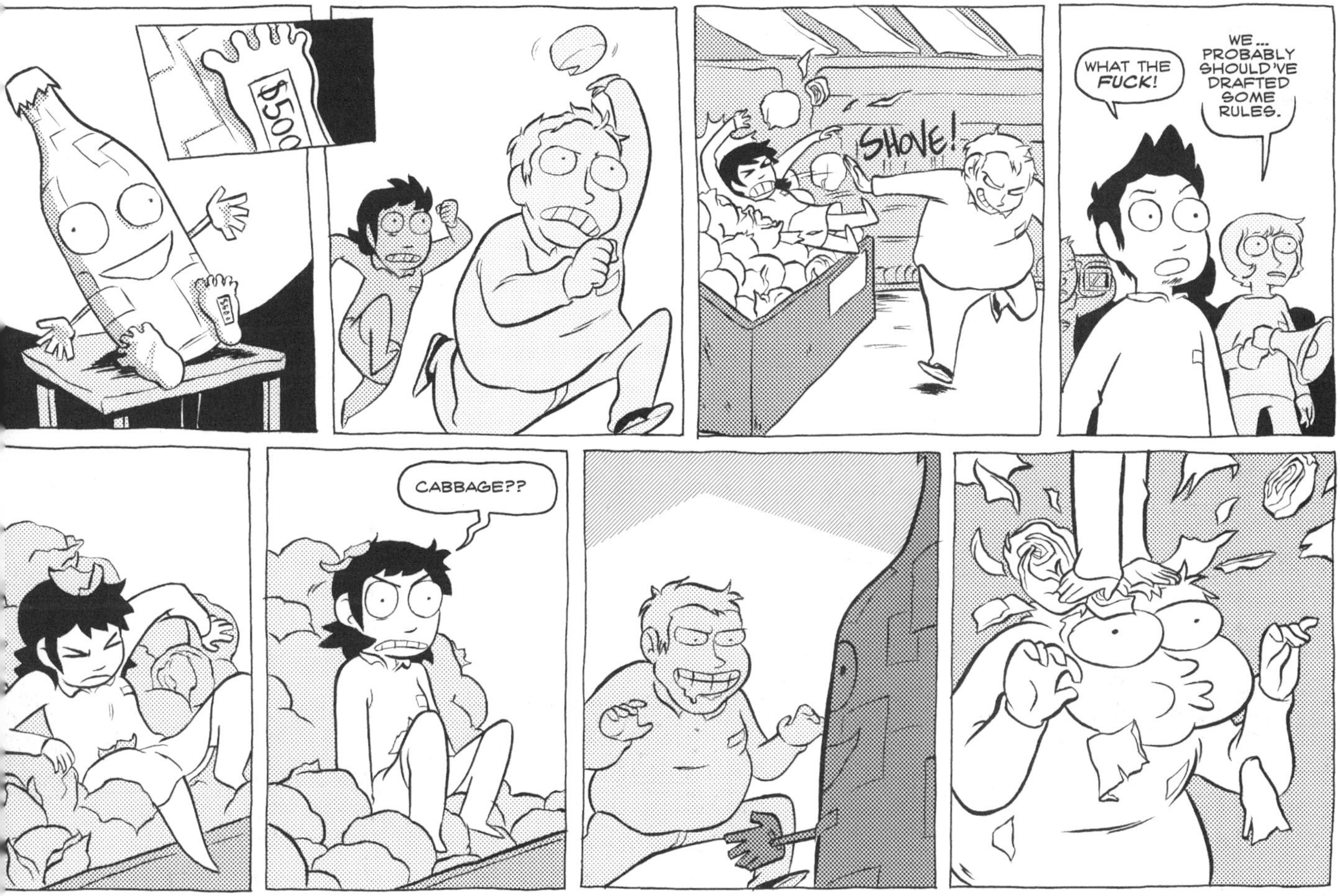
$500
SHOVE!
WHAT THE FUCK!
WE... PROBABLY SHOULD'VE DRAFTED SOME RULES.
CABBAGE??

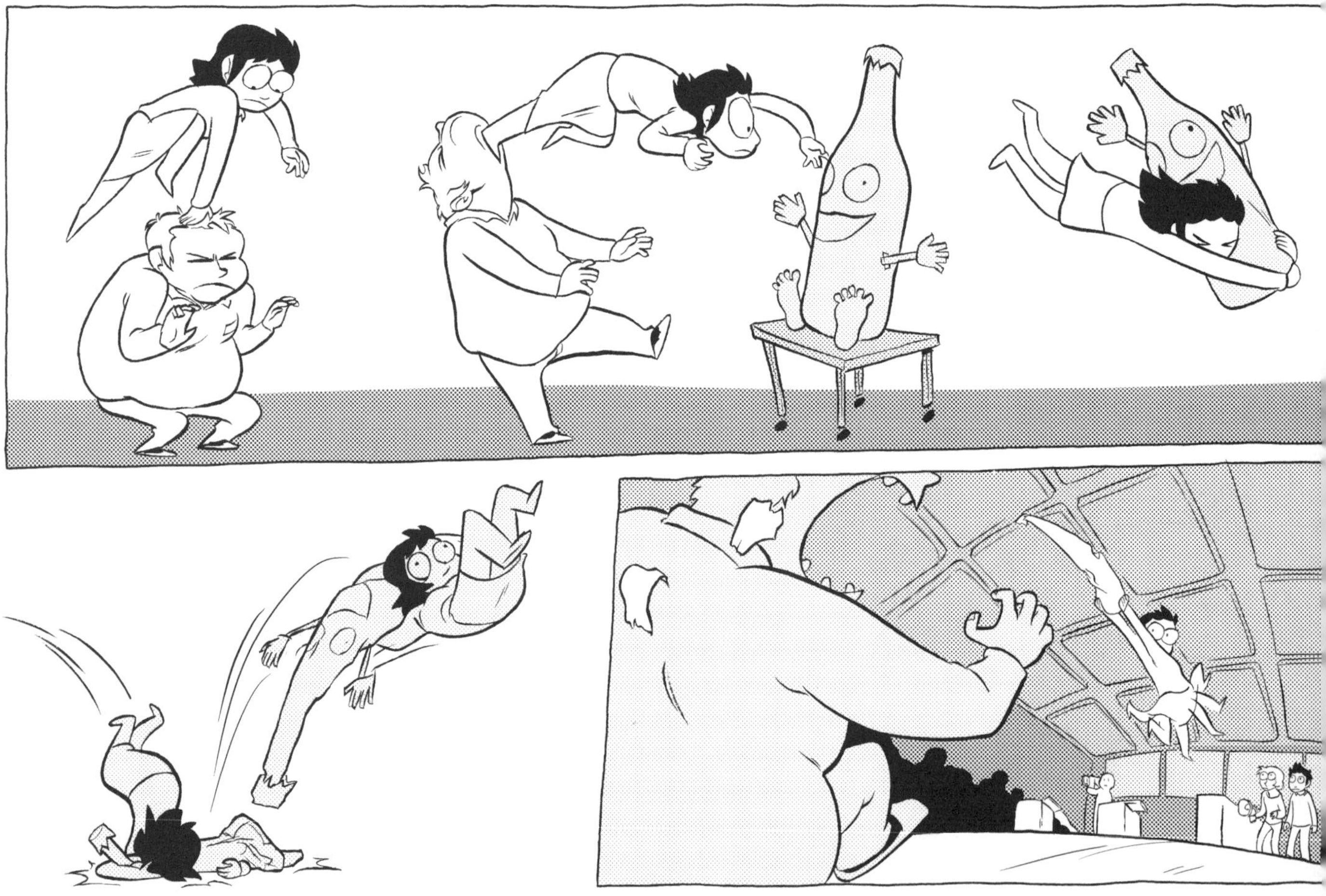

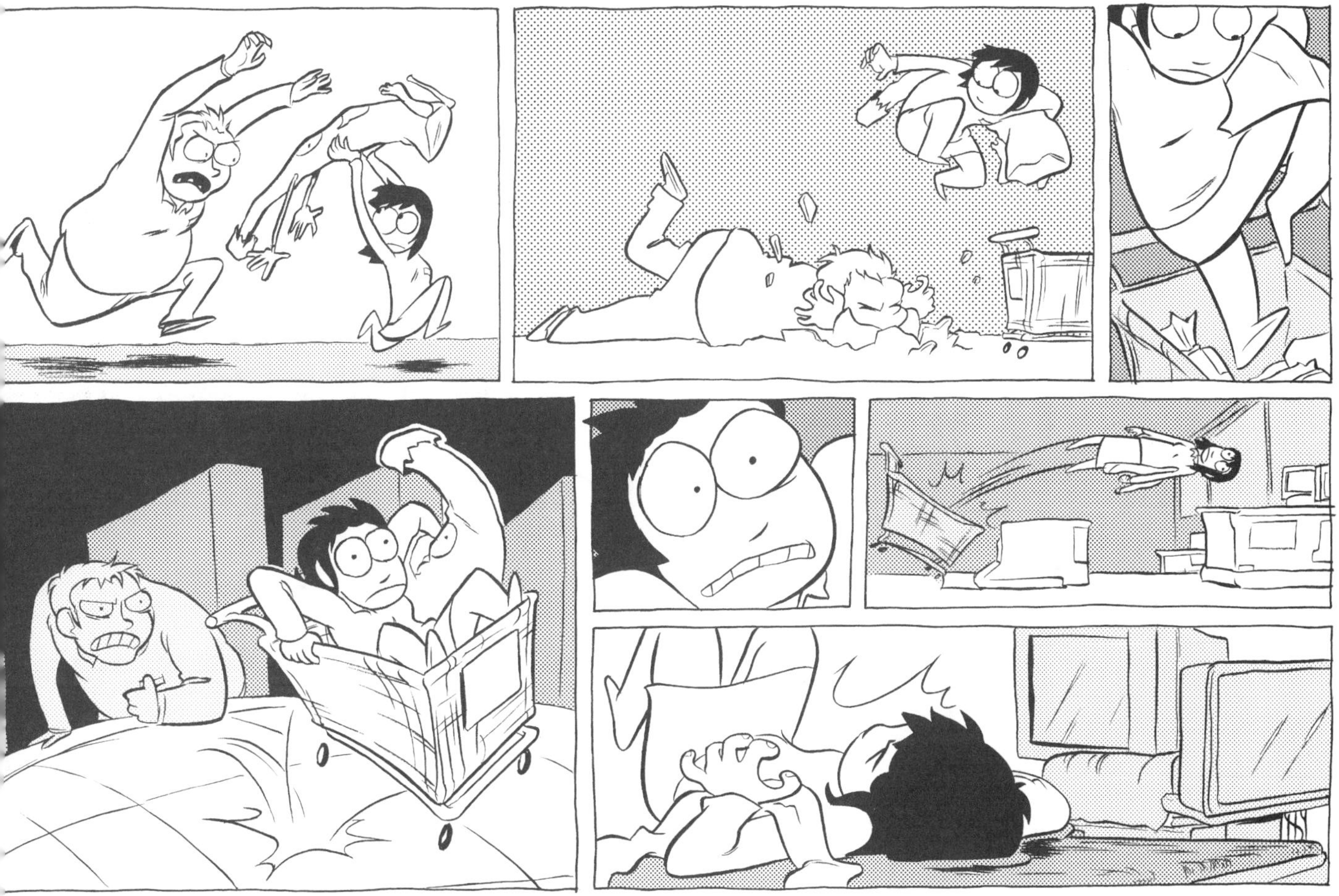

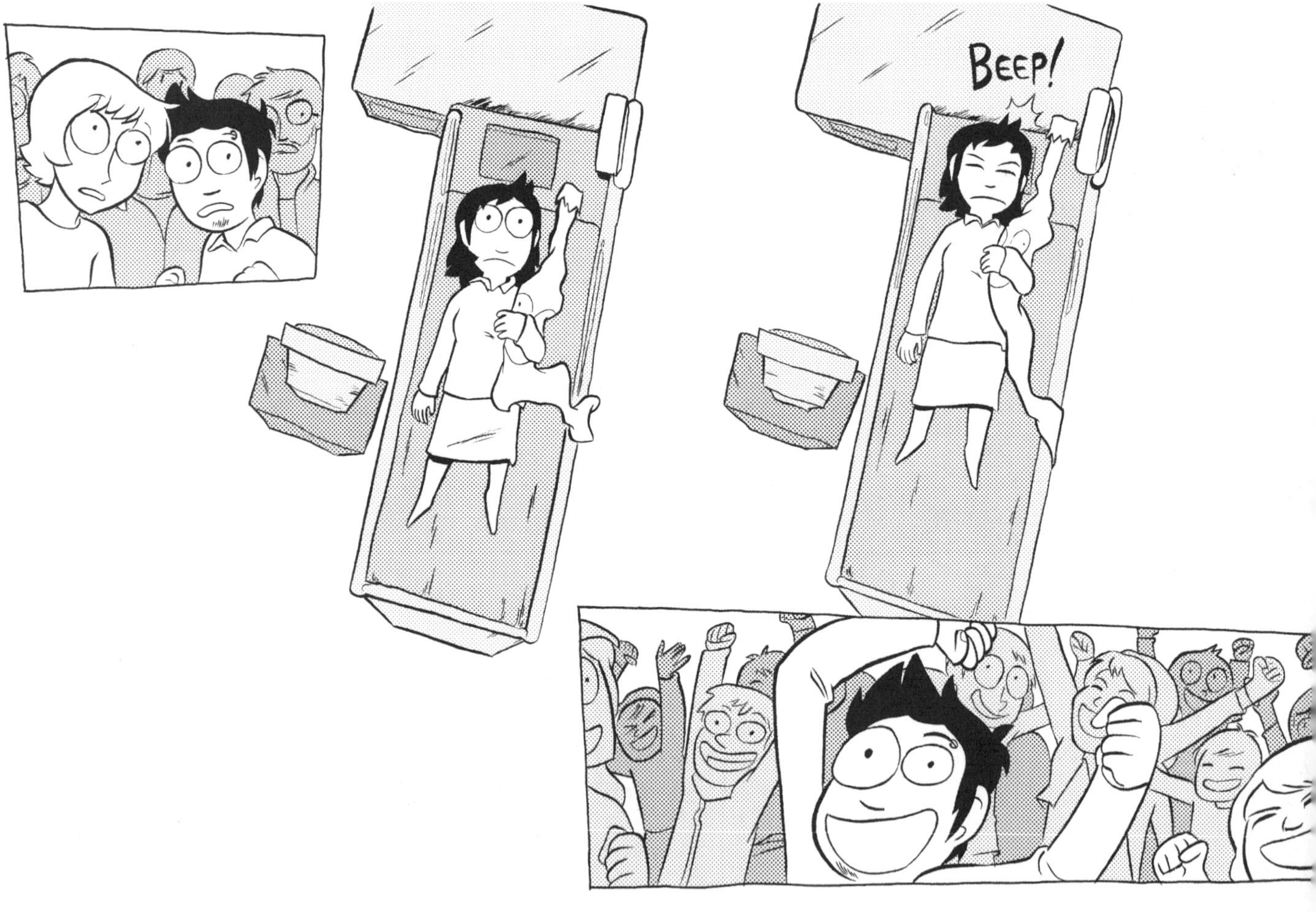
BEEP!

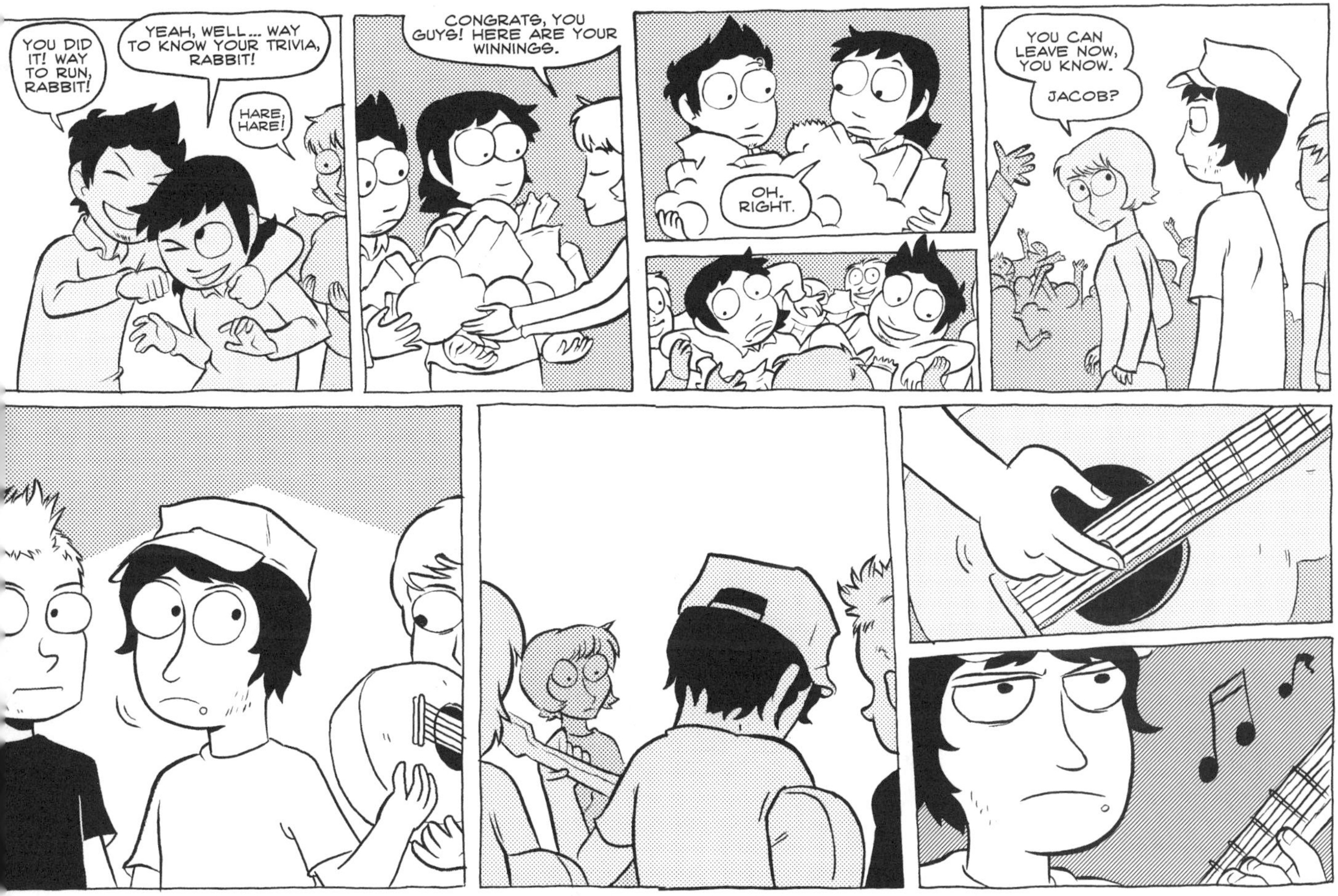
YOU DID IT! WAY TO RUN, RABBIT!
YEAH, WELL... WAY TO KNOW YOUR TRIVIA, RABBIT!
HARE, HARE!
CONGRATS, YOU GUYS! HERE ARE YOUR WINNINGS.
OH. RIGHT.
YOU CAN LEAVE NOW, YOU KNOW.
JACOB?

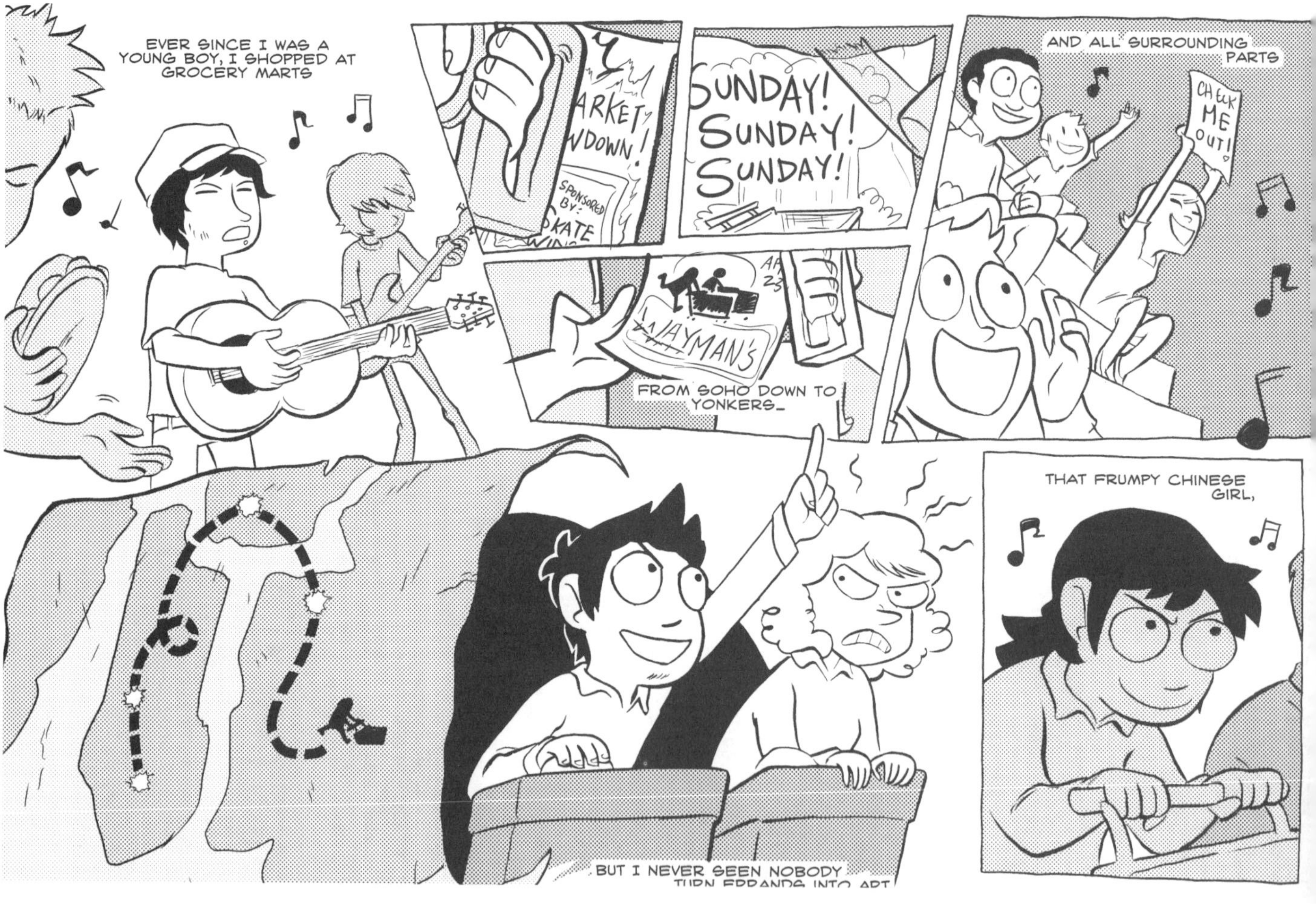
EVER SINCE I WAS A YOUNG BOY, I SHOPPED AT GROCERY MARTS
SPONSORED BY:
SUNDAY! SUNDAY! SUNDAY!
AND ALL SURROUNDING PARTS
CHECK ME OUT!
WAYMAN'S
FROM SOHO DOWN TO YONKERS_
THAT FRUMPY CHINESE GIRL,
BUT I NEVER SEEN NOBODY TURN ERRANDS INTO ART

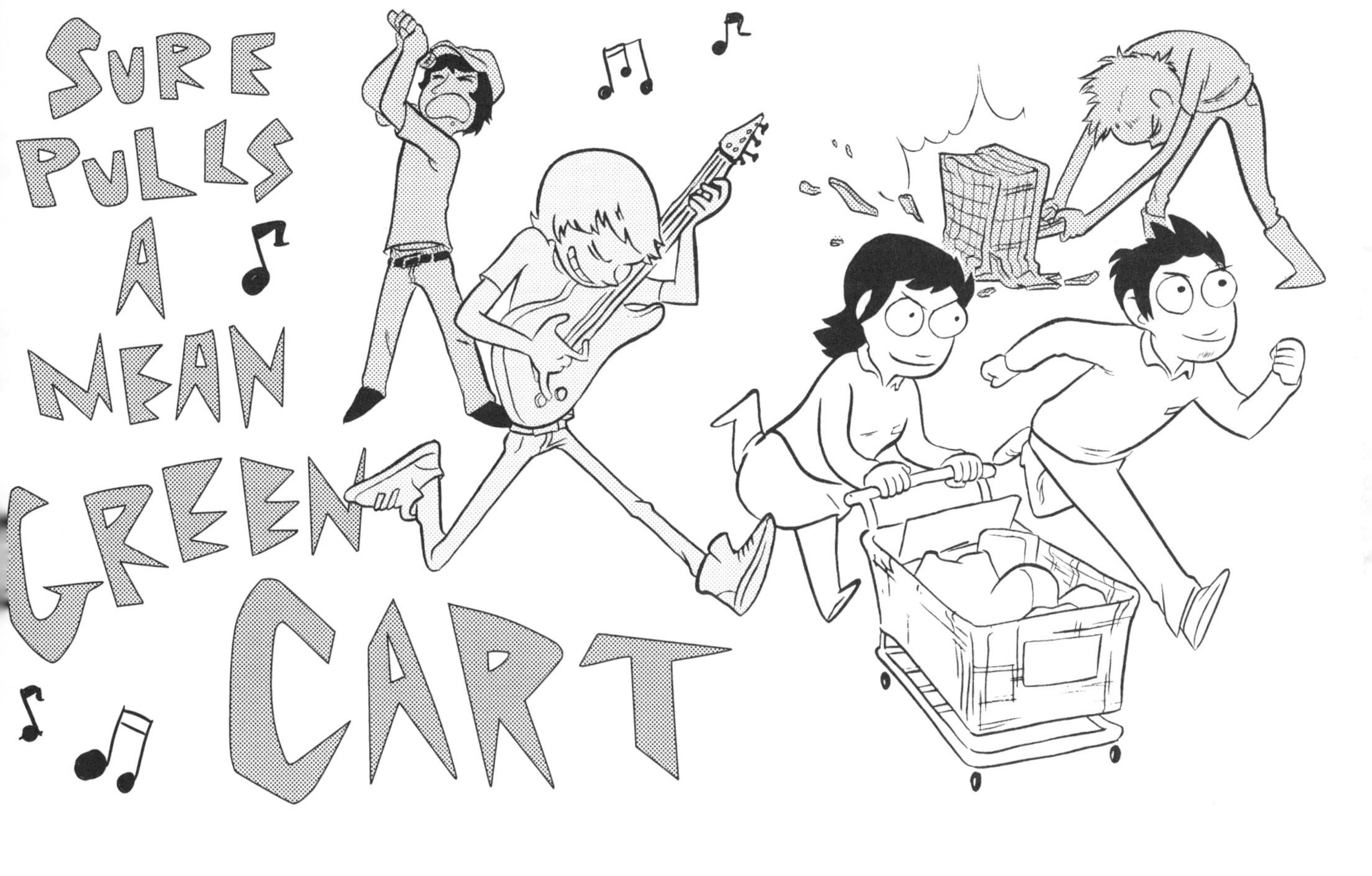
SURE
PULLS
A
MEAN
GREEN
CART

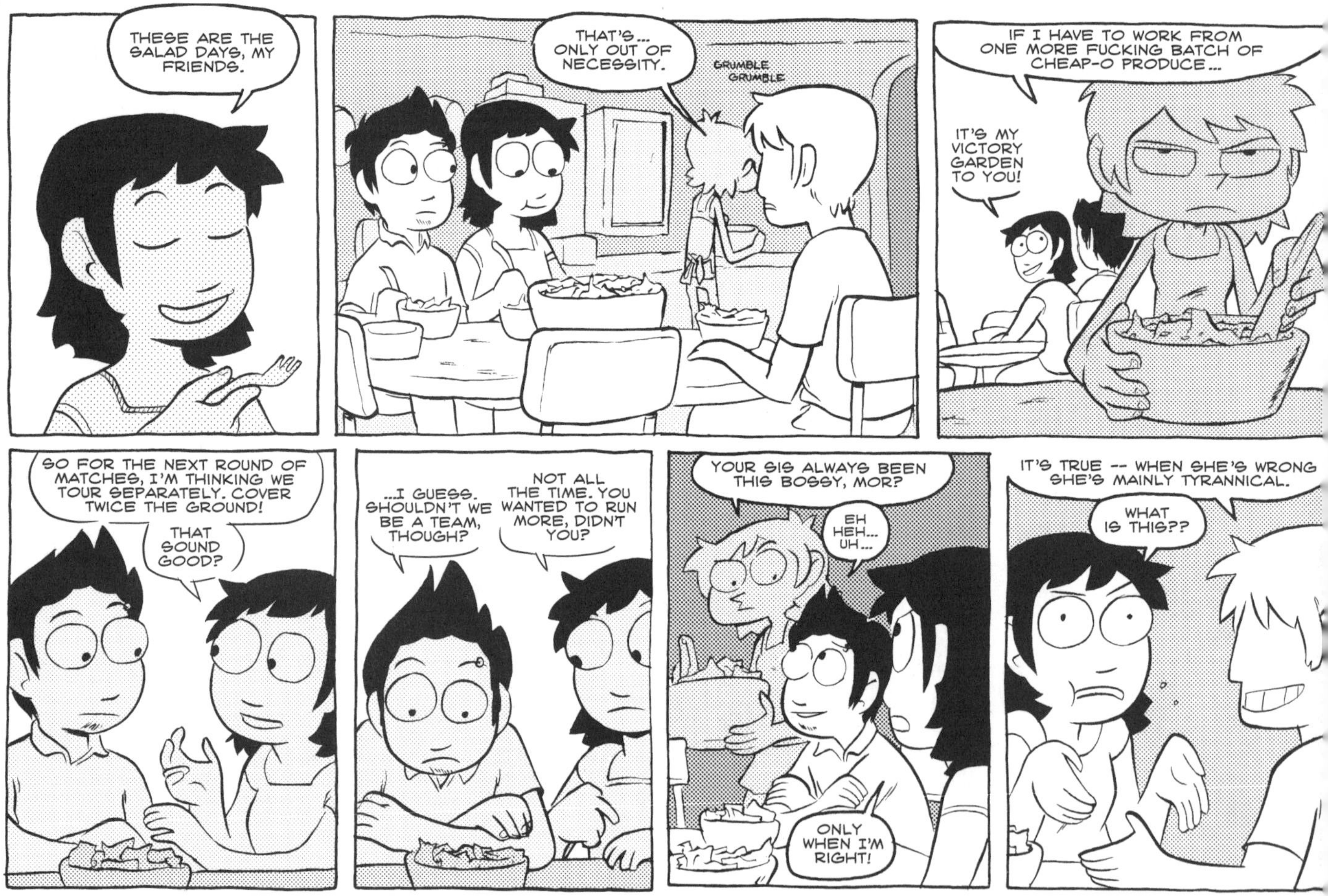
THESE ARE THE SALAD DAYS, MY FRIENDS.
THAT'S... ONLY OUT OF NECESSITY.
GRUMBLE GRUMBLE
IF I HAVE TO WORK FROM ONE MORE FUCKING BATCH OF CHEAP-O PRODUCE...
IT'S MY VICTORY GARDEN TO YOU!
SO FOR THE NEXT ROUND OF MATCHES, I'M THINKING WE TOUR SEPARATELY. COVER TWICE THE GROUND!
THAT SOUND GOOD?
...I GUESS. SHOULDN'T WE BE A TEAM, THOUGH?
NOT ALL THE TIME. YOU WANTED TO RUN MORE, DIDN'T YOU?
YOUR SIS ALWAYS BEEN THIS BOSSY, MOR?
EH HEH... UH...
ONLY WHEN I'M RIGHT!
IT'S TRUE -- WHEN SHE'S WRONG SHE'S MAINLY TYRANNICAL.
WHAT IS THIS??

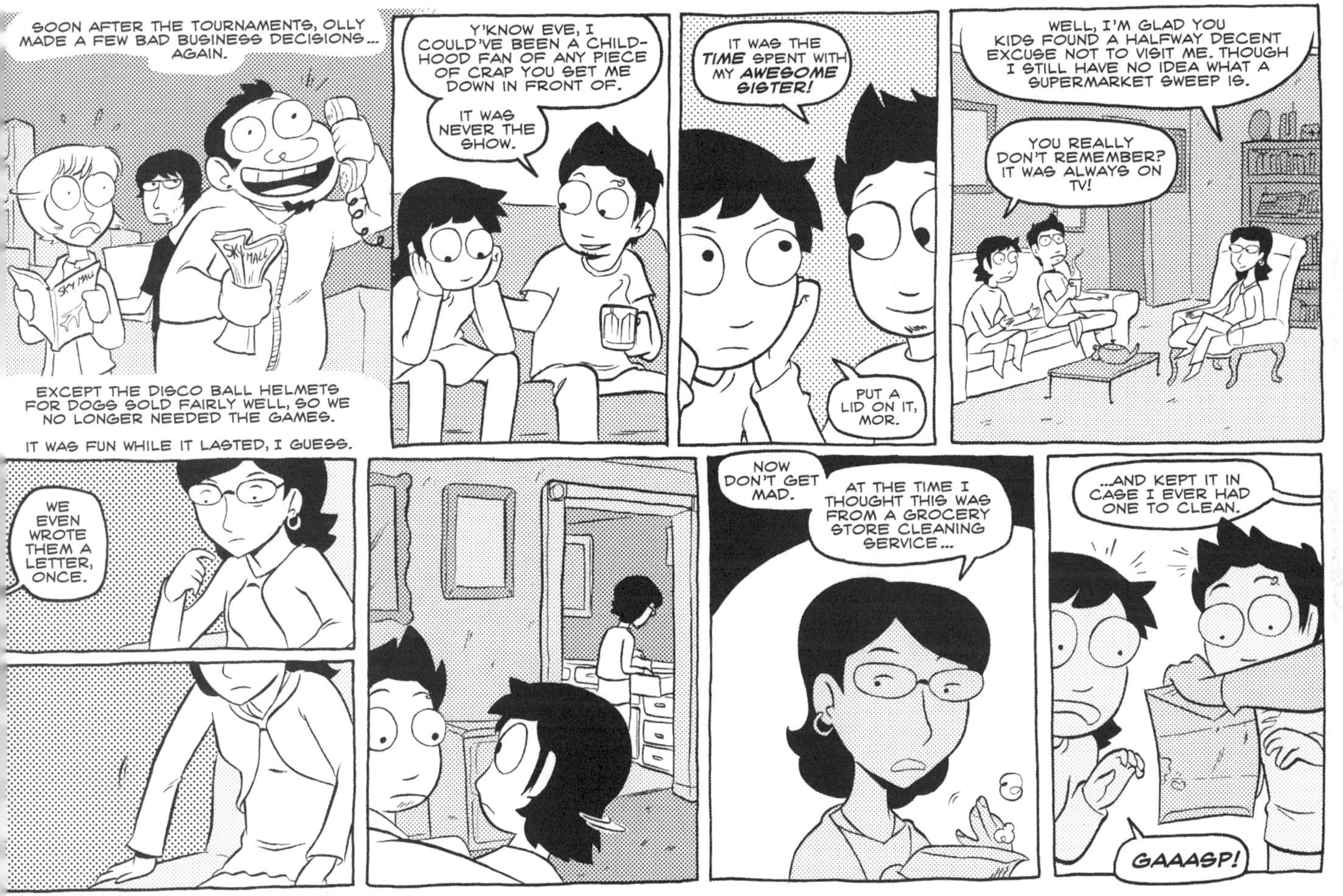
SOON AFTER THE TOURNAMENTS, OLLY MADE A FEW BAD BUSINESS DECISIONS... AGAIN.
SKY MALL
SKY MALL
EXCEPT THE DISCO BALL HELMETS FOR DOGS SOLD FAIRLY WELL, SO WE NO LONGER NEEDED THE GAMES.
IT WAS FUN WHILE IT LASTED, I GUESS.
Y'KNOW EVE, I COULD'VE BEEN A CHILDHOOD FAN OF ANY PIECE OF CRAP YOU SET ME DOWN IN FRONT OF.
IT WAS NEVER THE SHOW.
IT WAS THE *TIME* SPENT WITH MY *AWESOME SISTER!*
PUT A LID ON IT, MOR.
WELL, I'M GLAD YOU KIDS FOUND A HALFWAY DECENT EXCUSE NOT TO VISIT ME. THOUGH I STILL HAVE NO IDEA WHAT A SUPERMARKET SWEEP IS.
YOU REALLY DON'T REMEMBER? IT WAS ALWAYS ON TV!
WE EVEN WROTE THEM A LETTER, ONCE.
NOW DON'T GET MAD.
AT THE TIME I THOUGHT THIS WAS FROM A GROCERY STORE CLEANING SERVICE...
...AND KEPT IT IN CASE I EVER HAD ONE TO CLEAN.
GAAASP!

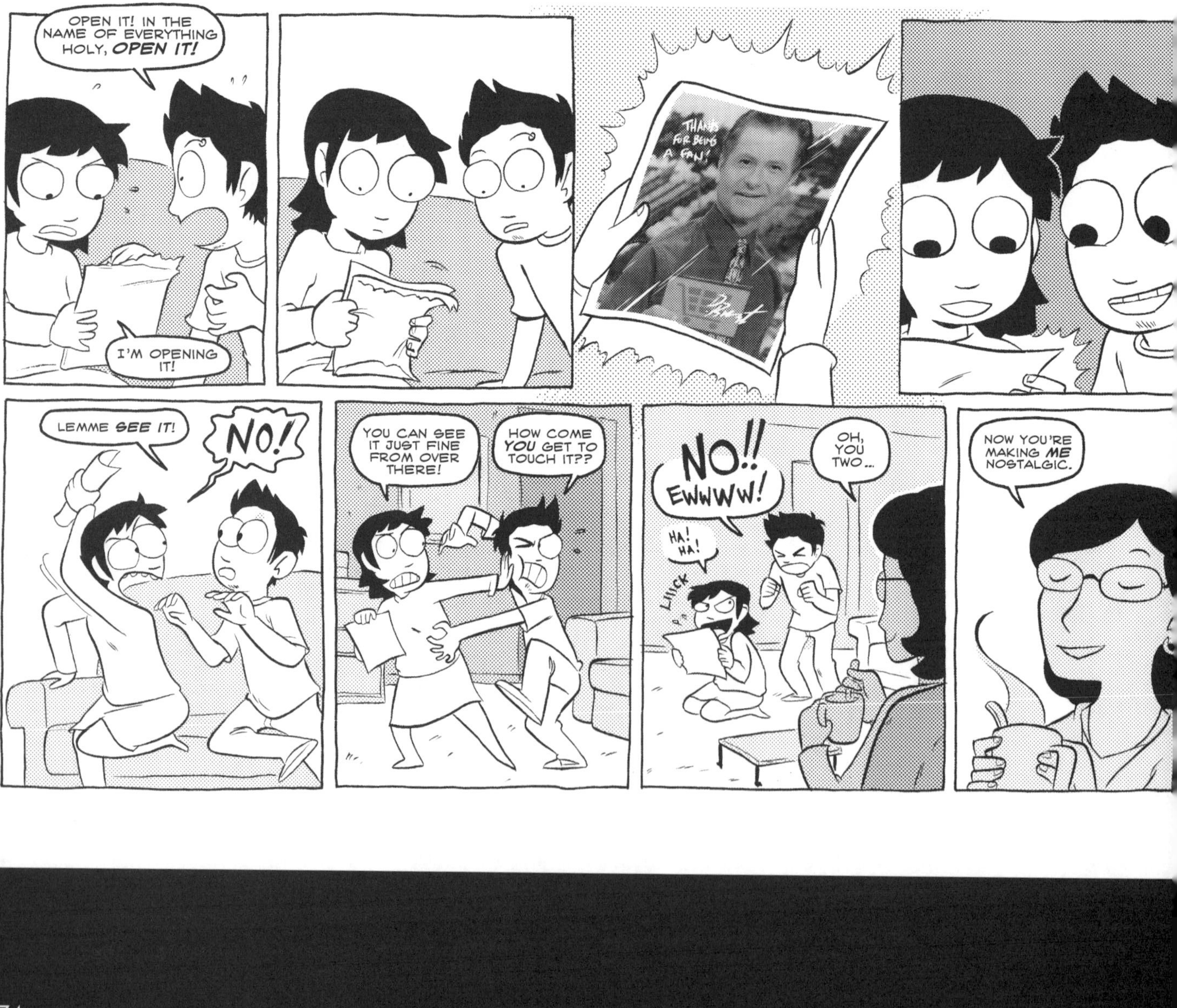
OPEN IT! IN THE NAME OF EVERYTHING HOLY, OPEN IT!
I'M OPENING IT!
THANKS FOR BEING A FAN!
LEMME SEE IT!
NO!
YOU CAN SEE IT JUST FINE FROM OVER THERE!
HOW COME YOU GET TO TOUCH IT??
NO!! EWWWW!
HA! HA!
LIIICK
OH, YOU TWO...
NOW YOU'RE MAKING ME NOSTALGIC.

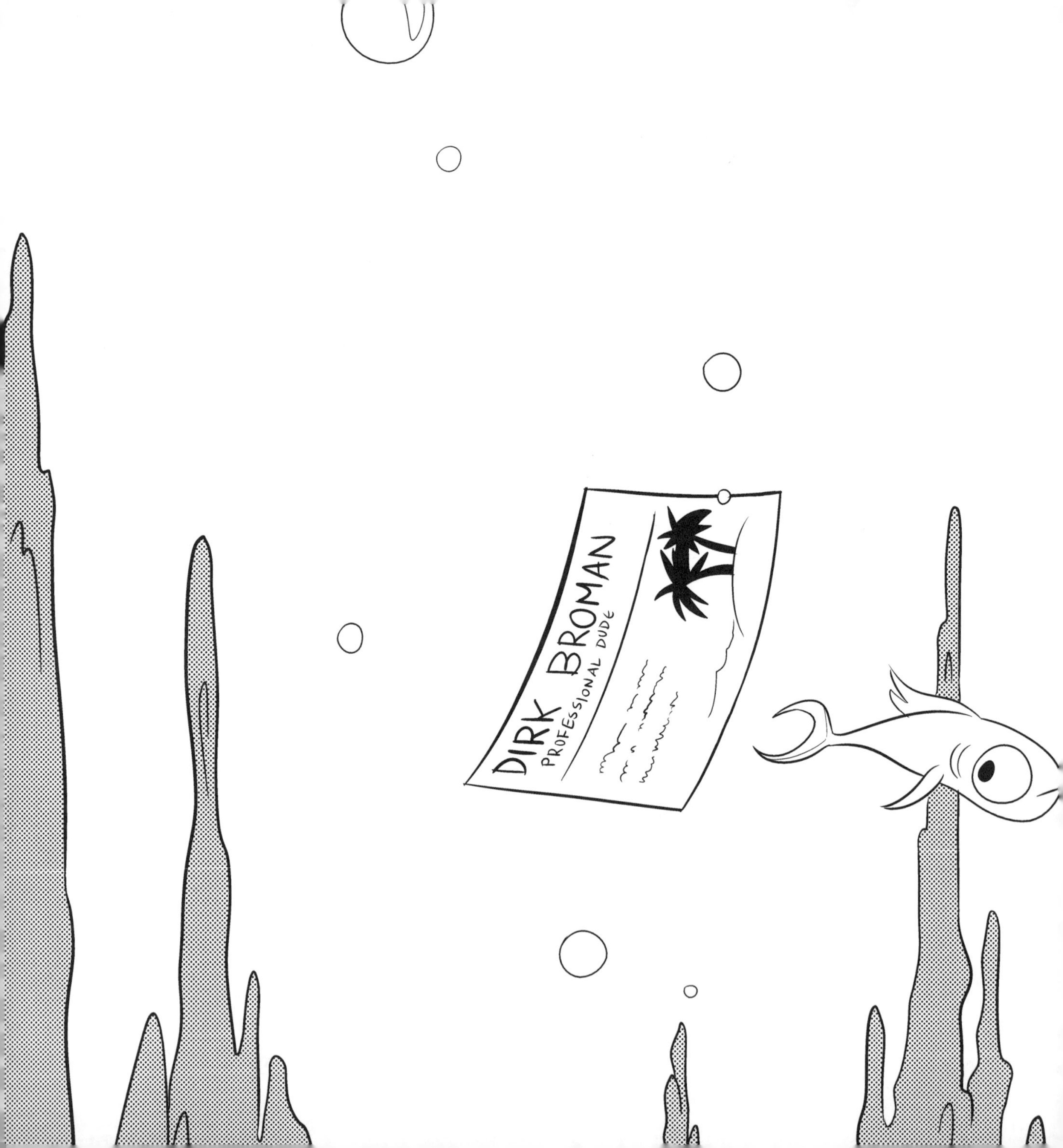
DIRK BROMAN
PROFESSIONAL DUDE

This Is How I Deal

This is a rare story where both Eve and Hanna are completely absent. I wanted to show Will and Marigold as a bumbling comedy team, and try to carry a story with their chemistry, or lack thereof. I'm not sure how fun it is to watch them, but I think the story communicates Marigold's perpetual dissatisfaction, and Will's longing for simplicity. It also reveals the banality of Will's drug dealing lifestyle, which I think takes a bit of the edge off his character.

There's an underlying theme in this story that audiences seek mediocrity when given the option for something truly good. I have mixed feelings about that presently. Pop culture is too fragmented to dwell on the tastes of others, but I think it's an easy attitude to adopt when you care enough about a craft, as Marigold does.

The "Max 9200 Dances" panel confused some people. This is a reference to the Kanye West track "Slow Jamz" in which Jamie Foxx describes a woman with unfulfilled desires.

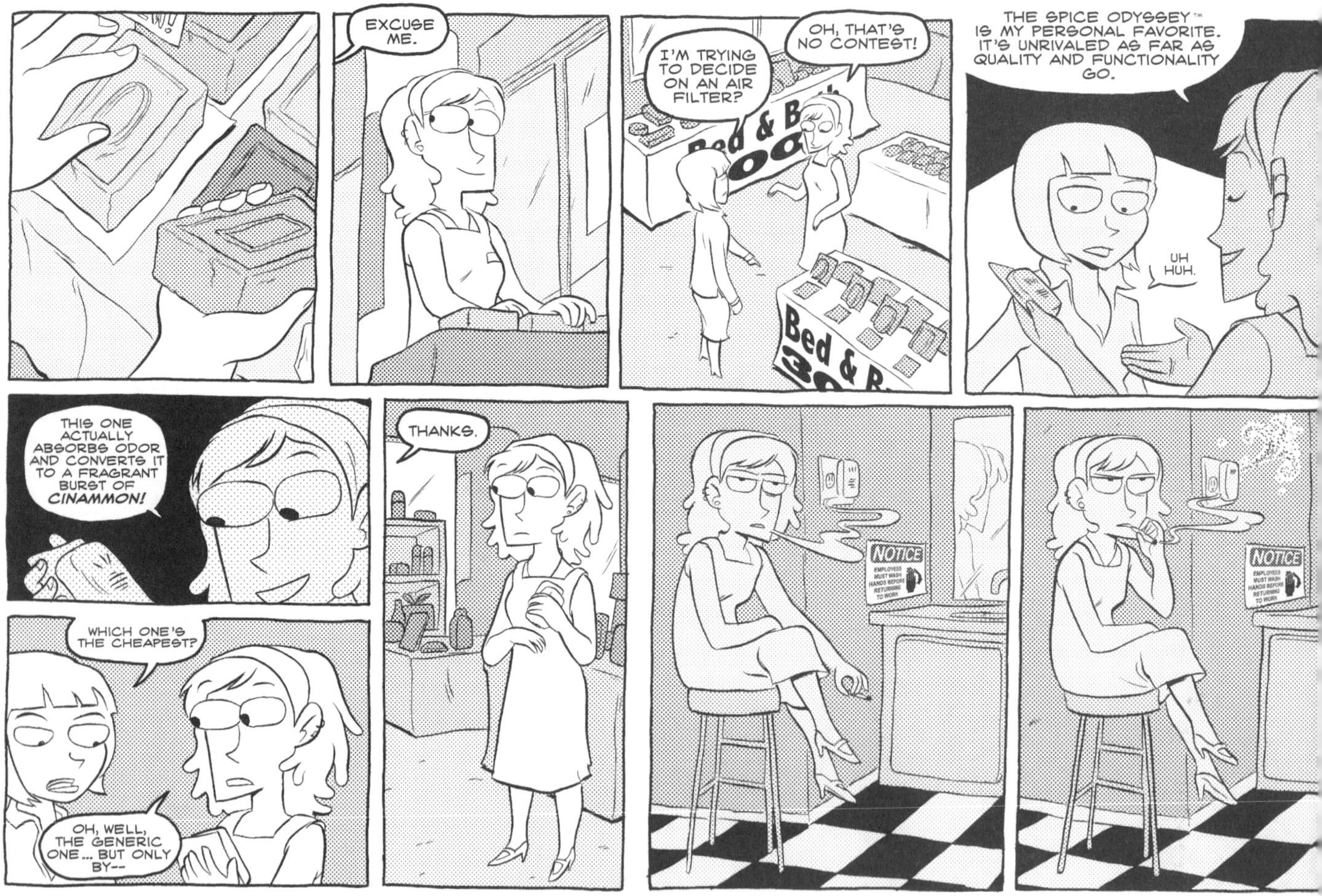

EXCUSE ME.
I'M TRYING TO DECIDE ON AN AIR FILTER?
OH, THAT'S NO CONTEST!
Bed & B
Bed & B
THE SPICE ODYSSEY™ IS MY PERSONAL FAVORITE. IT'S UNRIVALED AS FAR AS QUALITY AND FUNCTIONALITY GO.
UH HUH.
THIS ONE ACTUALLY ABSORBS ODOR AND CONVERTS IT TO A FRAGRANT BURST OF *CINAMMON!*
WHICH ONE'S THE CHEAPEST?
OH, WELL, THE GENERIC ONE... BUT ONLY BY--
THANKS.
NOTICE
EMPLOYEES MUST WASH HANDS BEFORE RETURNING TO WORK
NOTICE
EMPLOYEES MUST WASH HANDS BEFORE RETURNING TO WORK

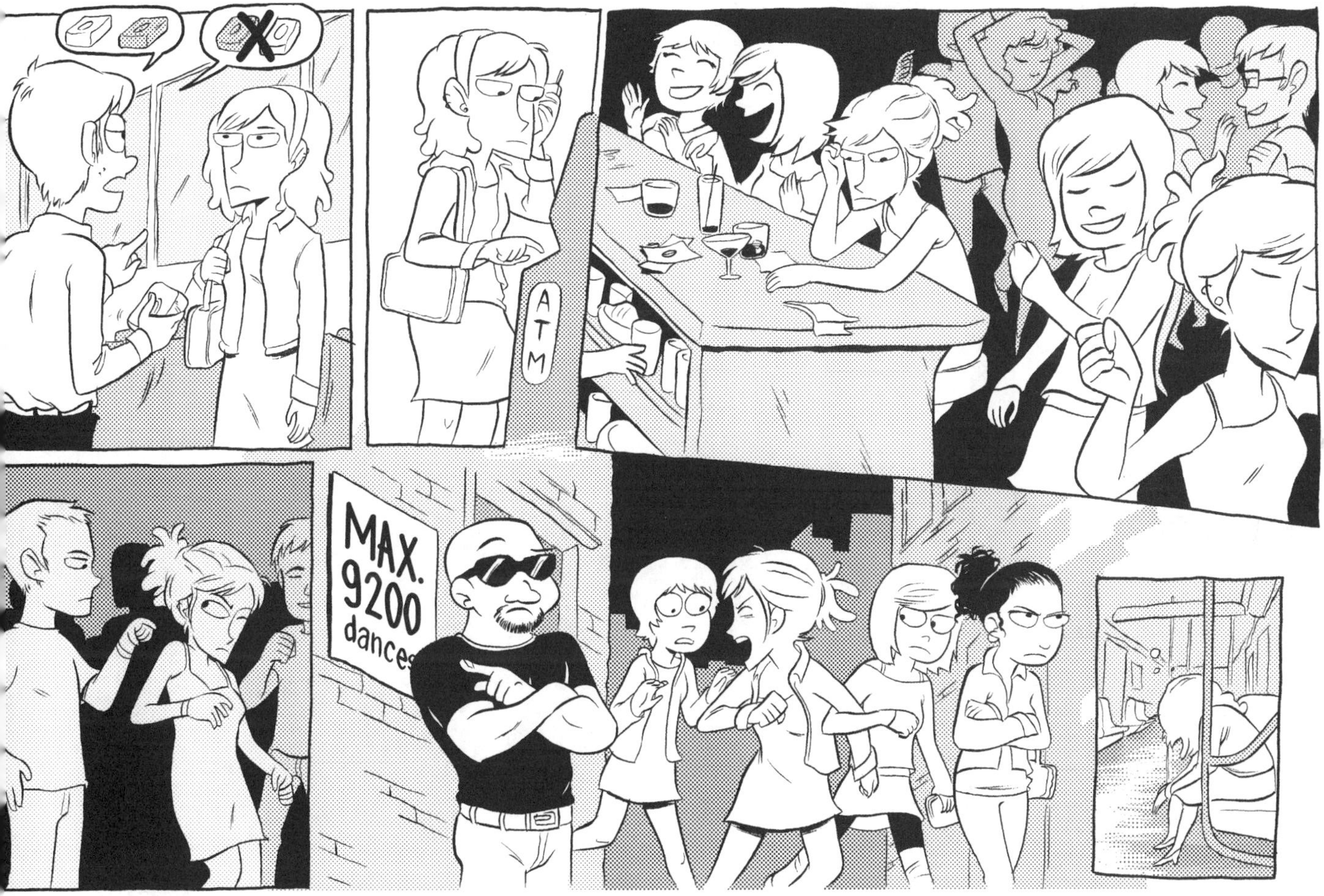
ATM
MAX.
9200
dances

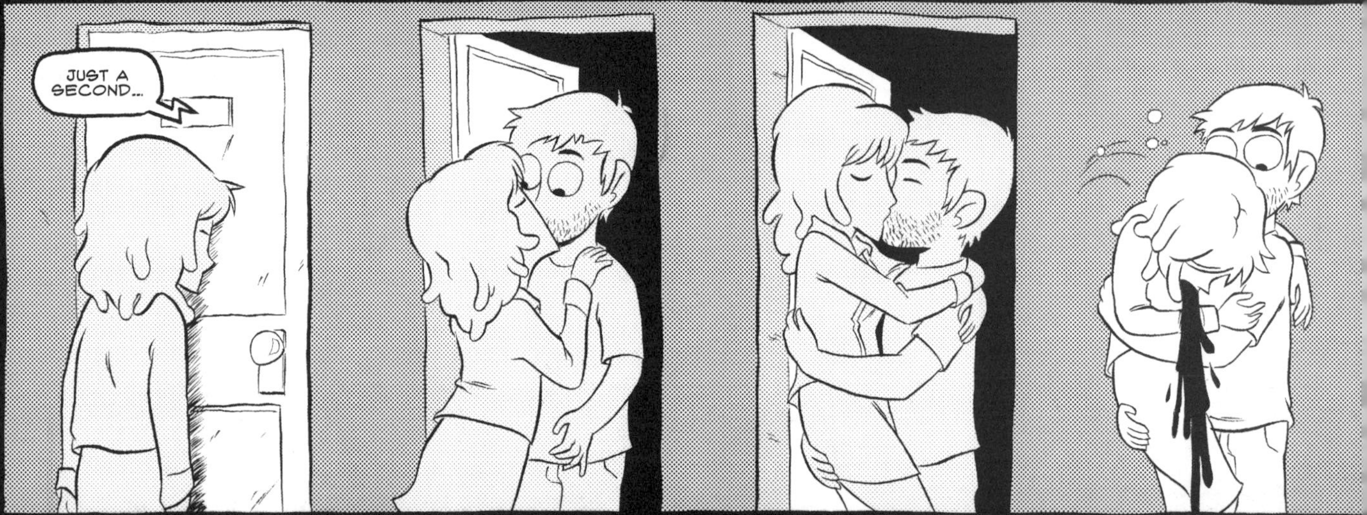
JUST A SECOND...

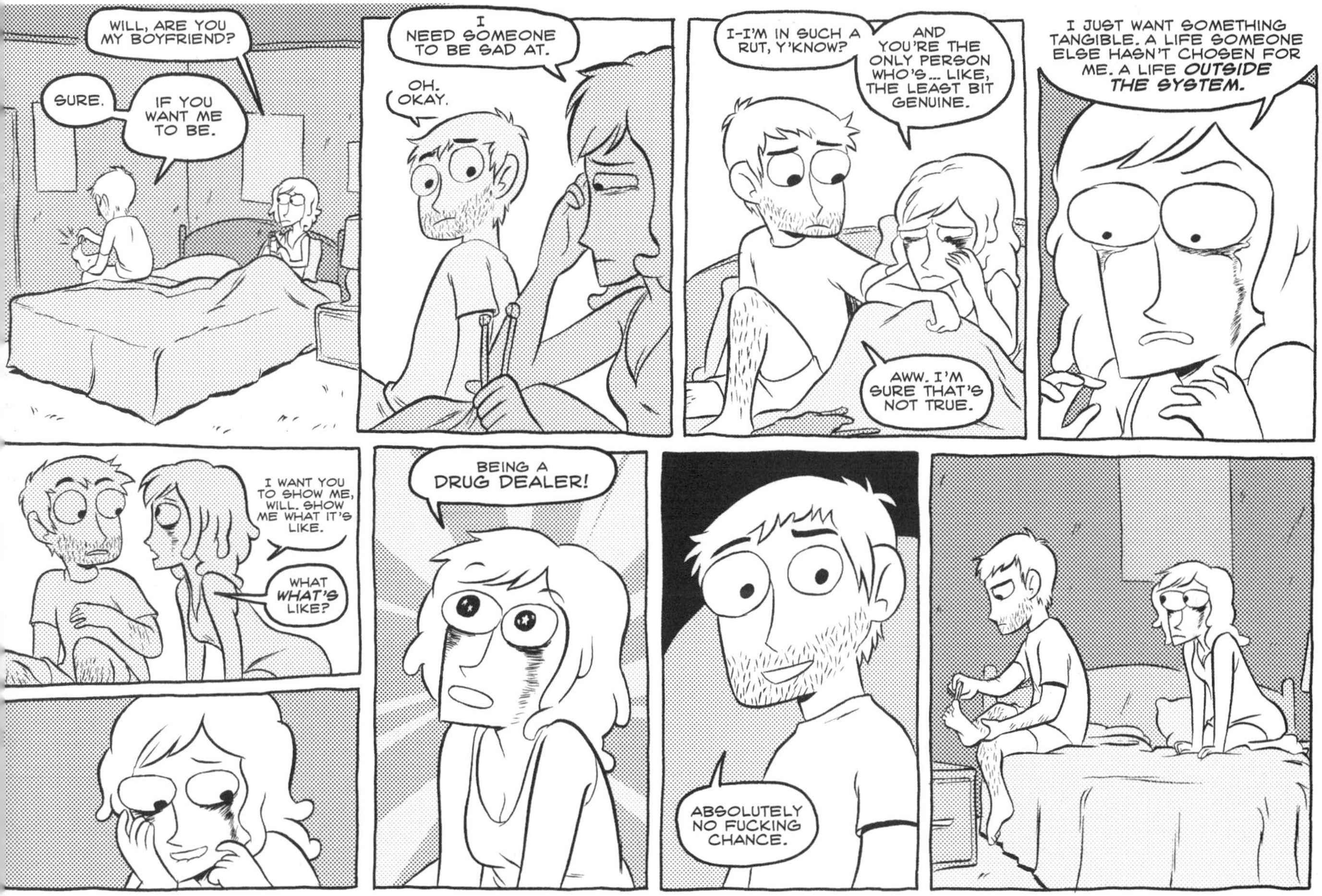
WILL, ARE YOU MY BOYFRIEND?
SURE.
IF YOU WANT ME TO BE.
I NEED SOMEONE TO BE SAD AT.
OH. OKAY.
I-I'M IN SUCH A RUT, Y'KNOW?
AND YOU'RE THE ONLY PERSON WHO'S... LIKE, THE LEAST BIT GENUINE.
AWW. I'M SURE THAT'S NOT TRUE.
I JUST WANT SOMETHING TANGIBLE. A LIFE SOMEONE ELSE HASN'T CHOSEN FOR ME. A LIFE *OUTSIDE THE SYSTEM.*
I WANT YOU TO SHOW ME, WILL. SHOW ME WHAT IT'S LIKE.
WHAT *WHAT'S* LIKE?
BEING A DRUG DEALER!
ABSOLUTELY NO FUCKING CHANCE.

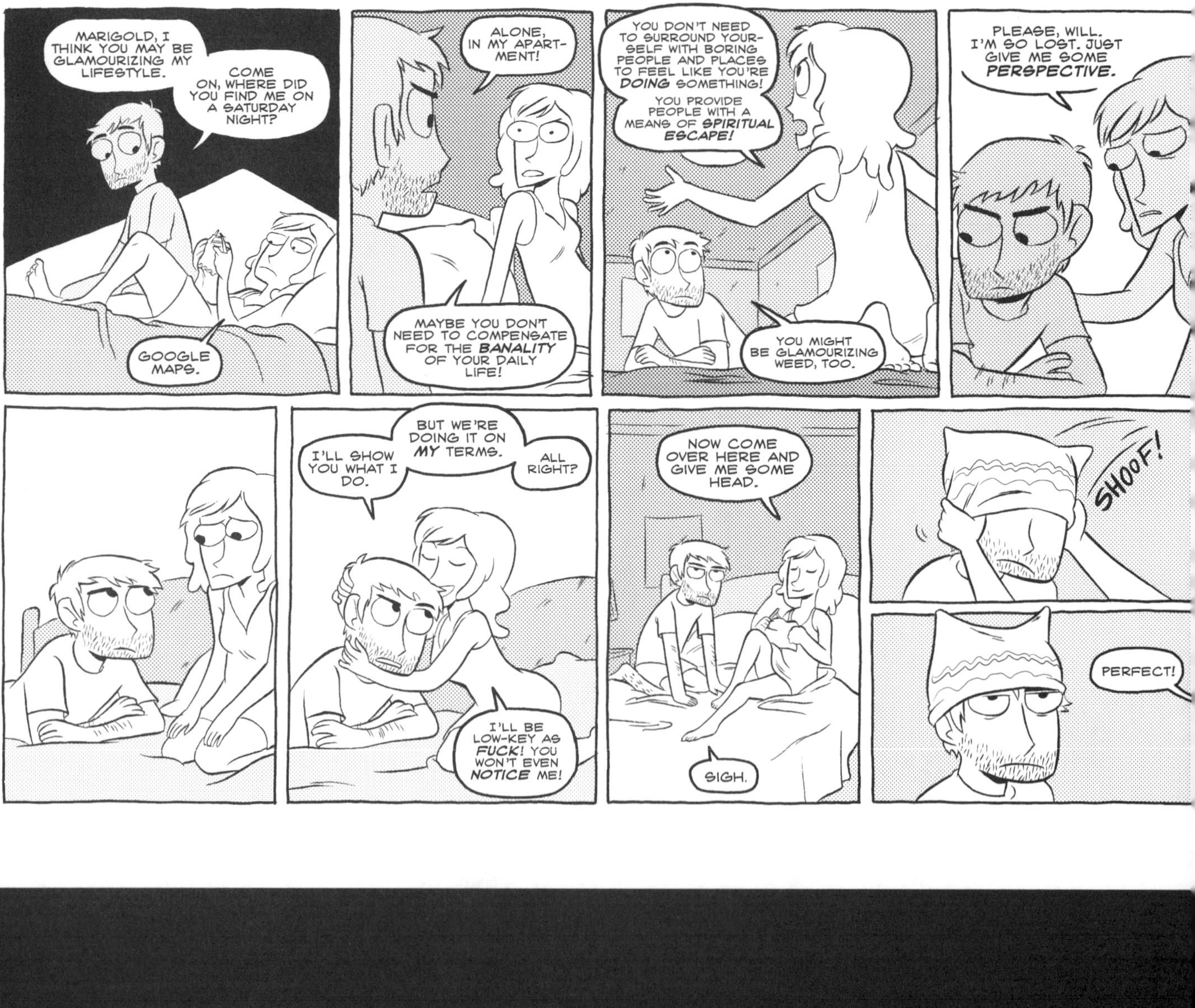
MARIGOLD, I THINK YOU MAY BE GLAMOURIZING MY LIFESTYLE.
COME ON, WHERE DID YOU FIND ME ON A SATURDAY NIGHT?
GOOGLE MAPS.
ALONE, IN MY APARTMENT!
MAYBE YOU DON'T NEED TO COMPENSATE FOR THE BANALITY OF YOUR DAILY LIFE!
YOU DON'T NEED TO SURROUND YOURSELF WITH BORING PEOPLE AND PLACES TO FEEL LIKE YOU'RE DOING SOMETHING!
YOU PROVIDE PEOPLE WITH A MEANS OF SPIRITUAL ESCAPE!
YOU MIGHT BE GLAMOURIZING WEED, TOO.
PLEASE, WILL. I'M SO LOST. JUST GIVE ME SOME PERSPECTIVE.
I'LL SHOW YOU WHAT I DO.
BUT WE'RE DOING IT ON MY TERMS.
ALL RIGHT?
I'LL BE LOW-KEY AS FUCK! YOU WON'T EVEN NOTICE ME!
NOW COME OVER HERE AND GIVE ME SOME HEAD.
SIGH.
SHOOF!
PERFECT!

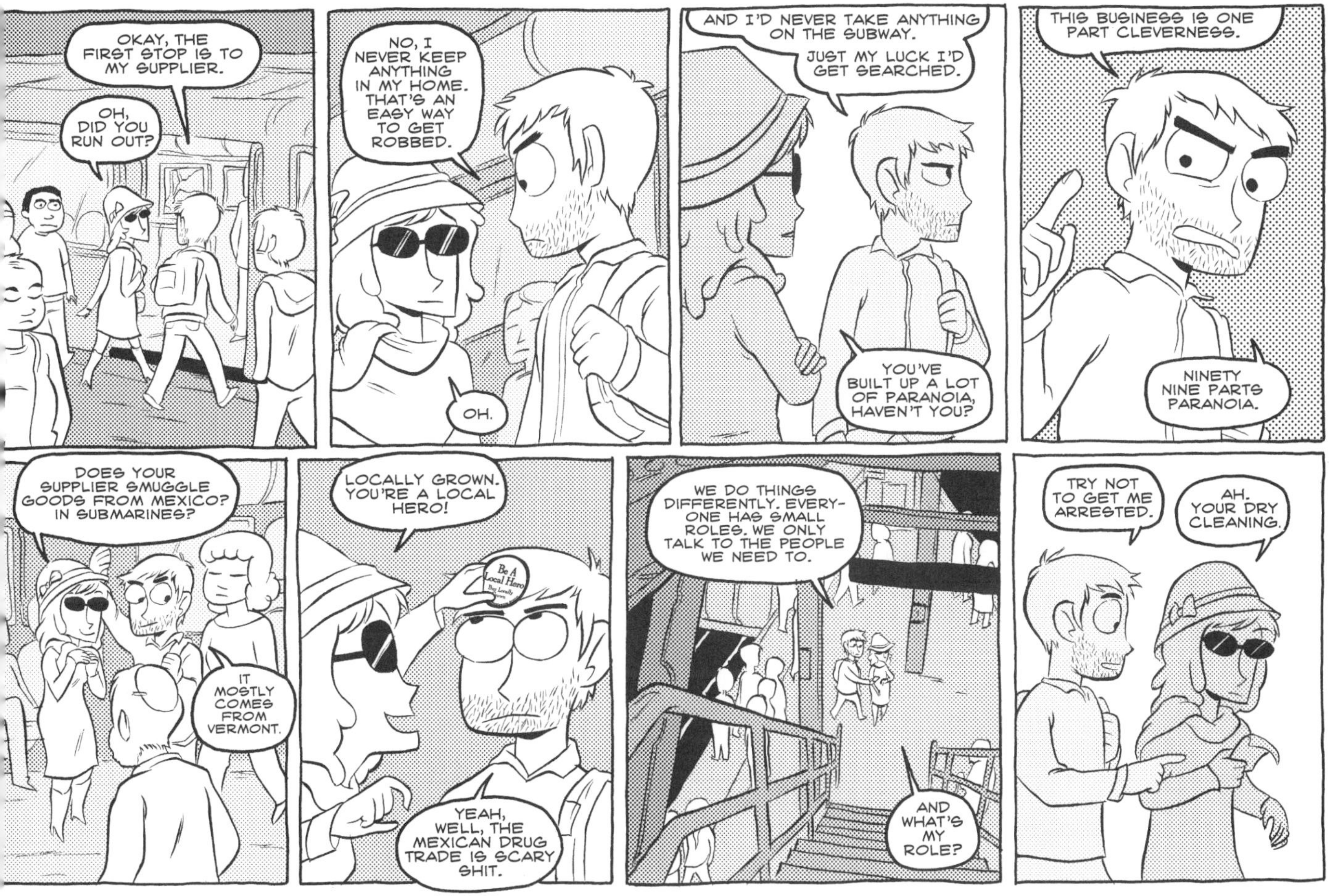
OKAY, THE FIRST STOP IS TO MY SUPPLIER.
OH, DID YOU RUN OUT?
NO, I NEVER KEEP ANYTHING IN MY HOME. THAT'S AN EASY WAY TO GET ROBBED.
OH.
AND I'D NEVER TAKE ANYTHING ON THE SUBWAY.
JUST MY LUCK I'D GET SEARCHED.
YOU'VE BUILT UP A LOT OF PARANOIA, HAVEN'T YOU?
THIS BUSINESS IS ONE PART CLEVERNESS.
NINETY NINE PARTS PARANOIA.
DOES YOUR SUPPLIER SMUGGLE GOODS FROM MEXICO? IN SUBMARINES?
IT MOSTLY COMES FROM VERMONT.
LOCALLY GROWN. YOU'RE A LOCAL HERO!
Be A Local Hero
YEAH, WELL, THE MEXICAN DRUG TRADE IS SCARY SHIT.
WE DO THINGS DIFFERENTLY. EVERY-ONE HAS SMALL ROLES. WE ONLY TALK TO THE PEOPLE WE NEED TO.
AND WHAT'S MY ROLE?
TRY NOT TO GET ME ARRESTED.
AH. YOUR DRY CLEANING.

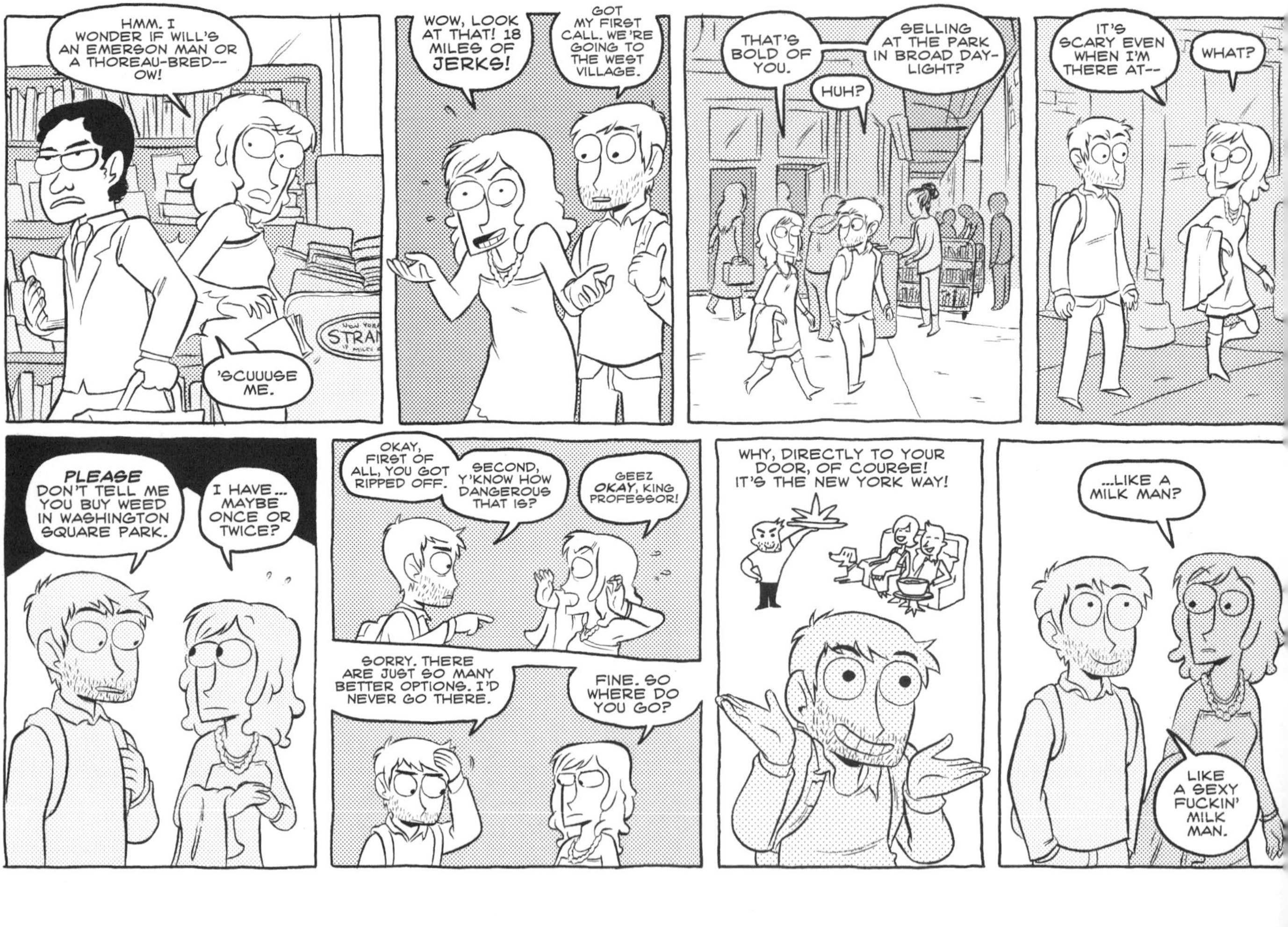
HMM. I WONDER IF WILL'S AN EMERSON MAN OR A THOREAU-BRED-- OW!
'SCUUUSE ME.
STRAN
WOW, LOOK AT THAT! 18 MILES OF JERKS!
GOT MY FIRST CALL. WE'RE GOING TO THE WEST VILLAGE.
SELLING AT THE PARK IN BROAD DAYLIGHT?
HUH?
THAT'S BOLD OF YOU.
IT'S SCARY EVEN WHEN I'M THERE AT--
WHAT?
PLEASE DON'T TELL ME YOU BUY WEED IN WASHINGTON SQUARE PARK.
I HAVE... MAYBE ONCE OR TWICE?
OKAY, FIRST OF ALL, YOU GOT RIPPED OFF.
SECOND, Y'KNOW HOW DANGEROUS THAT IS?
GEEZ OKAY, KING PROFESSOR!
SORRY. THERE ARE JUST SO MANY BETTER OPTIONS. I'D NEVER GO THERE.
FINE. SO WHERE DO YOU GO?
WHY, DIRECTLY TO YOUR DOOR, OF COURSE! IT'S THE NEW YORK WAY!
...LIKE A MILK MAN?
LIKE A SEXY FUCKIN' MILK MAN.

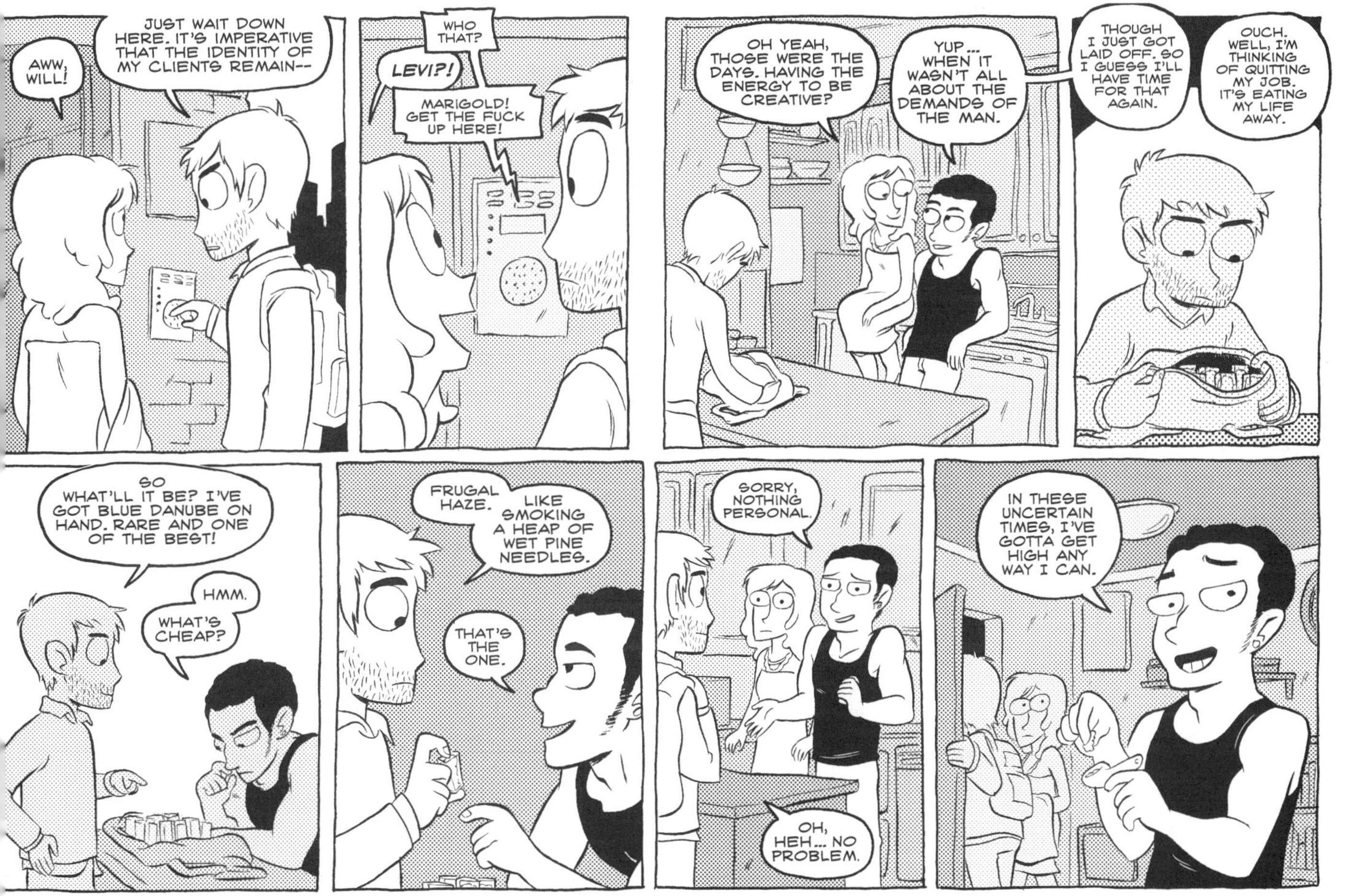
AWW, WILL!
JUST WAIT DOWN HERE. IT'S IMPERATIVE THAT THE IDENTITY OF MY CLIENTS REMAIN--
WHO THAT?
LEVI?!
MARIGOLD! GET THE FUCK UP HERE!
OH YEAH, THOSE WERE THE DAYS. HAVING THE ENERGY TO BE CREATIVE?
YUP... WHEN IT WASN'T ALL ABOUT THE DEMANDS OF THE MAN.
THOUGH I JUST GOT LAID OFF. SO I GUESS I'LL HAVE TIME FOR THAT AGAIN.
OUCH. WELL, I'M THINKING OF QUITTING MY JOB. IT'S EATING MY LIFE AWAY.
SO WHAT'LL IT BE? I'VE GOT BLUE DANUBE ON HAND. RARE AND ONE OF THE BEST!
HMM.
WHAT'S CHEAP?
FRUGAL HAZE.
LIKE SMOKING A HEAP OF WET PINE NEEDLES.
THAT'S THE ONE.
SORRY, NOTHING PERSONAL.
OH, HEH... NO PROBLEM.
IN THESE UNCERTAIN TIMES, I'VE GOTTA GET HIGH ANY WAY I CAN.

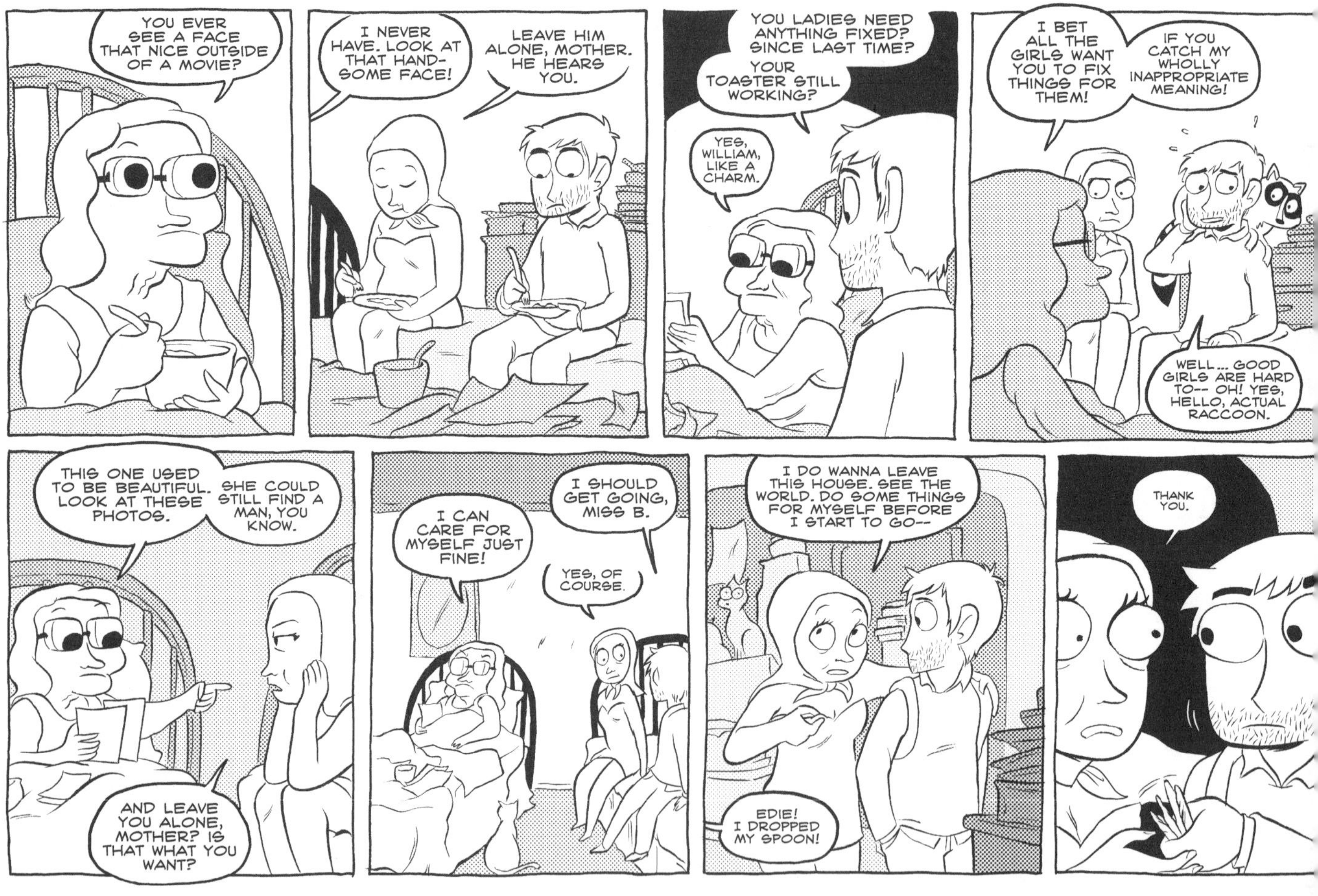
YOU EVER SEE A FACE THAT NICE OUTSIDE OF A MOVIE?
I NEVER HAVE. LOOK AT THAT HAND-SOME FACE!
LEAVE HIM ALONE, MOTHER. HE HEARS YOU.
YOU LADIES NEED ANYTHING FIXED? SINCE LAST TIME?
YOUR TOASTER STILL WORKING?
YES, WILLIAM, LIKE A CHARM.
I BET ALL THE GIRLS WANT YOU TO FIX THINGS FOR THEM!
IF YOU CATCH MY WHOLLY INAPPROPRIATE MEANING!
WELL... GOOD GIRLS ARE HARD TO-- OH! YES, HELLO, ACTUAL RACCOON.
THIS ONE USED TO BE BEAUTIFUL. LOOK AT THESE PHOTOS.
SHE COULD STILL FIND A MAN, YOU KNOW.
AND LEAVE YOU ALONE, MOTHER? IS THAT WHAT YOU WANT?
I CAN CARE FOR MYSELF JUST FINE!
I SHOULD GET GOING, MISS B.
YES, OF COURSE.
I DO WANNA LEAVE THIS HOUSE. SEE THE WORLD. DO SOME THINGS FOR MYSELF BEFORE I START TO GO--
EDIE! I DROPPED MY SPOON!
THANK YOU.

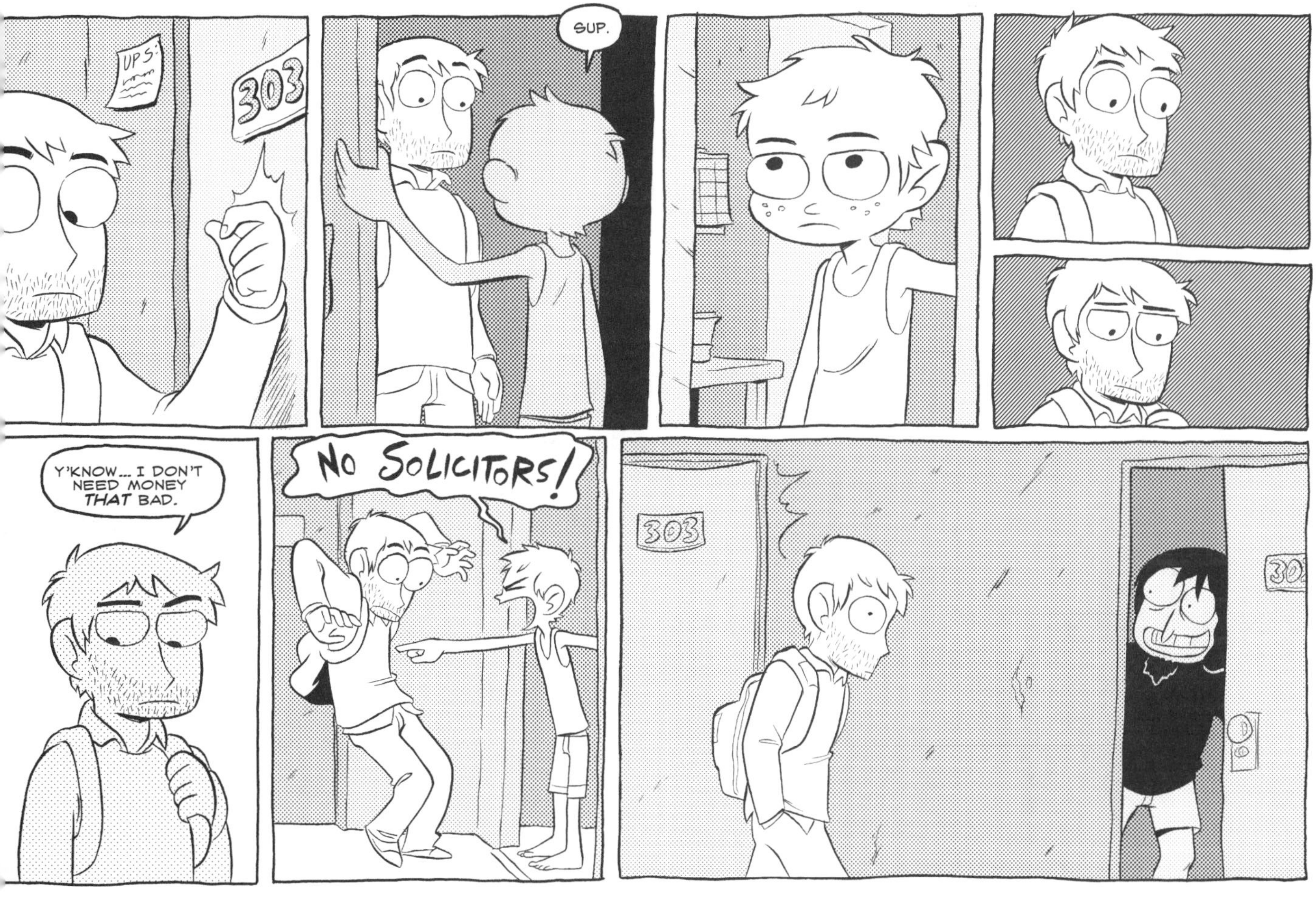
UPS
303
SUP.
Y'KNOW... I DON'T NEED MONEY THAT BAD.
NO SOLICITORS!
303
30

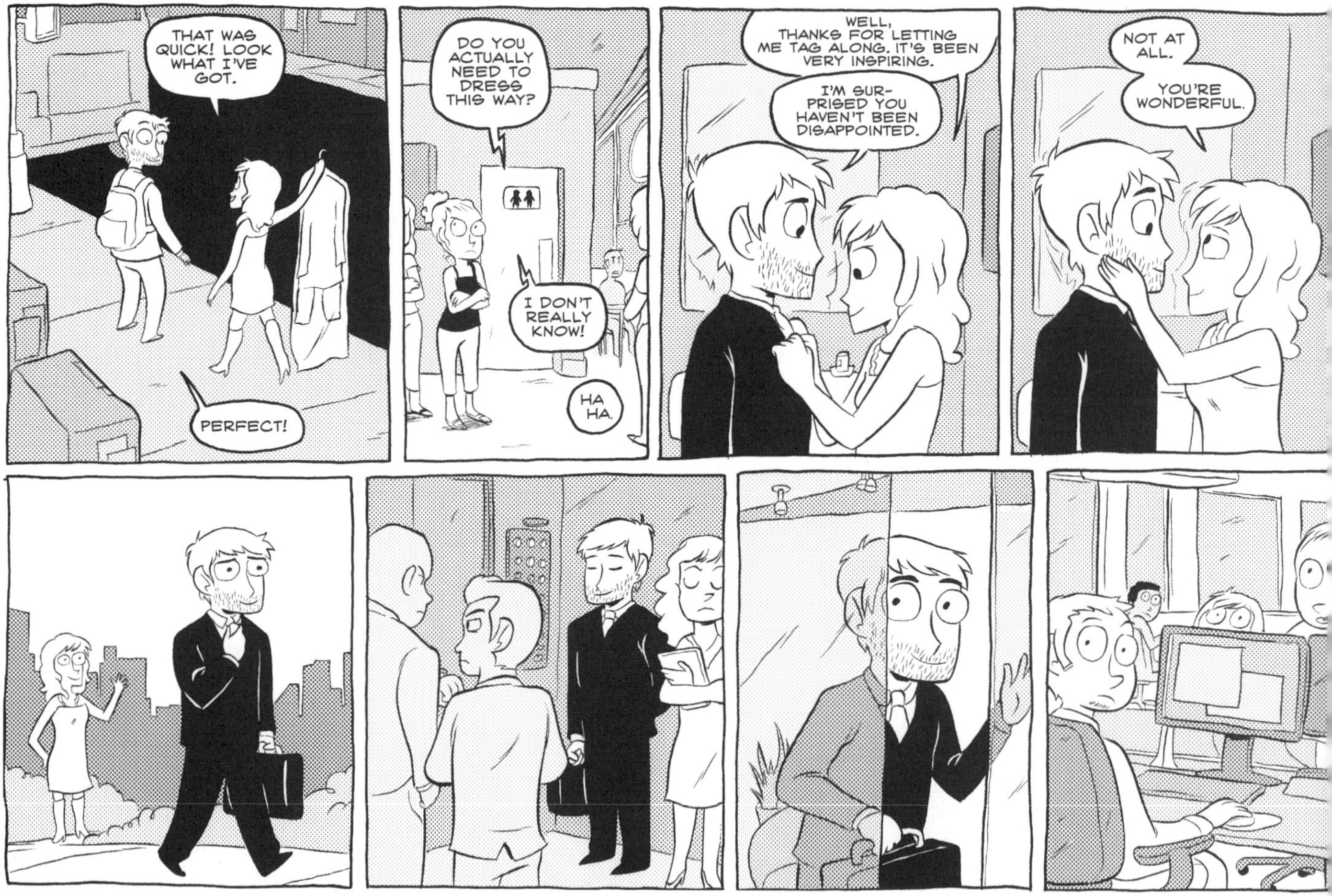
THAT WAS QUICK! LOOK WHAT I'VE GOT.
PERFECT!
DO YOU ACTUALLY NEED TO DRESS THIS WAY?
I DON'T REALLY KNOW!
HA HA.
WELL, THANKS FOR LETTING ME TAG ALONG. IT'S BEEN VERY INSPIRING.
I'M SUR-PRISED YOU HAVEN'T BEEN DISAPPOINTED.
NOT AT ALL.
YOU'RE WONDERFUL.

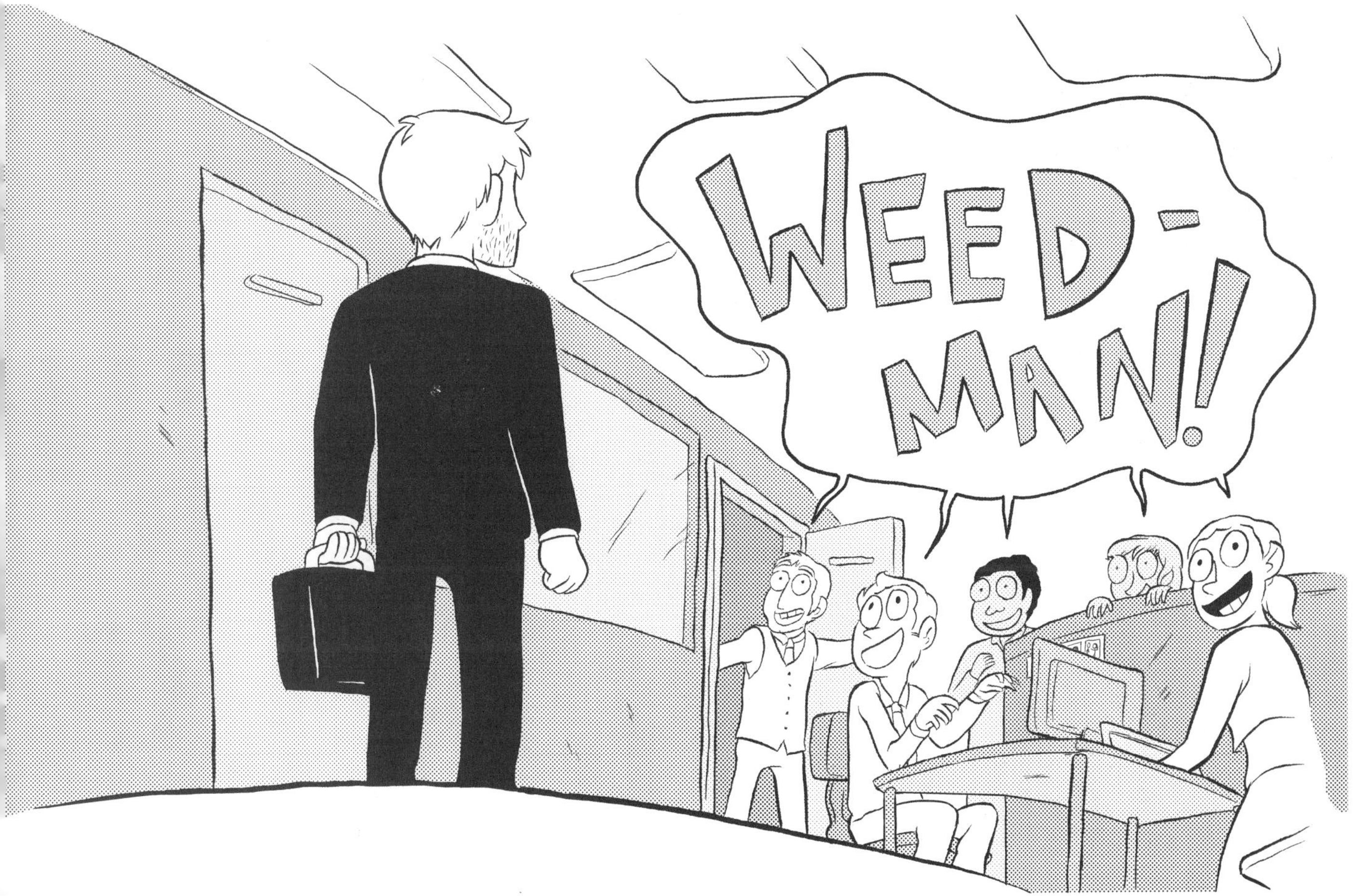
WEED-MAN!

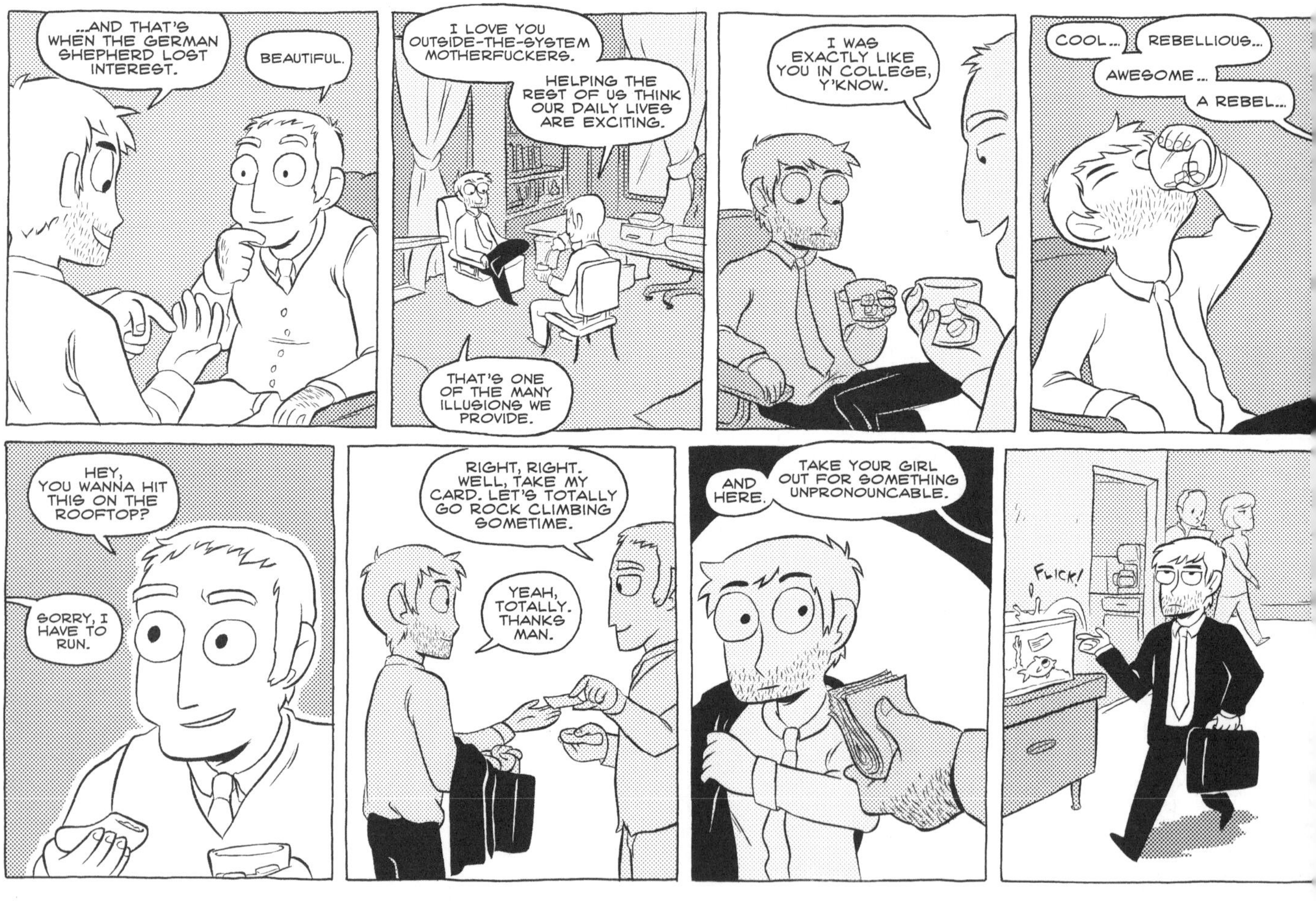
...AND THAT'S WHEN THE GERMAN SHEPHERD LOST INTEREST.
BEAUTIFUL.
I LOVE YOU OUTSIDE-THE-SYSTEM MOTHERFUCKERS.
HELPING THE REST OF US THINK OUR DAILY LIVES ARE EXCITING.
THAT'S ONE OF THE MANY ILLUSIONS WE PROVIDE.
I WAS EXACTLY LIKE YOU IN COLLEGE, Y'KNOW.
COOL...
REBELLIOUS...
AWESOME...
A REBEL...
HEY, YOU WANNA HIT THIS ON THE ROOFTOP?
SORRY, I HAVE TO RUN.
RIGHT, RIGHT. WELL, TAKE MY CARD. LET'S TOTALLY GO ROCK CLIMBING SOMETIME.
YEAH, TOTALLY. THANKS MAN.
AND HERE.
TAKE YOUR GIRL OUT FOR SOMETHING UNPRONOUNCABLE.
FLICK!

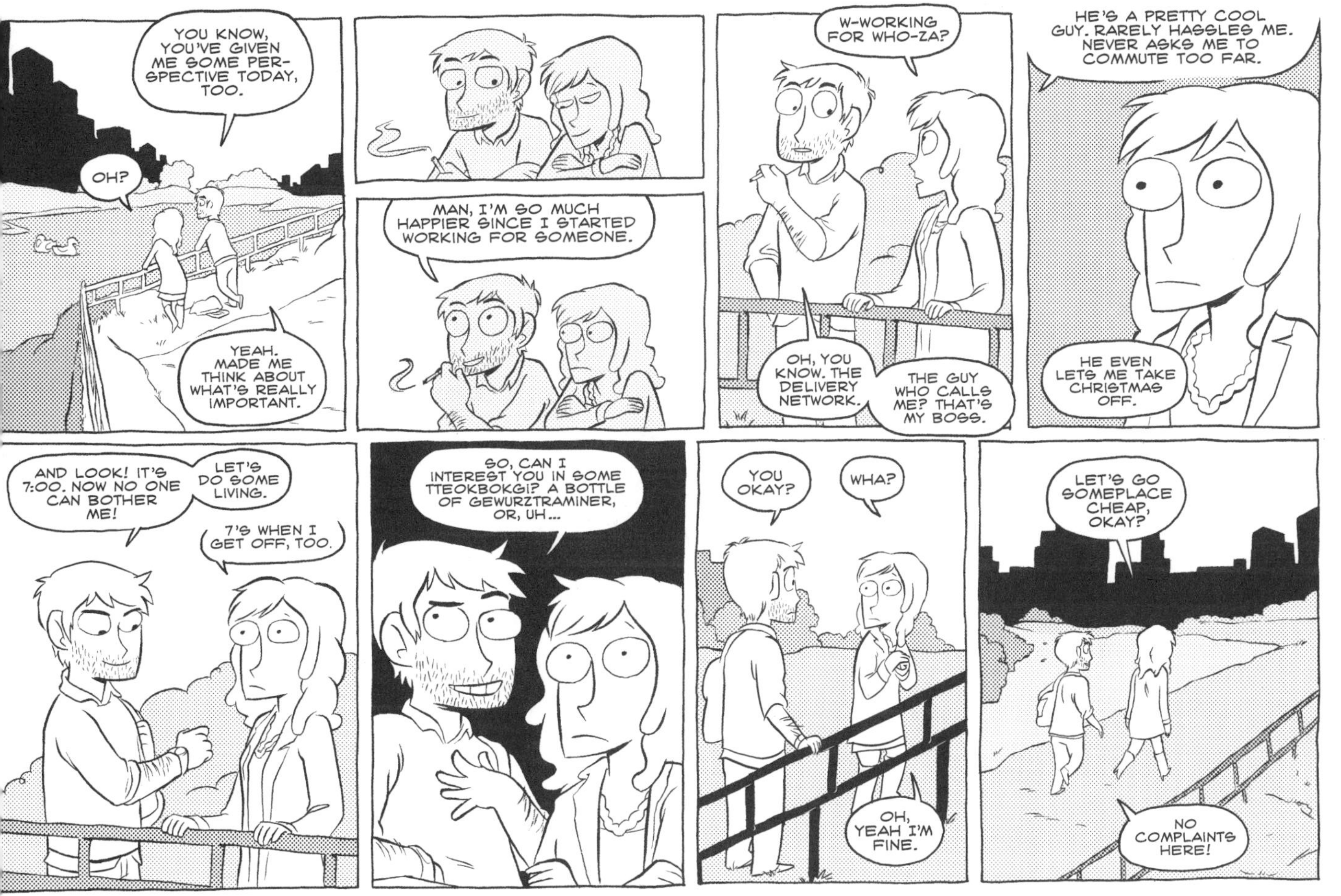
YOU KNOW, YOU'VE GIVEN ME SOME PER-SPECTIVE TODAY, TOO.
OH?
YEAH. MADE ME THINK ABOUT WHAT'S REALLY IMPORTANT.
MAN, I'M SO MUCH HAPPIER SINCE I STARTED WORKING FOR SOMEONE.
W-WORKING FOR WHO-ZA?
OH, YOU KNOW. THE DELIVERY NETWORK.
THE GUY WHO CALLS ME? THAT'S MY BOSS.
HE'S A PRETTY COOL GUY. RARELY HASSLES ME. NEVER ASKS ME TO COMMUTE TOO FAR.
HE EVEN LETS ME TAKE CHRISTMAS OFF.
AND LOOK! IT'S 7:00. NOW NO ONE CAN BOTHER ME!
LET'S DO SOME LIVING.
7'S WHEN I GET OFF, TOO.
SO, CAN I INTEREST YOU IN SOME TTEOKBOKGI? A BOTTLE OF GEWURZTRAMINER, OR, UH...
YOU OKAY?
WHA?
OH, YEAH I'M FINE.
LET'S GO SOMEPLACE CHEAP, OKAY?
NO COMPLAINTS HERE!

Snowy Patrol

I really, really wanted a dog when this story was written. In my mind a dog symbolized a level of comfort that people in their 20s try very hard to find. The comfort of being needed, of having responsibilities, of carving out a routine based around a place you call home. A home with a dog means, to some extent, figuring a few things out. This was the first story I wrote after my move to Portland, a time when I was actively trying to restructure my life, and there's a familiar feeling of tension on the characters' minds.

This isn't the first story where Hanna's controlling ways backfire on her, but it's the first time we see the futility of her efforts. It's nice to be able to show Hanna losing control once in a while, particularly by her own hand. She has the potential to grow, albeit slowly.

I wanted this arc to show Park in a well-meaning light, rather than the antagonistic boyfriend I felt he was becoming. He wants to do well by others by doing well for himself. Hanna (and hopefully, the reader) gains a little respect for him in the end, even if it means making Eve the bad guy.

I've since adopted a dog. She's totally the best.

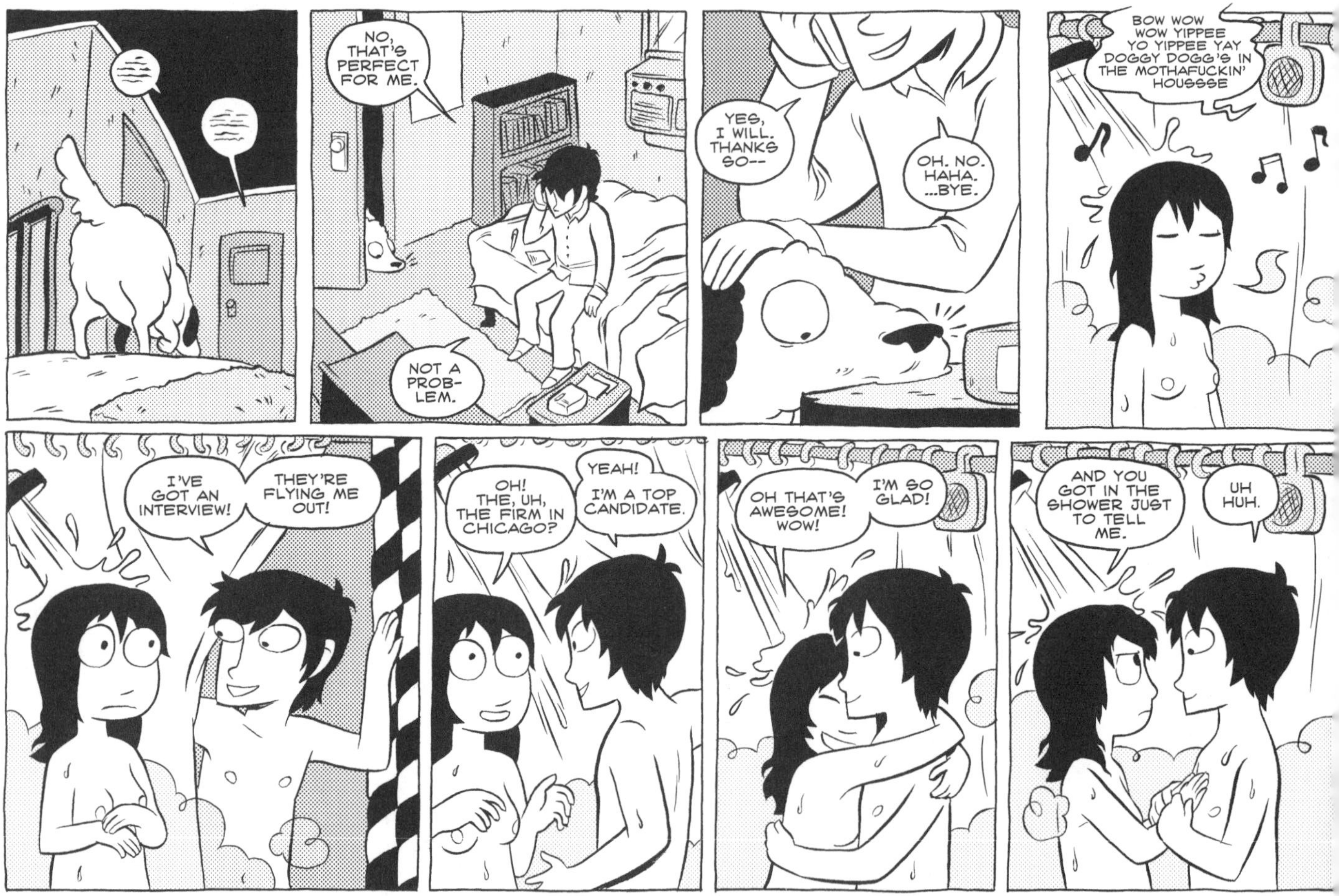
NO, THAT'S PERFECT FOR ME.
NOT A PROB-LEM.
YES, I WILL. THANKS SO--
OH. NO. HAHA. ...BYE.
BOW WOW WOW YIPPEE YO YIPPEE YAY DOGGY DOGG'S IN THE MOTHAFUCKIN' HOUSSSE
I'VE GOT AN INTERVIEW!
THEY'RE FLYING ME OUT!
OH! THE, UH, THE FIRM IN CHICAGO?
YEAH!
I'M A TOP CANDIDATE.
OH THAT'S AWESOME! WOW!
I'M SO GLAD!
AND YOU GOT IN THE SHOWER JUST TO TELL ME.
UH HUH.

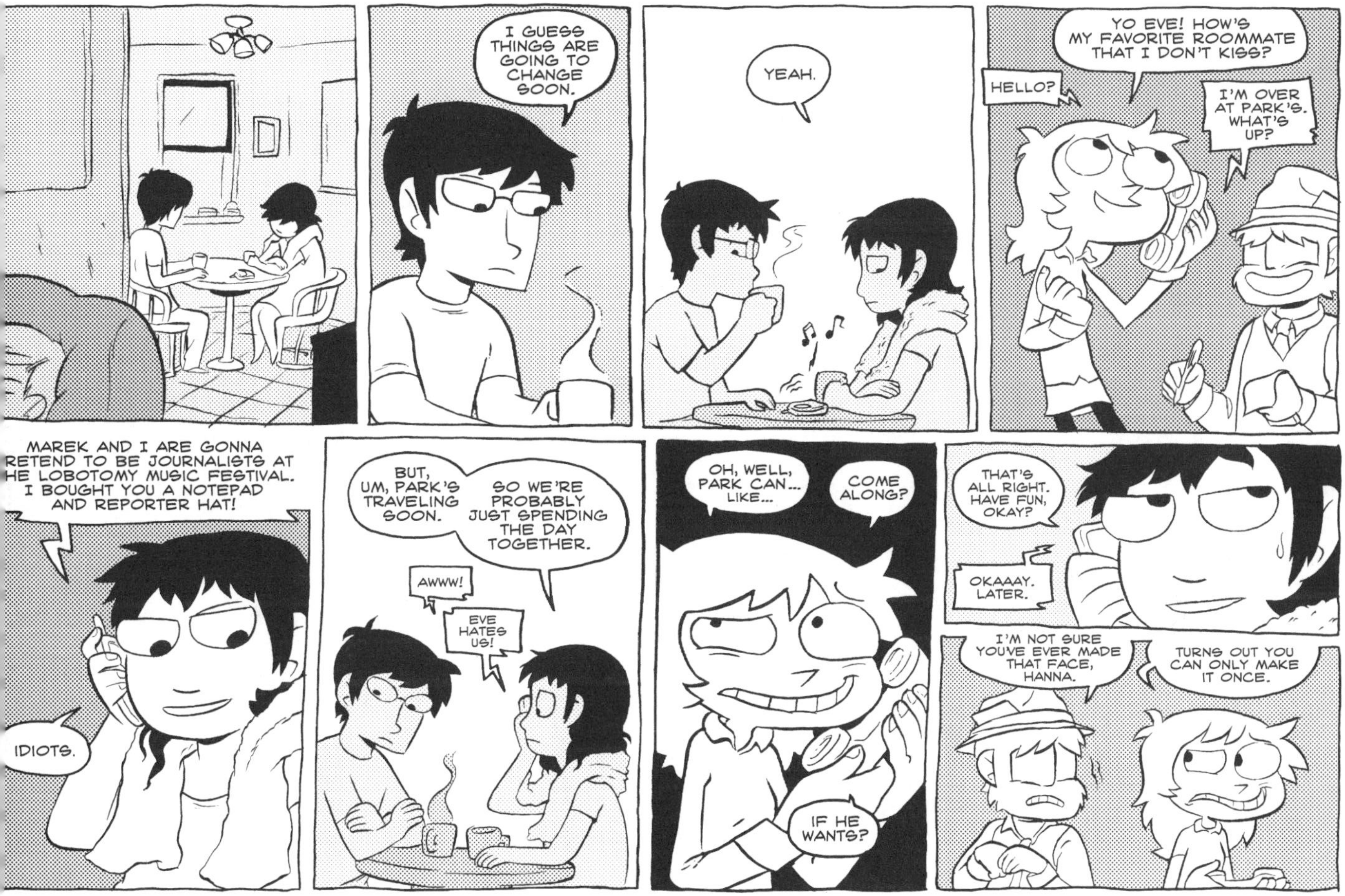
I GUESS THINGS ARE GOING TO CHANGE SOON.
YEAH.
HELLO?
YO EVE! HOW'S MY FAVORITE ROOMMATE THAT I DON'T KISS?
I'M OVER AT PARK'S. WHAT'S UP?
MAREK AND I ARE GONNA RETEND TO BE JOURNALISTS AT HE LOBOTOMY MUSIC FESTIVAL. I BOUGHT YOU A NOTEPAD AND REPORTER HAT!
IDIOTS.
BUT, UM, PARK'S TRAVELING SOON.
SO WE'RE PROBABLY JUST SPENDING THE DAY TOGETHER.
AWWW!
EVE HATES US!
OH, WELL, PARK CAN... LIKE...
COME ALONG?
IF HE WANTS?
THAT'S ALL RIGHT. HAVE FUN, OKAY?
OKAAAY. LATER.
I'M NOT SURE YOU'VE EVER MADE THAT FACE, HANNA.
TURNS OUT YOU CAN ONLY MAKE IT ONCE.

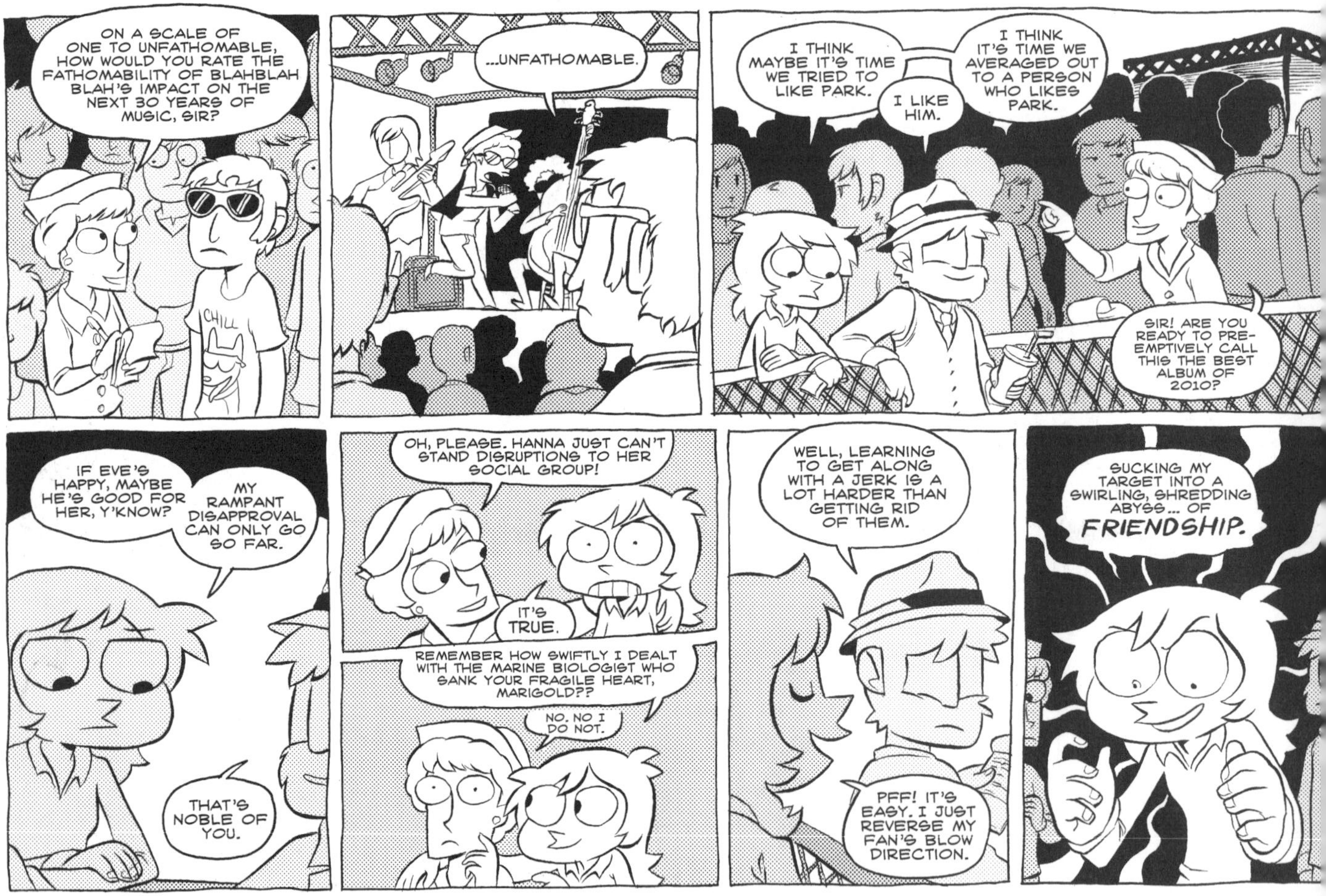
ON A SCALE OF ONE TO UNFATHOMABLE, HOW WOULD YOU RATE THE FATHOMABILITY OF BLAHBLAH BLAH'S IMPACT ON THE NEXT 30 YEARS OF MUSIC, SIR?
CHILL
...UNFATHOMABLE.
I THINK MAYBE IT'S TIME WE TRIED TO LIKE PARK.
I LIKE HIM.
I THINK IT'S TIME WE AVERAGED OUT TO A PERSON WHO LIKES PARK.
SIR! ARE YOU READY TO PRE-EMPTIVELY CALL THIS THE BEST ALBUM OF 2010?
IF EVE'S HAPPY, MAYBE HE'S GOOD FOR HER, Y'KNOW?
MY RAMPANT DISAPPROVAL CAN ONLY GO SO FAR.
THAT'S NOBLE OF YOU.
OH, PLEASE. HANNA JUST CAN'T STAND DISRUPTIONS TO HER SOCIAL GROUP!
IT'S TRUE.
REMEMBER HOW SWIFTLY I DEALT WITH THE MARINE BIOLOGIST WHO SANK YOUR FRAGILE HEART, MARIGOLD??
NO. NO I DO NOT.
WELL, LEARNING TO GET ALONG WITH A JERK IS A LOT HARDER THAN GETTING RID OF THEM.
PFF! IT'S EASY. I JUST REVERSE MY FAN'S BLOW DIRECTION.
SUCKING MY TARGET INTO A SWIRLING, SHREDDING ABYSS... OF FRIENDSHIP.

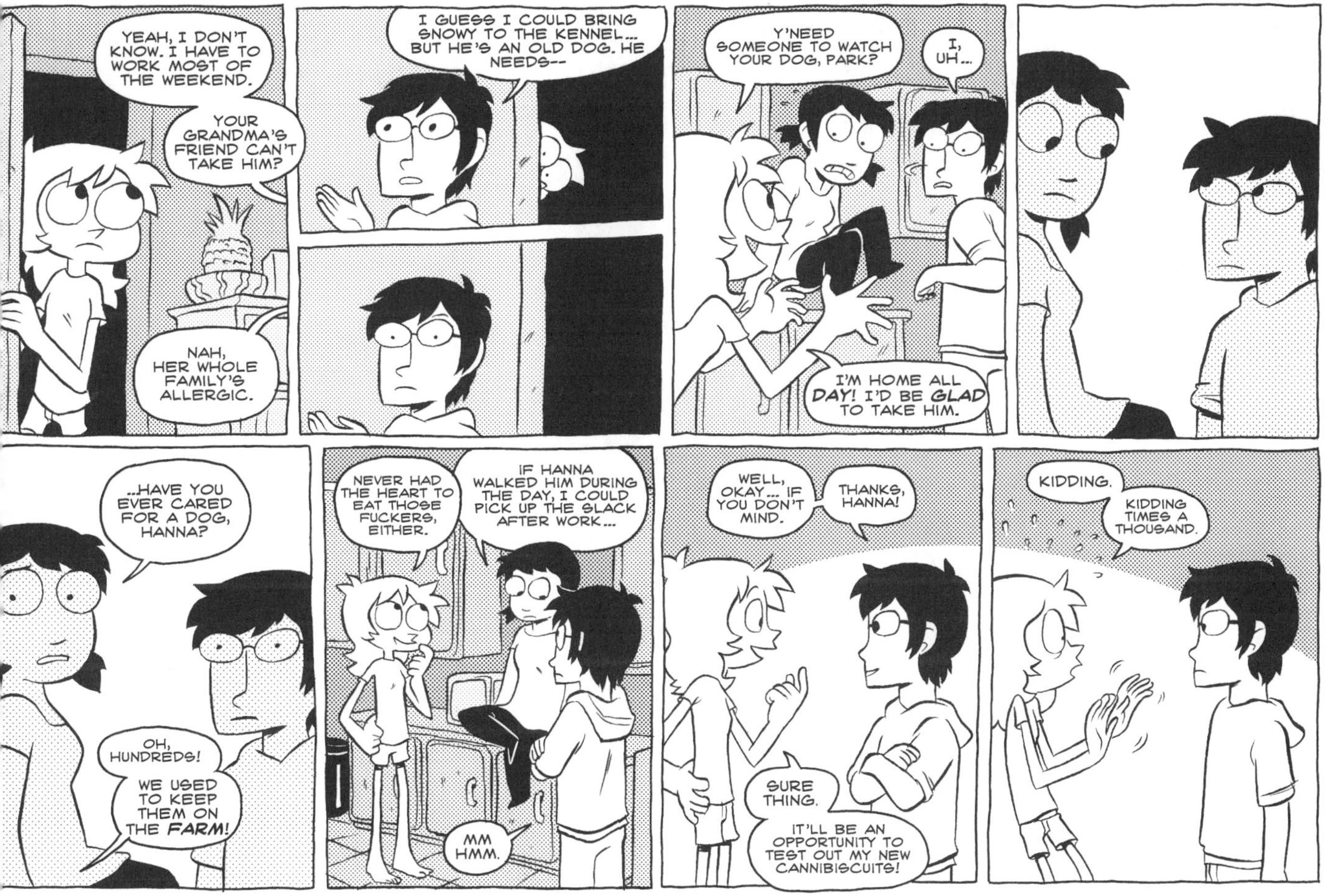
YEAH, I DON'T KNOW. I HAVE TO WORK MOST OF THE WEEKEND.
YOUR GRANDMA'S FRIEND CAN'T TAKE HIM?
NAH, HER WHOLE FAMILY'S ALLERGIC.
I GUESS I COULD BRING SNOWY TO THE KENNEL... BUT HE'S AN OLD DOG. HE NEEDS--
Y'NEED SOMEONE TO WATCH YOUR DOG, PARK?
I, UH...
I'M HOME ALL DAY! I'D BE GLAD TO TAKE HIM.
...HAVE YOU EVER CARED FOR A DOG, HANNA?
OH, HUNDREDS!
WE USED TO KEEP THEM ON THE FARM!
NEVER HAD THE HEART TO EAT THOSE FUCKERS, EITHER.
IF HANNA WALKED HIM DURING THE DAY, I COULD PICK UP THE SLACK AFTER WORK...
MM HMM.
WELL, OKAY... IF YOU DON'T MIND.
THANKS, HANNA!
SURE THING.
IT'LL BE AN OPPORTUNITY TO TEST OUT MY NEW CANNIBISCUITS!
KIDDING.
KIDDING TIMES A THOUSAND.

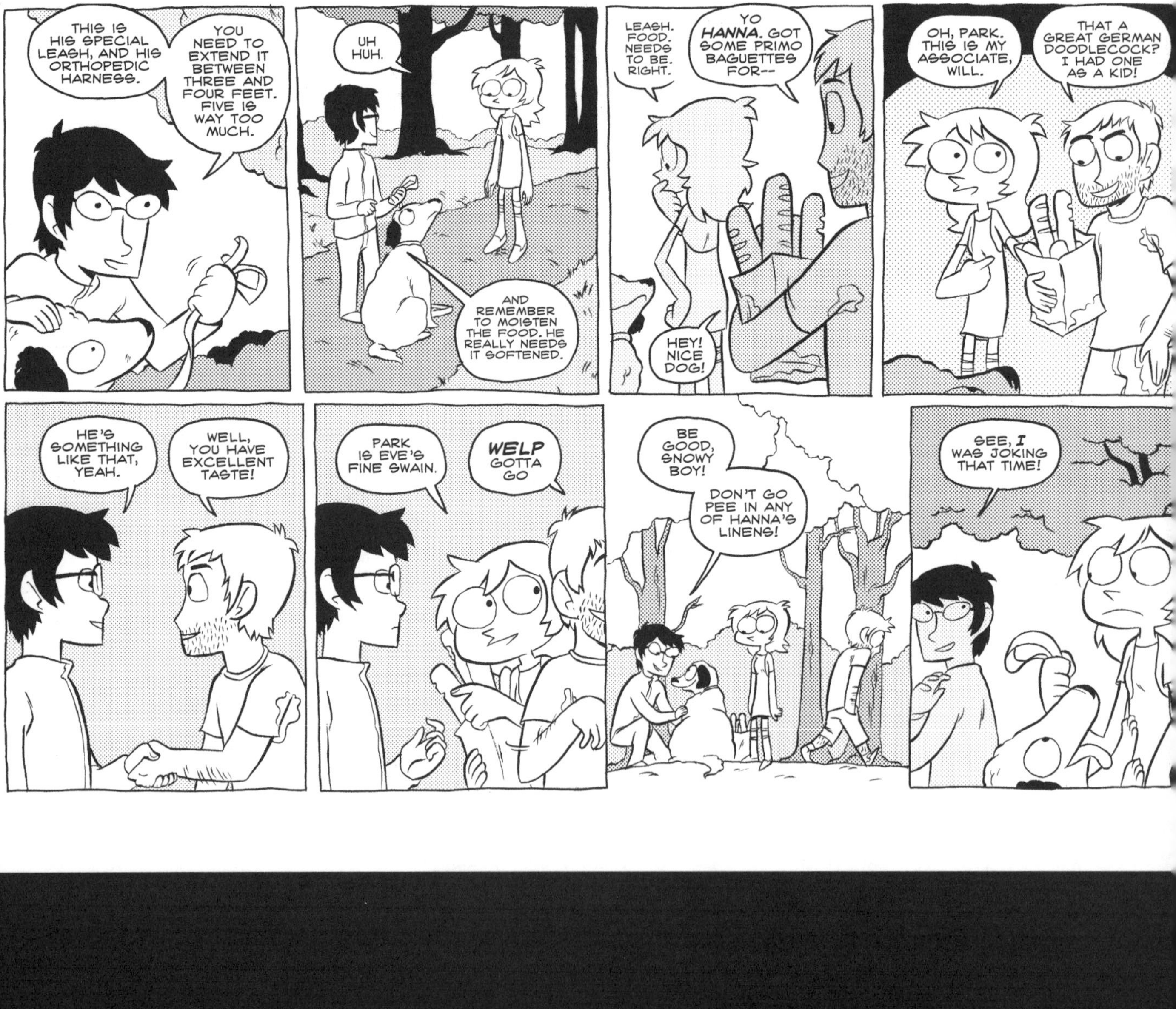
THIS IS HIS SPECIAL LEASH, AND HIS ORTHOPEDIC HARNESS.
YOU NEED TO EXTEND IT BETWEEN THREE AND FOUR FEET. FIVE IS WAY TOO MUCH.
UH HUH.
AND REMEMBER TO MOISTEN THE FOOD. HE REALLY NEEDS IT SOFTENED.
LEASH. FOOD. NEEDS TO BE. RIGHT.
YO *HANNA.* GOT SOME PRIMO BAGUETTES FOR--
HEY! NICE DOG!
OH, PARK. THIS IS MY ASSOCIATE, WILL.
THAT A GREAT GERMAN DOODLECOCK? I HAD ONE AS A KID!
HE'S SOMETHING LIKE THAT, YEAH.
WELL, YOU HAVE EXCELLENT TASTE!
PARK IS EVE'S FINE SWAIN.
WELP GOTTA GO
BE GOOD, SNOWY BOY!
DON'T GO PEE IN ANY OF HANNA'S LINENS!
SEE, *I* WAS JOKING THAT TIME!

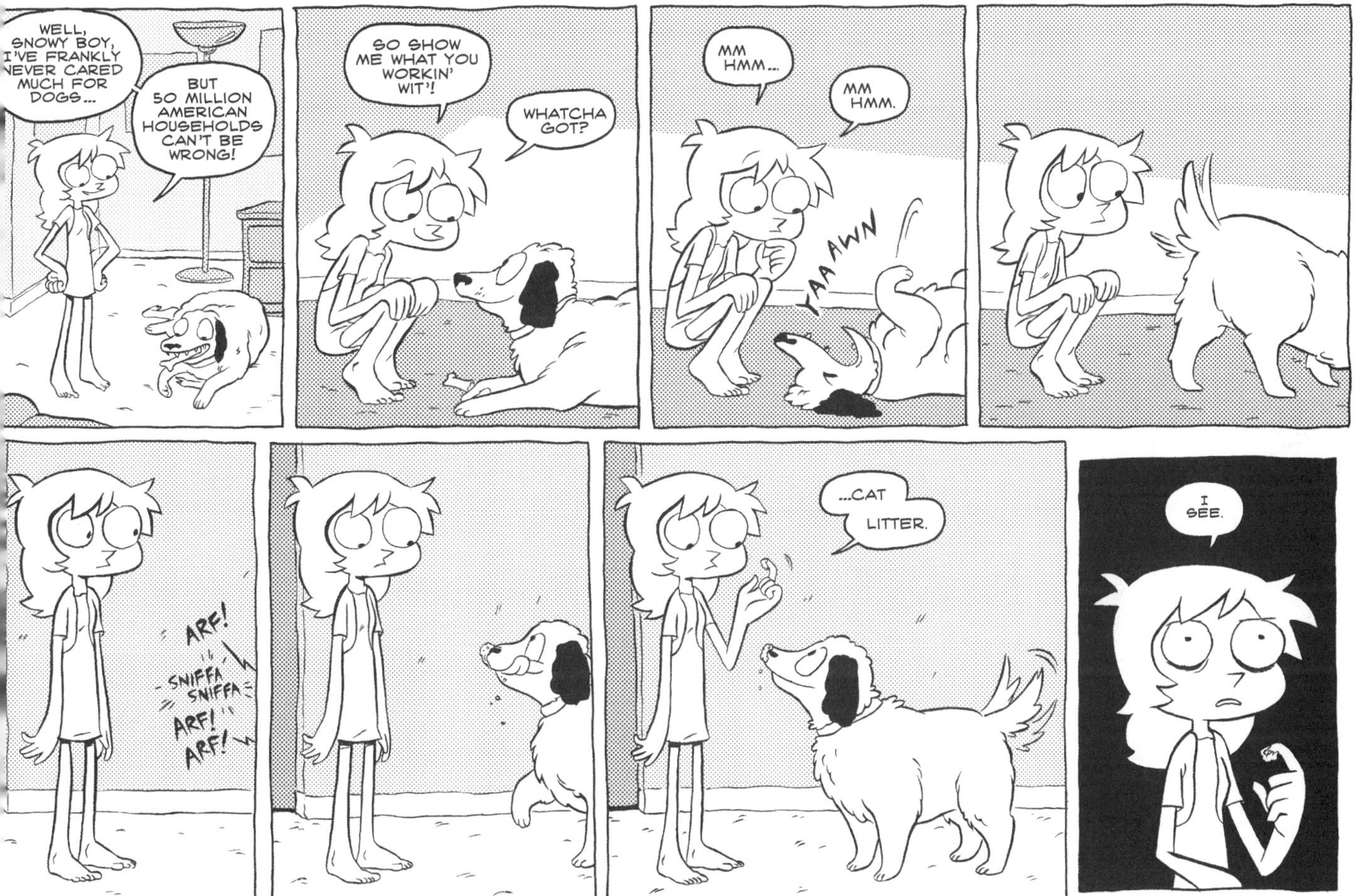
WELL, SNOWY BOY, I'VE FRANKLY NEVER CARED MUCH FOR DOGS...
BUT 50 MILLION AMERICAN HOUSEHOLDS CAN'T BE WRONG!
SO SHOW ME WHAT YOU WORKIN' WIT'!
WHATCHA GOT?
MM HMM...
MM HMM.
YAAAWN
ARF!
SNIFFA SNIFFA
ARF!
ARF!
...CAT LITTER.
I SEE.

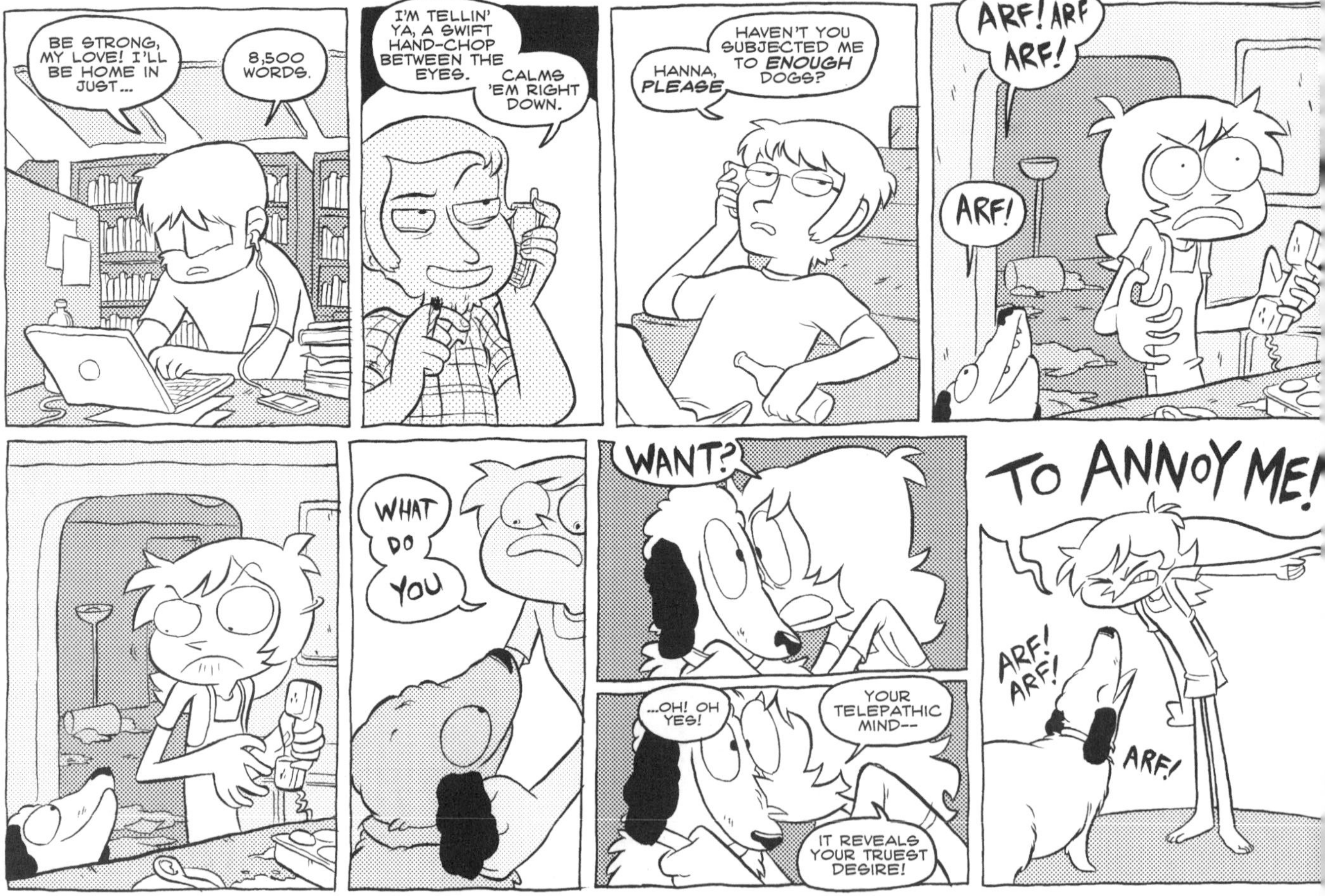
BE STRONG, MY LOVE! I'LL BE HOME IN JUST...
8,500 WORDS.
I'M TELLIN' YA, A SWIFT HAND-CHOP BETWEEN THE EYES.
CALMS 'EM RIGHT DOWN.
HANNA, PLEASE
HAVEN'T YOU SUBJECTED ME TO ENOUGH DOGS?
ARF! ARF ARF!
ARF!
WHAT DO YOU
WANT?
...OH! OH YES!
YOUR TELEPATHIC MIND--
IT REVEALS YOUR TRUEST DESIRE!
TO ANNOY ME!
ARF! ARF!
ARF!

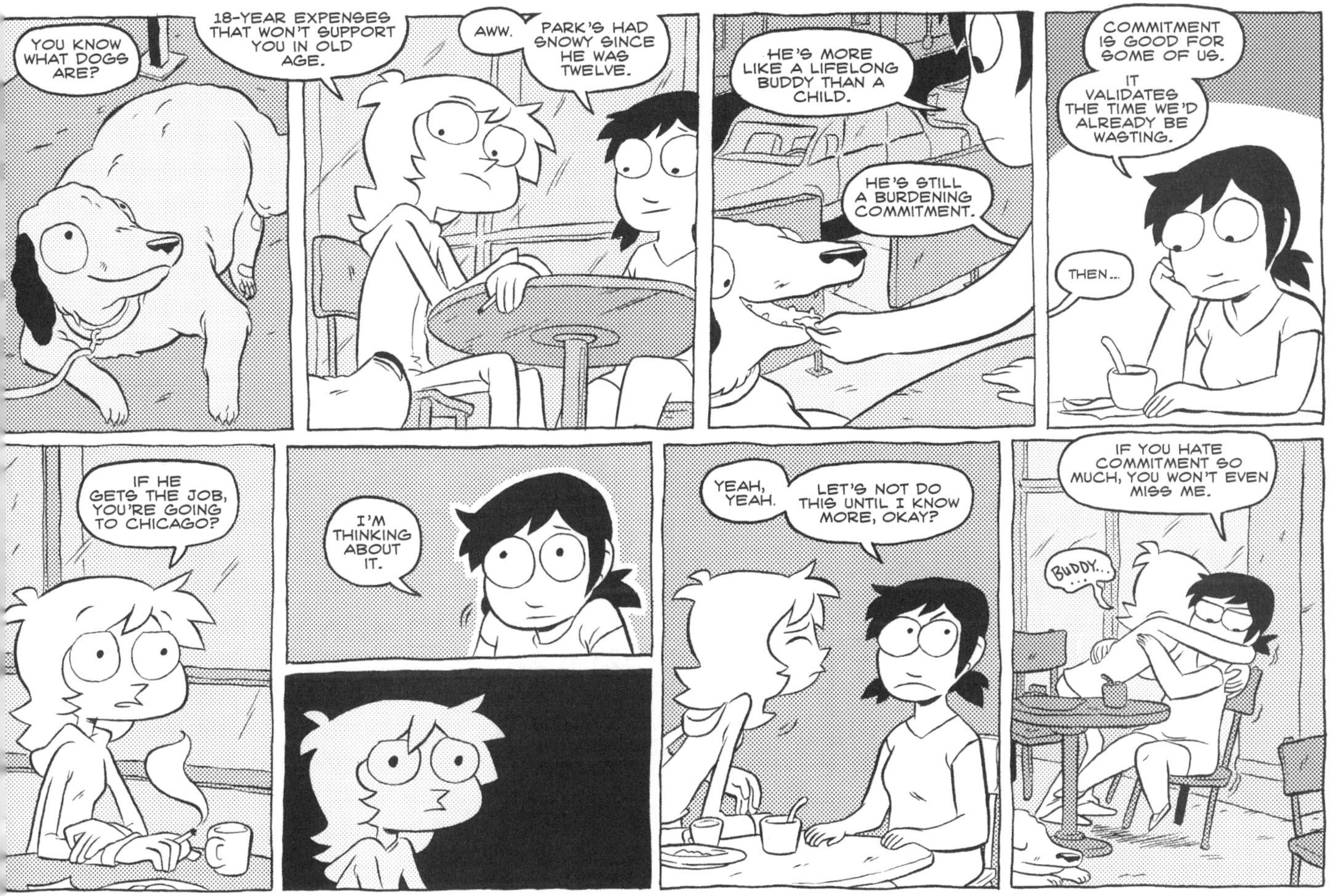
YOU KNOW WHAT DOGS ARE?
18-YEAR EXPENSES THAT WON'T SUPPORT YOU IN OLD AGE.
AWW.
PARK'S HAD SNOWY SINCE HE WAS TWELVE.
HE'S MORE LIKE A LIFELONG BUDDY THAN A CHILD.
HE'S STILL A BURDENING COMMITMENT.
COMMITMENT IS GOOD FOR SOME OF US.
IT VALIDATES THE TIME WE'D ALREADY BE WASTING.
THEN...
IF HE GETS THE JOB, YOU'RE GOING TO CHICAGO?
I'M THINKING ABOUT IT.
YEAH, YEAH.
LET'S NOT DO THIS UNTIL I KNOW MORE, OKAY?
IF YOU HATE COMMITMENT SO MUCH, YOU WON'T EVEN MISS ME.
BUDDY...

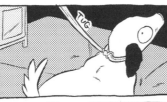

YOU DON'T THINK MUCH ABOUT THE PAST OR THE FUTURE, DO YOU?

MUST BE NICE.

NOT TO WORRY ABOUT HAPPINESS...

LET ALONE THE HAPPINESS OF OTHERS.

OR FEEL THE NEED TO INFLUENCE YOUR FRIENDS' FOOLISH DECISIONS.

OR WONDER IF, BY SAYING NOTHING

YOU'RE BEING ANY KIND OF FRIEND AT ALL.

THAT'S IT. I WANNA EAT KITTY SHIT FOR A LIVING.

TEACH ME YOUR WAYS, SNOWY.

SNOWY?

SNOWY!

SNOOOOWYY!!!

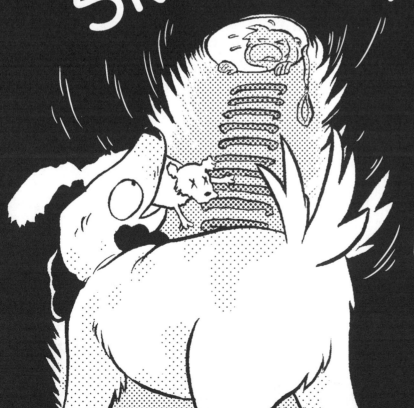

I'VE NEVER SEEN YOU SO UPSET ABOUT A HUMAN BEING, LET ALONE A DOG!

YEAH, YEAH.

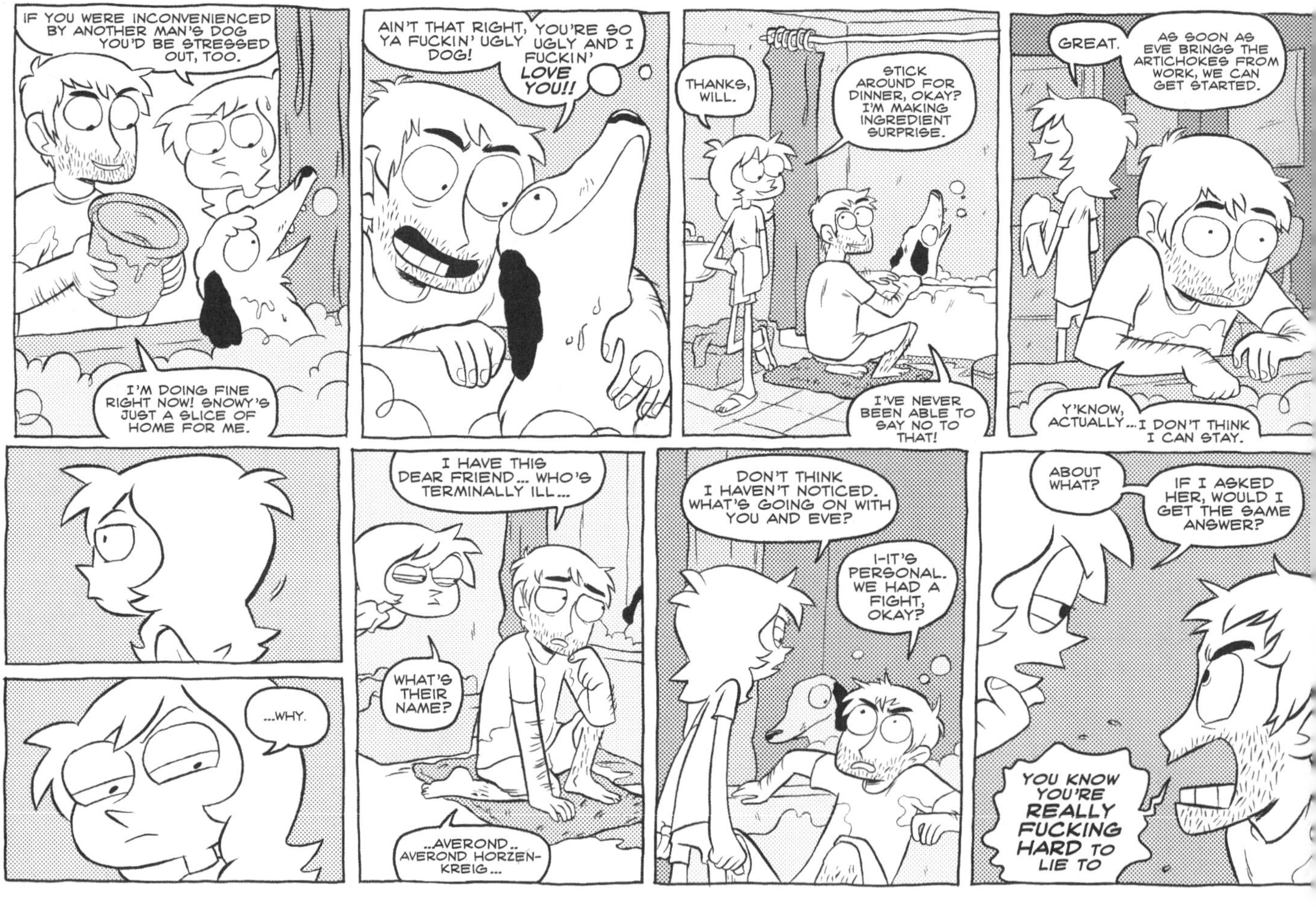
IF YOU WERE INCONVENIENCED BY ANOTHER MAN'S DOG YOU'D BE STRESSED OUT, TOO.
I'M DOING FINE RIGHT NOW! SNOWY'S JUST A SLICE OF HOME FOR ME.
AIN'T THAT RIGHT, YA FUCKIN' UGLY DOG!
YOU'RE SO UGLY AND I FUCKIN' LOVE YOU!!
THANKS, WILL.
STICK AROUND FOR DINNER, OKAY? I'M MAKING INGREDIENT SURPRISE.
I'VE NEVER BEEN ABLE TO SAY NO TO THAT!
GREAT.
AS SOON AS EVE BRINGS THE ARTICHOKES FROM WORK, WE CAN GET STARTED.
Y'KNOW, ACTUALLY... I DON'T THINK I CAN STAY.
...WHY.
I HAVE THIS DEAR FRIEND... WHO'S TERMINALLY ILL...
WHAT'S THEIR NAME?
...AVEROND.. AVEROND HORZEN-KREIG...
DON'T THINK I HAVEN'T NOTICED. WHAT'S GOING ON WITH YOU AND EVE?
I-IT'S PERSONAL. WE HAD A FIGHT, OKAY?
ABOUT WHAT?
IF I ASKED HER, WOULD I GET THE SAME ANSWER?
YOU KNOW YOU'RE REALLY FUCKING HARD TO LIE TO

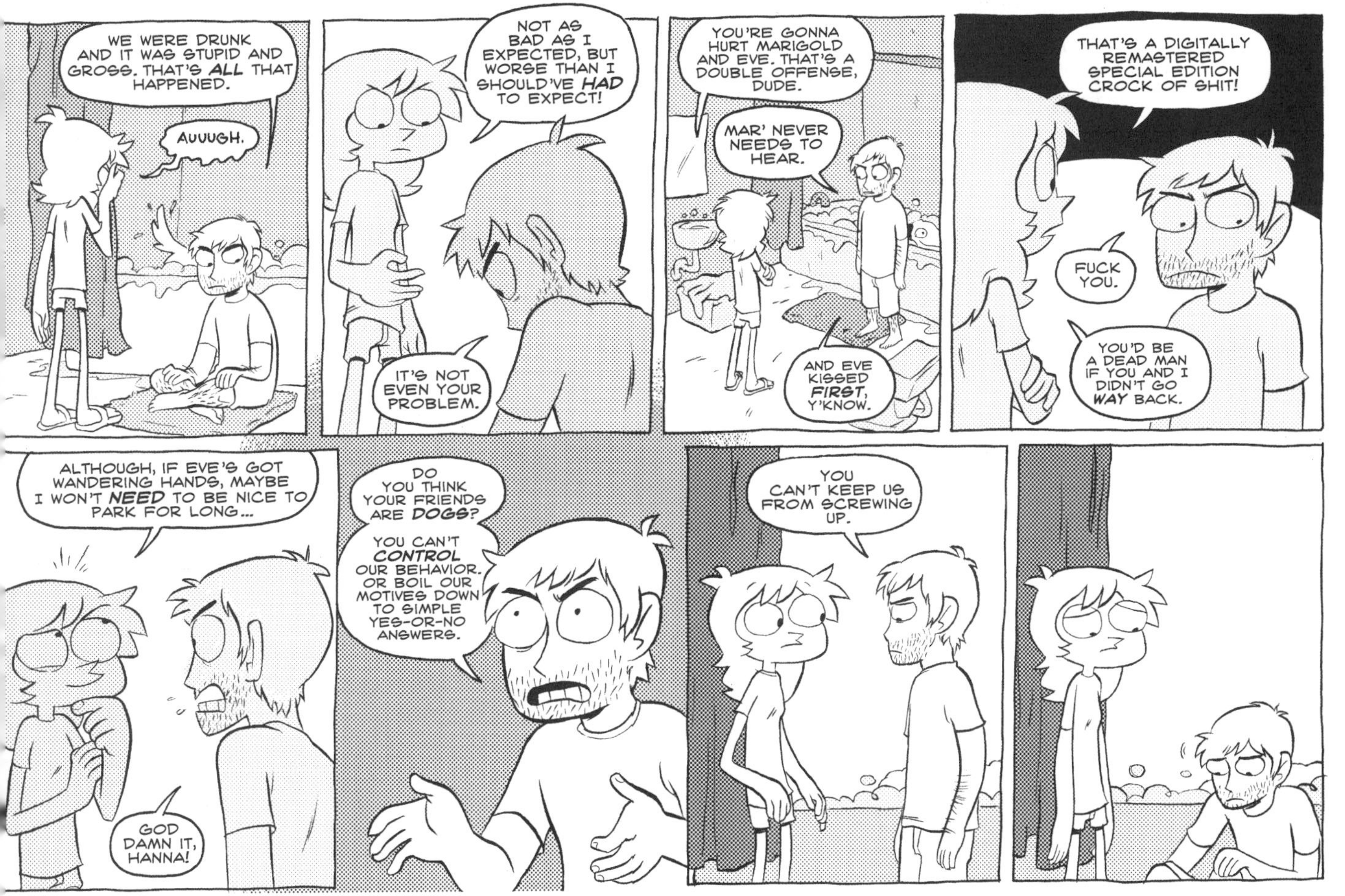
WE WERE DRUNK AND IT WAS STUPID AND GROSS. THAT'S ALL THAT HAPPENED.
AUUUGH.
NOT AS BAD AS I EXPECTED, BUT WORSE THAN I SHOULD'VE HAD TO EXPECT!
IT'S NOT EVEN YOUR PROBLEM.
YOU'RE GONNA HURT MARIGOLD AND EVE. THAT'S A DOUBLE OFFENSE, DUDE.
MAR' NEVER NEEDS TO HEAR.
AND EVE KISSED FIRST, Y'KNOW.
THAT'S A DIGITALLY REMASTERED SPECIAL EDITION CROCK OF SHIT!
FUCK YOU.
YOU'D BE A DEAD MAN IF YOU AND I DIDN'T GO WAY BACK.
ALTHOUGH, IF EVE'S GOT WANDERING HANDS, MAYBE I WON'T NEED TO BE NICE TO PARK FOR LONG...
GOD DAMN IT, HANNA!
DO YOU THINK YOUR FRIENDS ARE DOGS?
YOU CAN'T CONTROL OUR BEHAVIOR. OR BOIL OUR MOTIVES DOWN TO SIMPLE YES-OR-NO ANSWERS.
YOU CAN'T KEEP US FROM SCREWING UP.

HOW ARE YOU GOING TO DEAL WITH THIS?
BY FORGETTING ABOUT IT.
UNTIL YOU DREDGED IT UP, I WAS DOING JUST **FINE**.
WERE YOU?
AWW, WILL.
I KNOW.
WHO'D'VE THOUGHT YOUR MOST **BORING** FRIENDS WOULD CREATE THE MOST **DRAMA**?
EH... THAT'S USUALLY HOW IT GOES.

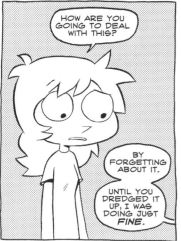

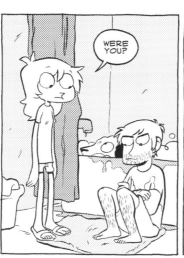

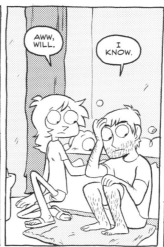

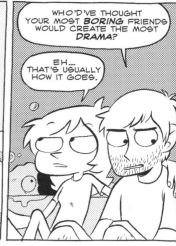

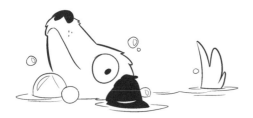

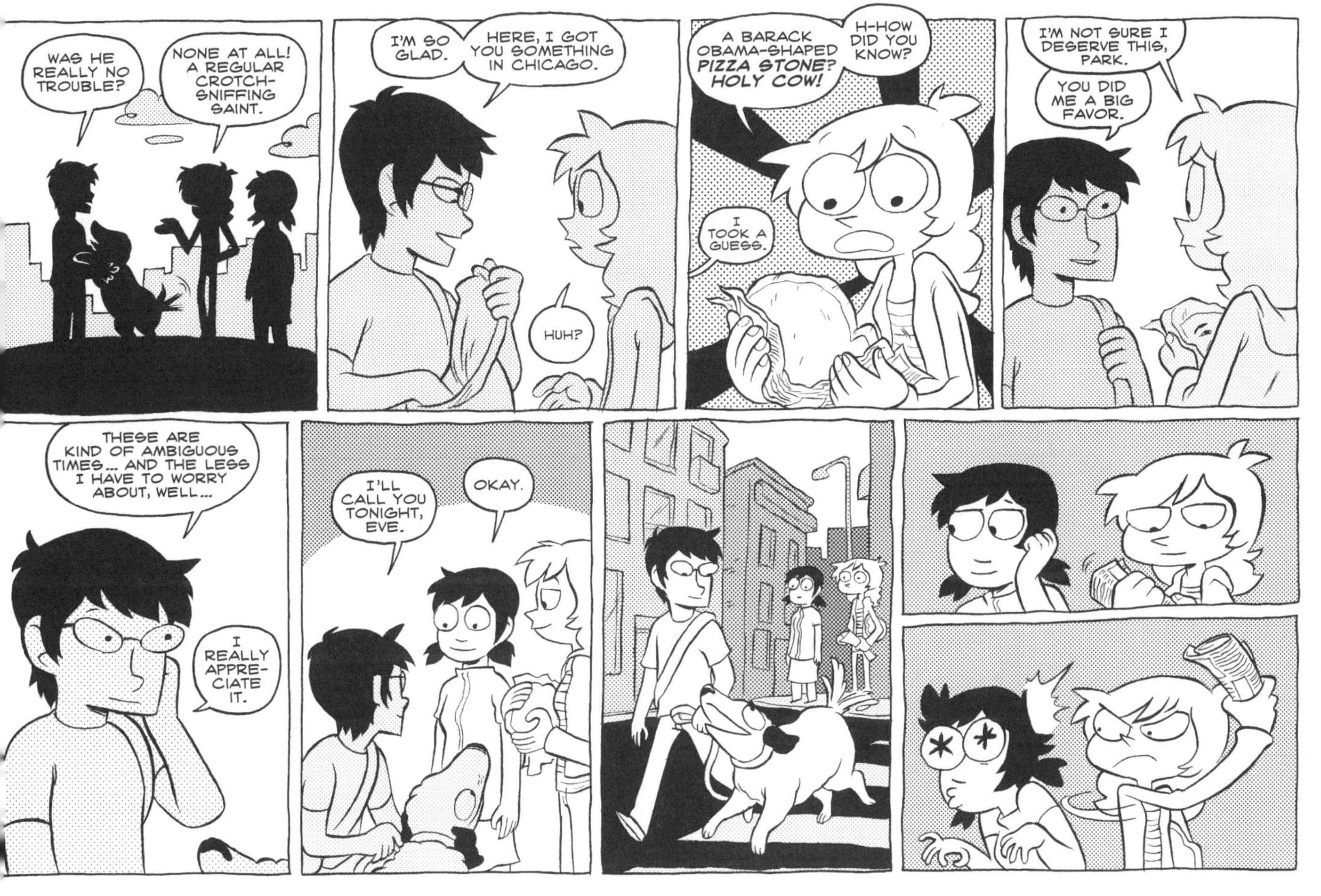
WAS HE REALLY NO TROUBLE?
NONE AT ALL! A REGULAR CROTCH-SNIFFING SAINT.
I'M SO GLAD.
HERE, I GOT YOU SOMETHING IN CHICAGO.
HUH?
A BARACK OBAMA-SHAPED PIZZA STONE? HOLY COW!
H-HOW DID YOU KNOW?
I TOOK A GUESS.
I'M NOT SURE I DESERVE THIS, PARK.
YOU DID ME A BIG FAVOR.
THESE ARE KIND OF AMBIGUOUS TIMES... AND THE LESS I HAVE TO WORRY ABOUT, WELL...
I REALLY APPRECIATE IT.
I'LL CALL YOU TONIGHT, EVE.
OKAY.

Beer Your Own Boss

This is a short, simple story I wrote while my housemates in Portland were beginning their foray into homemade beer. I got to taste a few of their homebrews, and some of it was very good. But I don't have the patience to attempt it myself. Living the dream through comics, once again.

It's a pleasure to show the grocery store kids thrown into a problem together, and getting a collective beatdown from Olly. I also enjoy writing Will as the sage bartender. And I got to draw flapper clothes. Fun times!

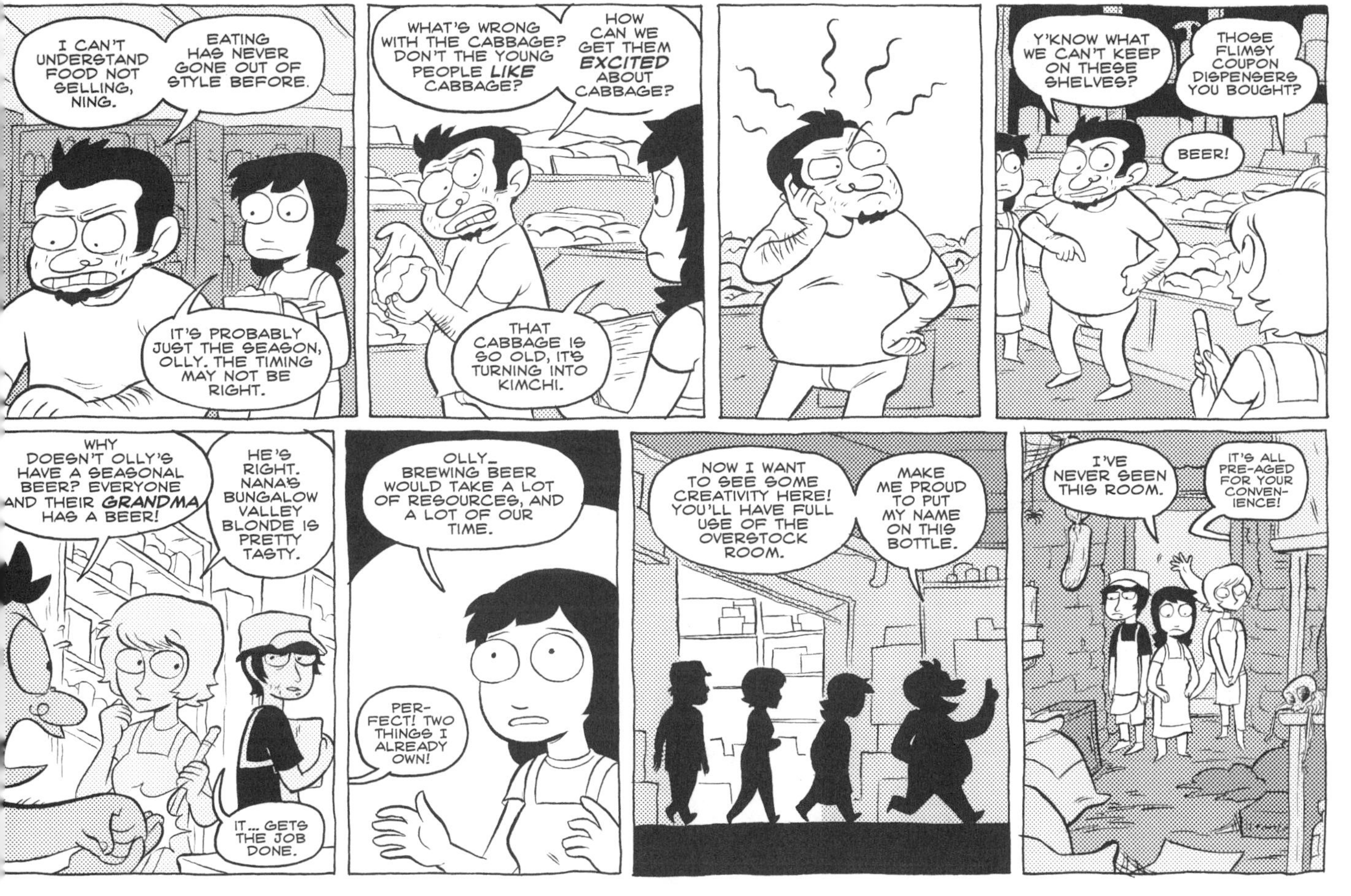
I CAN'T UNDERSTAND FOOD NOT SELLING, NING.
EATING HAS NEVER GONE OUT OF STYLE BEFORE.
IT'S PROBABLY JUST THE SEASON, OLLY. THE TIMING MAY NOT BE RIGHT.
WHAT'S WRONG WITH THE CABBAGE? DON'T THE YOUNG PEOPLE LIKE CABBAGE?
HOW CAN WE GET THEM EXCITED ABOUT CABBAGE?
THAT CABBAGE IS SO OLD, IT'S TURNING INTO KIMCHI.
Y'KNOW WHAT WE CAN'T KEEP ON THESE SHELVES?
THOSE FLIMSY COUPON DISPENSERS YOU BOUGHT?
BEER!
WHY DOESN'T OLLY'S HAVE A SEASONAL BEER? EVERYONE AND THEIR GRANDMA HAS A BEER!
HE'S RIGHT. NANA'S BUNGALOW VALLEY BLONDE IS PRETTY TASTY.
IT... GETS THE JOB DONE.
OLLY... BREWING BEER WOULD TAKE A LOT OF RESOURCES, AND A LOT OF OUR TIME.
PER-FECT! TWO THINGS I ALREADY OWN!
NOW I WANT TO SEE SOME CREATIVITY HERE! YOU'LL HAVE FULL USE OF THE OVERSTOCK ROOM.
MAKE ME PROUD TO PUT MY NAME ON THIS BOTTLE.
I'VE NEVER SEEN THIS ROOM.
IT'S ALL PRE-AGED FOR YOUR CONVEN-IENCE!

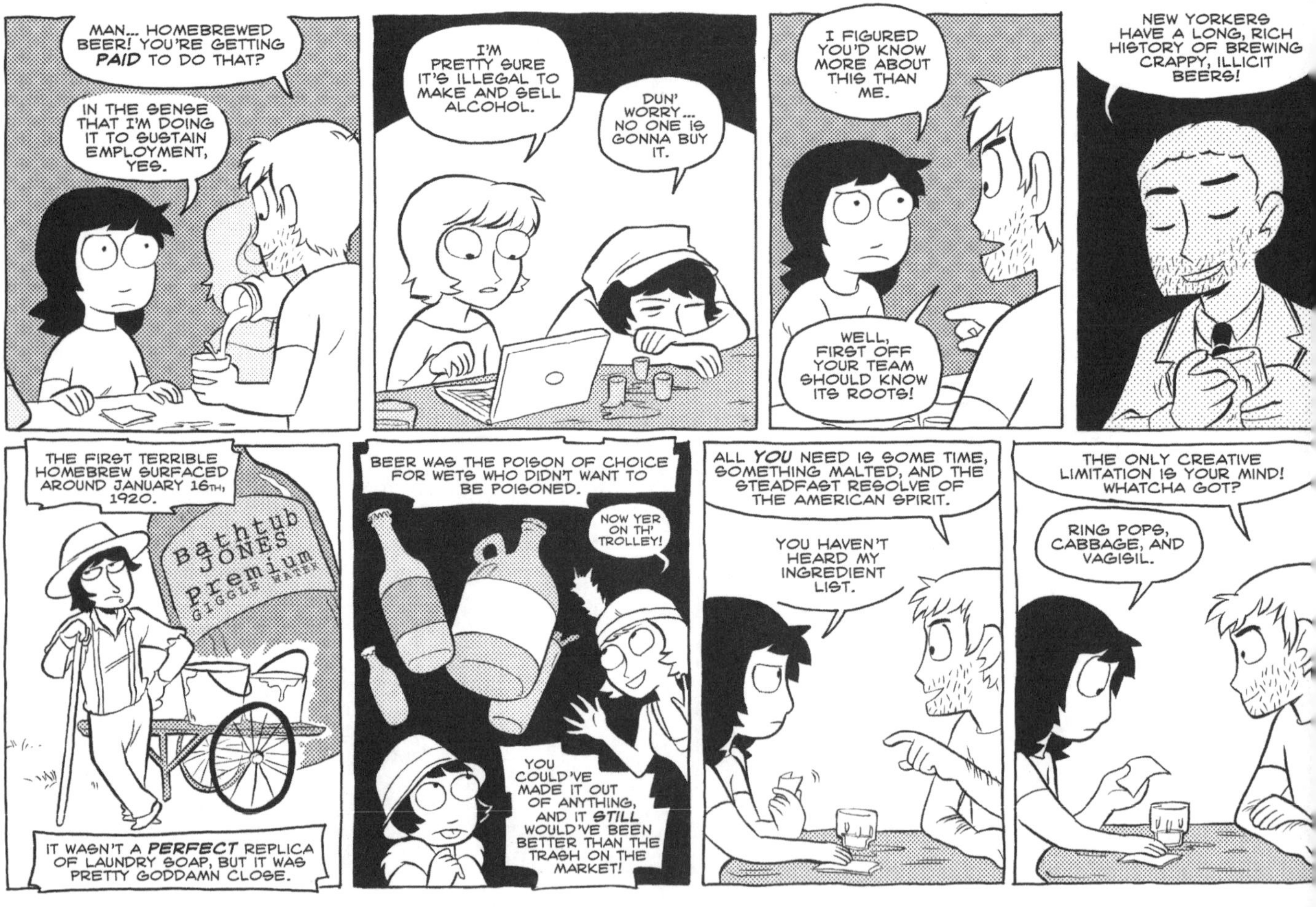
MAN... HOMEBREWED BEER! YOU'RE GETTING PAID TO DO THAT?
IN THE SENSE THAT I'M DOING IT TO SUSTAIN EMPLOYMENT, YES.
I'M PRETTY SURE IT'S ILLEGAL TO MAKE AND SELL ALCOHOL.
DUN' WORRY... NO ONE IS GONNA BUY IT.
I FIGURED YOU'D KNOW MORE ABOUT THIS THAN ME.
WELL, FIRST OFF YOUR TEAM SHOULD KNOW ITS ROOTS!
NEW YORKERS HAVE A LONG, RICH HISTORY OF BREWING CRAPPY, ILLICIT BEERS!
THE FIRST TERRIBLE HOMEBREW SURFACED AROUND JANUARY 16TH, 1920.
Bathtub JONES premium GIGGLE WATER
IT WASN'T A PERFECT REPLICA OF LAUNDRY SOAP, BUT IT WAS PRETTY GODDAMN CLOSE.
BEER WAS THE POISON OF CHOICE FOR WETS WHO DIDN'T WANT TO BE POISONED.
NOW YER ON TH' TROLLEY!
YOU COULD'VE MADE IT OUT OF ANYTHING, AND IT STILL WOULD'VE BEEN BETTER THAN THE TRASH ON THE MARKET!
ALL YOU NEED IS SOME TIME, SOMETHING MALTED, AND THE STEADFAST RESOLVE OF THE AMERICAN SPIRIT.
YOU HAVEN'T HEARD MY INGREDIENT LIST.
THE ONLY CREATIVE LIMITATION IS YOUR MIND! WHATCHA GOT?
RING POPS, CABBAGE, AND VAGISIL.

Julie Clark's quick n' dirty DYI Beer Recipe

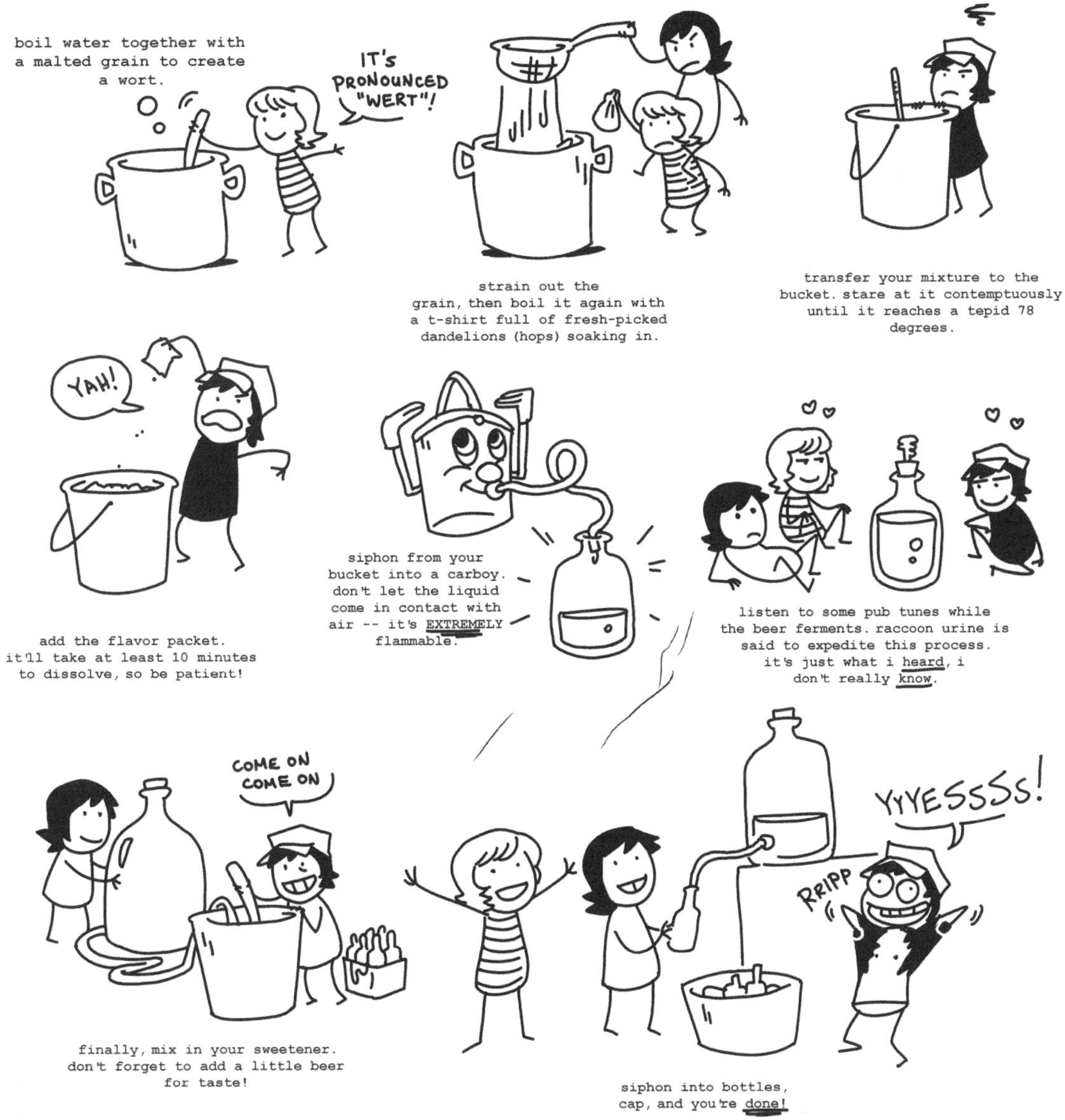
boil water together with a malted grain to create a wort.
IT's PRONOUNCED "WERT"!
strain out the grain, then boil it again with a t-shirt full of fresh-picked dandelions (hops) soaking in.
transfer your mixture to the bucket. stare at it contemptuously until it reaches a tepid 78 degrees.
YAH!
add the flavor packet. it'll take at least 10 minutes to dissolve, so be patient!
siphon from your bucket into a carboy. don't let the liquid come in contact with air -- it's EXTREMELY flammable.
listen to some pub tunes while the beer ferments. raccoon urine is said to expedite this process. it's just what i heard, i don't really know.
COME ON COME ON
finally, mix in your sweetener. don't forget to add a little beer for taste!
YYYESSSSS!
RRIPP
siphon into bottles, cap, and you're done!

now wait like a month.

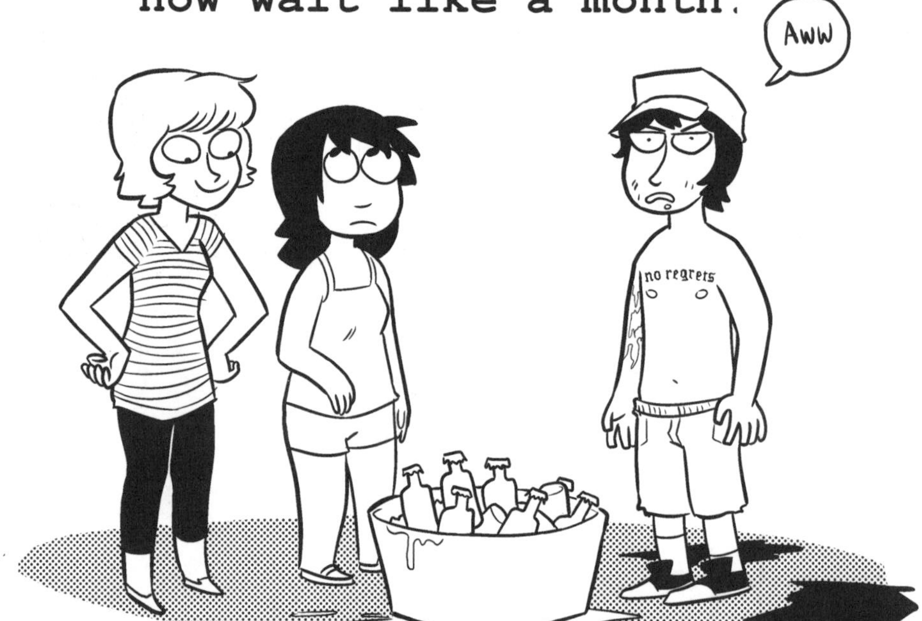
AWW
no regrets

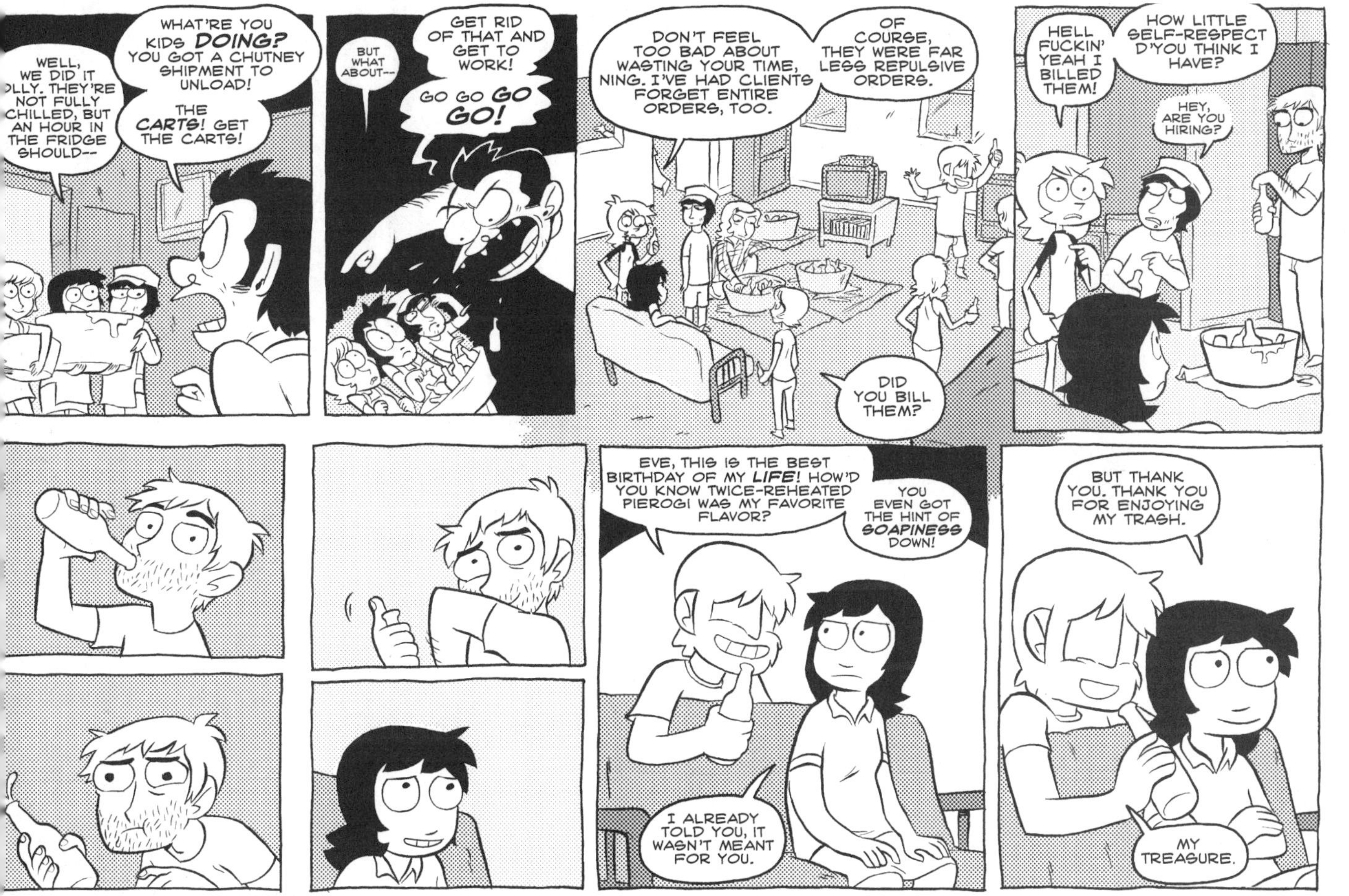
WELL, WE DID IT OLLY. THEY'RE NOT FULLY CHILLED, BUT AN HOUR IN THE FRIDGE SHOULD--
WHAT'RE YOU KIDS DOING? YOU GOT A CHUTNEY SHIPMENT TO UNLOAD!
THE CARTS! GET THE CARTS!
BUT WHAT ABOUT--
GET RID OF THAT AND GET TO WORK!
GO GO GO GO!
DON'T FEEL TOO BAD ABOUT WASTING YOUR TIME, NING. I'VE HAD CLIENTS FORGET ENTIRE ORDERS, TOO.
OF COURSE, THEY WERE FAR LESS REPULSIVE ORDERS.
DID YOU BILL THEM?
HELL FUCKIN' YEAH I BILLED THEM!
HOW LITTLE SELF-RESPECT D'YOU THINK I HAVE?
HEY, ARE YOU HIRING?
EVE, THIS IS THE BEST BIRTHDAY OF MY LIFE! HOW'D YOU KNOW TWICE-REHEATED PIEROGI WAS MY FAVORITE FLAVOR?
YOU EVEN GOT THE HINT OF SOAPINESS DOWN!
I ALREADY TOLD YOU, IT WASN'T MEANT FOR YOU.
BUT THANK YOU. THANK YOU FOR ENJOYING MY TRASH.
MY TREASURE.

FEAR

Eve's fear of the night is based on my own, and the general fear felt by women in urban environments. During college in New York I'd hesitate to go out alone, or walk in the dark for more time than absolutely necessary. Even fumbling at the entrance with my keys was enough to get my heart pounding. It would be years before I could break down the sources of my fears, and understand (or dismiss) the logic behind them.

My intention in this story was to show this fear as a mental construction. Eve hesitates to discuss her fears with Park (and admit there's a problem) because she doubts his ability to understand. And despite his empathy, it's difficult for Park to offer anything but protection on his own terms. In the end Eve is given the choice between dealing with her fears, or compromising her freedom for a sense of security.

I was living in Portland, a notoriously bike-friendly town, when I wrote this story, and I chose bicycles as a subject because I saw them as a device of empowerment: economically, environmentally, and physically. Bikes have been a strong symbol of feminine power since the early 20th century, one which seems relevant as ever today.

My favorite sequence in this one is Hanna and Marek laughing at a 1942 Chuck Jones cartoon "The Dover Boys at Pimento University". It's a film for the ages, and has some hilarious commentary on heroes and damsels.

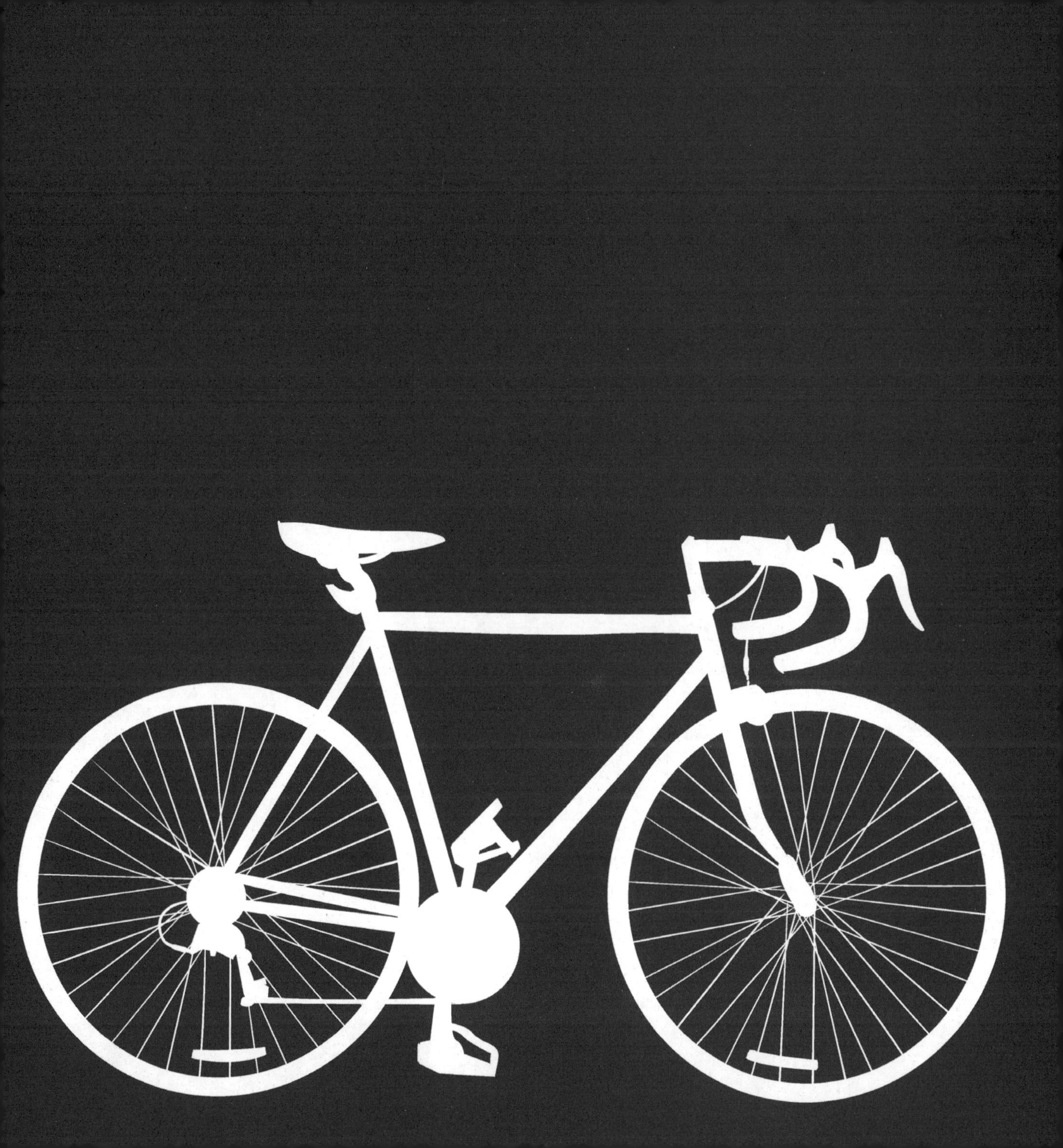

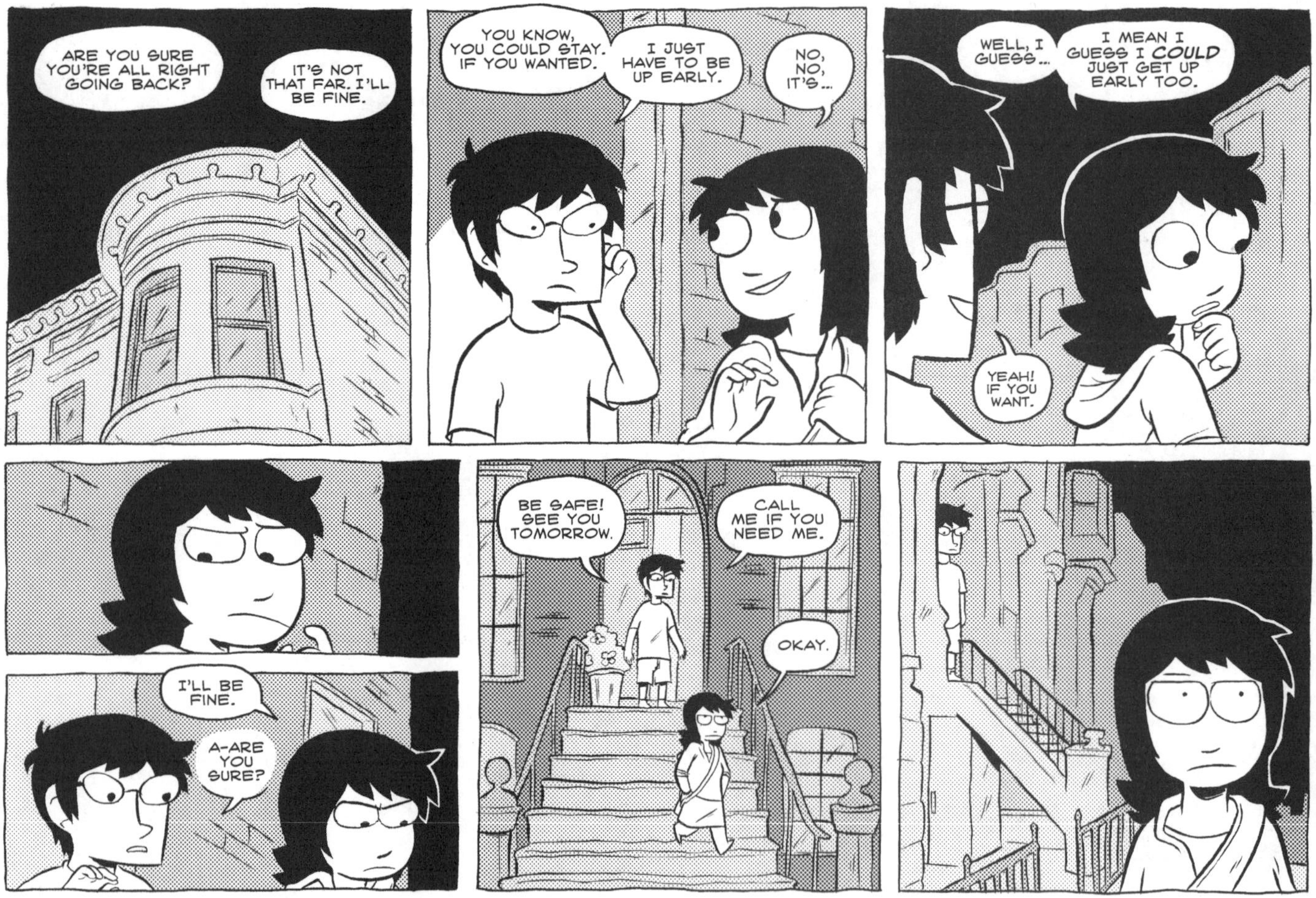
ARE YOU SURE YOU'RE ALL RIGHT GOING BACK?
IT'S NOT THAT FAR. I'LL BE FINE.
YOU KNOW, YOU COULD STAY. IF YOU WANTED.
I JUST HAVE TO BE UP EARLY.
NO, NO, IT'S...
WELL, I GUESS...
I MEAN I GUESS I COULD JUST GET UP EARLY TOO.
YEAH! IF YOU WANT.
I'LL BE FINE.
A-ARE YOU SURE?
BE SAFE! SEE YOU TOMORROW.
CALL ME IF YOU NEED ME.
OKAY.

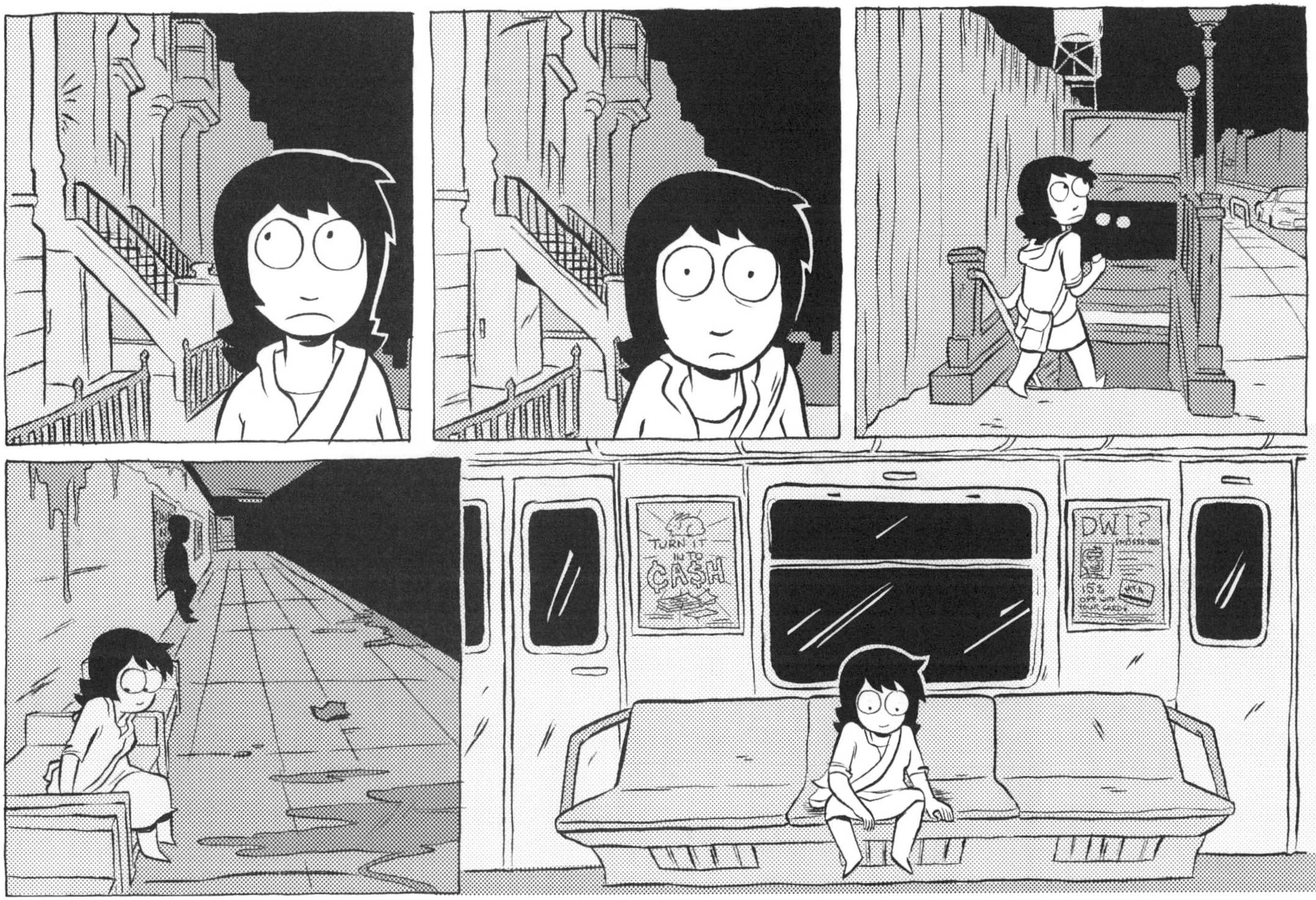
TURN IT INTO CA$H
DWI?
15% OFF WITH YOUR CARD
MTA

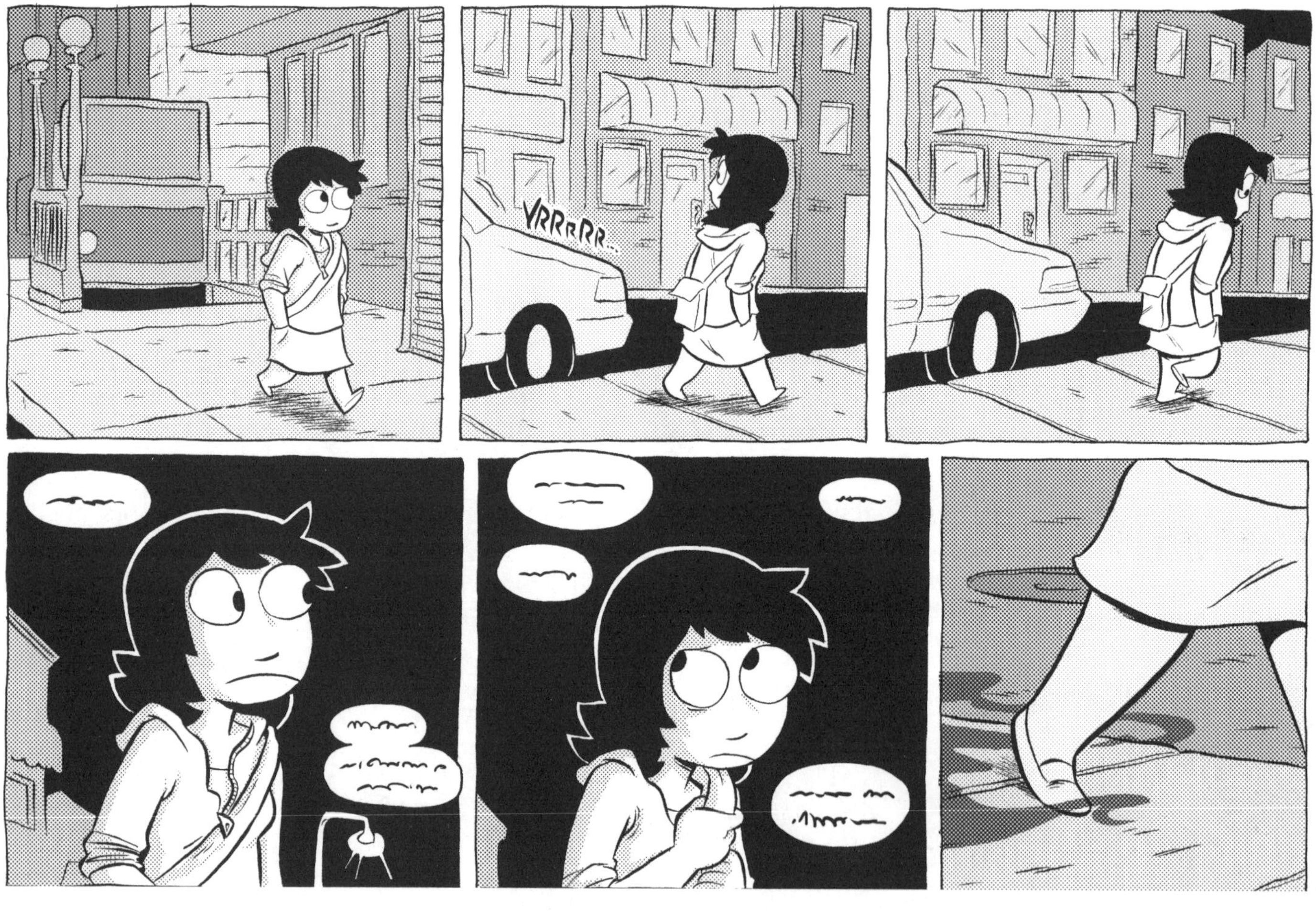
VRRrRR...

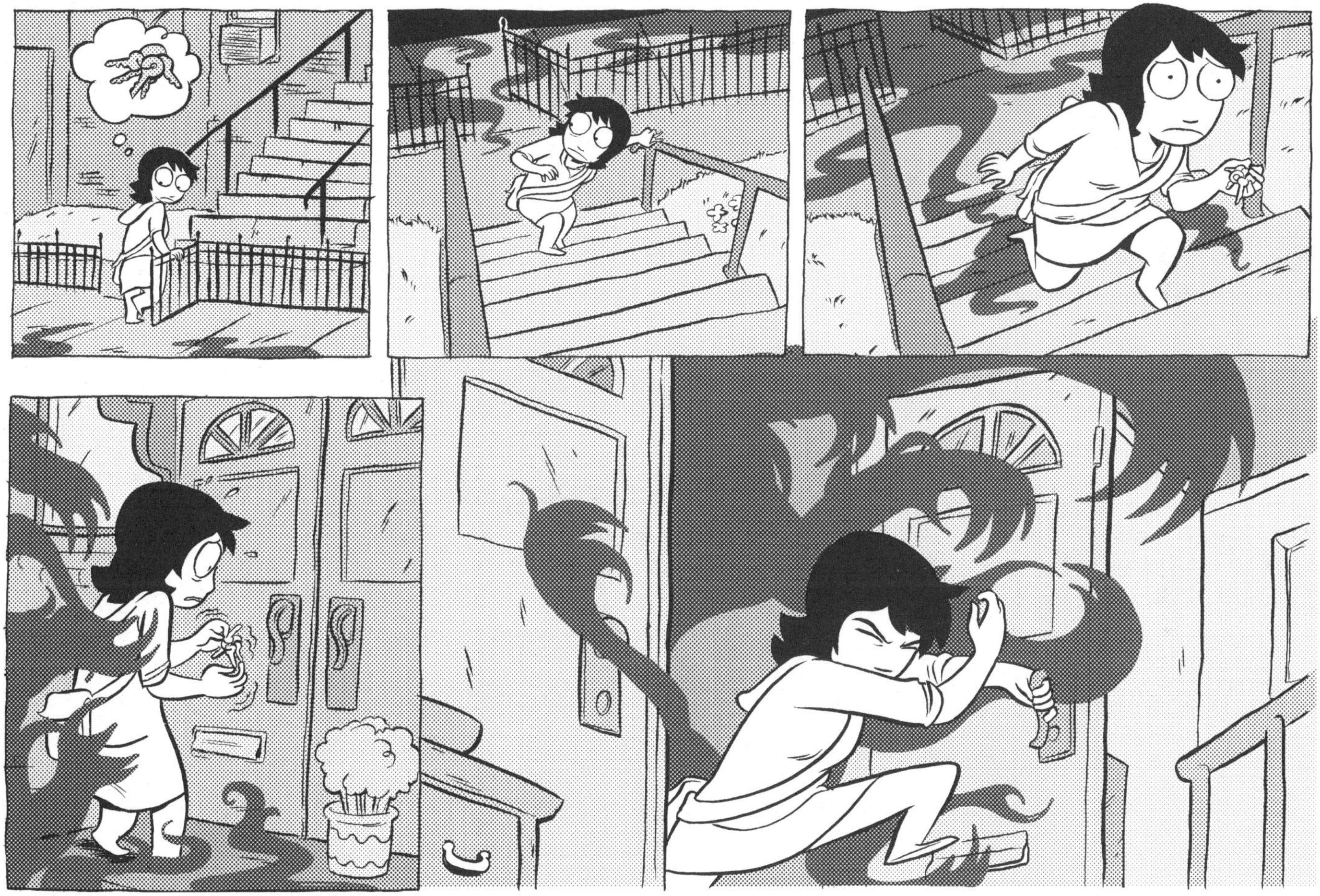

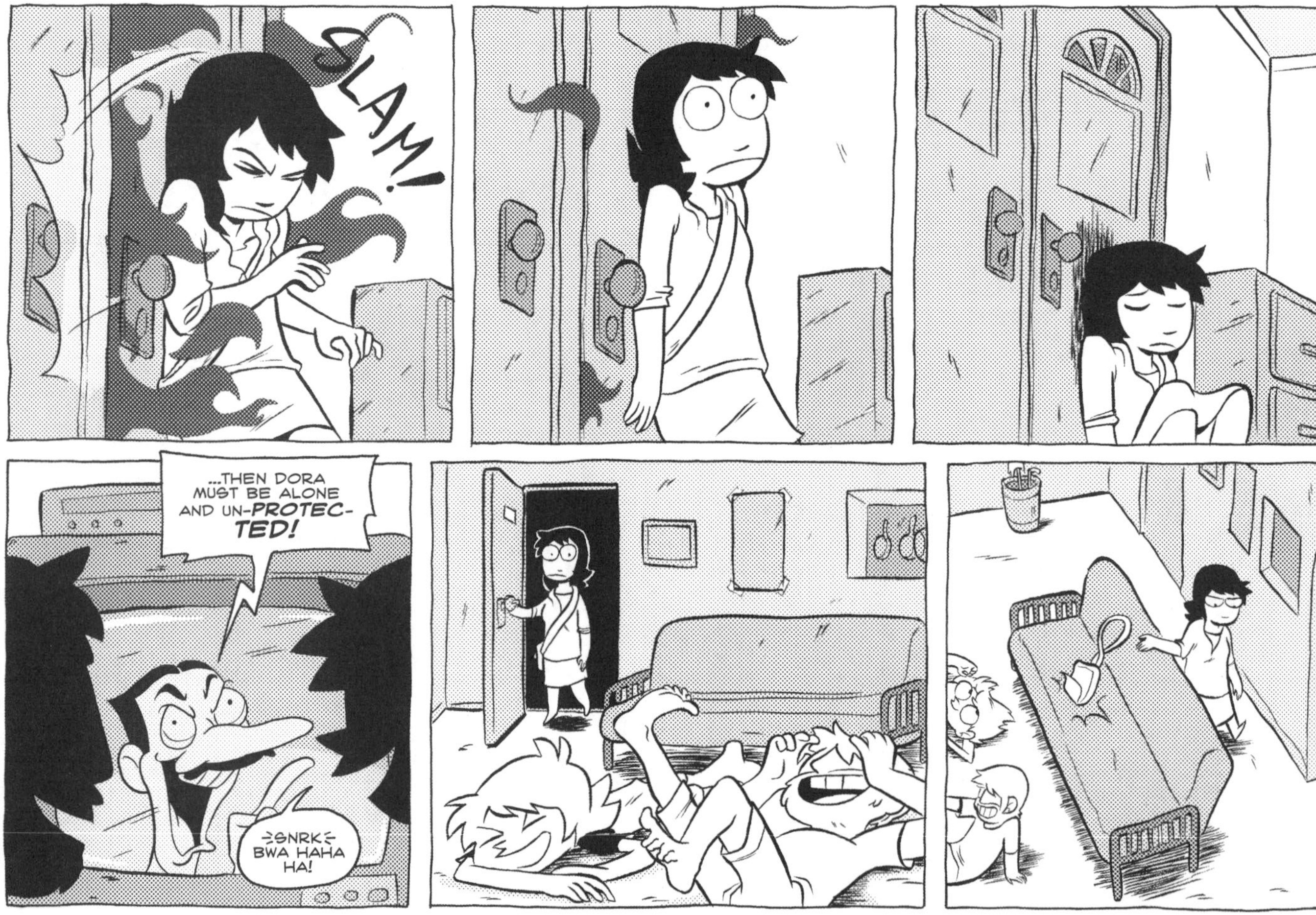
SLAM!
...THEN DORA MUST BE ALONE AND UN-PROTEC-TED!
SNRK BWA HAHA HA!

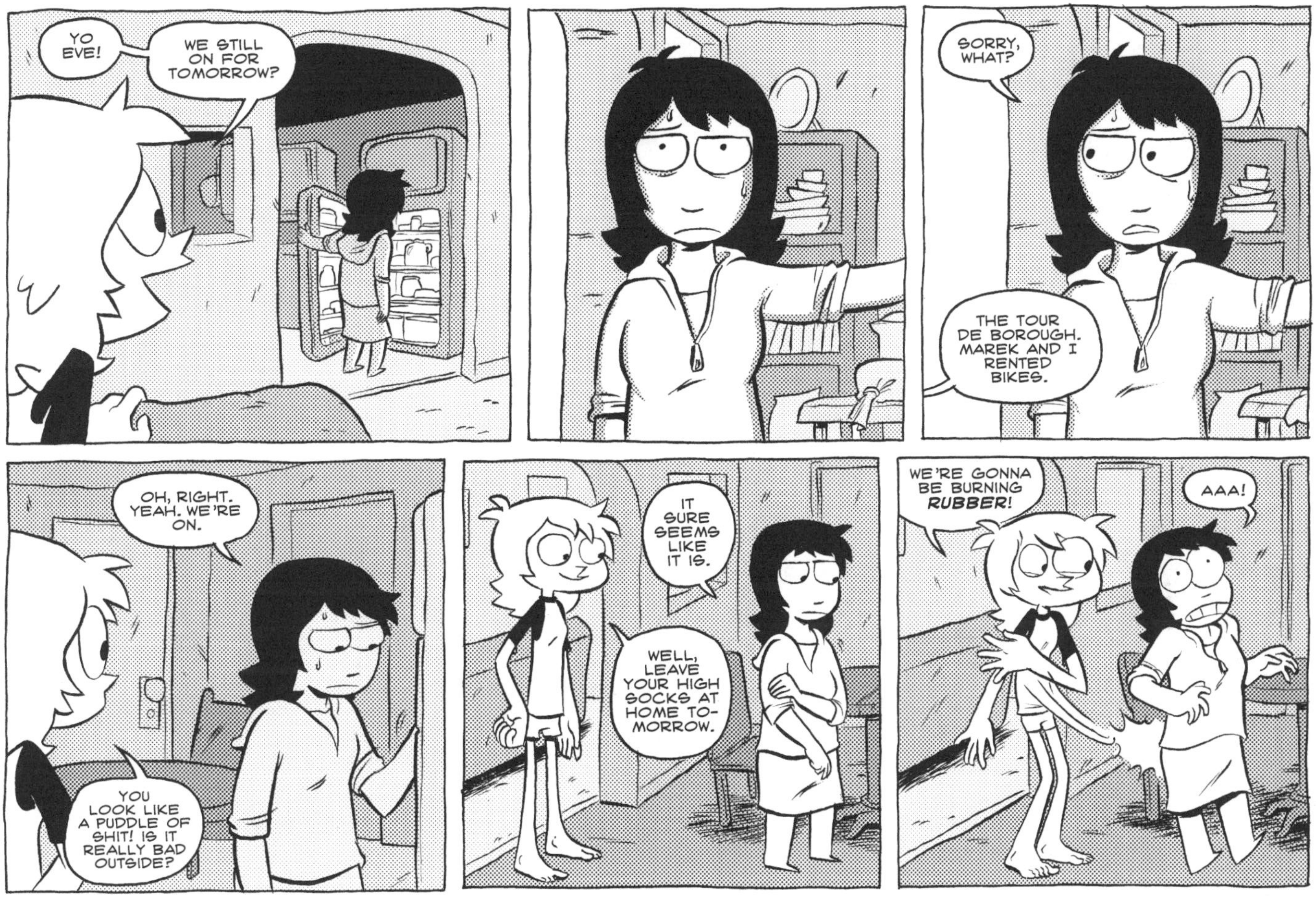
YO EVE!
WE STILL ON FOR TOMORROW?
SORRY, WHAT?
THE TOUR DE BOROUGH. MAREK AND I RENTED BIKES.
OH, RIGHT. YEAH. WE'RE ON.
YOU LOOK LIKE A PUDDLE OF SHIT! IS IT REALLY BAD OUTSIDE?
IT SURE SEEMS LIKE IT IS.
WELL, LEAVE YOUR HIGH SOCKS AT HOME TO-MORROW.
WE'RE GONNA BE BURNING *RUBBER*!
AAA!

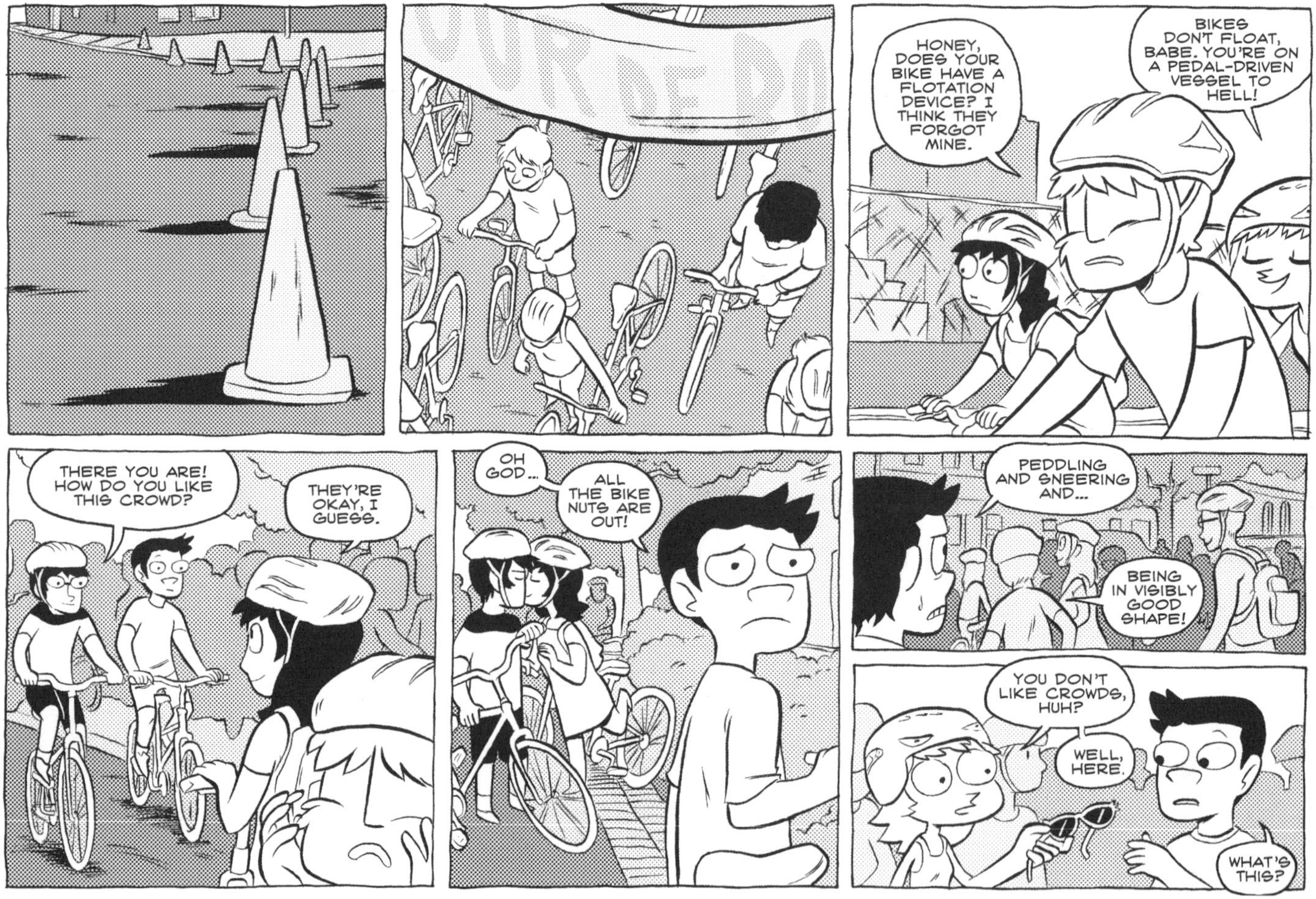
HONEY, DOES YOUR BIKE HAVE A FLOTATION DEVICE? I THINK THEY FORGOT MINE.
BIKES DON'T FLOAT, BABE. YOU'RE ON A PEDAL-DRIVEN VESSEL TO HELL!
THERE YOU ARE! HOW DO YOU LIKE THIS CROWD?
THEY'RE OKAY, I GUESS.
OH GOD...
ALL THE BIKE NUTS ARE OUT!
PEDDLING AND SNEERING AND...
BEING IN VISIBLY GOOD SHAPE!
YOU DON'T LIKE CROWDS, HUH?
WELL, HERE.
WHAT'S THIS?

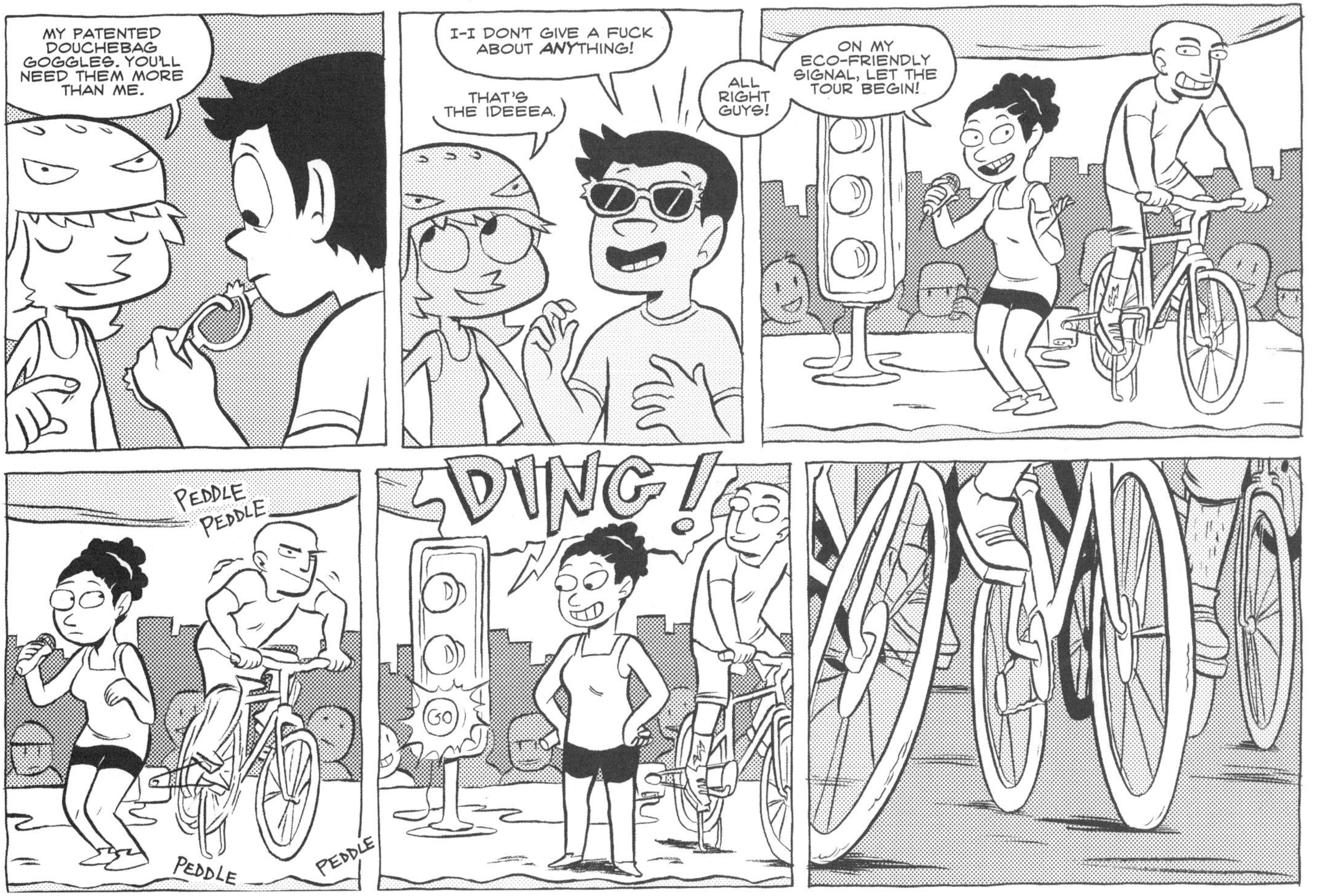
MY PATENTED DOUCHEBAG GOGGLES. YOU'LL NEED THEM MORE THAN ME.
I-I DON'T GIVE A FUCK ABOUT ANYTHING!
THAT'S THE IDEEEA.
ALL RIGHT GUYS!
ON MY ECO-FRIENDLY SIGNAL, LET THE TOUR BEGIN!
PEDDLE PEDDLE
PEDDLE
PEDDLE
DING!
GO

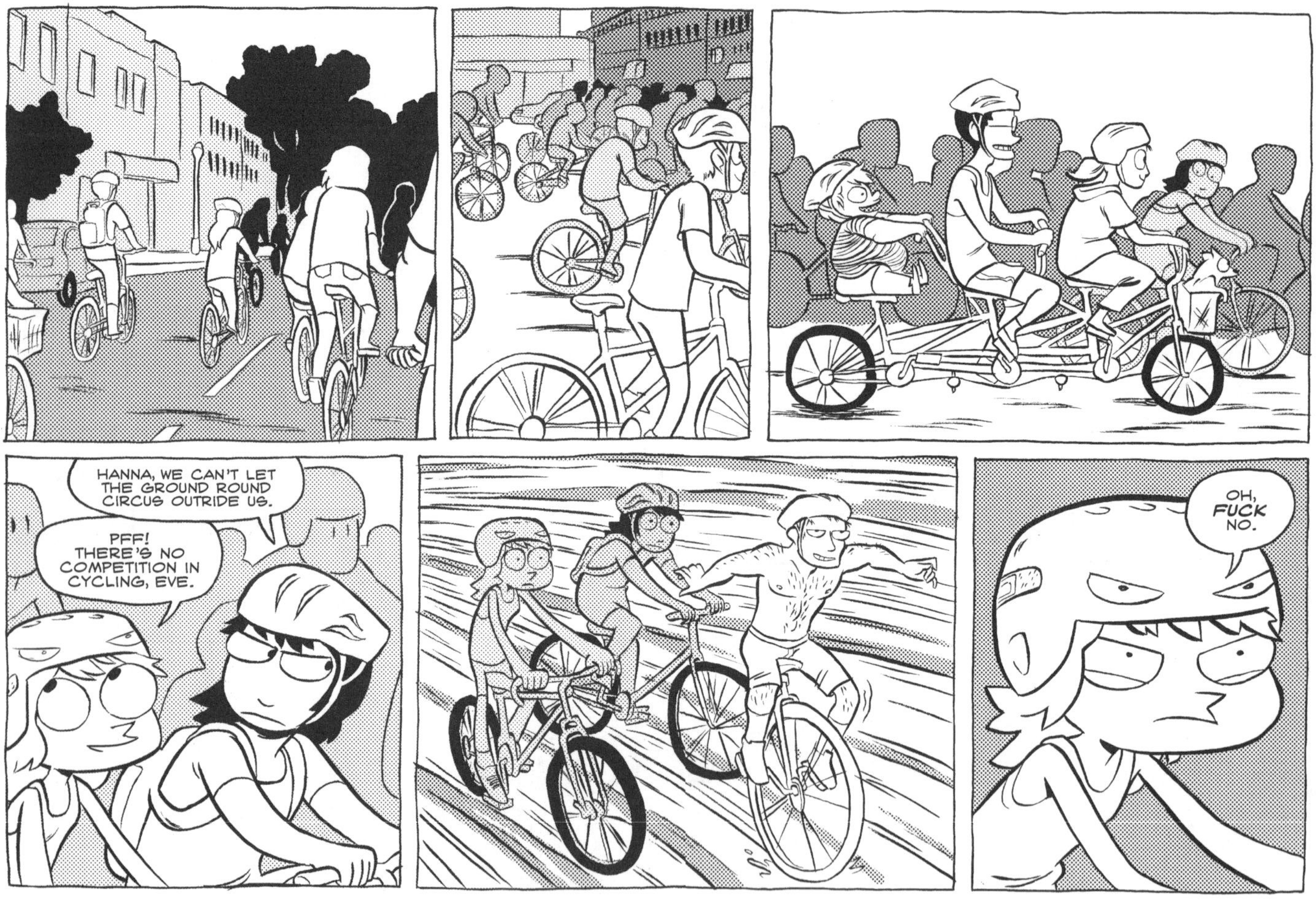
HANNA, WE CAN'T LET THE GROUND ROUND CIRCUS OUTRIDE US.
PFF! THERE'S NO COMPETITION IN CYCLING, EVE.
OH, **FUCK** NO.

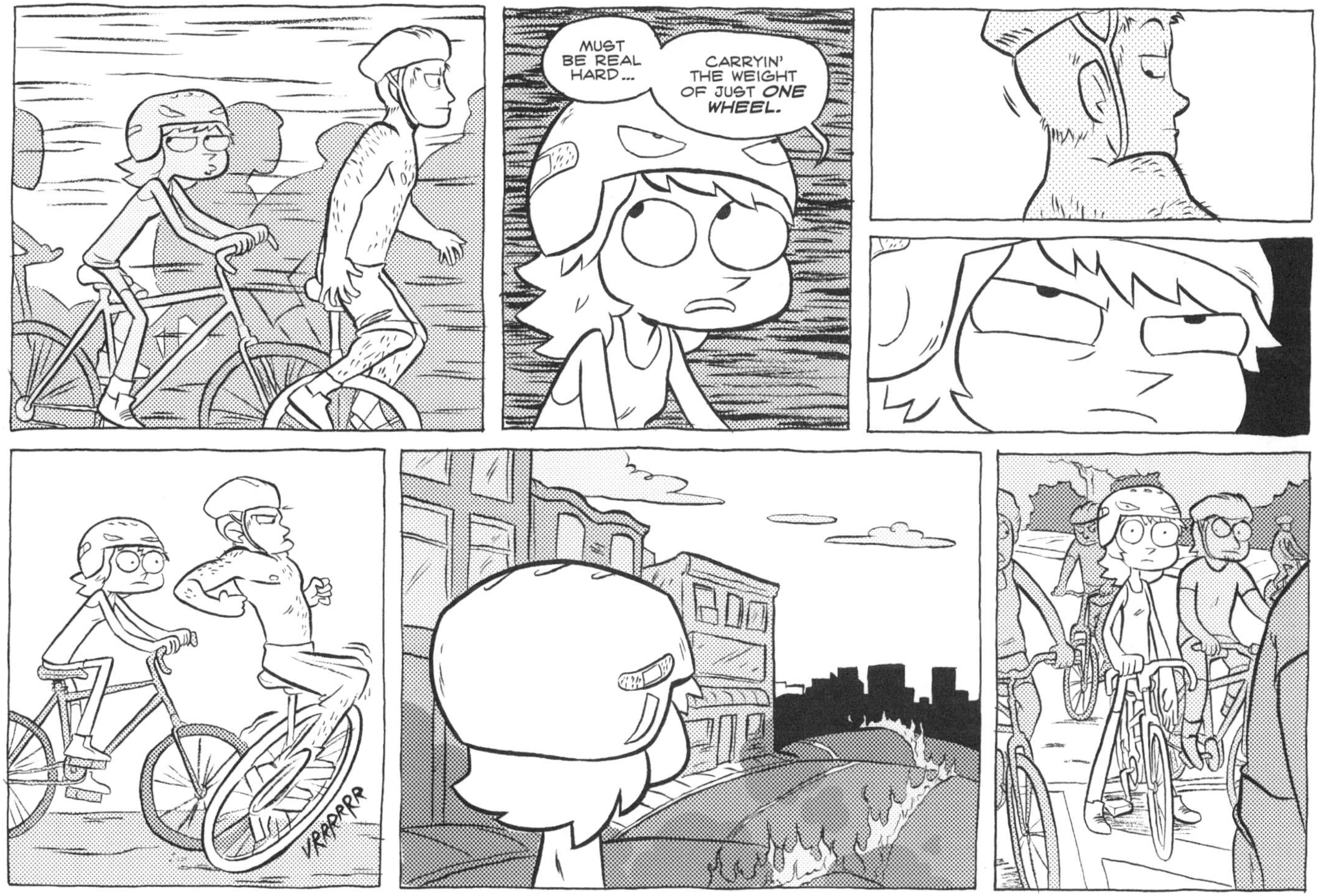
MUST BE REAL HARD...
CARRYIN' THE WEIGHT OF JUST *ONE WHEEL.*
VRRRRRR

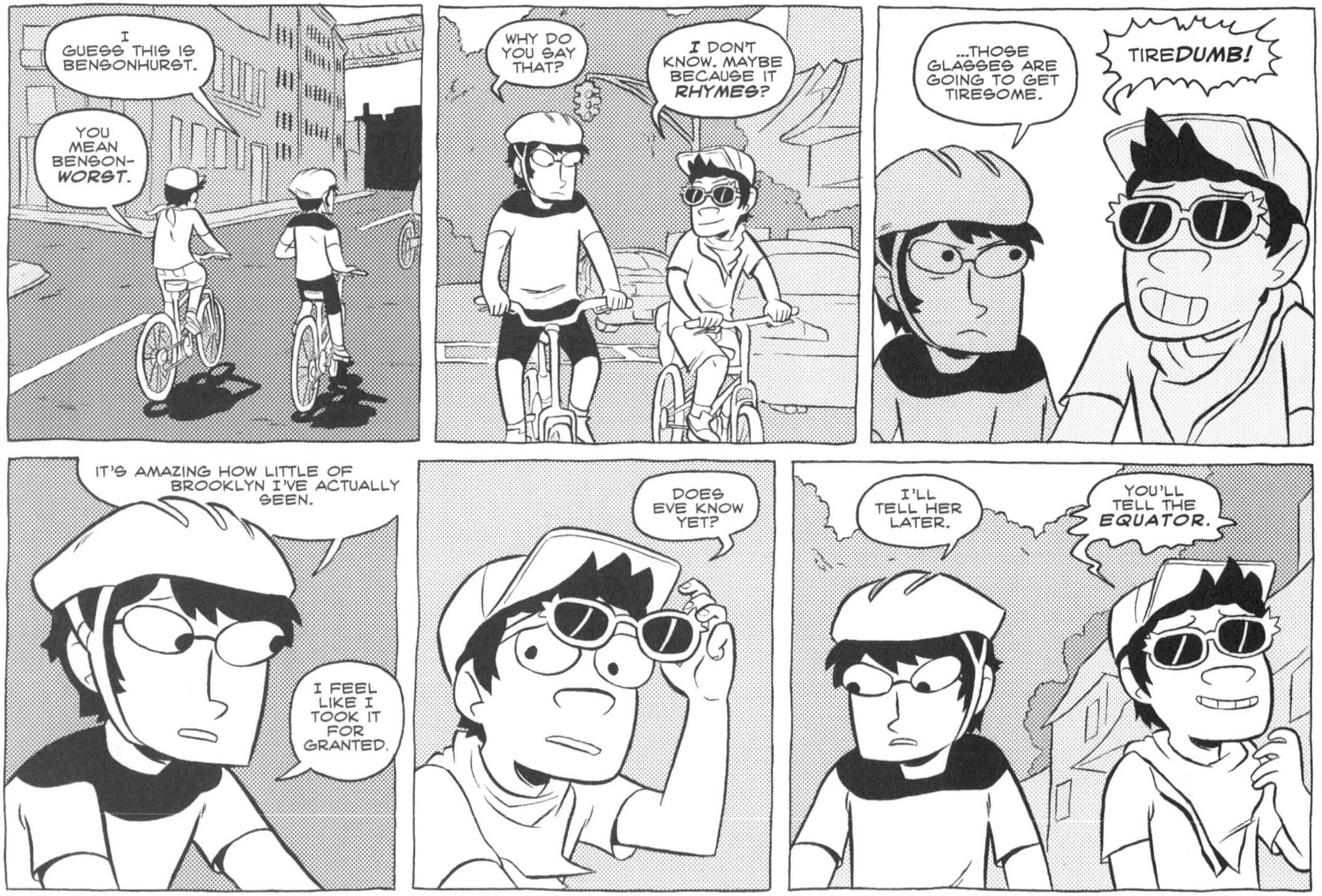
I GUESS THIS IS BENSONHURST.
YOU MEAN BENSON-WORST.
WHY DO YOU SAY THAT?
I DON'T KNOW. MAYBE BECAUSE IT RHYMES?
...THOSE GLASSES ARE GOING TO GET TIRESOME.
TIREDUMB!
IT'S AMAZING HOW LITTLE OF BROOKLYN I'VE ACTUALLY SEEN.
I FEEL LIKE I TOOK IT FOR GRANTED.
DOES EVE KNOW YET?
I'LL TELL HER LATER.
YOU'LL TELL THE EQUATOR.

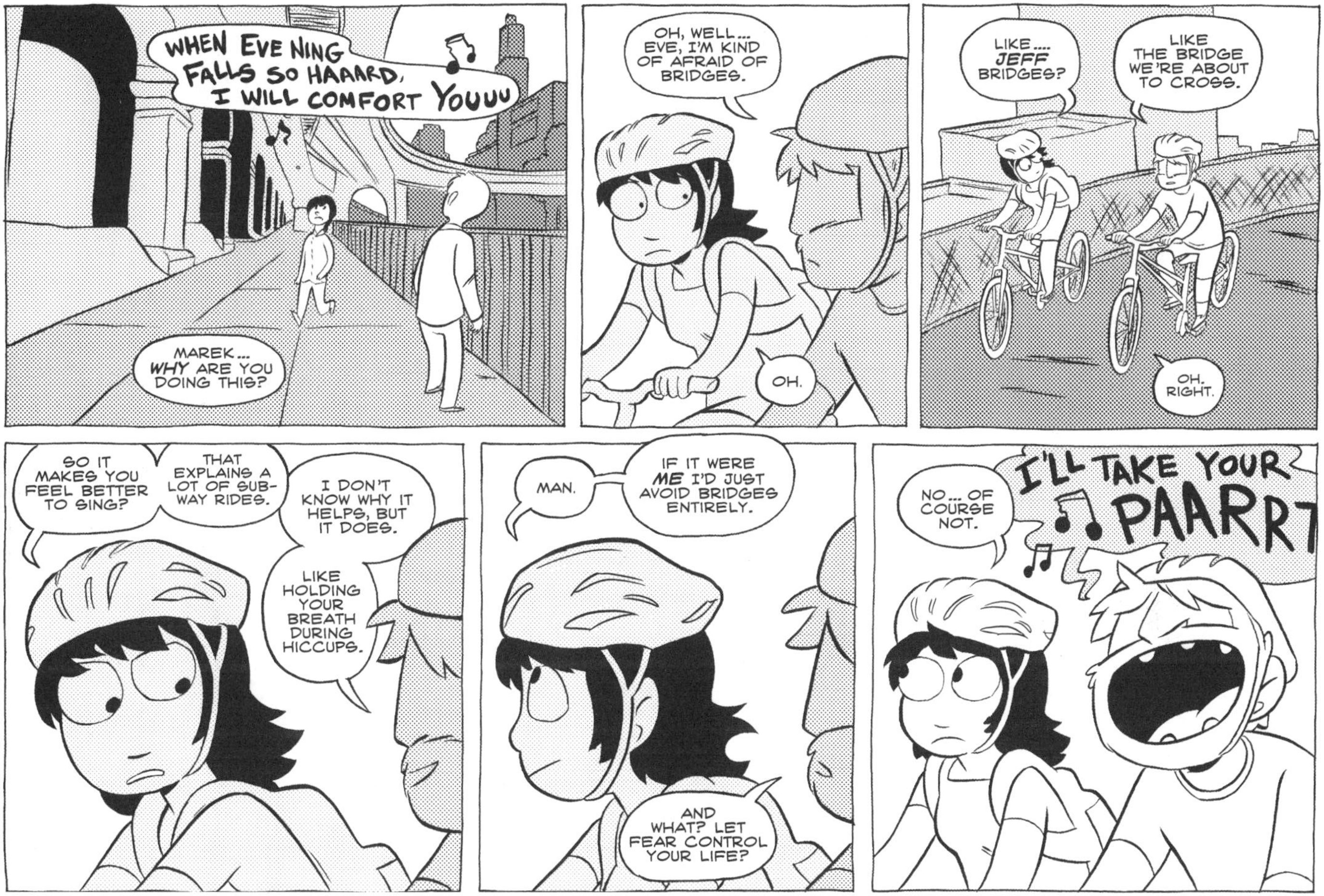
WHEN EVE NING FALLS SO HAAARD, I WILL COMFORT YOUUU
MAREK... WHY ARE YOU DOING THIS?
OH, WELL... EVE, I'M KIND OF AFRAID OF BRIDGES.
OH.
LIKE.... JEFF BRIDGES?
LIKE THE BRIDGE WE'RE ABOUT TO CROSS.
OH. RIGHT.
SO IT MAKES YOU FEEL BETTER TO SING?
THAT EXPLAINS A LOT OF SUB-WAY RIDES.
I DON'T KNOW WHY IT HELPS, BUT IT DOES.
LIKE HOLDING YOUR BREATH DURING HICCUPS.
MAN.
IF IT WERE ME I'D JUST AVOID BRIDGES ENTIRELY.
AND WHAT? LET FEAR CONTROL YOUR LIFE?
NO... OF COURSE NOT.
I'LL TAKE YOUR PAARRT

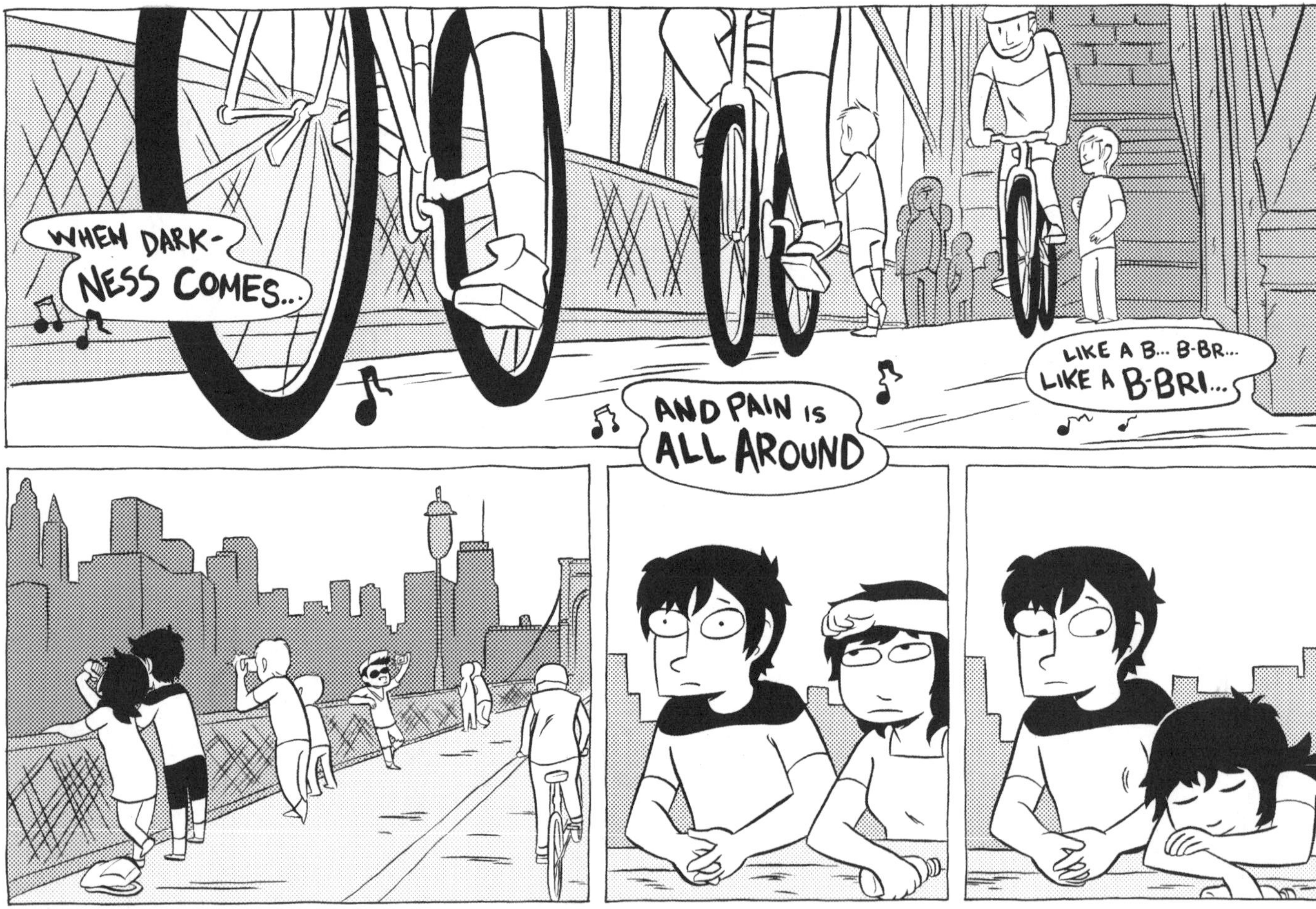
WHEN DARK-
NESS COMES...
AND PAIN IS
ALL AROUND
LIKE A B... B-BR...
LIKE A B-BRI...

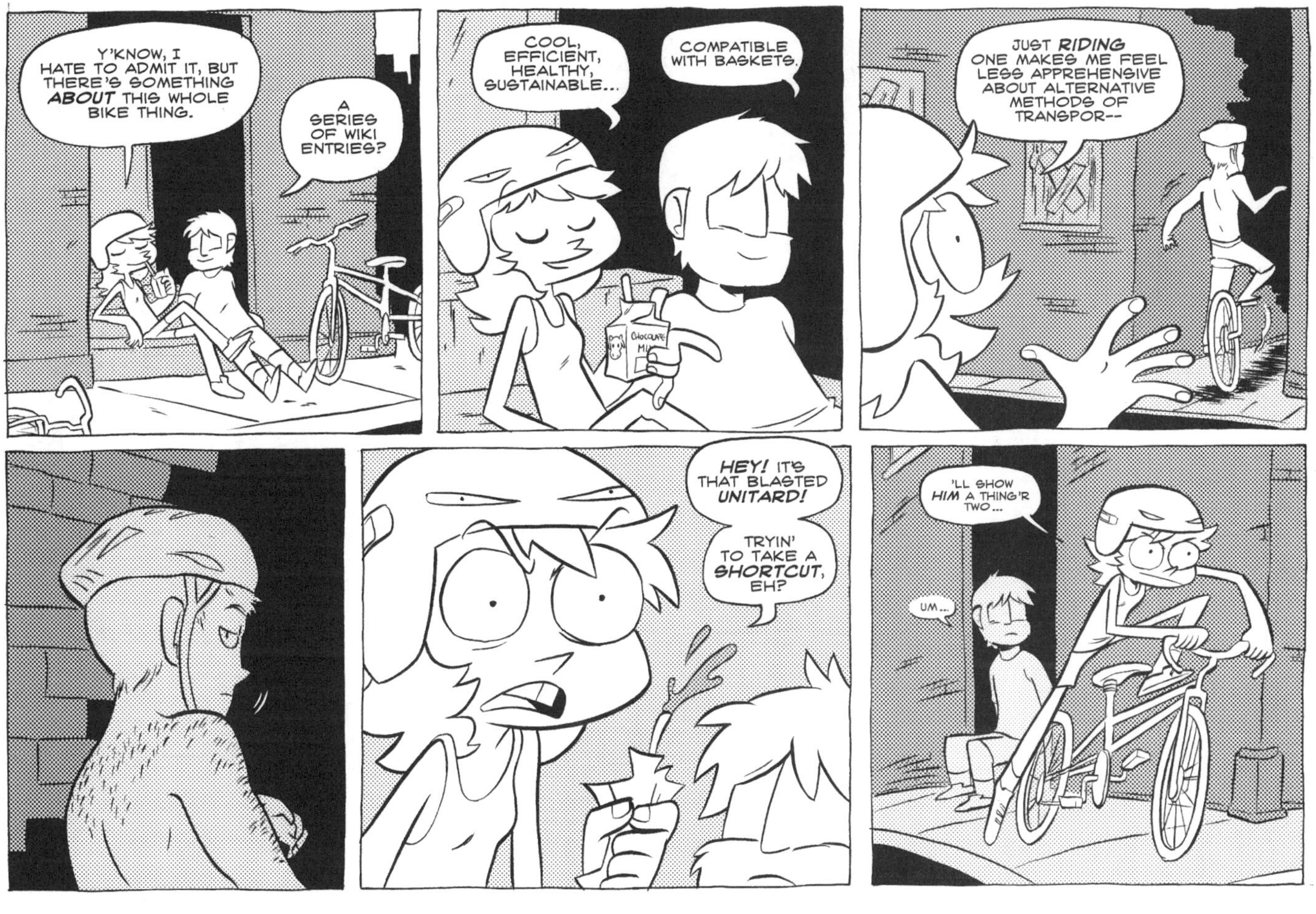
Y'KNOW, I HATE TO ADMIT IT, BUT THERE'S SOMETHING ABOUT THIS WHOLE BIKE THING.
A SERIES OF WIKI ENTRIES?
COOL, EFFICIENT, HEALTHY, SUSTAINABLE...
COMPATIBLE WITH BASKETS.
JUST RIDING ONE MAKES ME FEEL LESS APPREHENSIVE ABOUT ALTERNATIVE METHODS OF TRANSPOR--
HEY! IT'S THAT BLASTED UNITARD!
TRYIN' TO TAKE A SHORTCUT, EH?
'LL SHOW HIM A THING'R TWO...
UM...

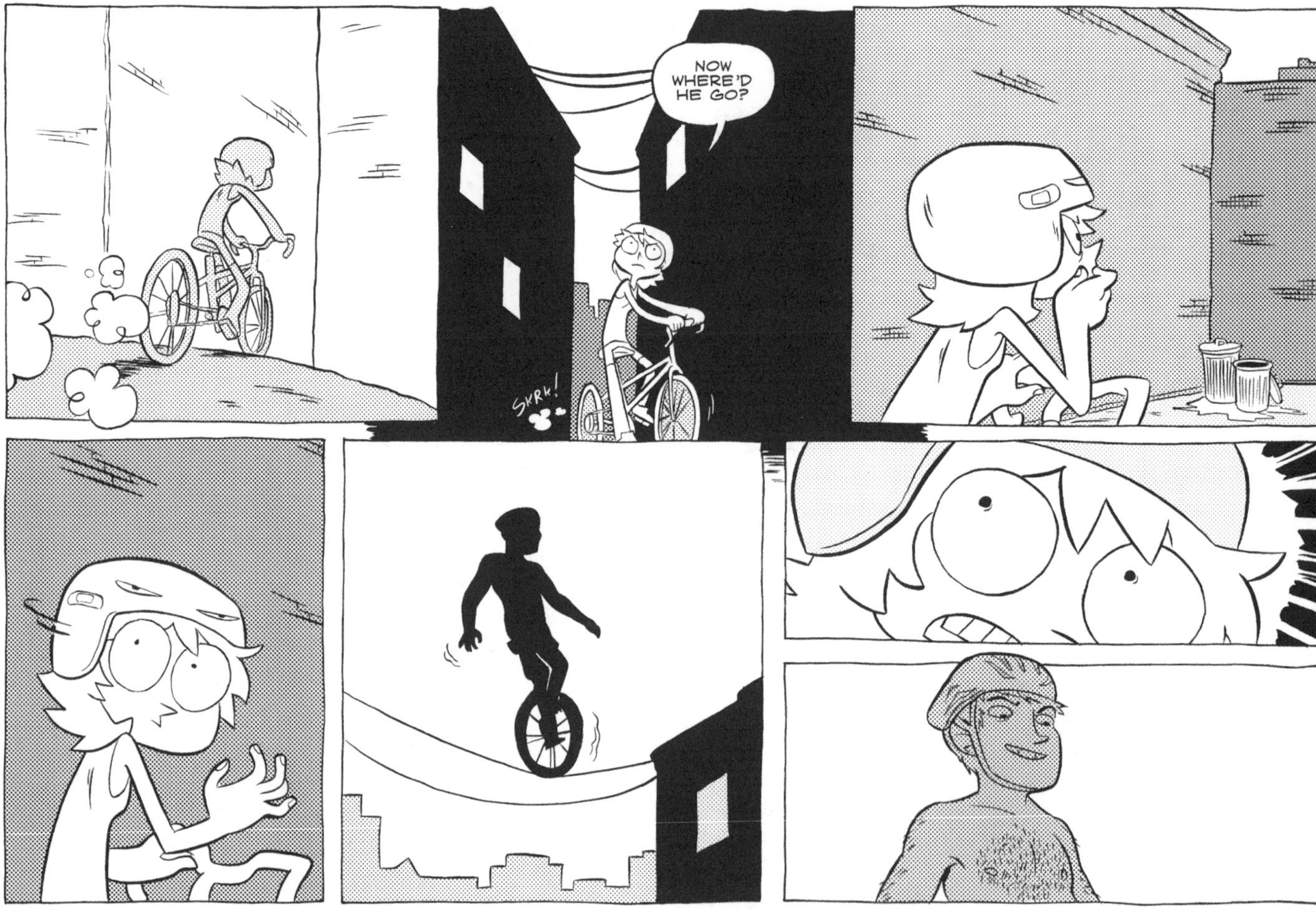
NOW WHERE'D HE GO?
SKRK!

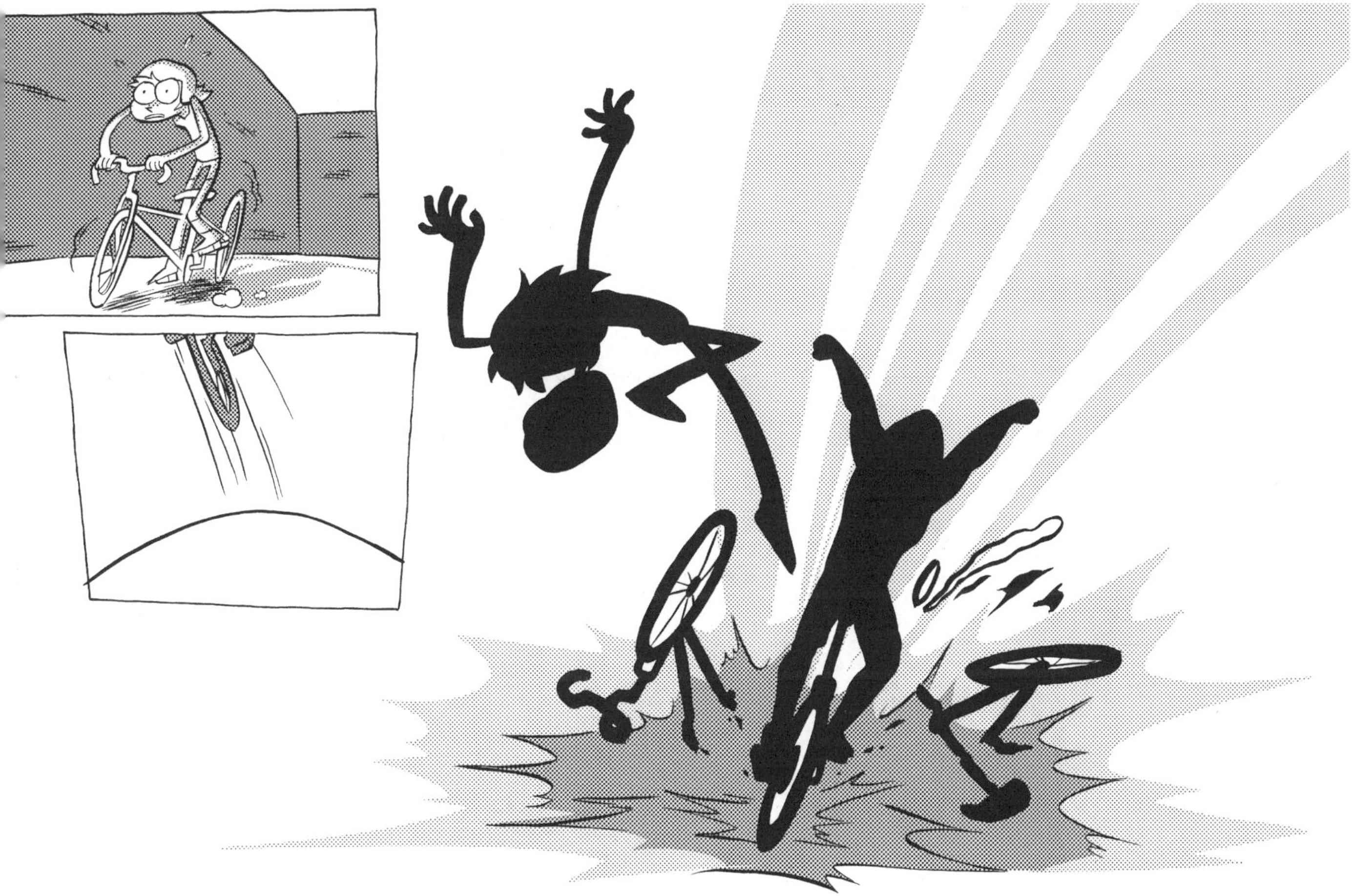

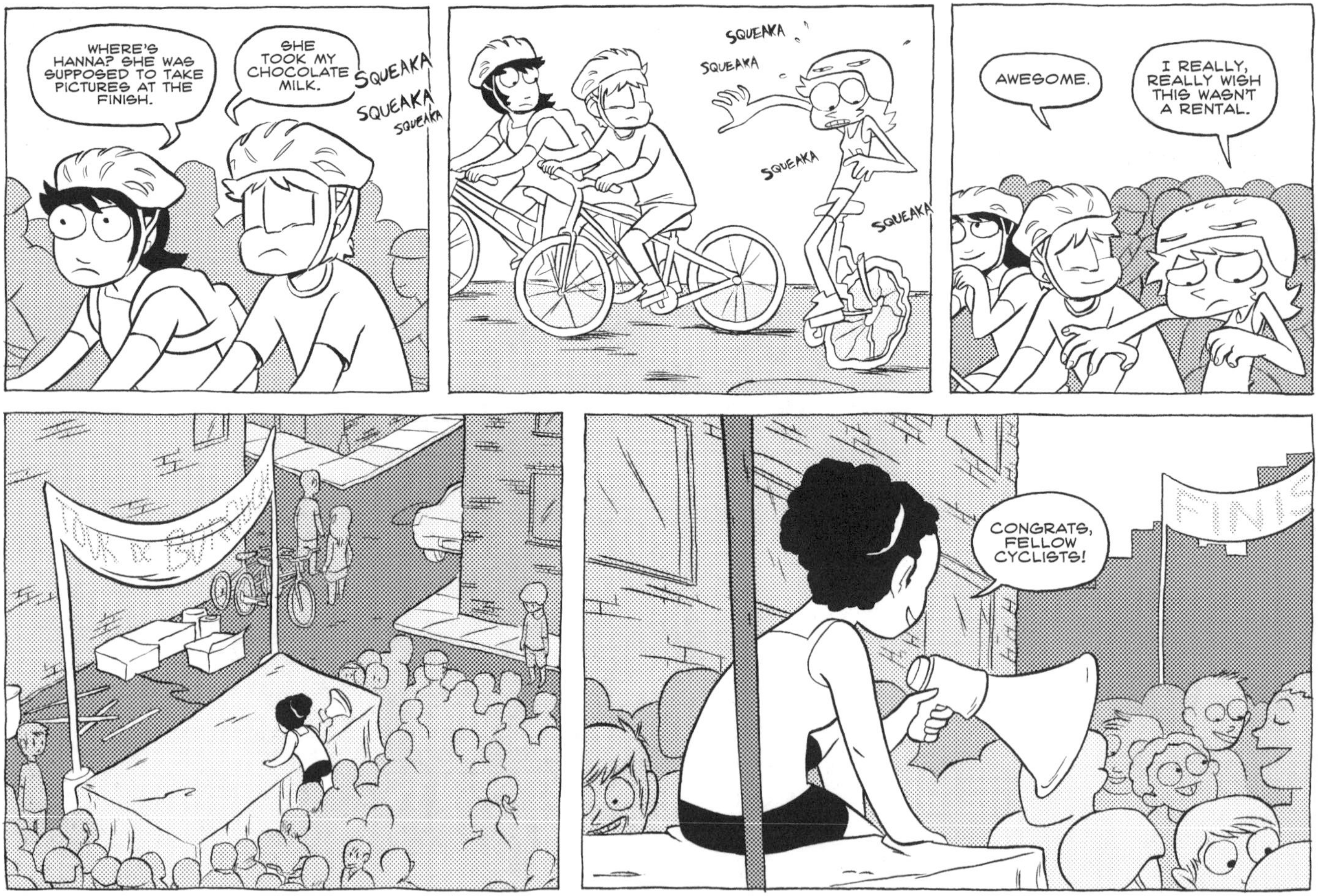

WHERE'S HANNA? SHE WAS SUPPOSED TO TAKE PICTURES AT THE FINISH.
SHE TOOK MY CHOCOLATE MILK.
SQUEAKA
SQUEAKA
SQUEAKA
SQUEAKA
SQUEAKA
SQUEAKA
SQUEAKA
AWESOME.
I REALLY, REALLY WISH THIS WASN'T A RENTAL.
FINIS
CONGRATS, FELLOW CYCLISTS!

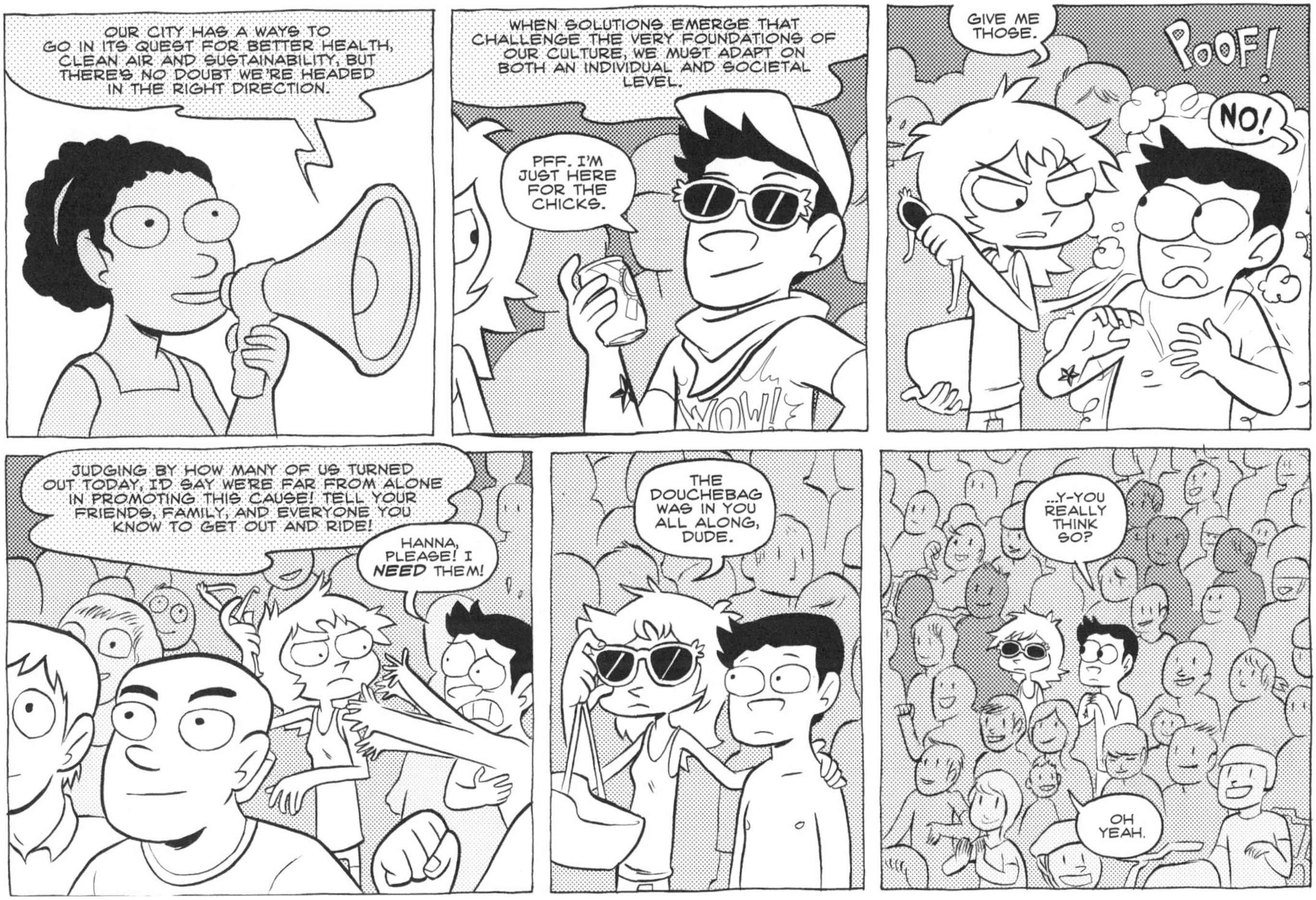
OUR CITY HAS A WAYS TO GO IN ITS QUEST FOR BETTER HEALTH, CLEAN AIR AND SUSTAINABILITY, BUT THERE'S NO DOUBT WE'RE HEADED IN THE RIGHT DIRECTION.
WHEN SOLUTIONS EMERGE THAT CHALLENGE THE VERY FOUNDATIONS OF OUR CULTURE, WE MUST ADAPT ON BOTH AN INDIVIDUAL AND SOCIETAL LEVEL.
PFF. I'M JUST HERE FOR THE CHICKS.
WOW!
GIVE ME THOSE.
POOF!
NO!
JUDGING BY HOW MANY OF US TURNED OUT TODAY, I'D SAY WE'RE FAR FROM ALONE IN PROMOTING THIS CAUSE! TELL YOUR FRIENDS, FAMILY, AND EVERYONE YOU KNOW TO GET OUT AND RIDE!
HANNA, PLEASE! I ***NEED*** THEM!
THE DOUCHEBAG WAS IN YOU ALL ALONG, DUDE.
...Y-YOU REALLY THINK SO?
OH YEAH.

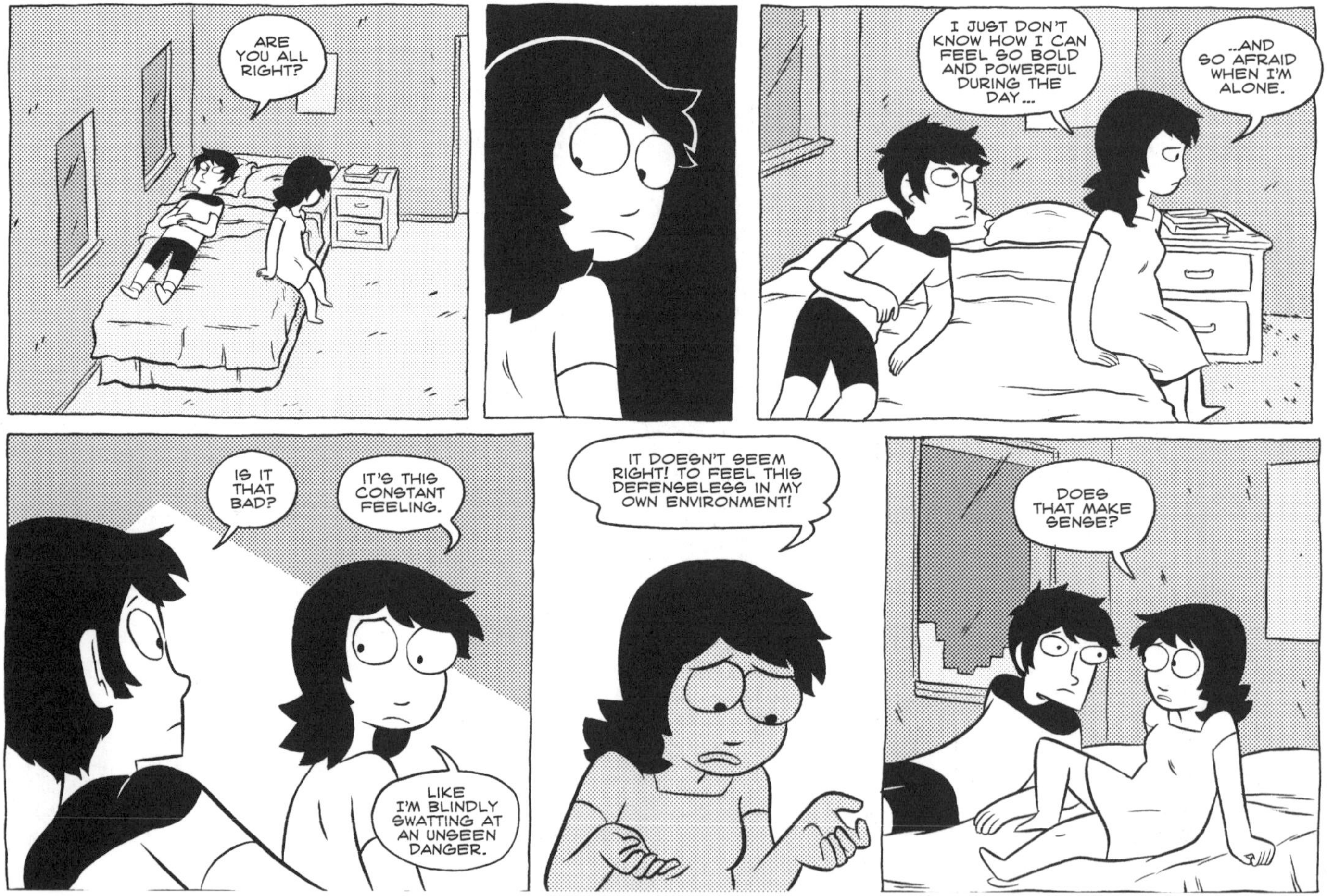
ARE YOU ALL RIGHT?
I JUST DON'T KNOW HOW I CAN FEEL SO BOLD AND POWERFUL DURING THE DAY...
...AND SO AFRAID WHEN I'M ALONE.
IS IT THAT BAD?
IT'S THIS CONSTANT FEELING.
LIKE I'M BLINDLY SWATTING AT AN UNSEEN DANGER.
IT DOESN'T SEEM RIGHT! TO FEEL THIS DEFENSELESS IN MY OWN ENVIRONMENT!
DOES THAT MAKE SENSE?

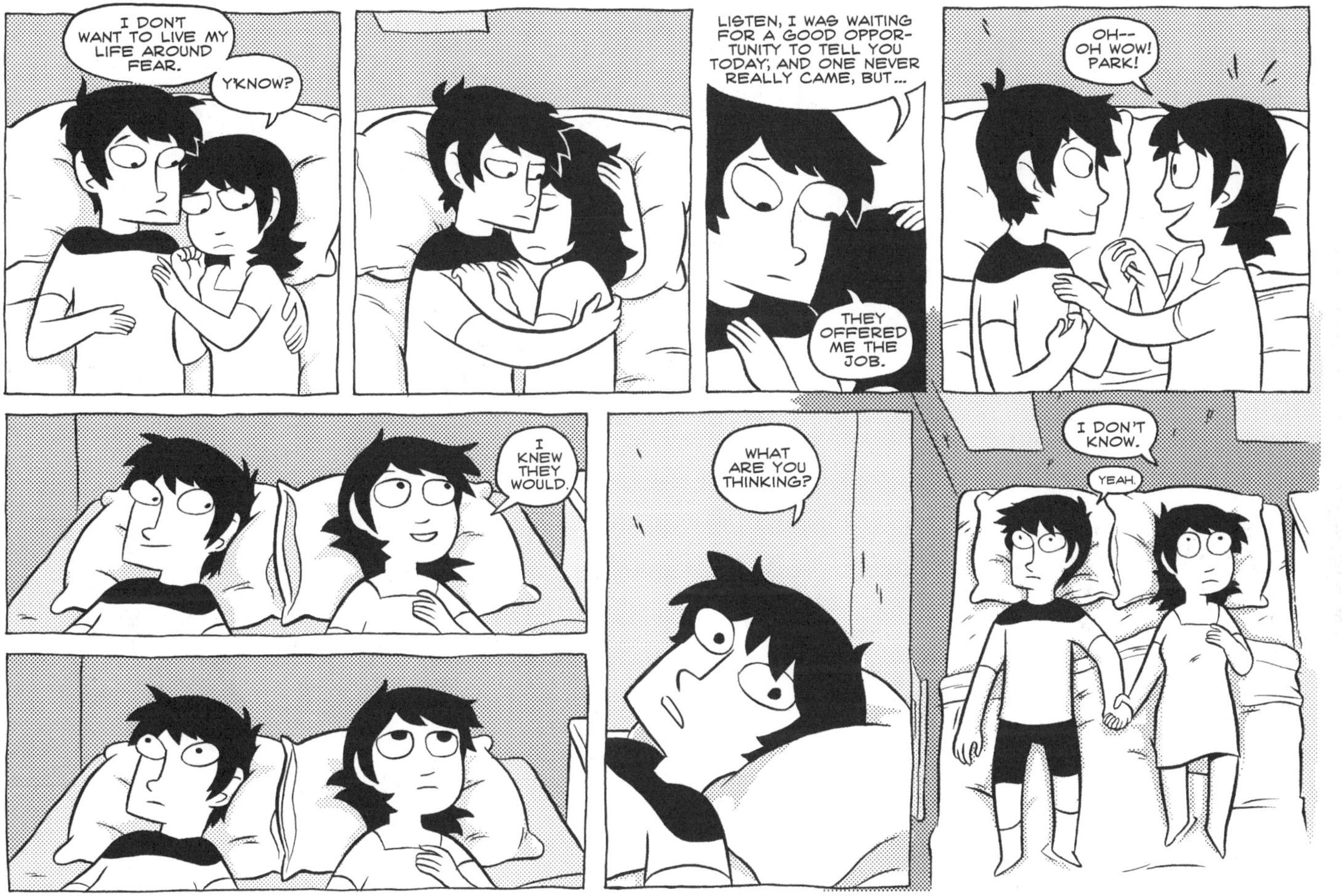
I DON'T WANT TO LIVE MY LIFE AROUND FEAR.
Y'KNOW?
LISTEN, I WAS WAITING FOR A GOOD OPPORTUNITY TO TELL YOU TODAY; AND ONE NEVER REALLY CAME, BUT...
THEY OFFERED ME THE JOB.
OH-- OH WOW! PARK!
I KNEW THEY WOULD.
WHAT ARE YOU THINKING?
I DON'T KNOW.
YEAH.

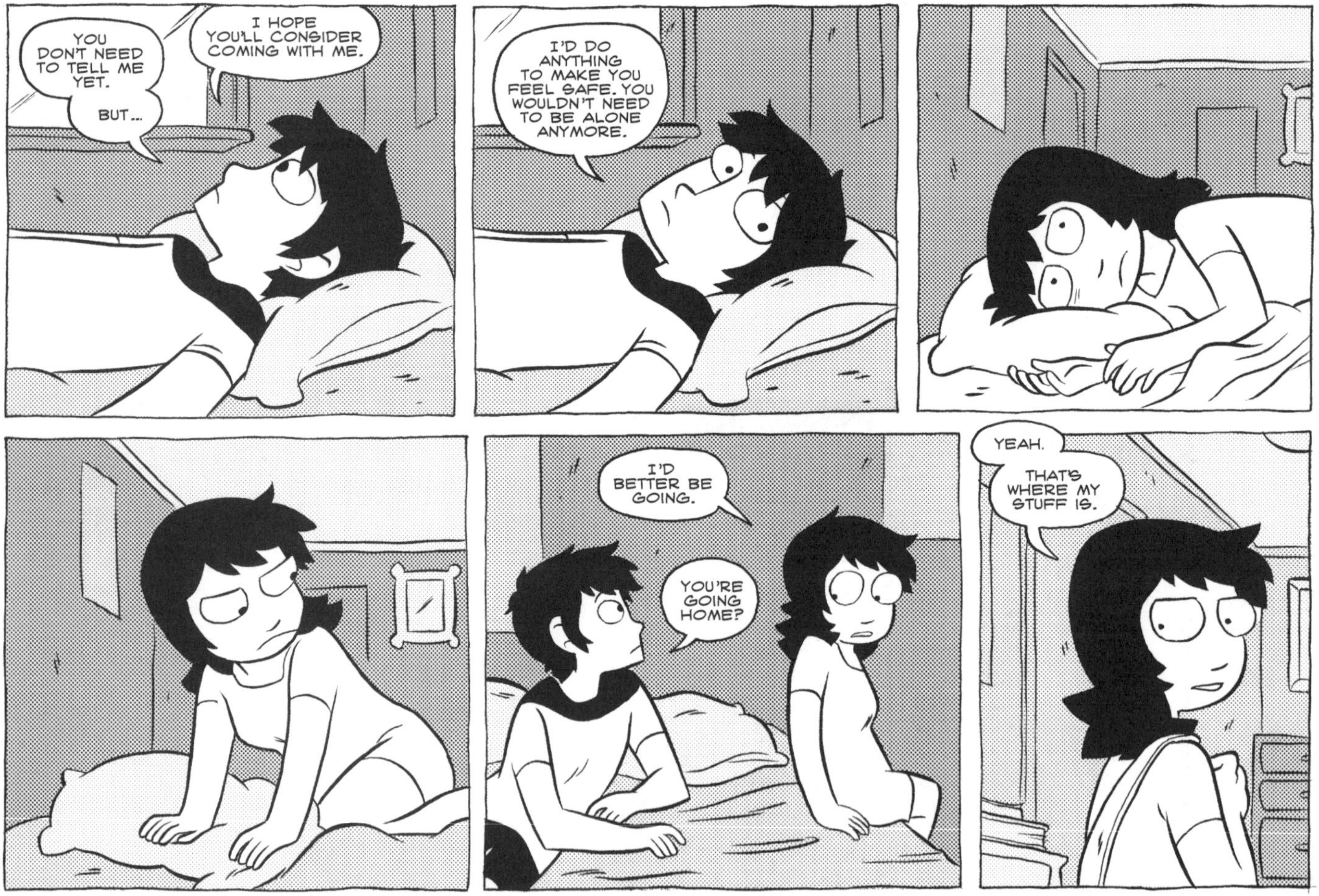
YOU DON'T NEED TO TELL ME YET.
BUT...
I HOPE YOU'LL CONSIDER COMING WITH ME.
I'D DO ANYTHING TO MAKE YOU FEEL SAFE. YOU WOULDN'T NEED TO BE ALONE ANYMORE.
I'D BETTER BE GOING.
YOU'RE GOING HOME?
YEAH.
THAT'S WHERE MY STUFF IS.

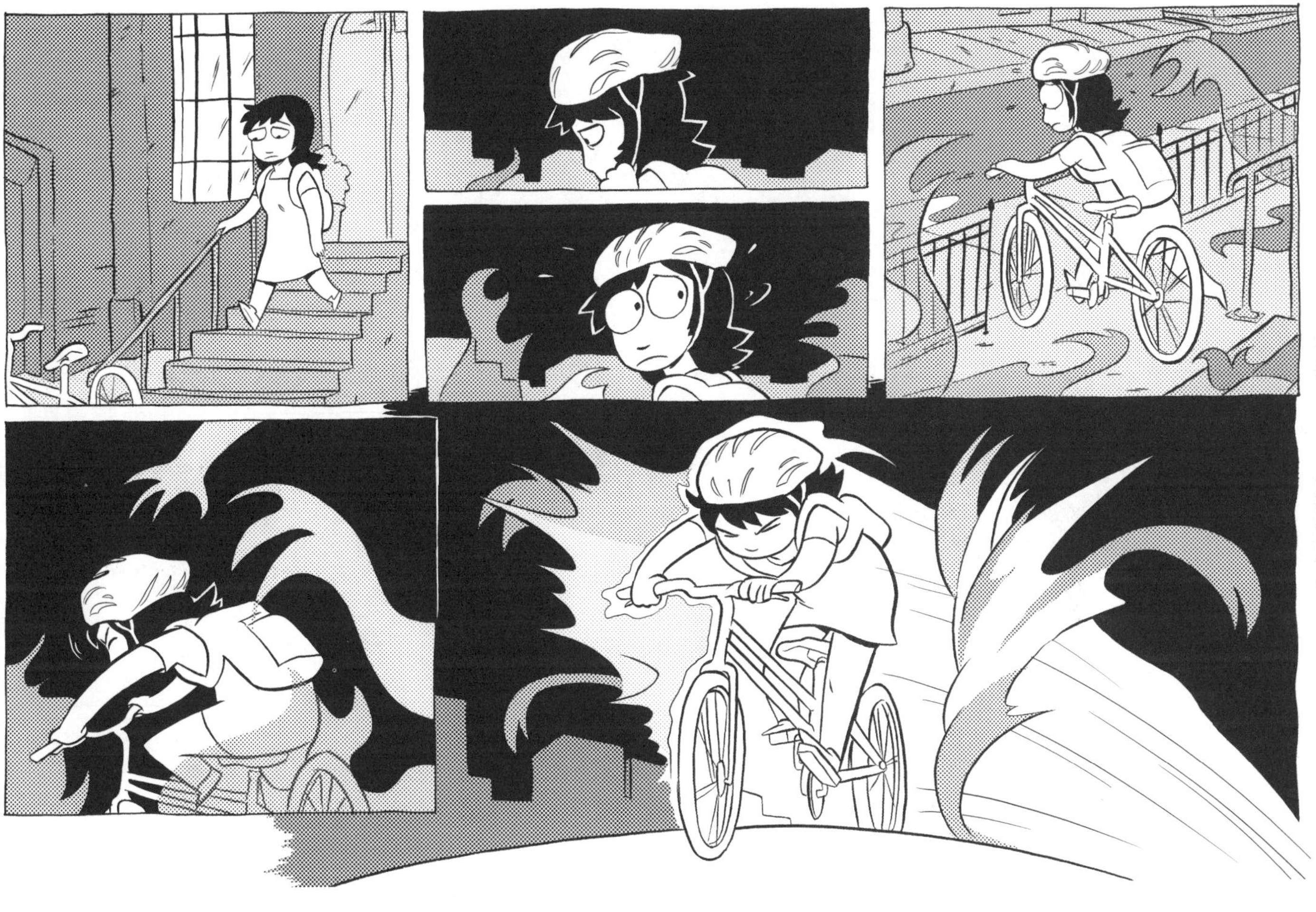

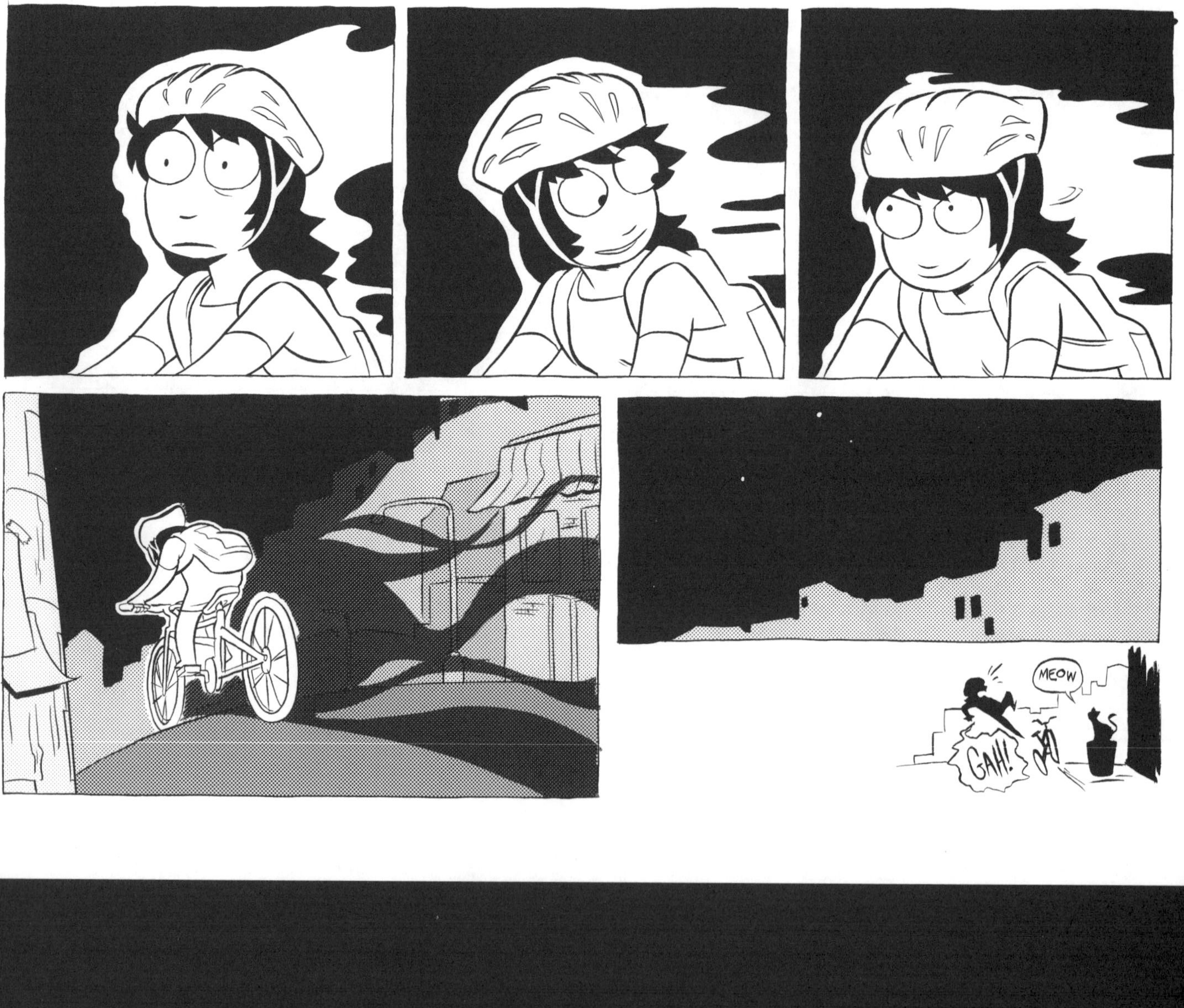
MEOW
GAH!

Who Are Parents

In the winter of 2007 I left my friends and family in New York to live in Western Massachusetts. I worked at home and was alone most of the time. During the snowiest weeks I holed myself up with a great deal of music — including The Shaggs, with whom I briefly became obsessed.

It's impossible to prepare for the sound of The Shaggs. Their shortcomings go so far beyond lack of technical skill that the music becomes entirely its own thing. I laughed at them and with them, longed for their distorted teenage fantasies, and wept for their good intentions. In particular the track "Who Are Parents" stood out. It's the band's 100% earnest endorsement of the people they were trying desperately to please (who were, tragically, forcing them to make music).

I started to think about the reasons I'd grown distant from my own family, how painful certain subjects had become over the years, and how not speaking at all often seemed like the best option. In this story, Eve is made to reflect on the emotional distance between she and her mother, and whether or not any aspect of their communication is salvageable. Hanna's parents are caring and involved, influential on her lifestyle, and miraculously in love with each other. They're the sort of family that, at my loneliest, I imagined everyone else must have.

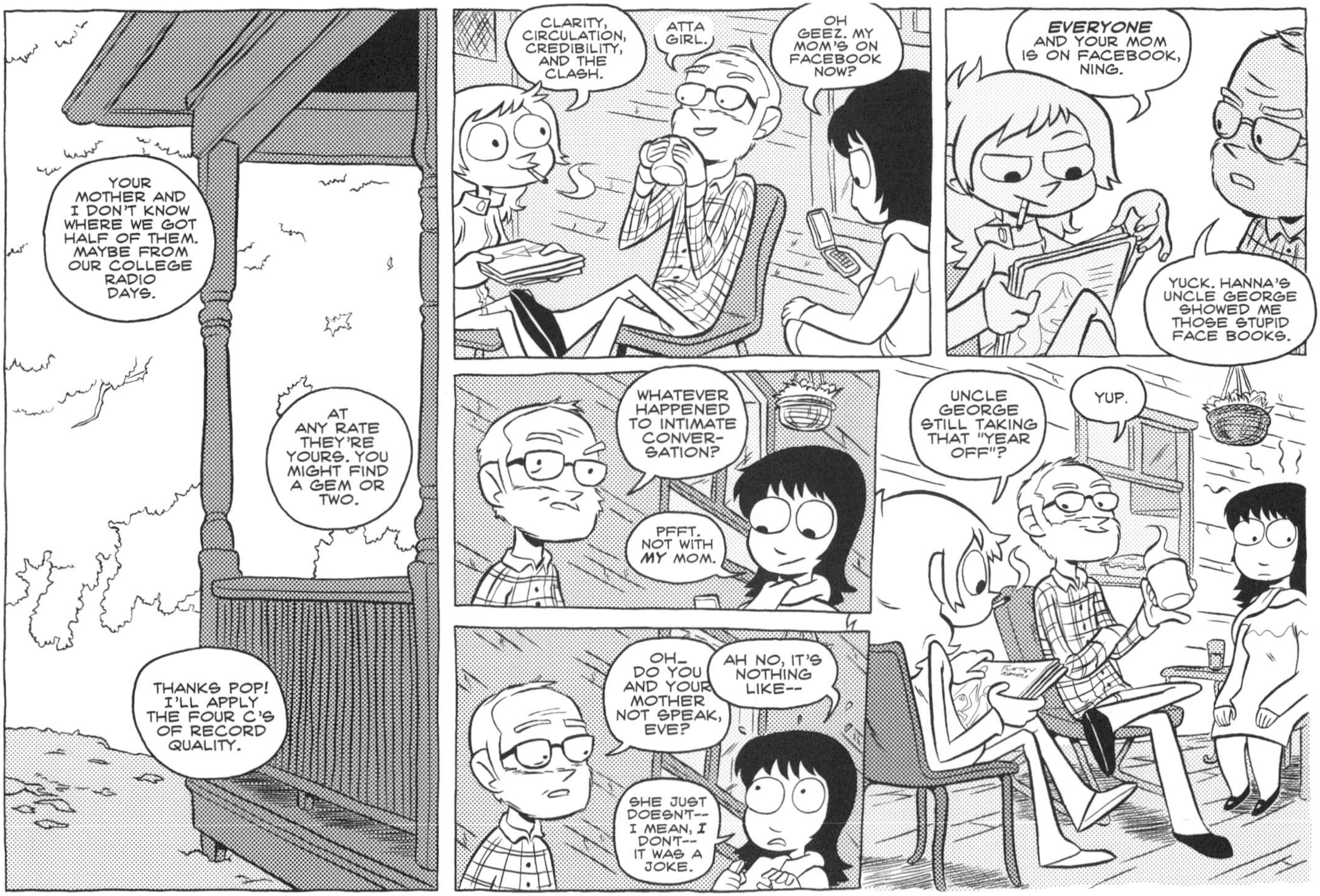
YOUR MOTHER AND I DON'T KNOW WHERE WE GOT HALF OF THEM. MAYBE FROM OUR COLLEGE RADIO DAYS.
AT ANY RATE THEY'RE YOURS. YOU MIGHT FIND A GEM OR TWO.
THANKS POP! I'LL APPLY THE FOUR C'S OF RECORD QUALITY.
CLARITY, CIRCULATION, CREDIBILITY, AND THE CLASH.
ATTA GIRL.
OH GEEZ. MY MOM'S ON FACEBOOK NOW?
EVERYONE AND YOUR MOM IS ON FACEBOOK, NING.
YUCK. HANNA'S UNCLE GEORGE SHOWED ME THOSE STUPID FACE BOOKS.
WHATEVER HAPPENED TO INTIMATE CONVER-SATION?
PFFT. NOT WITH *MY* MOM.
UNCLE GEORGE STILL TAKING THAT "YEAR OFF"?
YUP.
OH_ DO YOU AND YOUR MOTHER NOT SPEAK, EVE?
AH NO, IT'S NOTHING LIKE--
SHE JUST DOESN'T-- I MEAN, *I* DONT-- IT WAS A JOKE.

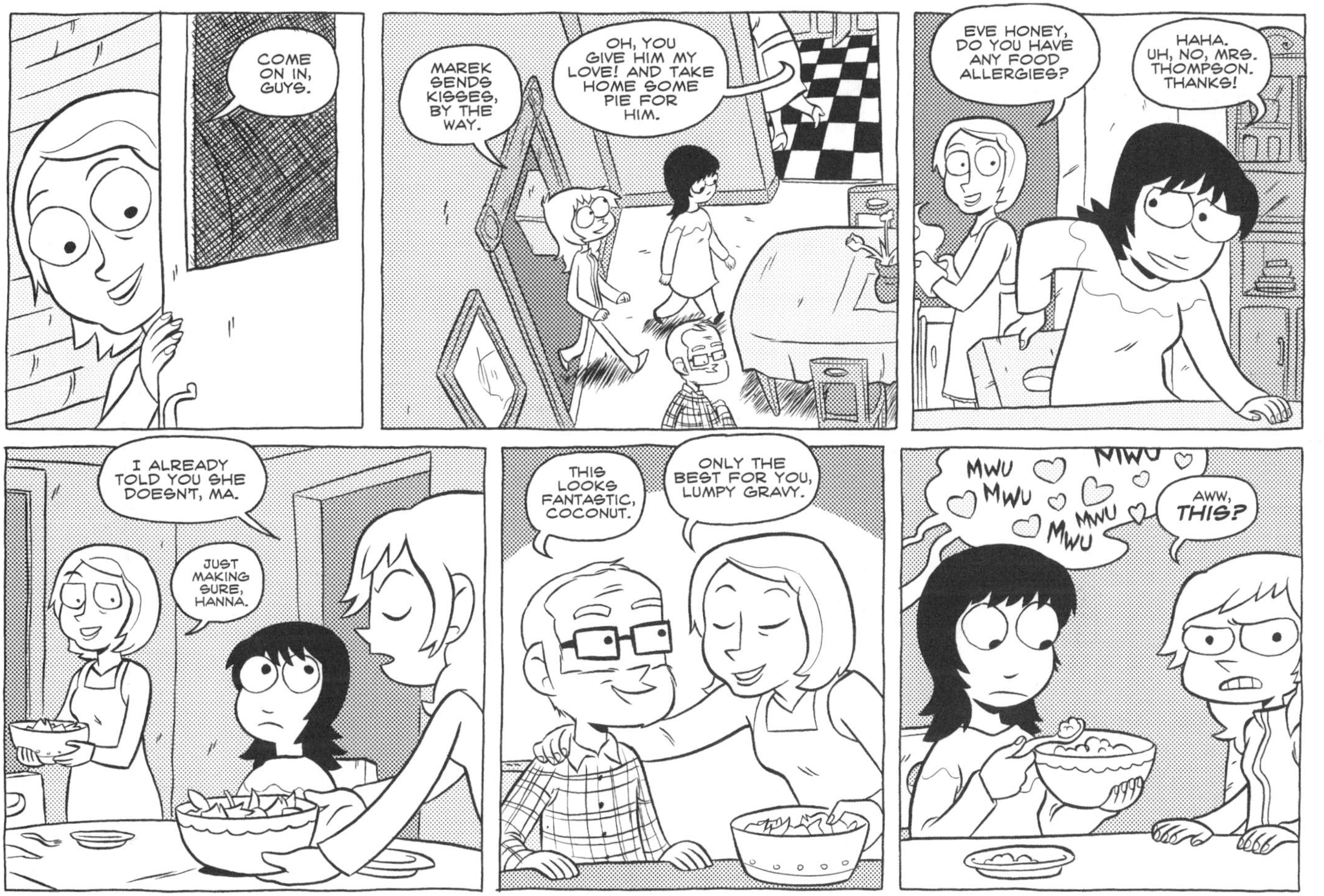
COME ON IN, GUYS.
MAREK SENDS KISSES, BY THE WAY.
OH, YOU GIVE HIM MY LOVE! AND TAKE HOME SOME PIE FOR HIM.
EVE HONEY, DO YOU HAVE ANY FOOD ALLERGIES?
HAHA. UH, NO, MRS. THOMPSON. THANKS!
I ALREADY TOLD YOU SHE DOESN'T, MA.
JUST MAKING SURE, HANNA.
THIS LOOKS FANTASTIC, COCONUT.
ONLY THE BEST FOR YOU, LUMPY GRAVY.
MWU MWU MWU MWU MWU MWU
AWW, THIS?

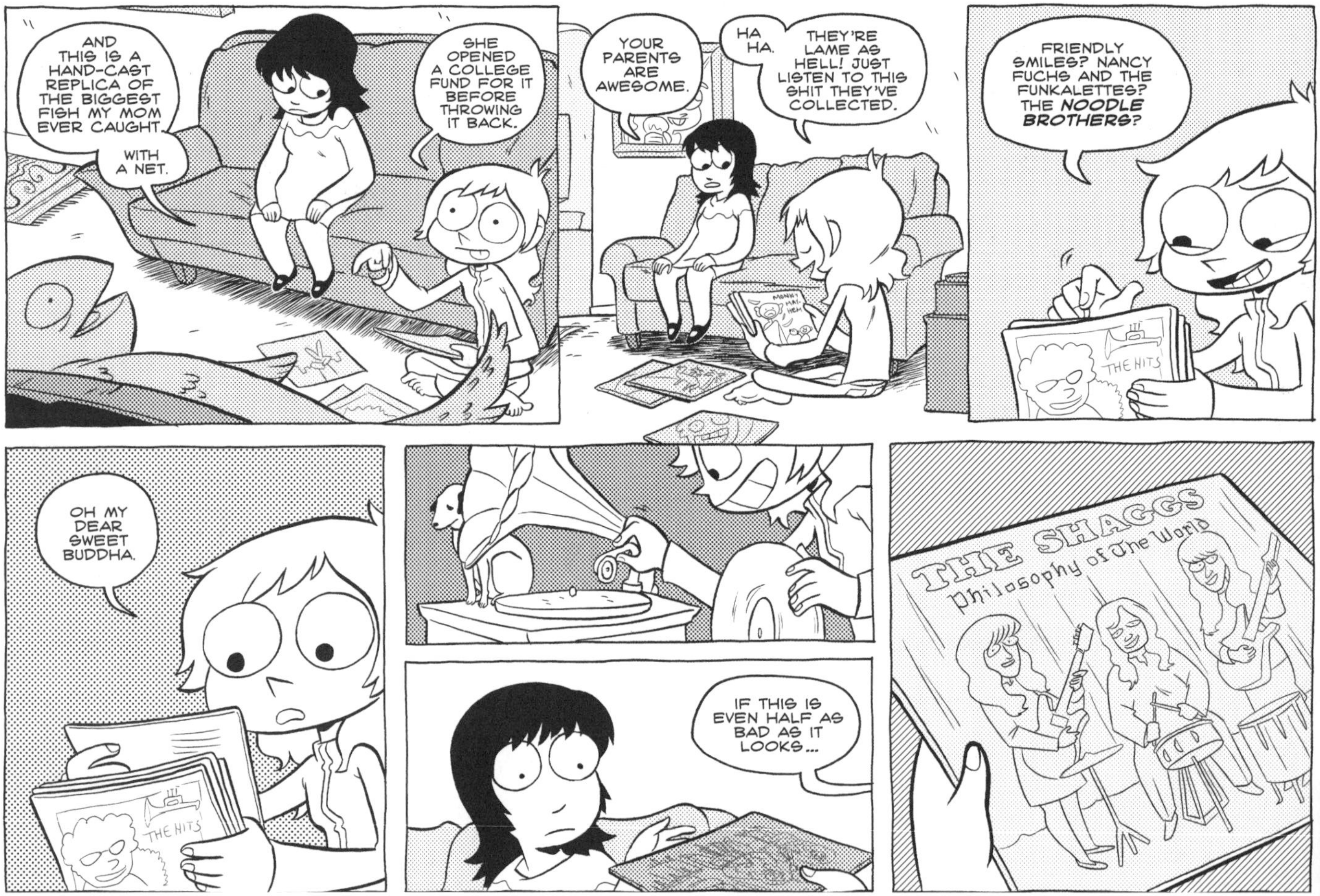
AND THIS IS A HAND-CAST REPLICA OF THE BIGGEST FISH MY MOM EVER CAUGHT.
WITH A NET.
SHE OPENED A COLLEGE FUND FOR IT BEFORE THROWING IT BACK.
YOUR PARENTS ARE AWESOME.
HA HA.
THEY'RE LAME AS HELL! JUST LISTEN TO THIS SHIT THEY'VE COLLECTED.
FRIENDLY SMILES? NANCY FUCHS AND THE FUNKALETTES? THE NOODLE BROTHERS?
THE HITS
OH MY DEAR SWEET BUDDHA.
THE HITS
IF THIS IS EVEN HALF AS BAD AS IT LOOKS...
THE SHAGGS
Philosophy of The World

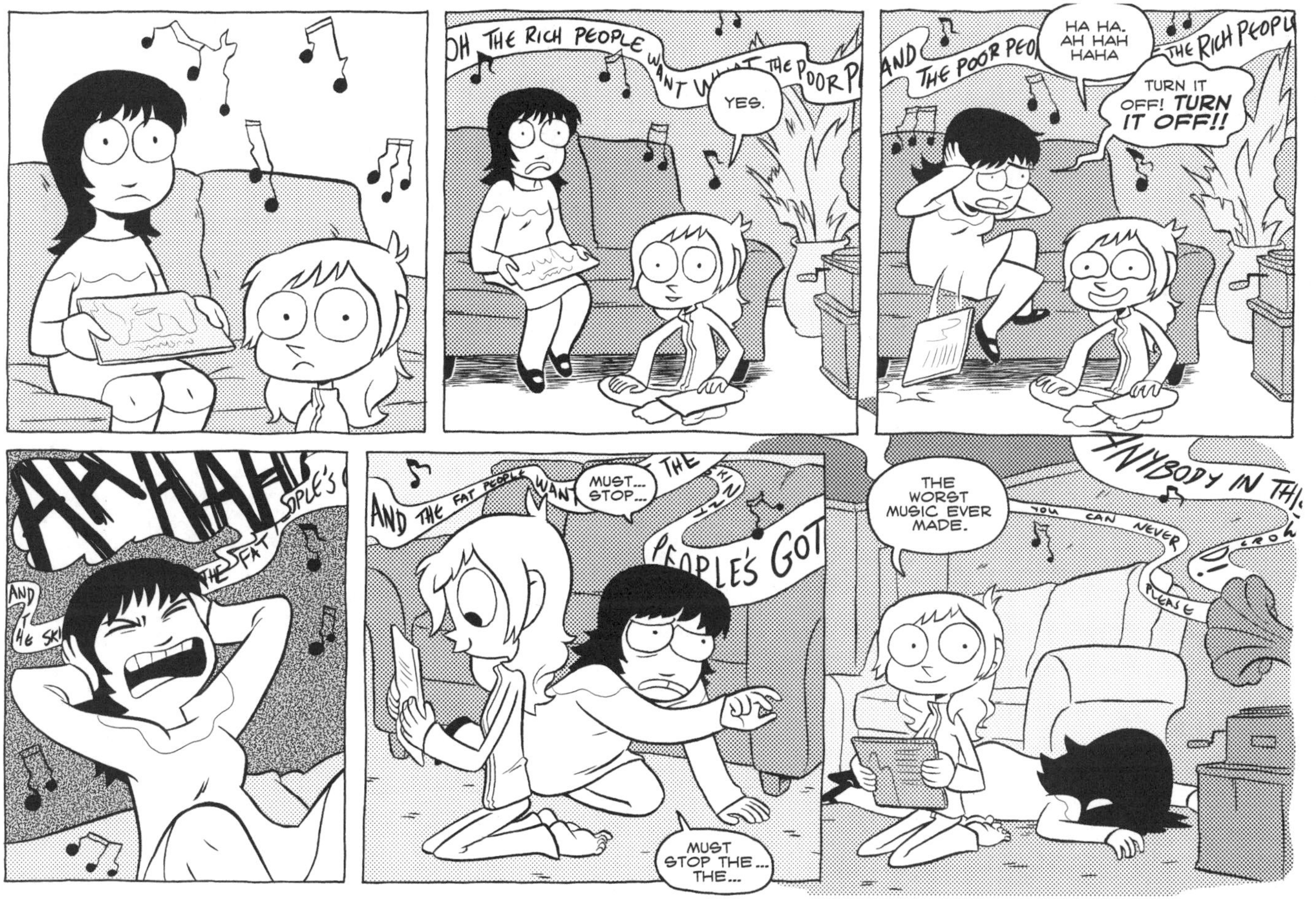

OH THE RICH PEOPLE WANT WHAT THE POOR P
YES.
AND THE POOR PEO
HA HA. AH HAH HAHA
THE RICH PEOPL
TURN IT OFF! TURN IT OFF!!
AND THE FAT PEOPLE WANT
MUST... STOP...
PEOPLE'S GOT
MUST STOP THE... THE...
ANYBODY IN TH
THE WORST MUSIC EVER MADE.
YOU CAN NEVER
PLEASE

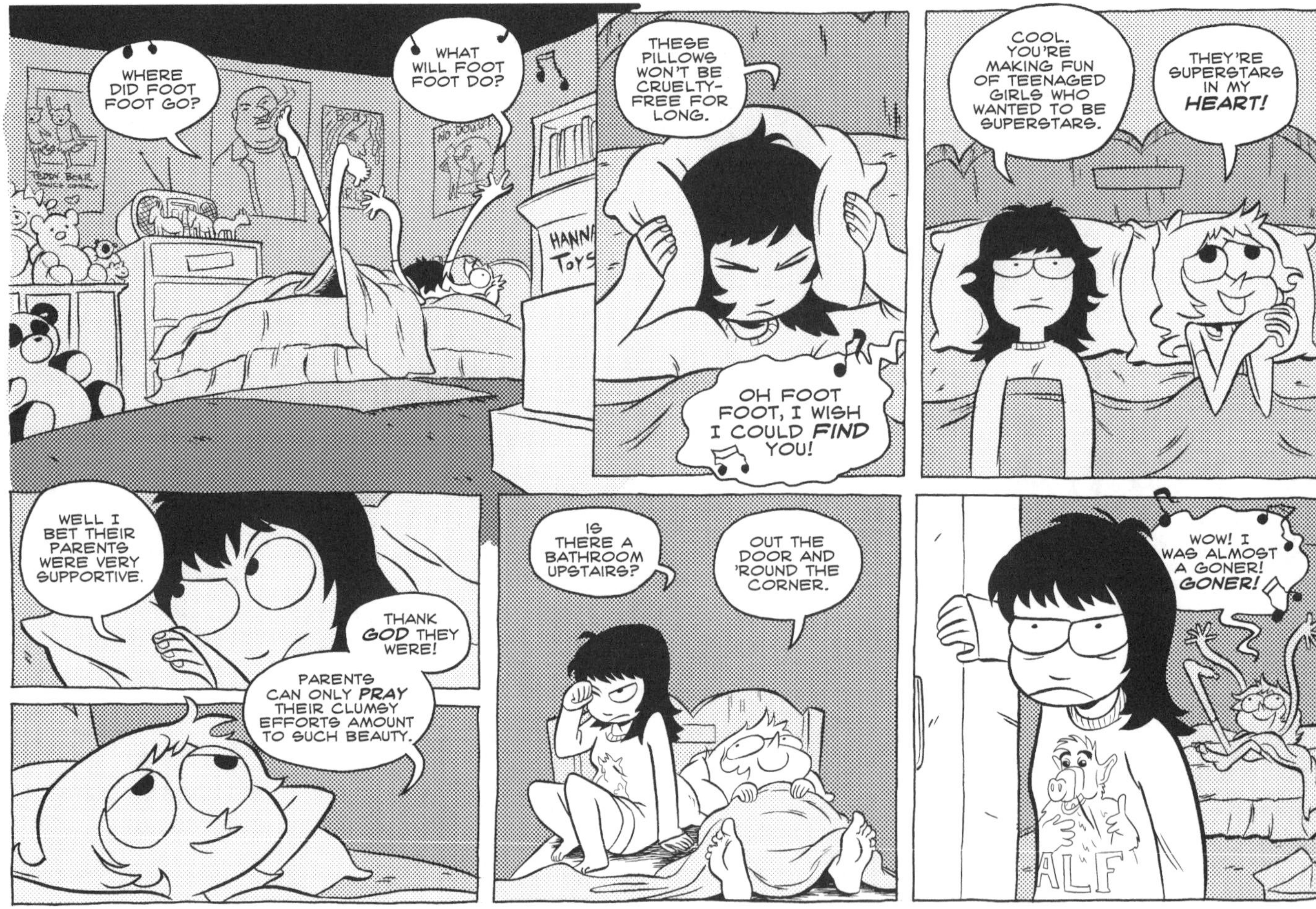

WHERE DID FOOT FOOT GO?
WHAT WILL FOOT FOOT DO?
HANNA TOYS
THESE PILLOWS WON'T BE CRUELTY-FREE FOR LONG.
OH FOOT FOOT, I WISH I COULD FIND YOU!
COOL. YOU'RE MAKING FUN OF TEENAGED GIRLS WHO WANTED TO BE SUPERSTARS.
THEY'RE SUPERSTARS IN MY HEART!
WELL I BET THEIR PARENTS WERE VERY SUPPORTIVE.
THANK GOD THEY WERE!
PARENTS CAN ONLY PRAY THEIR CLUMSY EFFORTS AMOUNT TO SUCH BEAUTY.
IS THERE A BATHROOM UPSTAIRS?
OUT THE DOOR AND 'ROUND THE CORNER.
WOW! I WAS ALMOST A GONER! GONER!
ALF

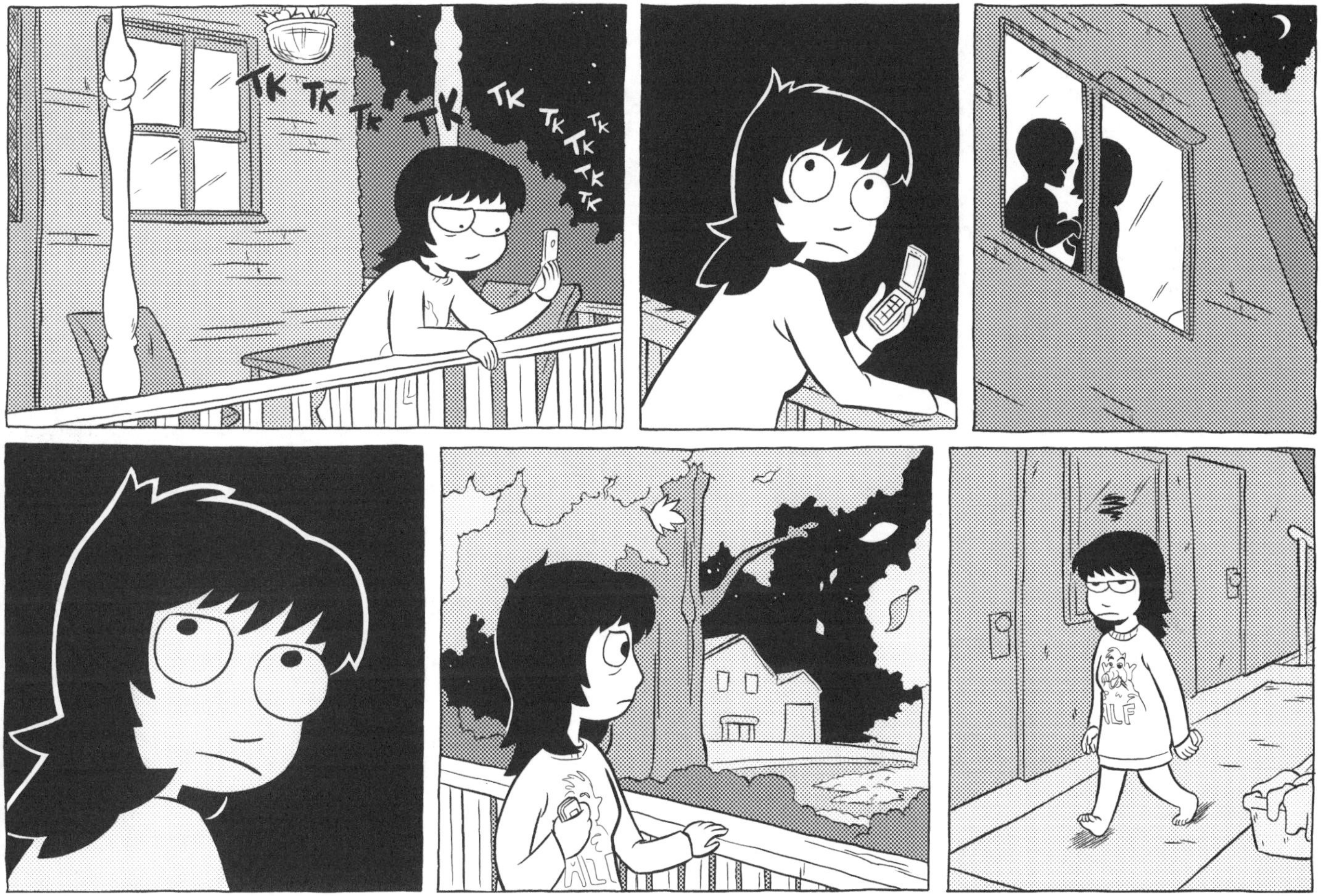
TK TK TK TK TK TK TK TK TK TK TK
ALF

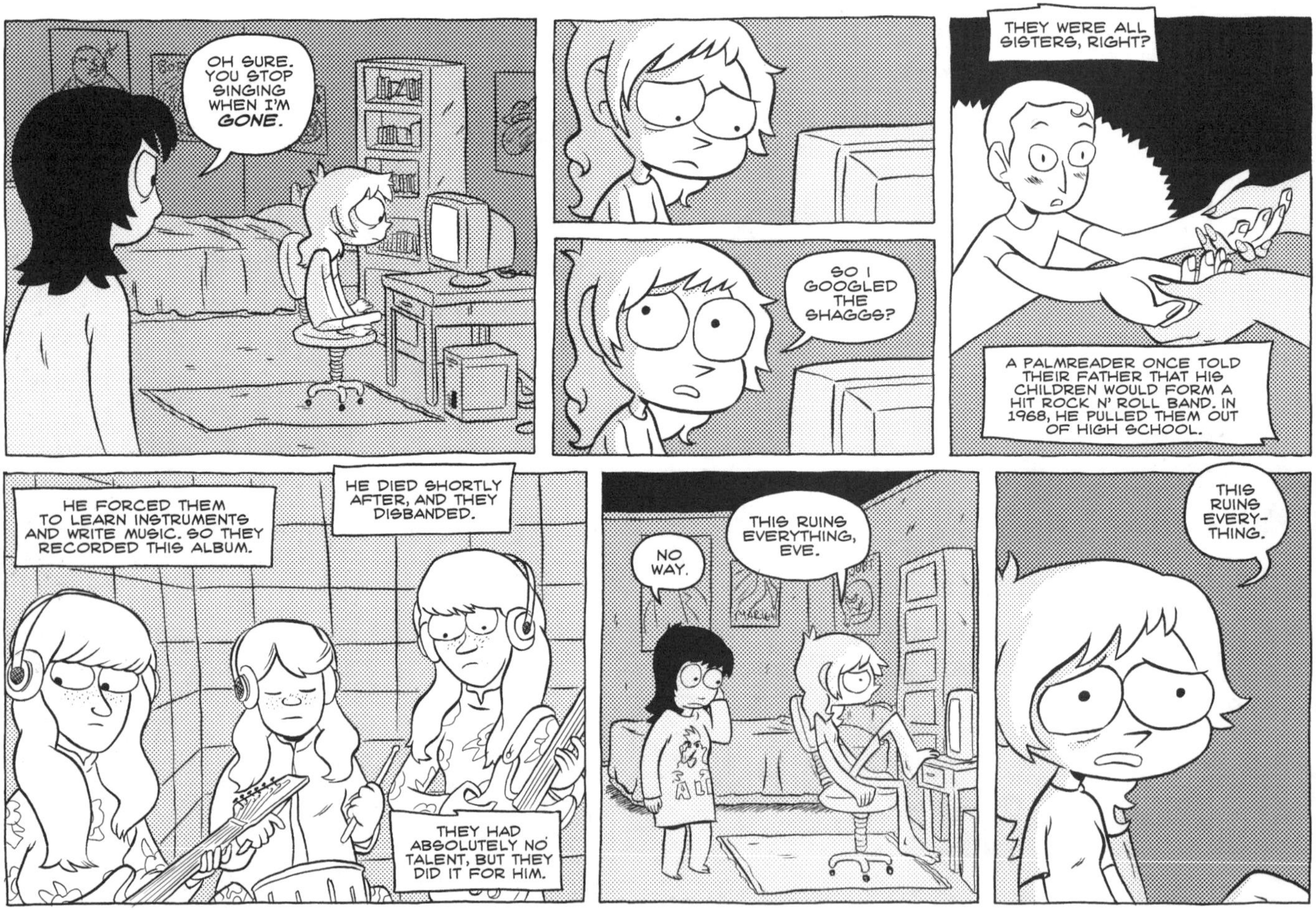
OH SURE. YOU STOP SINGING WHEN I'M GONE.
SO I GOOGLED THE SHAGGS?
THEY WERE ALL SISTERS, RIGHT?
A PALMREADER ONCE TOLD THEIR FATHER THAT HIS CHILDREN WOULD FORM A HIT ROCK N' ROLL BAND. IN 1968, HE PULLED THEM OUT OF HIGH SCHOOL.
HE FORCED THEM TO LEARN INSTRUMENTS AND WRITE MUSIC. SO THEY RECORDED THIS ALBUM.
HE DIED SHORTLY AFTER, AND THEY DISBANDED.
THEY HAD ABSOLUTELY NO TALENT, BUT THEY DID IT FOR HIM.
NO WAY.
THIS RUINS EVERYTHING, EVE.
THIS RUINS EVERY-THING.

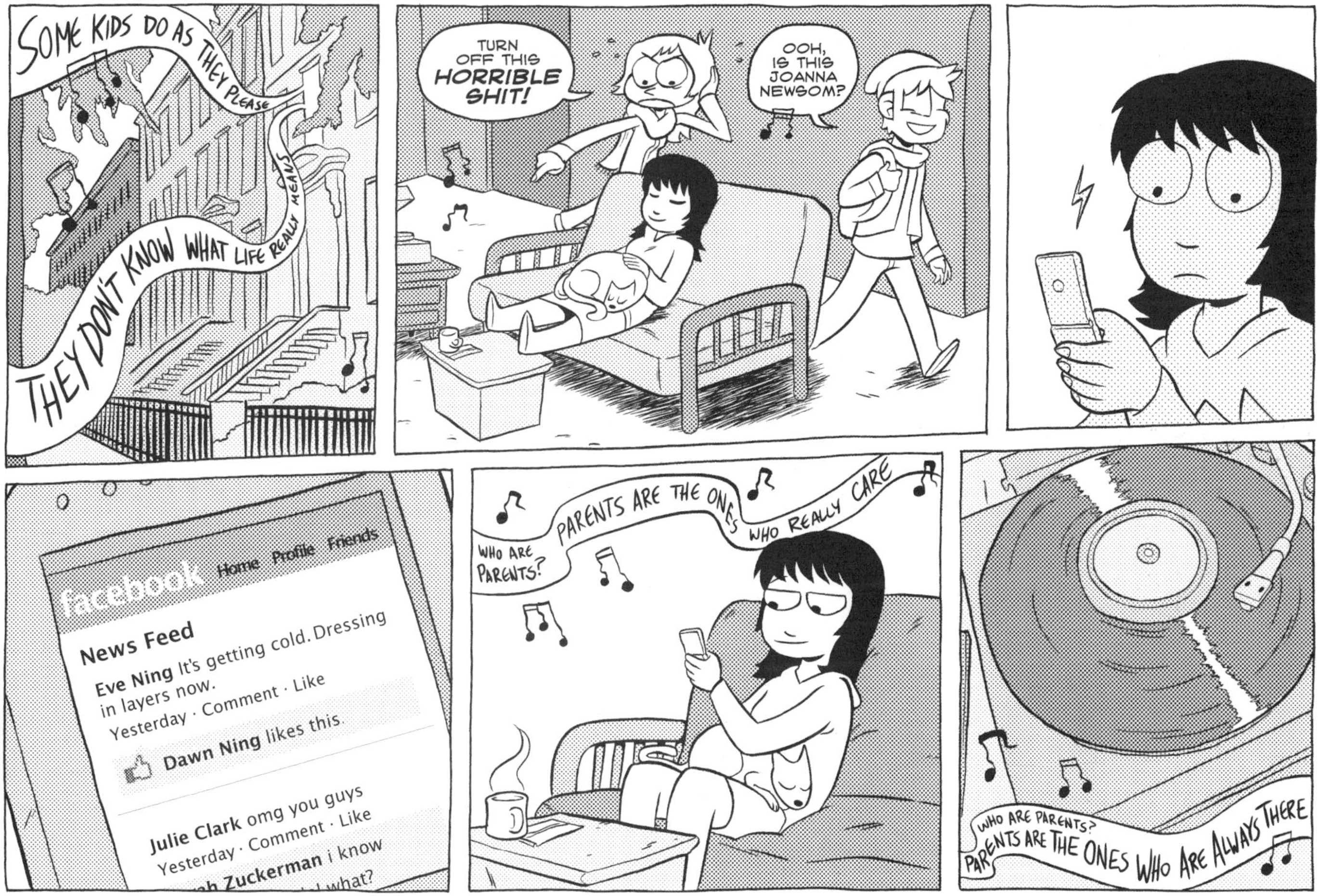
SOME KIDS DO AS THEY PLEASE
THEY DON'T KNOW WHAT LIFE REALLY MEANS
TURN OFF THIS HORRIBLE SHIT!
OOH, IS THIS JOANNA NEWSOM?
facebook Home Profile Friends
News Feed
Eve Ning It's getting cold. Dressing in layers now.
Yesterday · Comment · Like
Dawn Ning likes this.
Julie Clark omg you guys
Yesterday · Comment · Like
Zuckerman i know
WHO ARE PARENTS?
PARENTS ARE THE ONES WHO REALLY CARE
WHO ARE PARENTS?
PARENTS ARE THE ONES WHO ARE ALWAYS THERE

Couch Sitter

Okay, so we've all met someone we believed to be part of a group, who was later discovered to be a stranger. In my observation this has generally been a comfort, especially when the person was kind of a weirdo. But on rare occasions it's been a sad awakening: the realization that they've left without a trace, that we'll never be able to find them again. Social networks allow us to trace friends-of-exes-of-cousins-of-friends with stalker precision, so it's rare and distressing to truly miss a connection. It's at this point that our heroes begin to wish they'd known more about Victor, or gotten his full name...or confirmed that Victor was his name at all.

It's been suggested by readers that Victor is someone we've all met, that he's a thief and a mooch, that he's a folk hero, that he's a symbolic manifestation of our need for guidance. I began writing with the intent of the former, and it evolved into the latter. The reader is invited to interpret it in any of these ways.

Victor is instantly relatable to most of the cast, barring Will, to whom he is apparently invisible. By this I meant to suggest that Will needs no guidance, for better or worse. Though, perhaps Will just rejects hero worship, and can't "see" past the hype. Or maybe there are too many drunk people in the way. This is also possible.

I was inspired by the hero of John Steinbeck's "Tortilla Flat," who is immortalized by his friends during the story's climactic party scene, to stage Victor's departure. His feats are so impressive that they create a void in his absence. Before his hosts even know Victor has left, they're already struggling to get along without him.

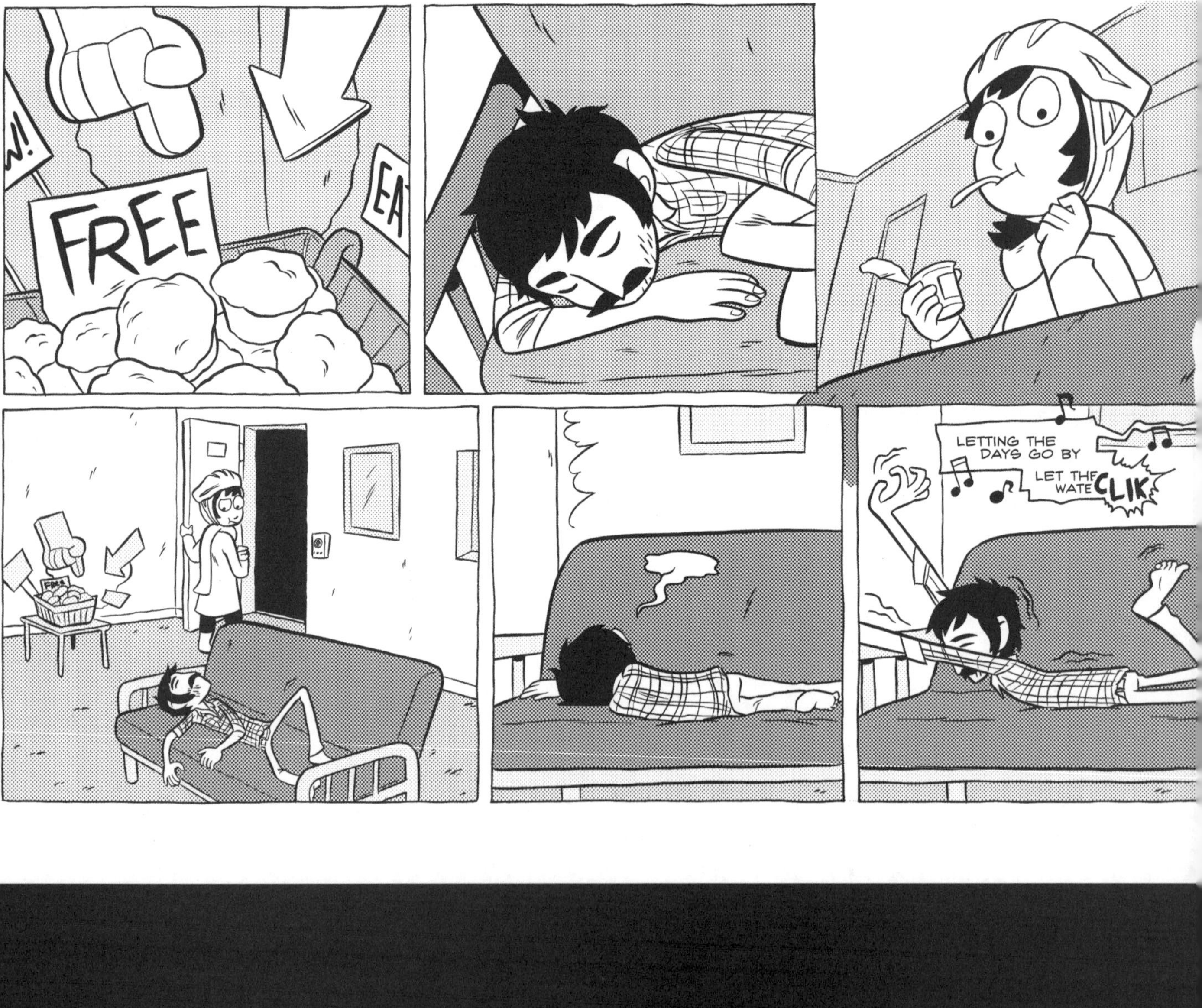
FREE
LETTING THE DAYS GO BY
LET THE WATE
CLIK

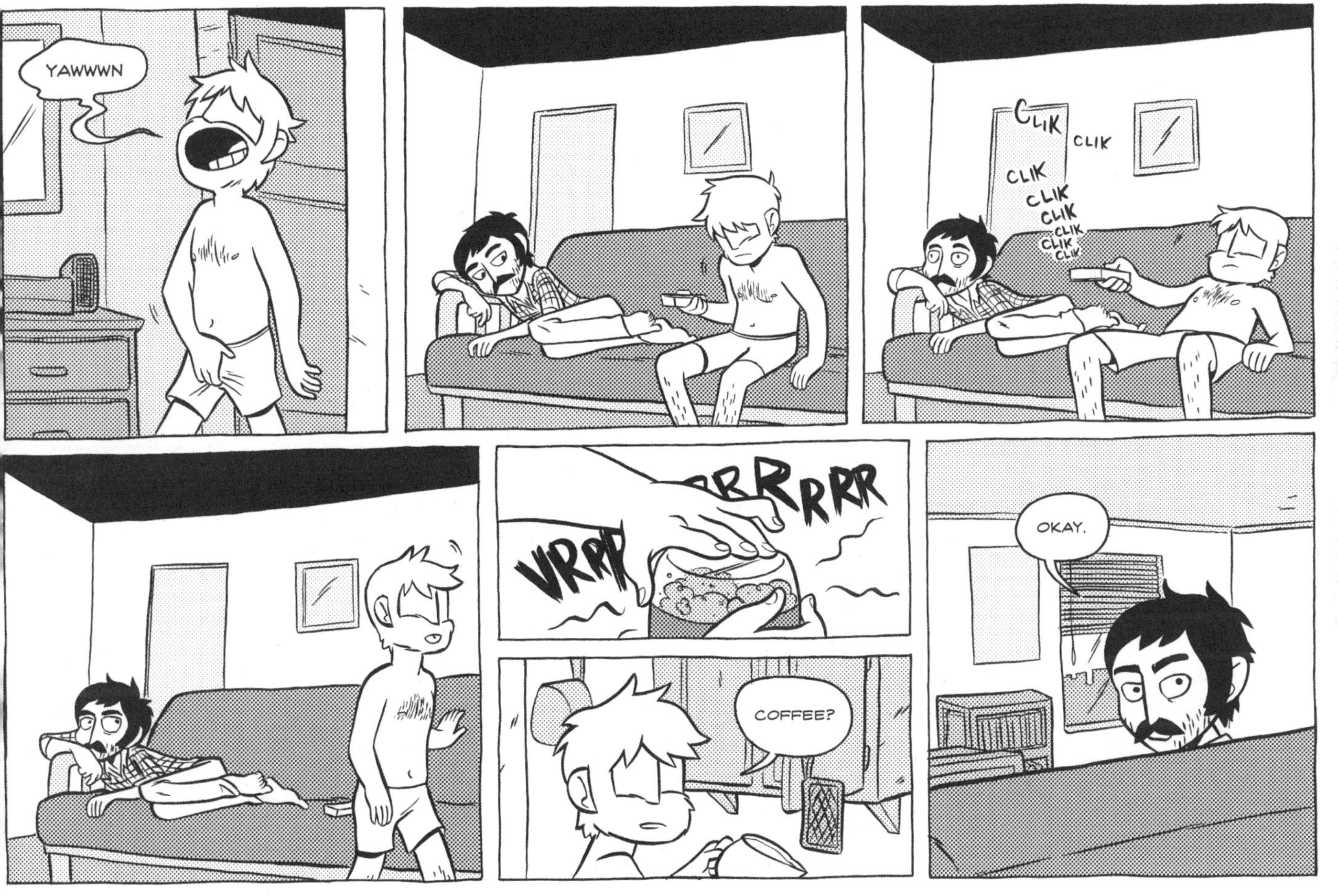
YAWWWN
CLIK
CLIK
CLIK
CLIK
CLIK
CLIK
CLIK
CLIK
VRRR
RRRRRR
COFFEE?
OKAY.

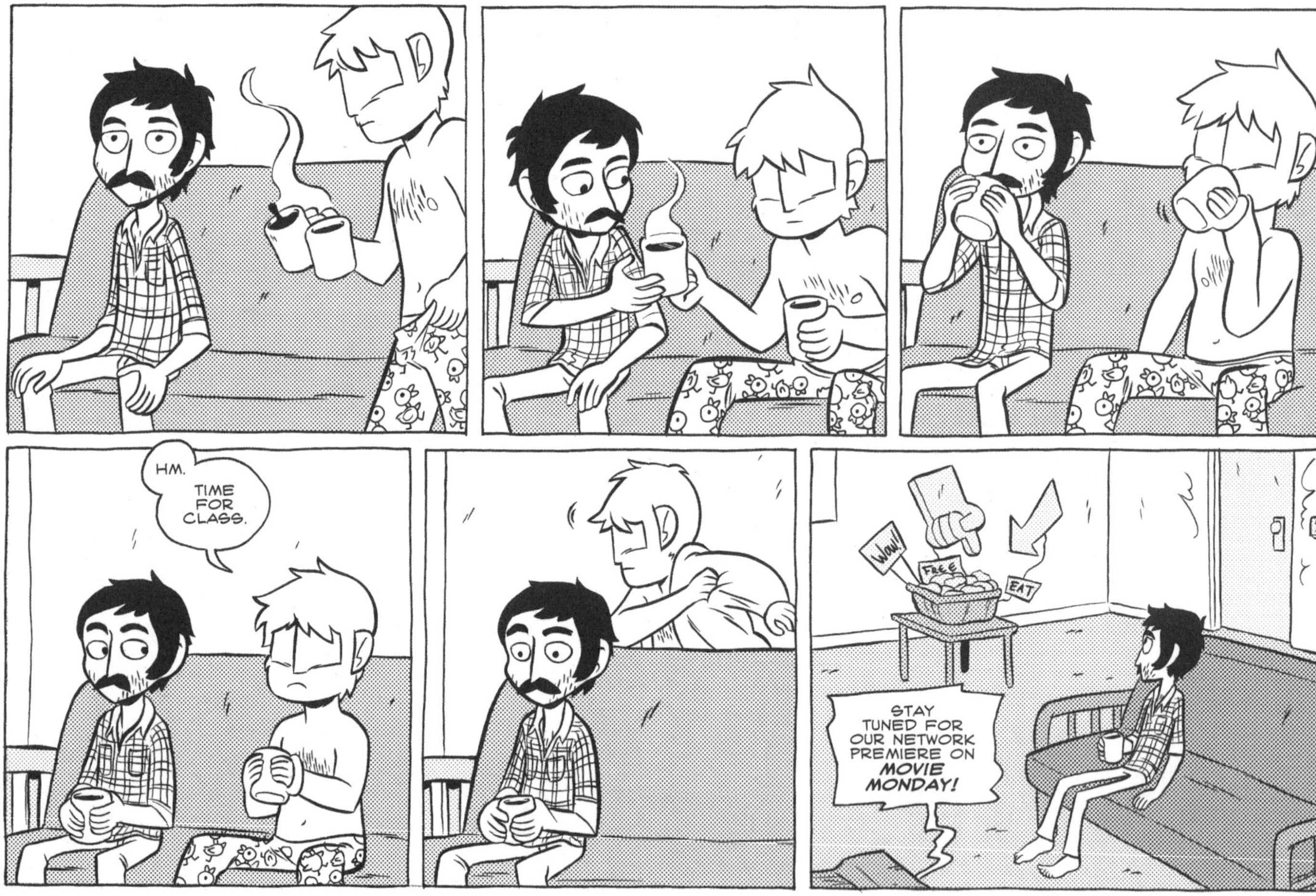
HM.
TIME FOR CLASS.
WOW!
FREE
EAT
STAY TUNED FOR OUR NETWORK PREMIERE ON MOVIE MONDAY!

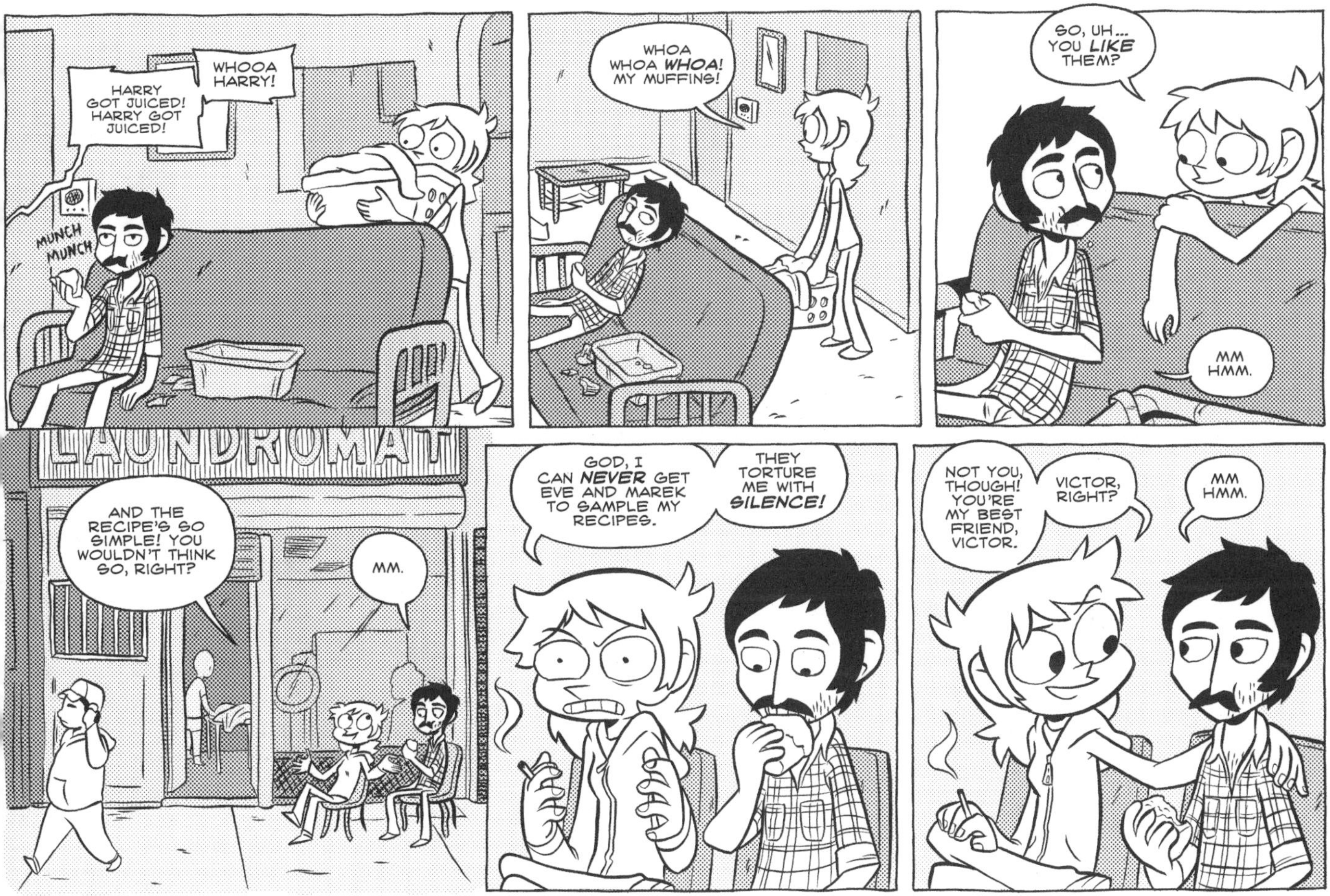
HARRY GOT JUICED! HARRY GOT JUICED!
WHOOA HARRY!
MUNCH MUNCH
WHOA WHOA WHOA! MY MUFFINS!
SO, UH... YOU LIKE THEM?
MM HMM.
LAUNDROMAT
AND THE RECIPE'S SO SIMPLE! YOU WOULDN'T THINK SO, RIGHT?
MM.
GOD, I CAN NEVER GET EVE AND MAREK TO SAMPLE MY RECIPES.
THEY TORTURE ME WITH SILENCE!
NOT YOU, THOUGH! YOU'RE MY BEST FRIEND, VICTOR.
VICTOR, RIGHT?
MM HMM.

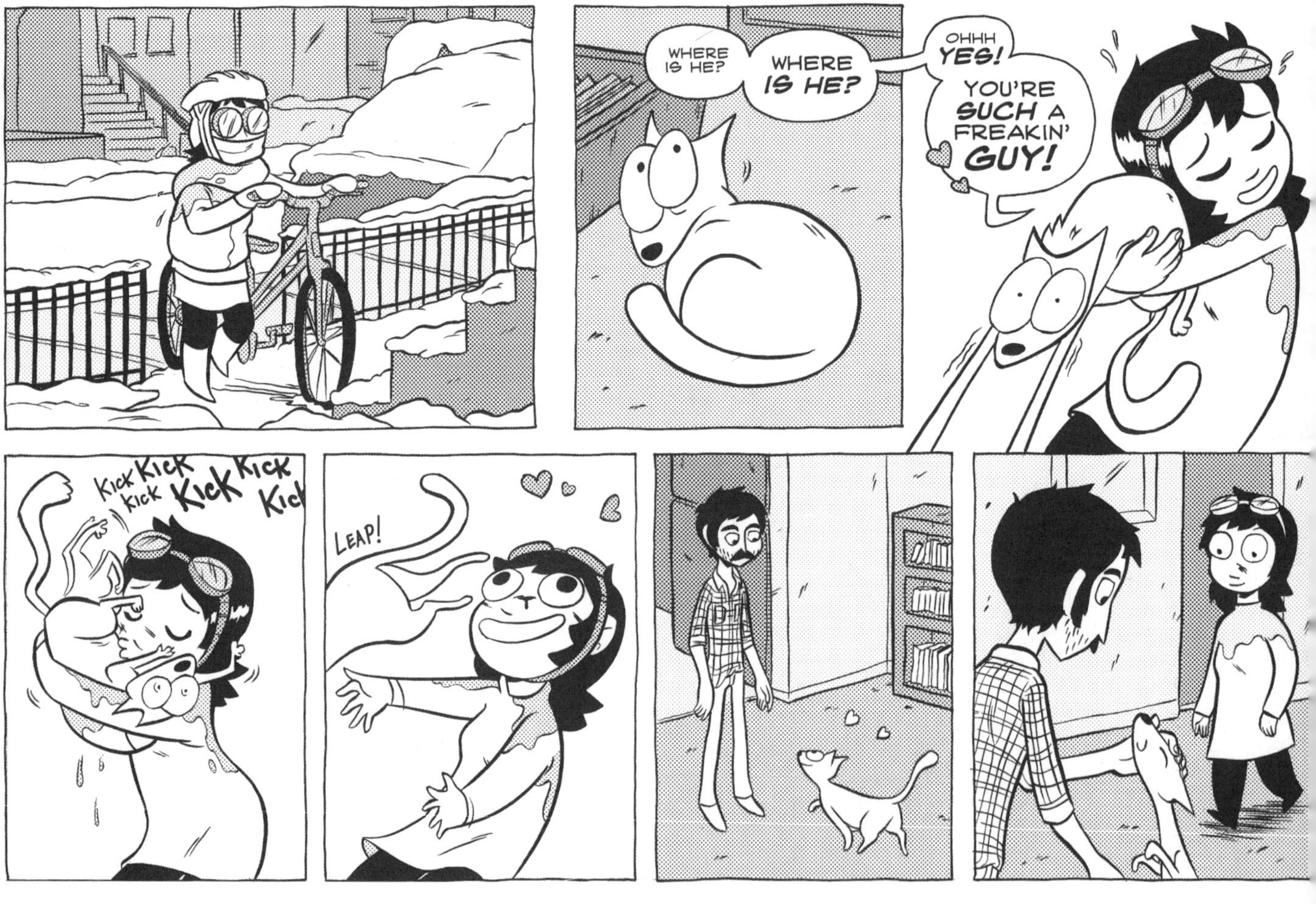
WHERE IS HE?
WHERE IS HE?
OHHH YES!
YOU'RE SUCH A FREAKIN' GUY!
KICK KICK KICK KICK KICK KICK
LEAP!

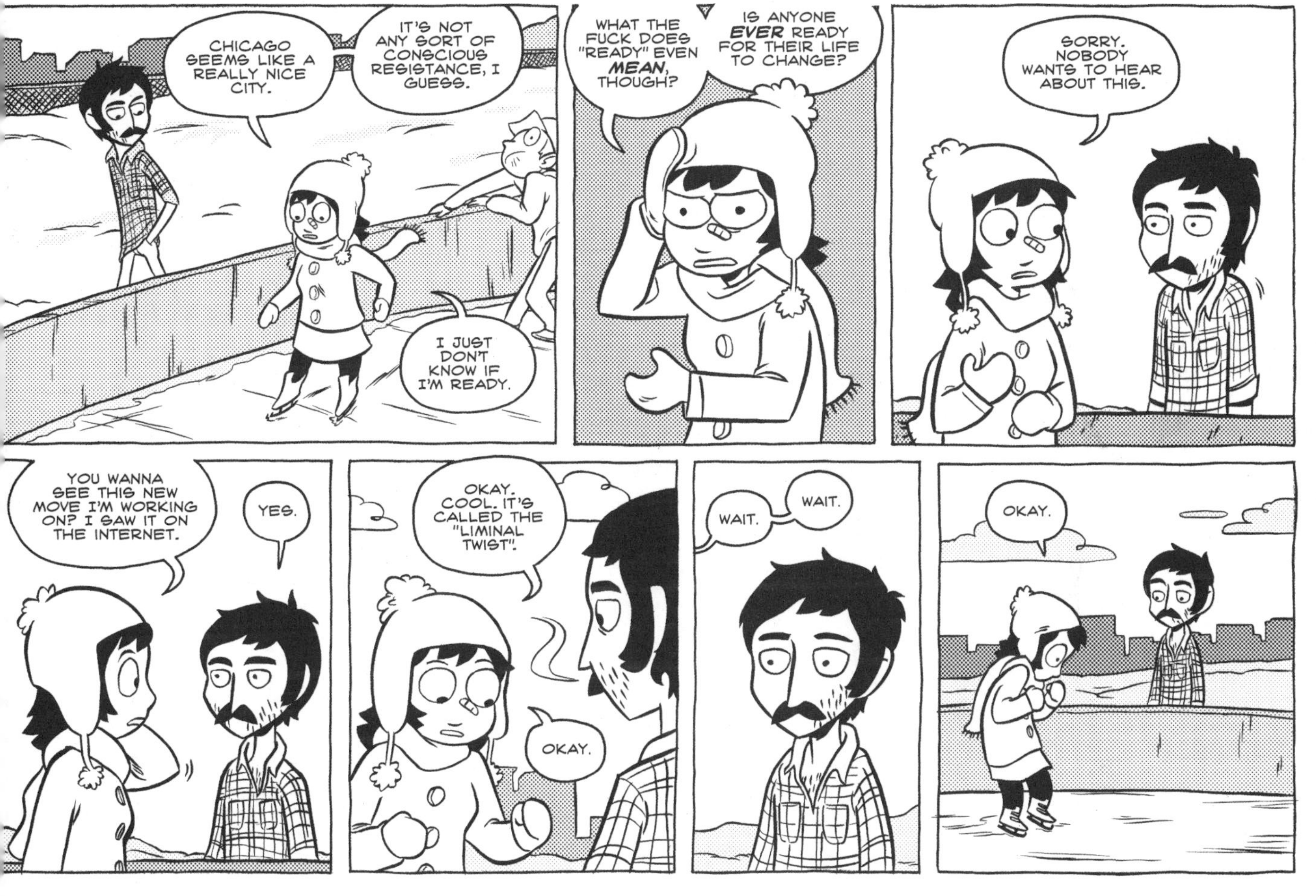
CHICAGO SEEMS LIKE A REALLY NICE CITY.
IT'S NOT ANY SORT OF CONSCIOUS RESISTANCE, I GUESS.
I JUST DON'T KNOW IF I'M READY.
WHAT THE FUCK DOES "READY" EVEN MEAN, THOUGH?
IS ANYONE EVER READY FOR THEIR LIFE TO CHANGE?
SORRY. NOBODY WANTS TO HEAR ABOUT THIS.
YOU WANNA SEE THIS NEW MOVE I'M WORKING ON? I SAW IT ON THE INTERNET.
YES.
OKAY. COOL. IT'S CALLED THE "LIMINAL TWIST".
OKAY.
WAIT.
WAIT.
OKAY.

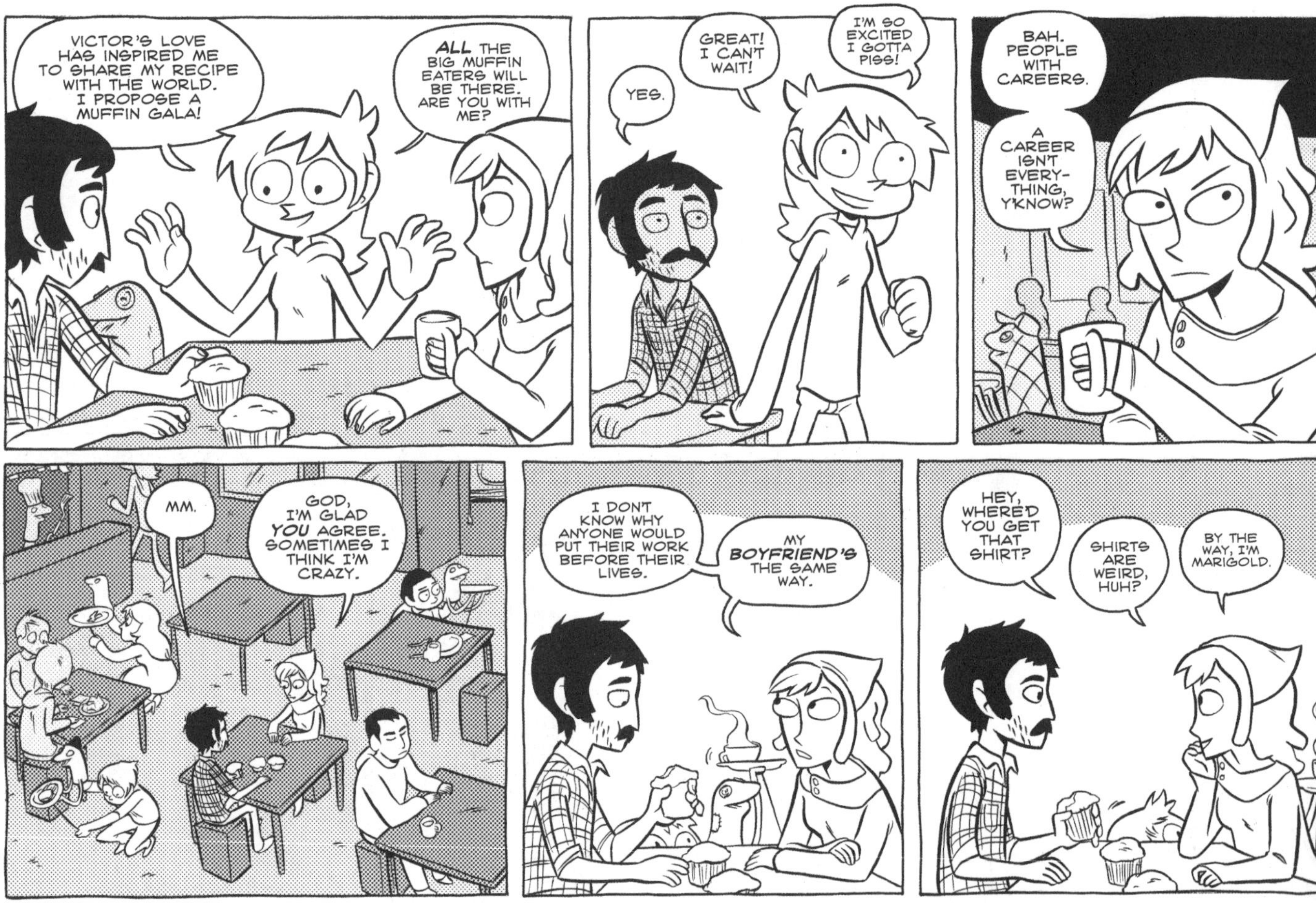

VICTOR'S LOVE HAS INSPIRED ME TO SHARE MY RECIPE WITH THE WORLD. I PROPOSE A MUFFIN GALA!
ALL THE BIG MUFFIN EATERS WILL BE THERE. ARE YOU WITH ME?
YES.
GREAT! I CAN'T WAIT!
I'M SO EXCITED I GOTTA PISS!
BAH. PEOPLE WITH CAREERS.
A CAREER ISN'T EVERY-THING, Y'KNOW?
MM.
GOD, I'M GLAD YOU AGREE. SOMETIMES I THINK I'M CRAZY.
I DON'T KNOW WHY ANYONE WOULD PUT THEIR WORK BEFORE THEIR LIVES.
MY BOYFRIEND'S THE SAME WAY.
HEY, WHERE'D YOU GET THAT SHIRT?
SHIRTS ARE WEIRD, HUH?
BY THE WAY, I'M MARIGOLD.

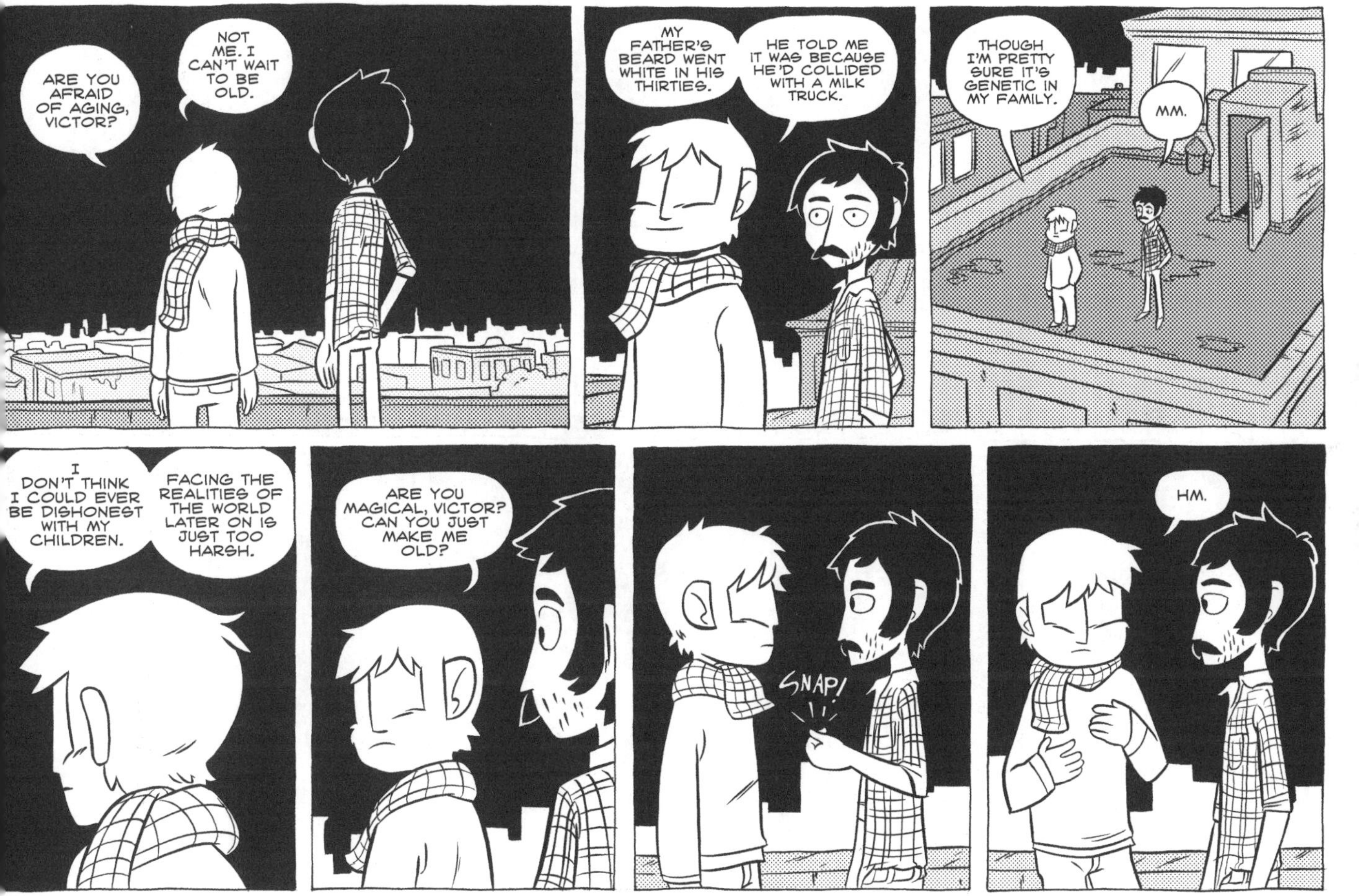
ARE YOU AFRAID OF AGING, VICTOR?
NOT ME. I CAN'T WAIT TO BE OLD.
MY FATHER'S BEARD WENT WHITE IN HIS THIRTIES.
HE TOLD ME IT WAS BECAUSE HE'D COLLIDED WITH A MILK TRUCK.
THOUGH I'M PRETTY SURE IT'S GENETIC IN MY FAMILY.
MM.
I DON'T THINK I COULD EVER BE DISHONEST WITH MY CHILDREN.
FACING THE REALITIES OF THE WORLD LATER ON IS JUST TOO HARSH.
ARE YOU MAGICAL, VICTOR? CAN YOU JUST MAKE ME OLD?
SNAP!
HM.

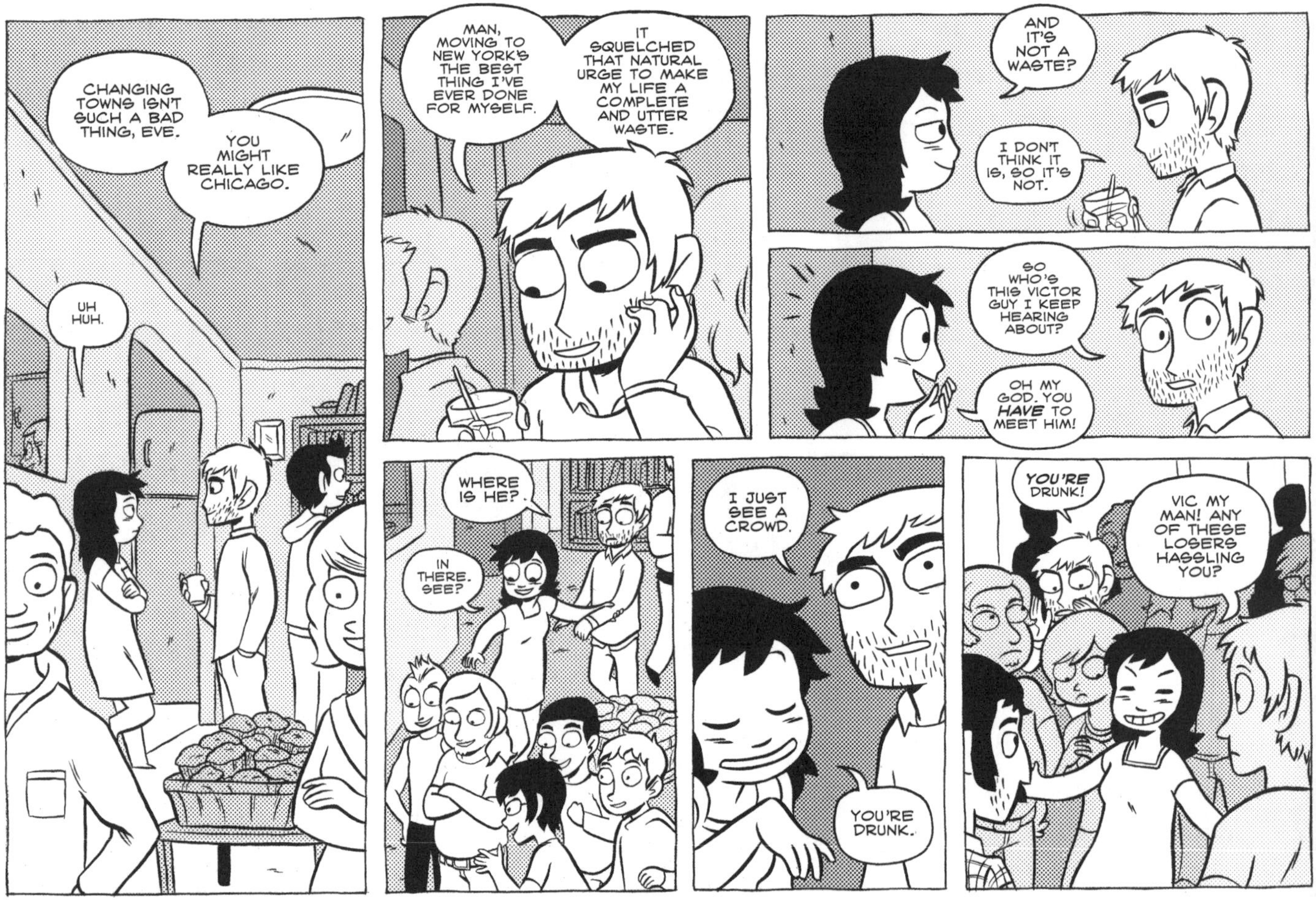

CHANGING TOWNS ISN'T SUCH A BAD THING, EVE.
YOU MIGHT REALLY LIKE CHICAGO.
UH HUH.
MAN, MOVING TO NEW YORK'S THE BEST THING I'VE EVER DONE FOR MYSELF.
IT SQUELCHED THAT NATURAL URGE TO MAKE MY LIFE A COMPLETE AND UTTER WASTE.
AND IT'S NOT A WASTE?
I DON'T THINK IT IS, SO IT'S NOT.
SO WHO'S THIS VICTOR GUY I KEEP HEARING ABOUT?
OH MY GOD. YOU ***HAVE*** TO MEET HIM!
WHERE IS HE?
IN THERE. SEE?
I JUST SEE A CROWD.
YOU'RE DRUNK.
YOU'RE DRUNK!
VIC MY MAN! ANY OF THESE LOSERS HASSLING YOU?

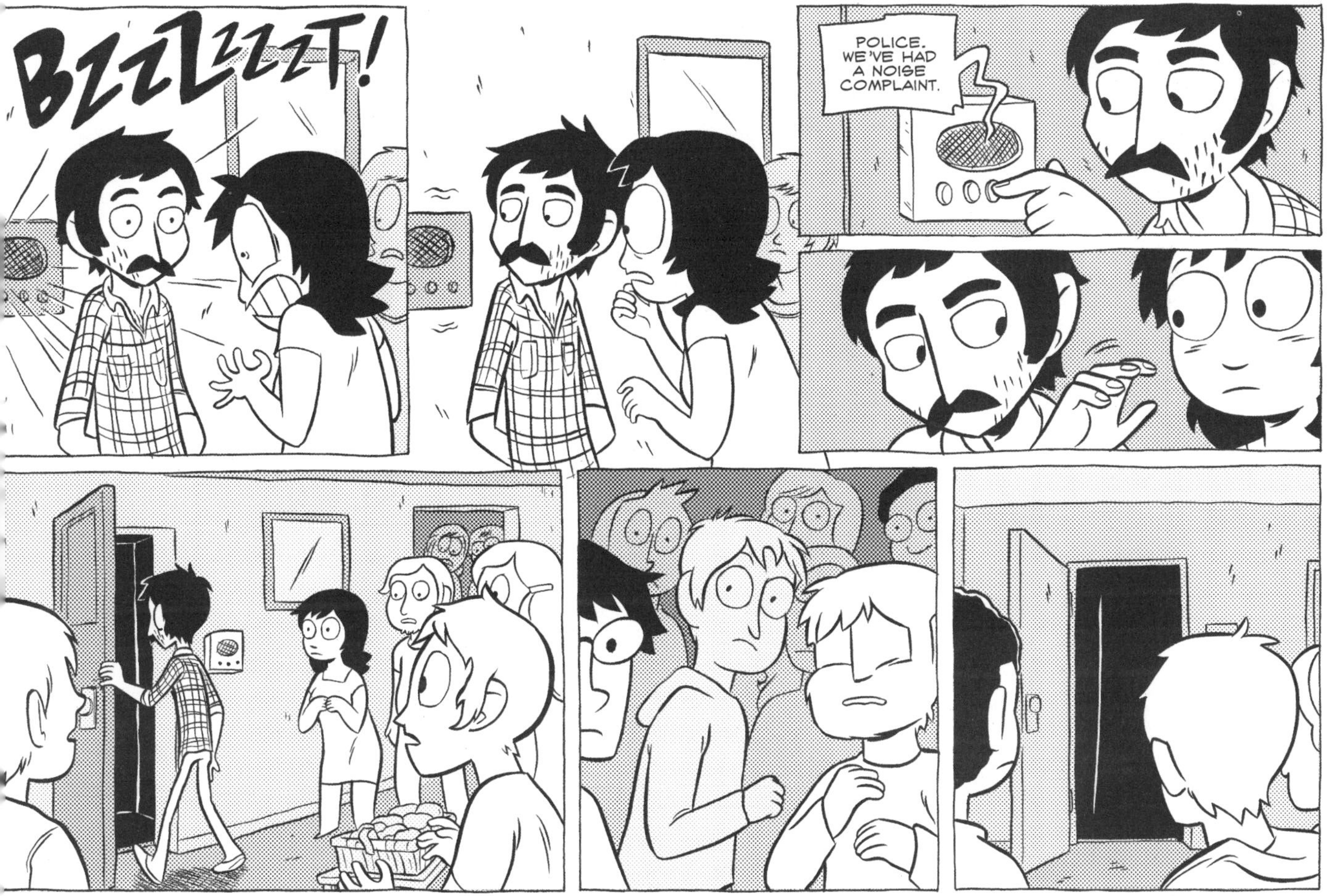
BZZZzzzzT!
POLICE. WE'VE HAD A NOISE COMPLAINT.

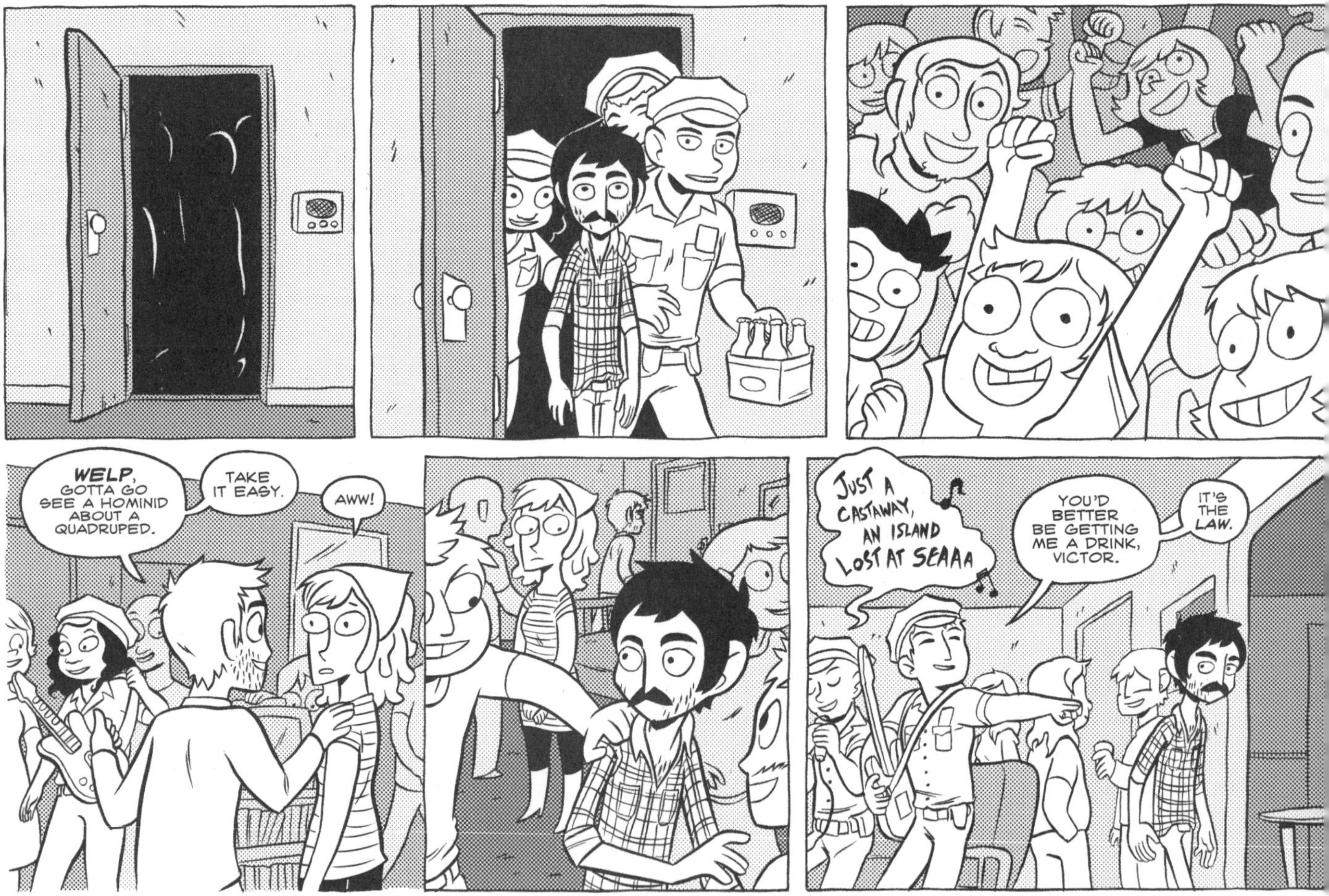
WELP, GOTTA GO SEE A HOMINID ABOUT A QUADRUPED.
TAKE IT EASY.
AWW!
JUST A CASTAWAY, AN ISLAND LOST AT SEAAA
YOU'D BETTER BE GETTING ME A DRINK, VICTOR.
IT'S THE LAW.

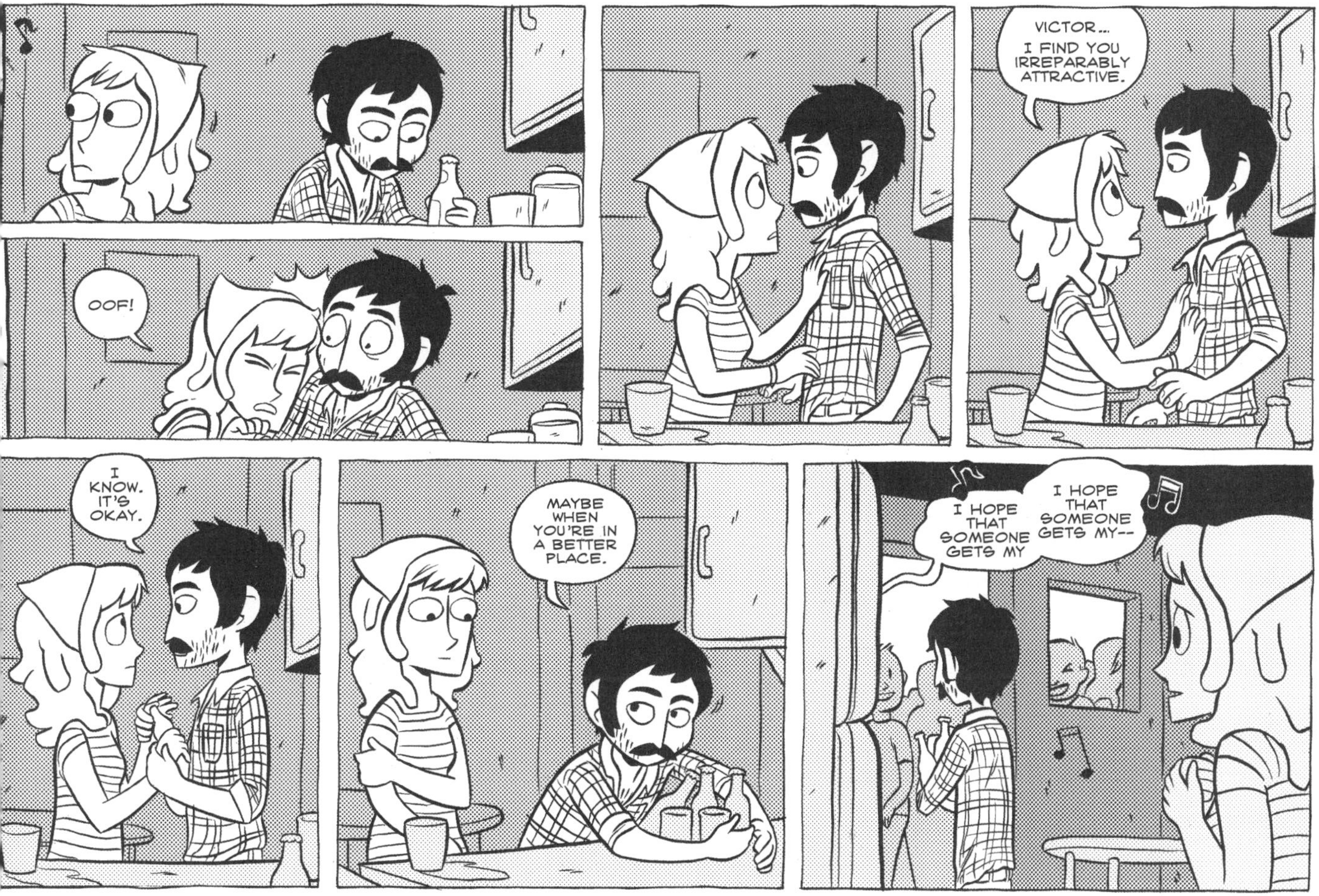
OOF!
VICTOR... I FIND YOU IRREPARABLY ATTRACTIVE.
I KNOW. IT'S OKAY.
MAYBE WHEN YOU'RE IN A BETTER PLACE.
I HOPE THAT SOMEONE GETS MY
I HOPE THAT SOMEONE GETS MY--

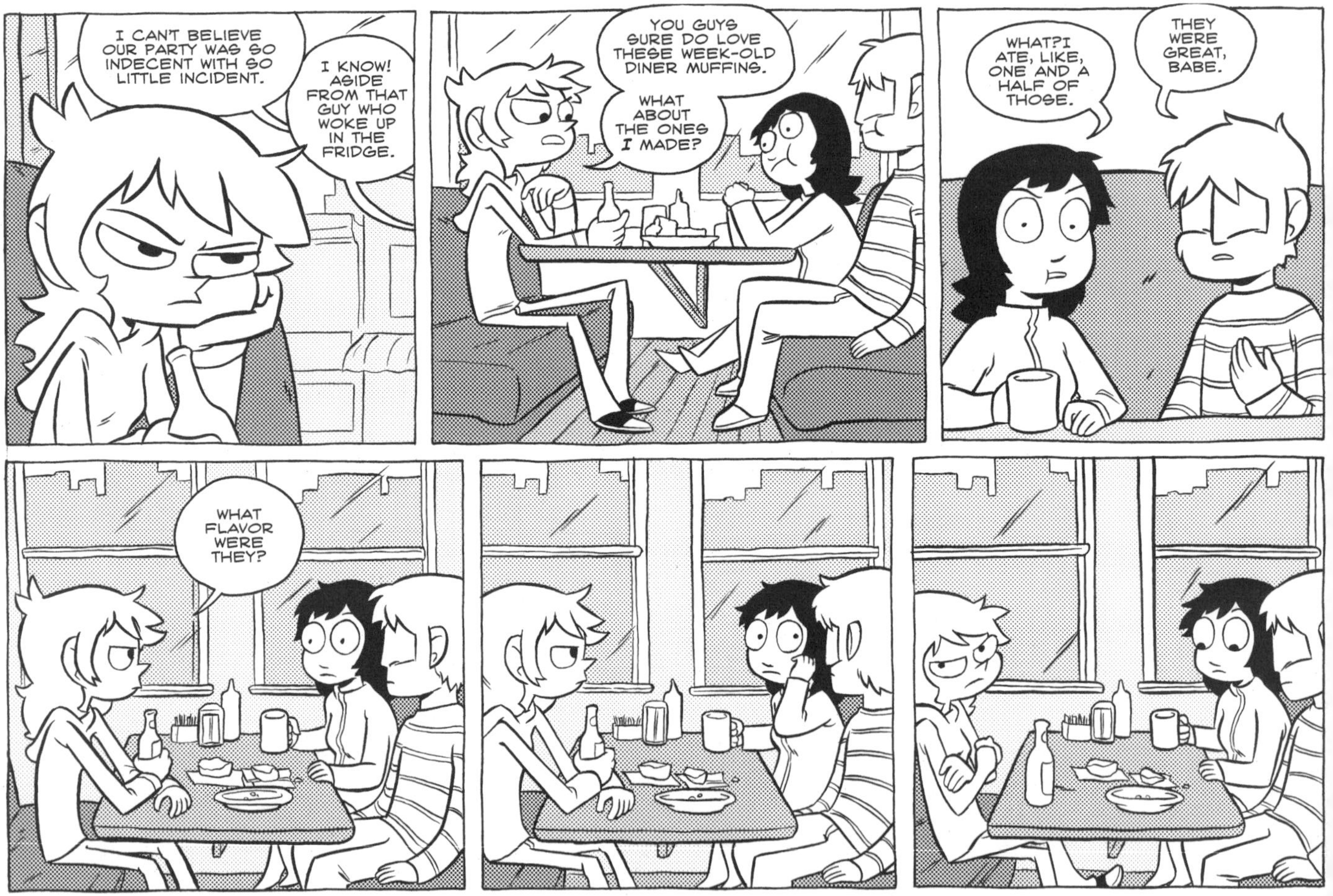
I CAN'T BELIEVE OUR PARTY WAS SO INDECENT WITH SO LITTLE INCIDENT.
I KNOW! ASIDE FROM THAT GUY WHO WOKE UP IN THE FRIDGE.
YOU GUYS SURE DO LOVE THESE WEEK-OLD DINER MUFFINS.
WHAT ABOUT THE ONES I MADE?
WHAT?I ATE, LIKE, ONE AND A HALF OF THOSE.
THEY WERE GREAT, BABE.
WHAT FLAVOR WERE THEY?

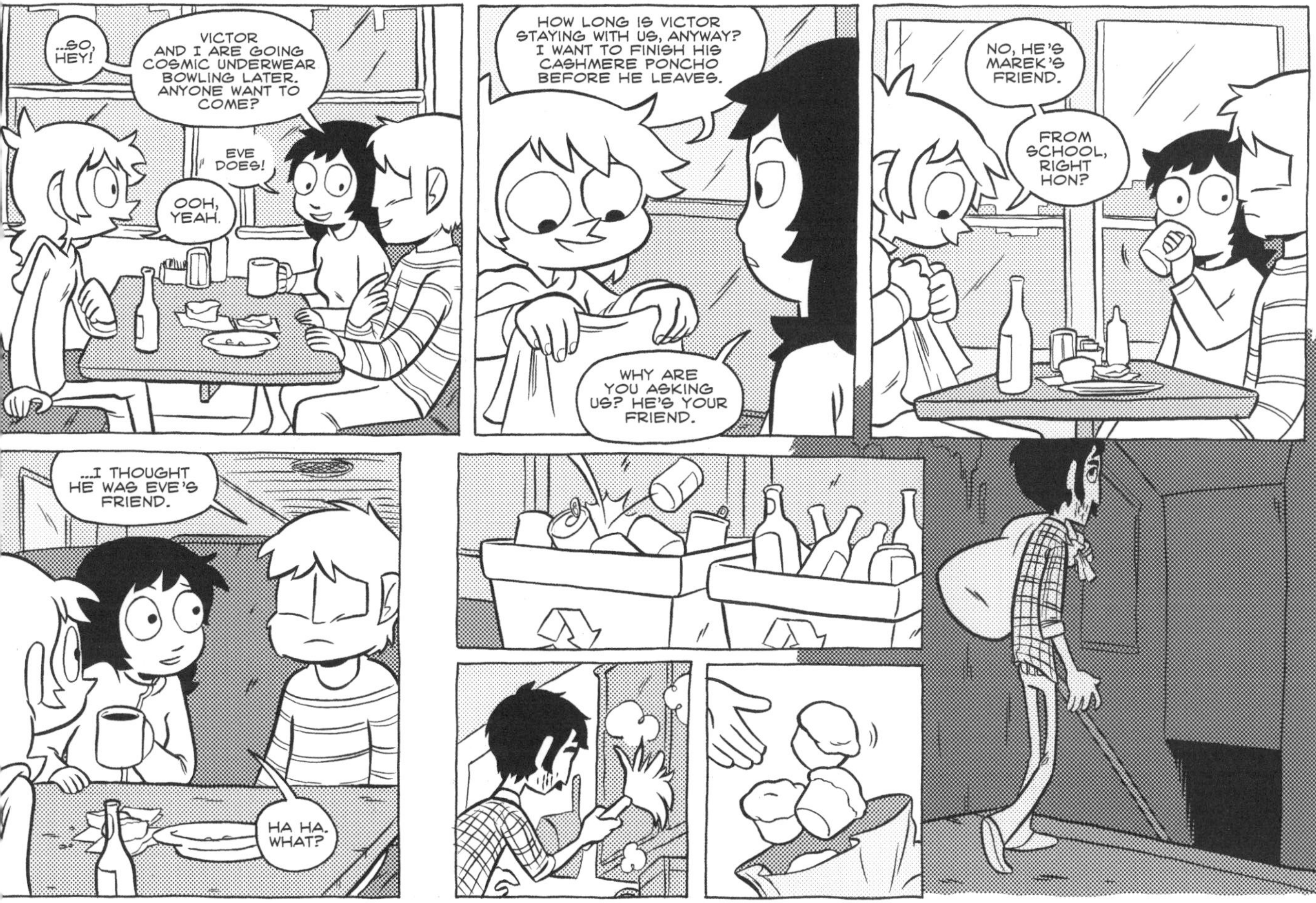
...SO, HEY!
VICTOR AND I ARE GOING COSMIC UNDERWEAR BOWLING LATER. ANYONE WANT TO COME?
EVE DOES!
OOH, YEAH.
HOW LONG IS VICTOR STAYING WITH US, ANYWAY? I WANT TO FINISH HIS CASHMERE PONCHO BEFORE HE LEAVES.
WHY ARE YOU ASKING US? HE'S YOUR FRIEND.
NO, HE'S MAREK'S FRIEND.
FROM SCHOOL, RIGHT HON?
...I THOUGHT HE WAS EVE'S FRIEND.
HA HA. WHAT?

Frontwards

Breakups are never easy stories to write. Done poorly, they feel forced and manipulative. The subject is so universal it's easy to let the reader fill in the blanks. I wanted Eve and Park's breakup to have an individual voice, one that the reader could understand whether they'd been through something similar or not.

The pain of leaving someone behind for life in a different city is a familiar one to me, and I tried to preserve some of that distance-spurred weariness in my characters. Or perhaps I tried to share the burden with them. It felt cathartic.

So much of Eve and Park's relationship is grounded in nostalgia that dropping one final bomb of childhood memories seemed appropriate. Nothing kills nostalgia, after all, like reliving the experience and realizing how crummy it was.

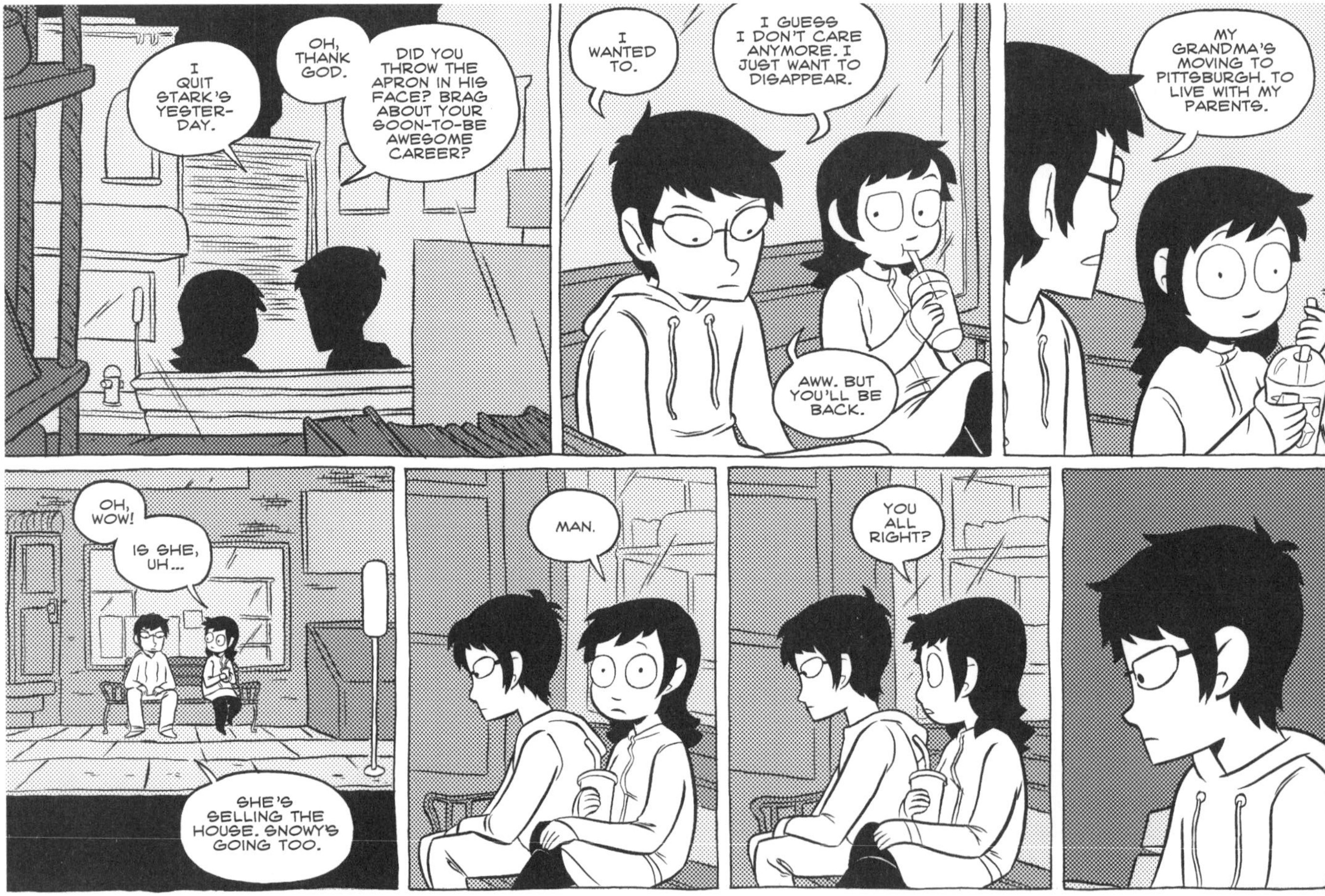
I QUIT STARK'S YESTER-DAY.
OH, THANK GOD.
DID YOU THROW THE APRON IN HIS FACE? BRAG ABOUT YOUR SOON-TO-BE AWESOME CAREER?
I WANTED TO.
I GUESS I DON'T CARE ANYMORE. I JUST WANT TO DISAPPEAR.
AWW. BUT YOU'LL BE BACK.
MY GRANDMA'S MOVING TO PITTSBURGH. TO LIVE WITH MY PARENTS.
OH, WOW!
IS SHE, UH...
SHE'S SELLING THE HOUSE. SNOWY'S GOING TOO.
MAN.
YOU ALL RIGHT?

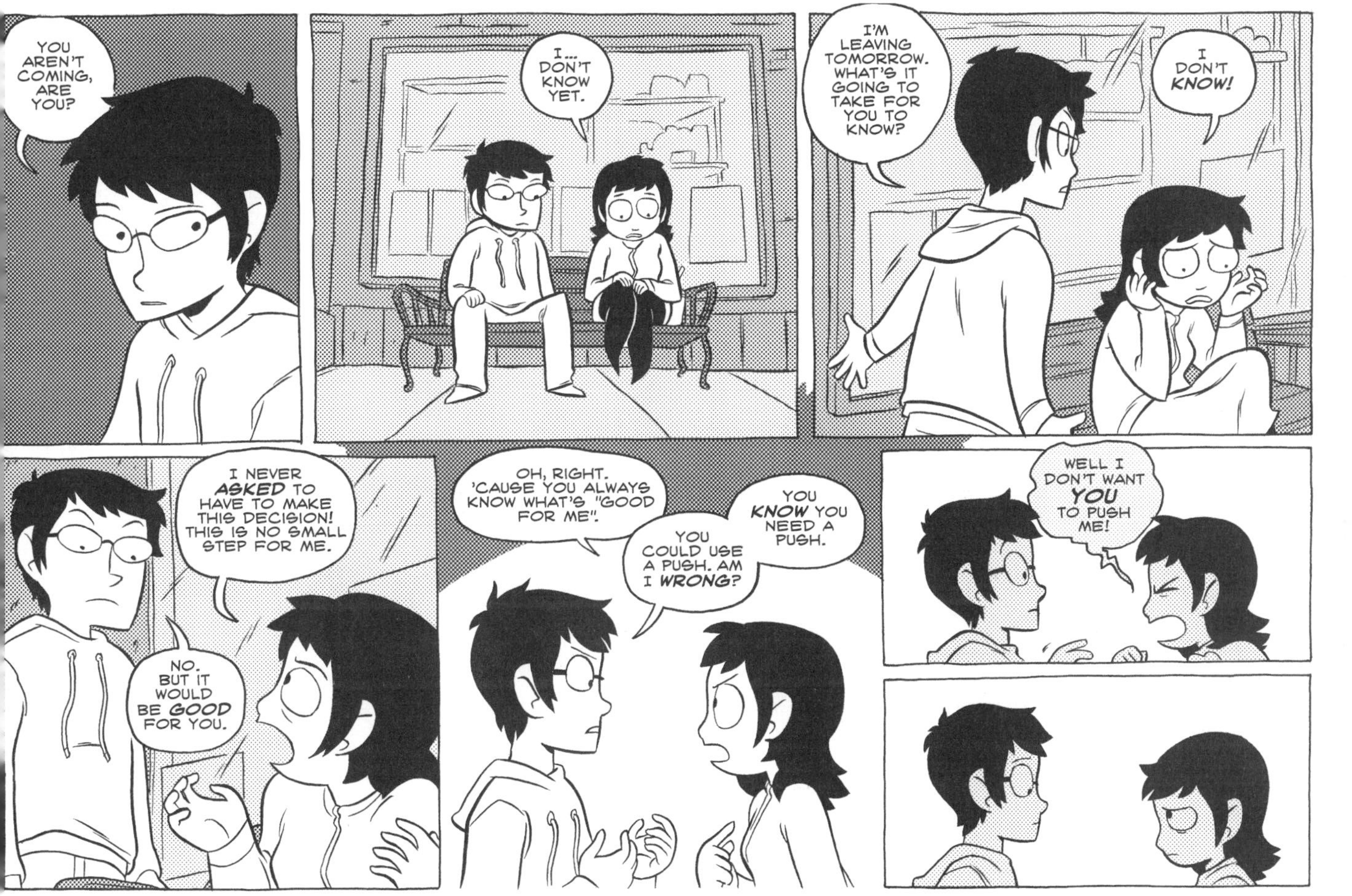
YOU AREN'T COMING, ARE YOU?
I... DON'T KNOW YET.
I'M LEAVING TOMORROW. WHAT'S IT GOING TO TAKE FOR YOU TO KNOW?
I DON'T **KNOW!**
I NEVER **ASKED** TO HAVE TO MAKE THIS DECISION! THIS IS NO SMALL STEP FOR ME.
NO. BUT IT WOULD BE **GOOD** FOR YOU.
OH, RIGHT. 'CAUSE YOU ALWAYS KNOW WHAT'S "GOOD FOR ME".
YOU COULD USE A PUSH. AM I **WRONG**?
YOU **KNOW** YOU NEED A PUSH.
WELL I DON'T WANT **YOU** TO PUSH ME!

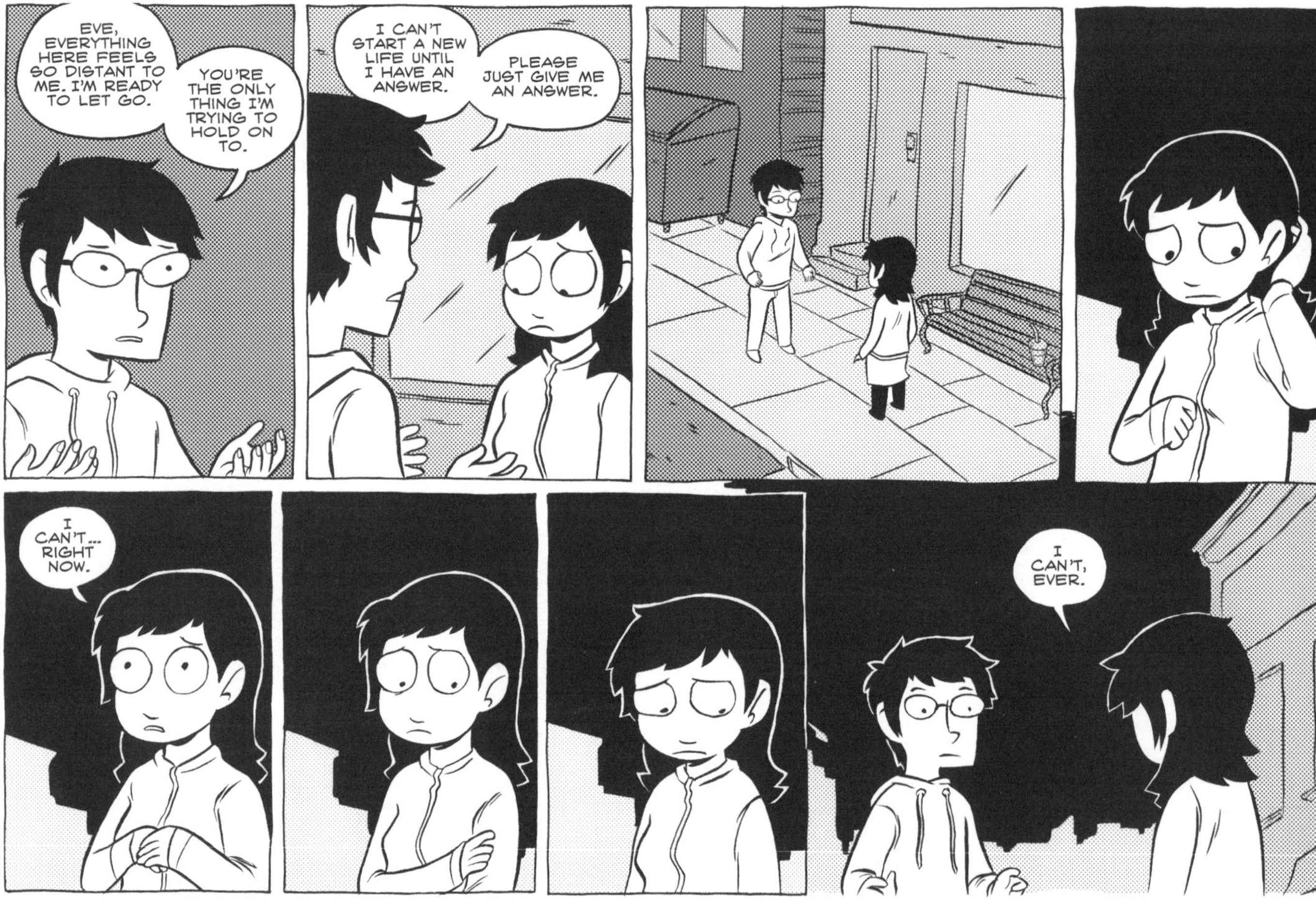
EVE, EVERYTHING HERE FEELS SO DISTANT TO ME. I'M READY TO LET GO.
YOU'RE THE ONLY THING I'M TRYING TO HOLD ON TO.
I CAN'T START A NEW LIFE UNTIL I HAVE AN ANSWER.
PLEASE JUST GIVE ME AN ANSWER.
I CAN'T... RIGHT NOW.
I CAN'T, EVER.

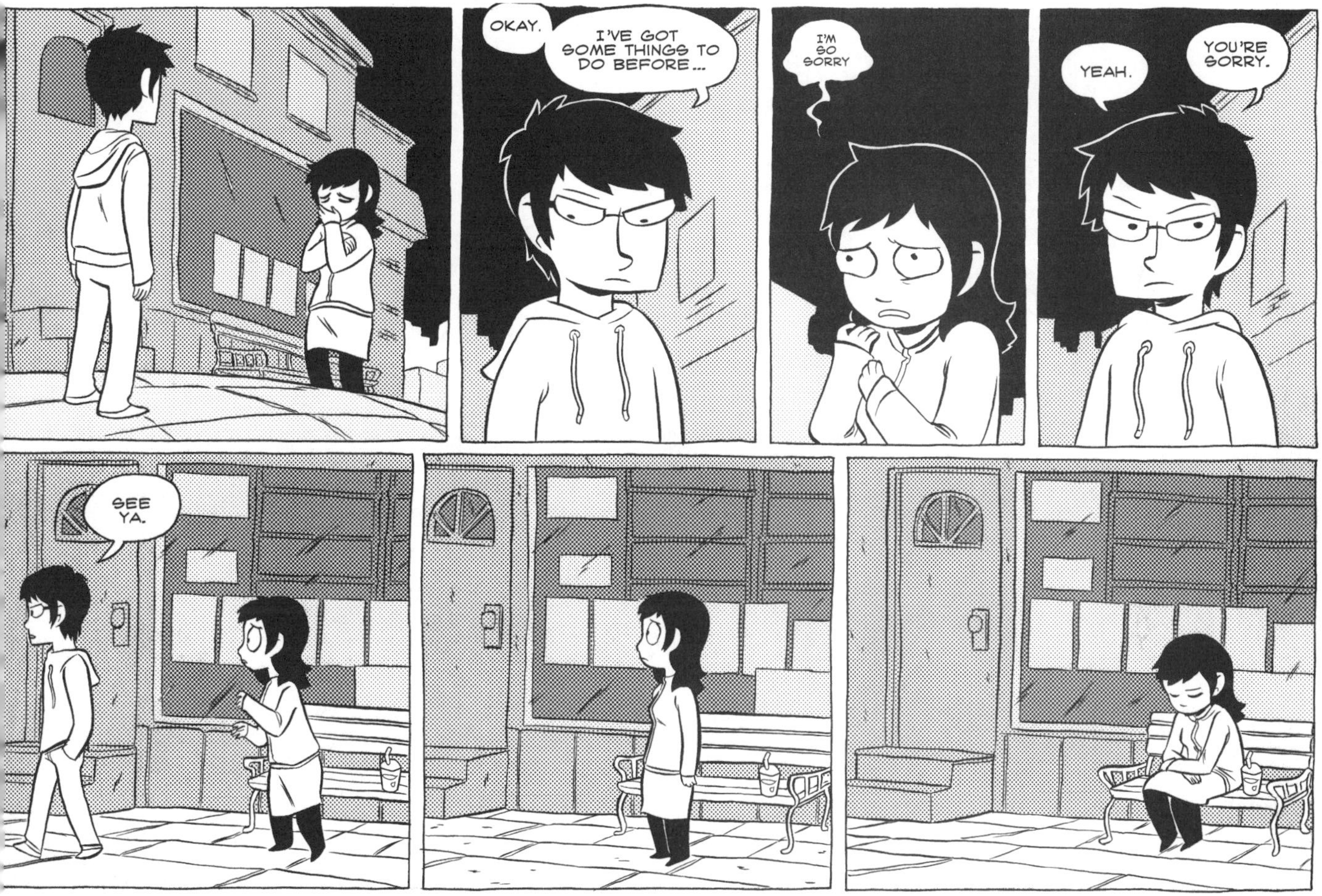
OKAY.
I'VE GOT SOME THINGS TO DO BEFORE...
I'M SO SORRY
YOU'RE SORRY.
YEAH.
SEE YA.

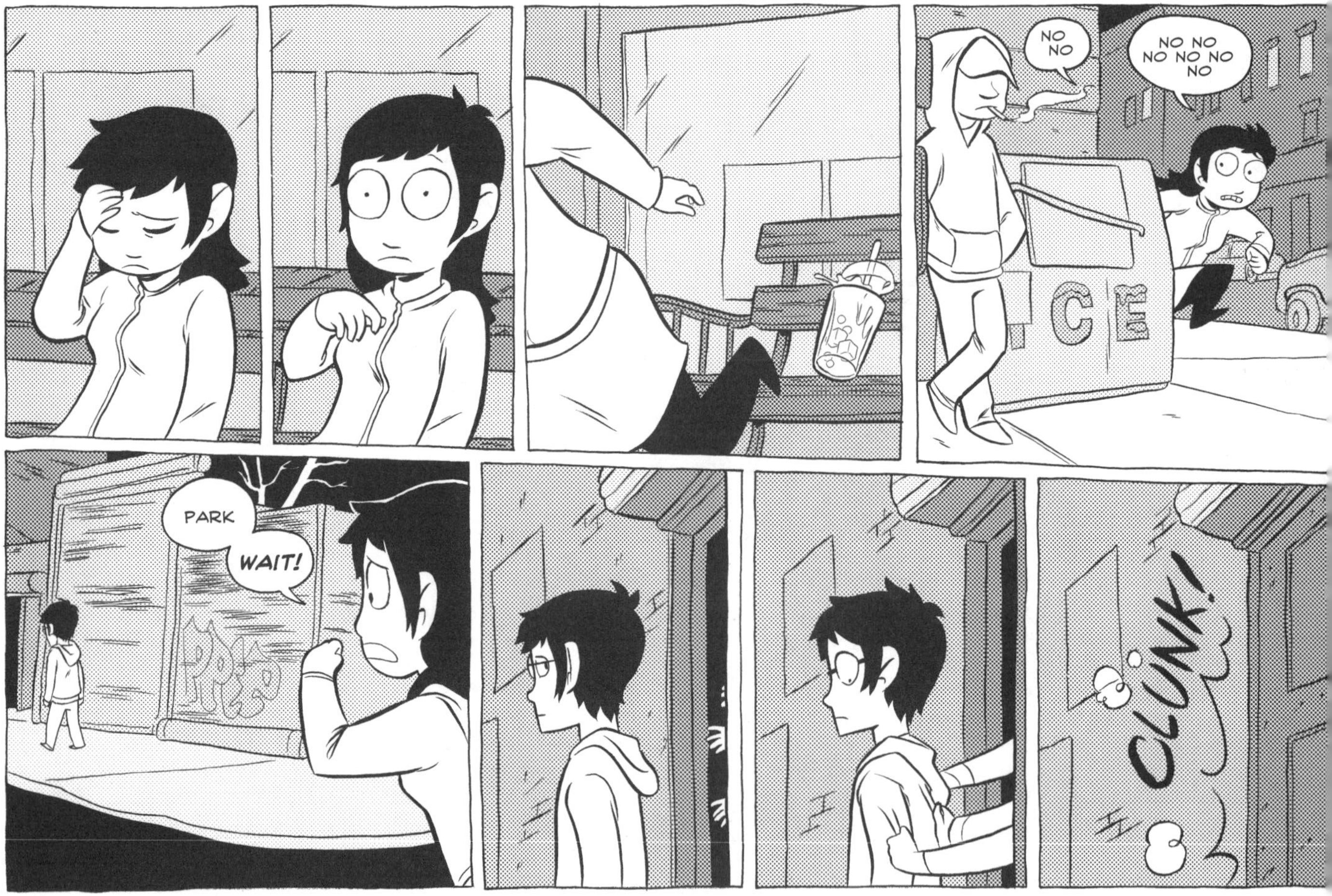
NO
NO
NO NO
NO NO NO
NO
CE
PARK
WAIT!
CLINK!

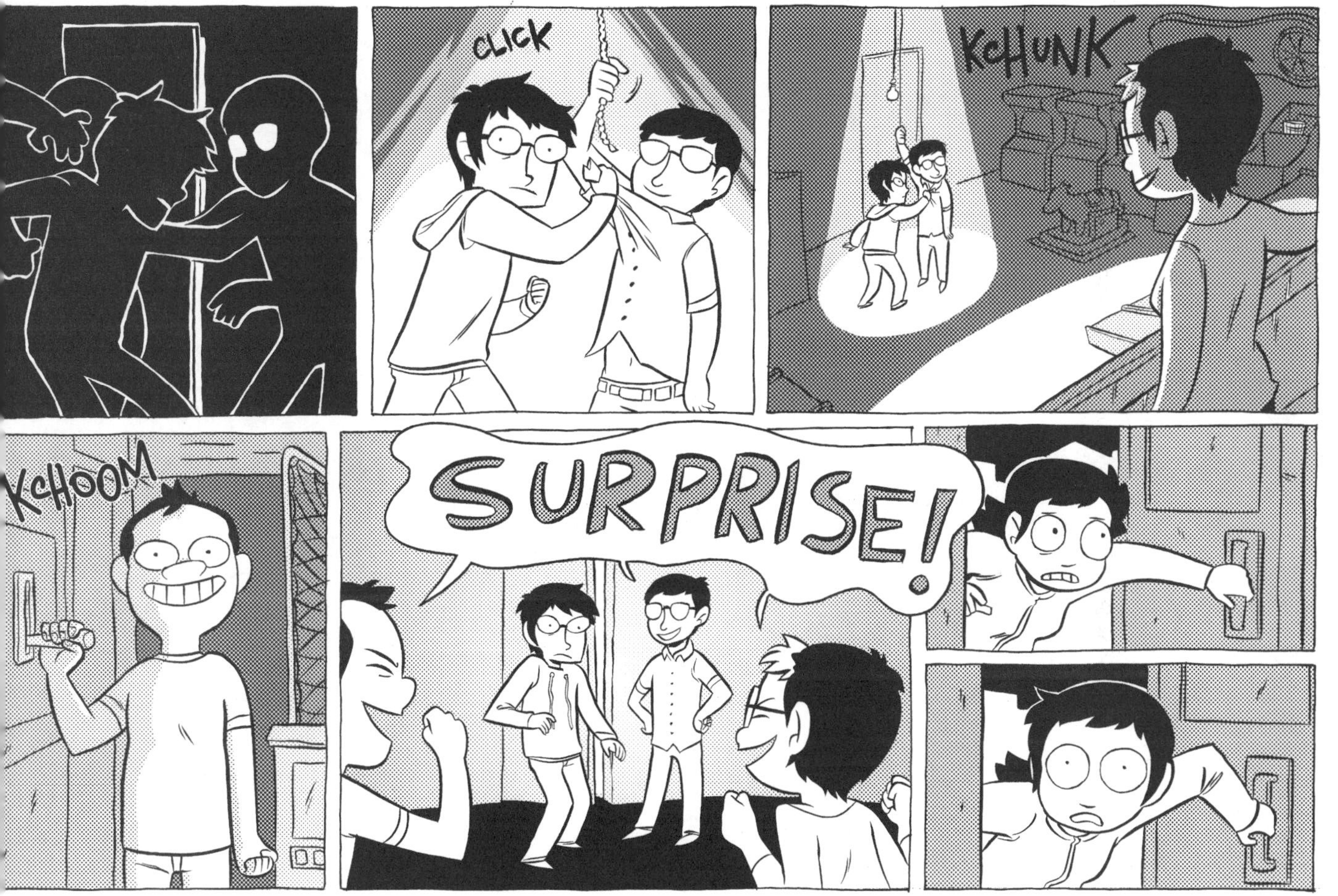
CLICK
KCHUNK
KCHOOM
SURPRISE!

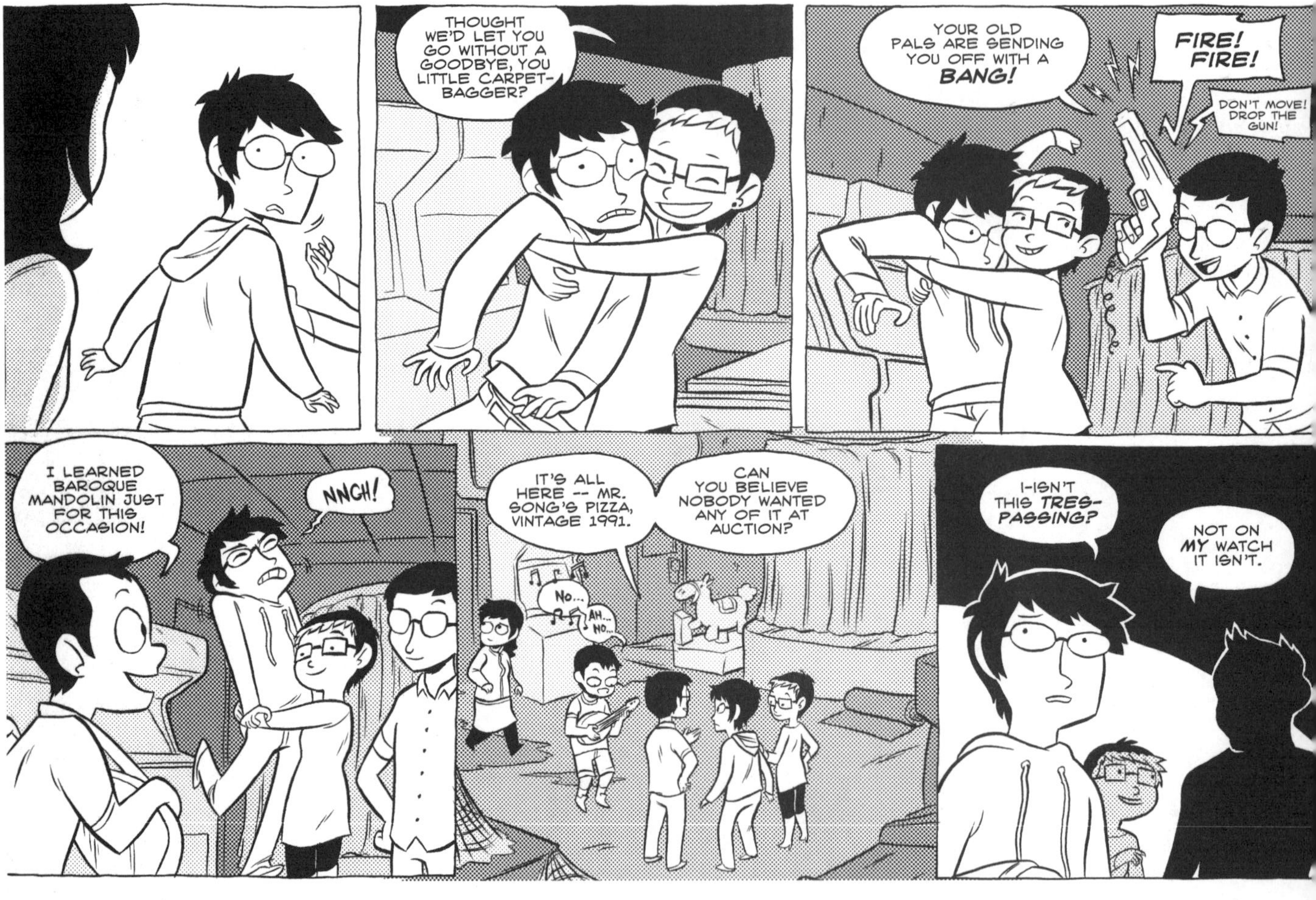

THOUGHT WE'D LET YOU GO WITHOUT A GOODBYE, YOU LITTLE CARPET-BAGGER?
YOUR OLD PALS ARE SENDING YOU OFF WITH A **BANG!**
FIRE! FIRE!
DON'T MOVE! DROP THE GUN!
I LEARNED BAROQUE MANDOLIN JUST FOR THIS OCCASION!
NNGH!
IT'S ALL HERE -- MR. SONG'S PIZZA, VINTAGE 1991.
CAN YOU BELIEVE NOBODY WANTED ANY OF IT AT AUCTION?
No...
AH... NO...
I-ISN'T THIS *TRES-PASSING?*
NOT ON *MY* WATCH IT ISN'T.

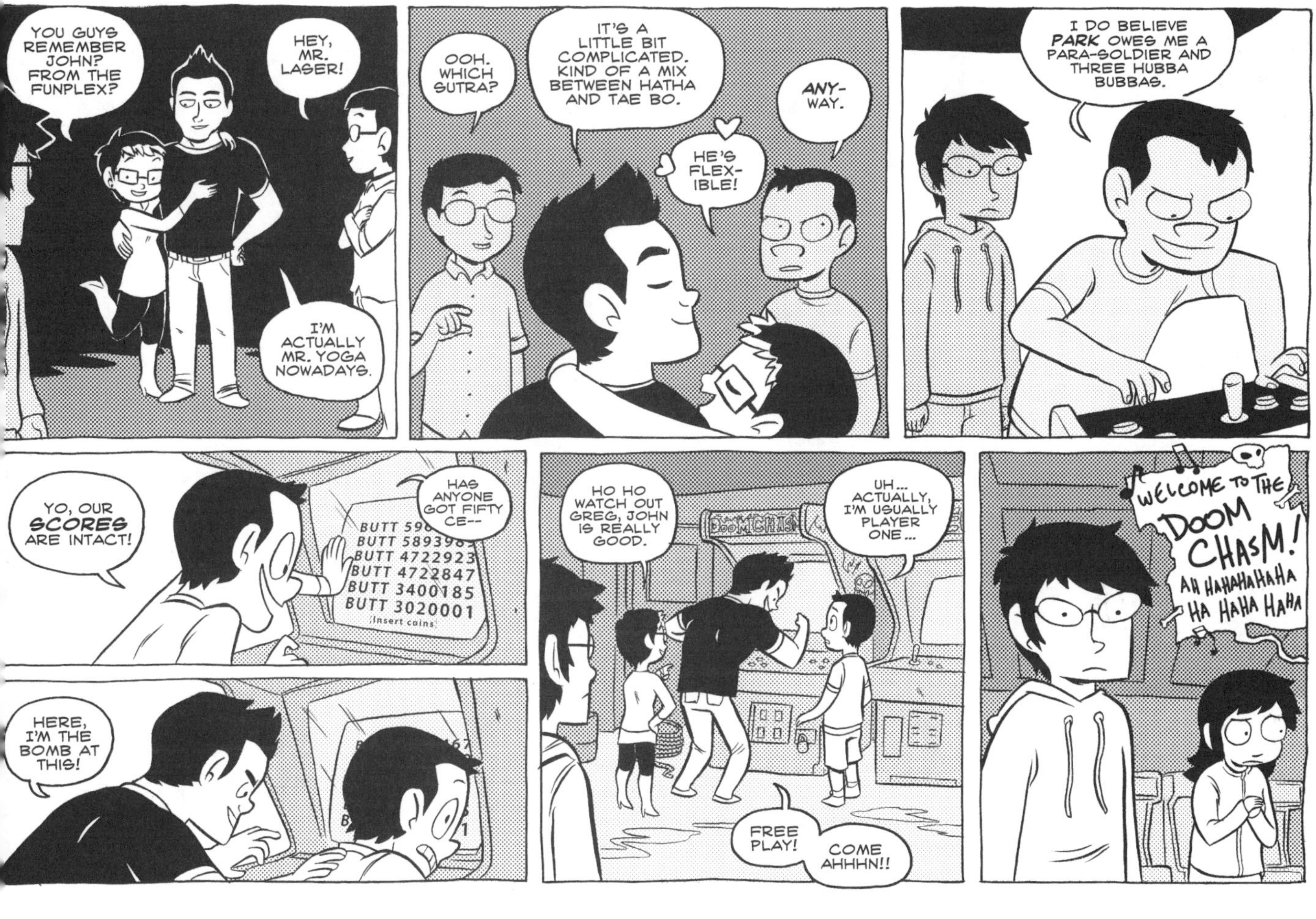
YOU GUYS REMEMBER JOHN? FROM THE FUNPLEX?
HEY, MR. LASER!
I'M ACTUALLY MR. YOGA NOWADAYS.
OOH. WHICH SUTRA?
IT'S A LITTLE BIT COMPLICATED. KIND OF A MIX BETWEEN HATHA AND TAE BO.
HE'S FLEX-IBLE!
ANY-WAY.
I DO BELIEVE PARK OWES ME A PARA-SOLDIER AND THREE HUBBA BUBBAS.
YO, OUR SCORES ARE INTACT!
HAS ANYONE GOT FIFTY CE--
BUTT 589398
BUTT 4722923
BUTT 4722847
BUTT 3400185
BUTT 3020001
Insert coins
HERE, I'M THE BOMB AT THIS!
HO HO WATCH OUT GREG, JOHN IS REALLY GOOD.
UH... ACTUALLY, I'M USUALLY PLAYER ONE...
DOOM CHASM
FREE PLAY!
COME AHHHN!!
WELCOME TO THE DOOM CHASM! AH HAHAHAHAHA HA HAHA HAHA

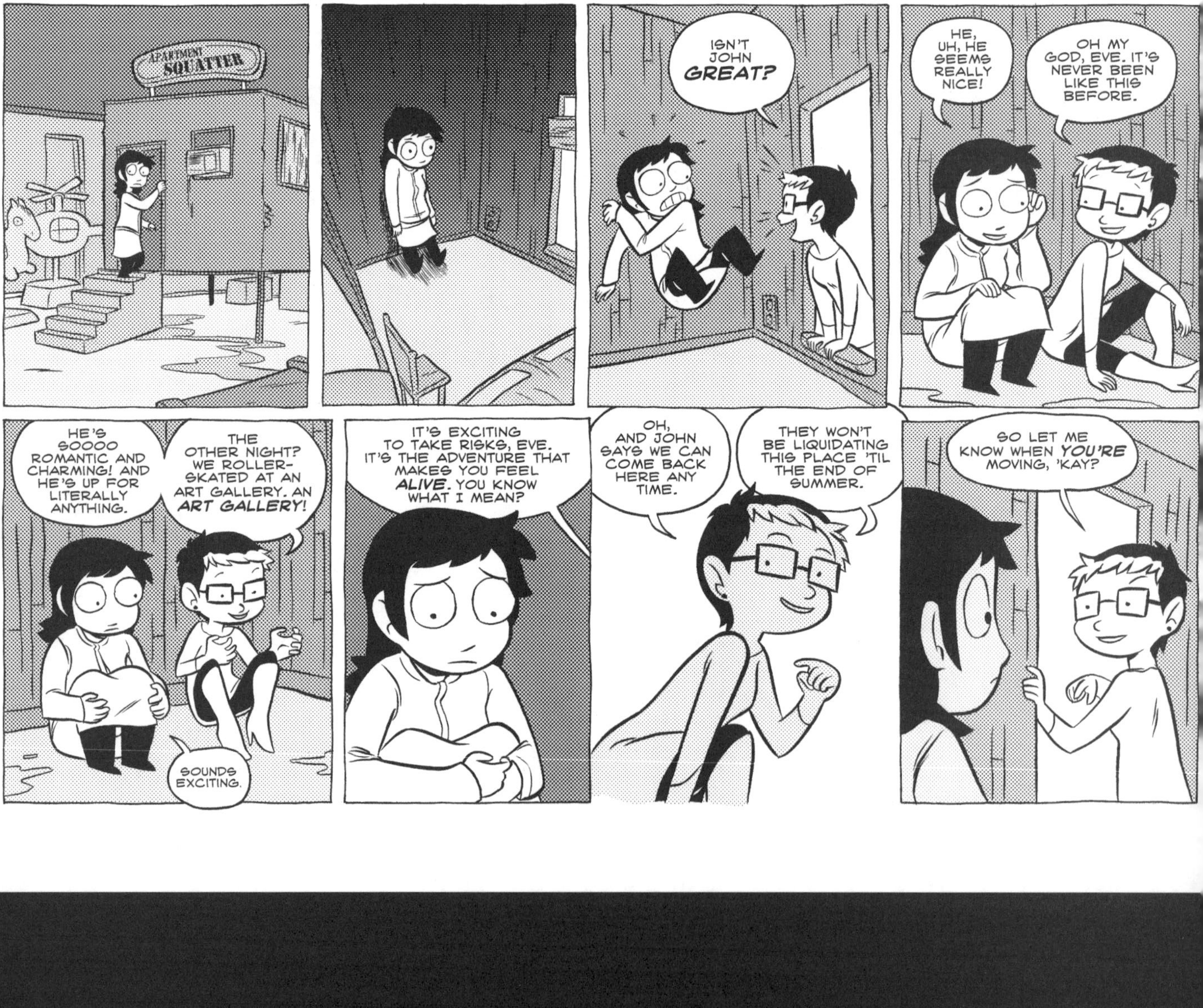
APARTMENT SQUATTER
ISN'T JOHN GREAT?
HE, UH, HE SEEMS REALLY NICE!
OH MY GOD, EVE. IT'S NEVER BEEN LIKE THIS BEFORE.
HE'S SOOOO ROMANTIC AND CHARMING! AND HE'S UP FOR LITERALLY ANYTHING.
THE OTHER NIGHT? WE ROLLER-SKATED AT AN ART GALLERY. AN ART GALLERY!
SOUNDS EXCITING.
IT'S EXCITING TO TAKE RISKS, EVE. IT'S THE ADVENTURE THAT MAKES YOU FEEL ALIVE. YOU KNOW WHAT I MEAN?
OH, AND JOHN SAYS WE CAN COME BACK HERE ANY TIME.
THEY WON'T BE LIQUIDATING THIS PLACE 'TIL THE END OF SUMMER.
SO LET ME KNOW WHEN YOU'RE MOVING, 'KAY?

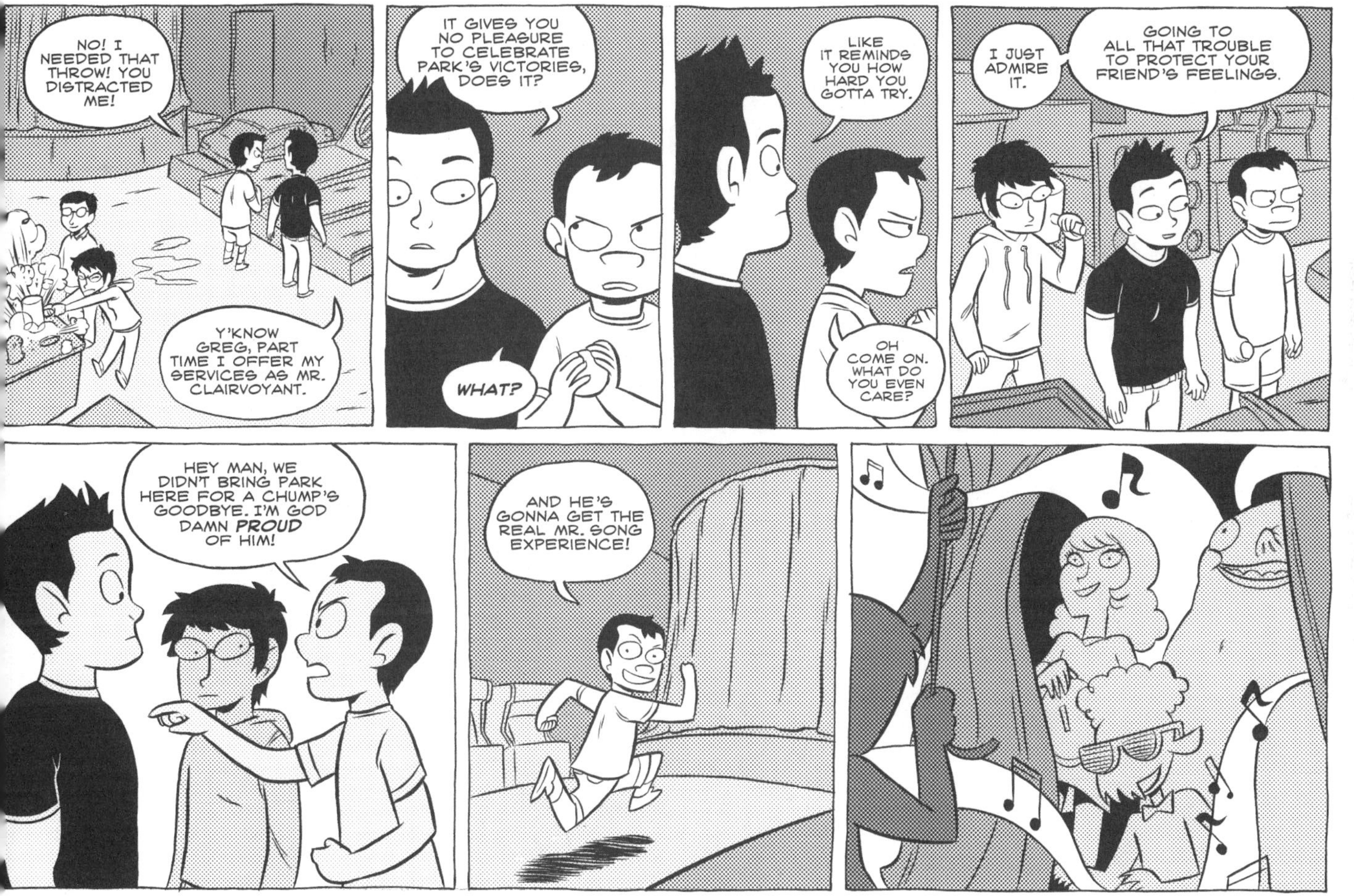
NO! I NEEDED THAT THROW! YOU DISTRACTED ME!
Y'KNOW GREG, PART TIME I OFFER MY SERVICES AS MR. CLAIRVOYANT.
IT GIVES YOU NO PLEASURE TO CELEBRATE PARK'S VICTORIES, DOES IT?
WHAT?
LIKE IT REMINDS YOU HOW HARD YOU GOTTA TRY.
OH COME ON. WHAT DO YOU EVEN CARE?
I JUST ADMIRE IT.
GOING TO ALL THAT TROUBLE TO PROTECT YOUR FRIEND'S FEELINGS.
HEY MAN, WE DIDN'T BRING PARK HERE FOR A CHUMP'S GOODBYE. I'M GOD DAMN PROUD OF HIM!
AND HE'S GONNA GET THE REAL MR. SONG EXPERIENCE!

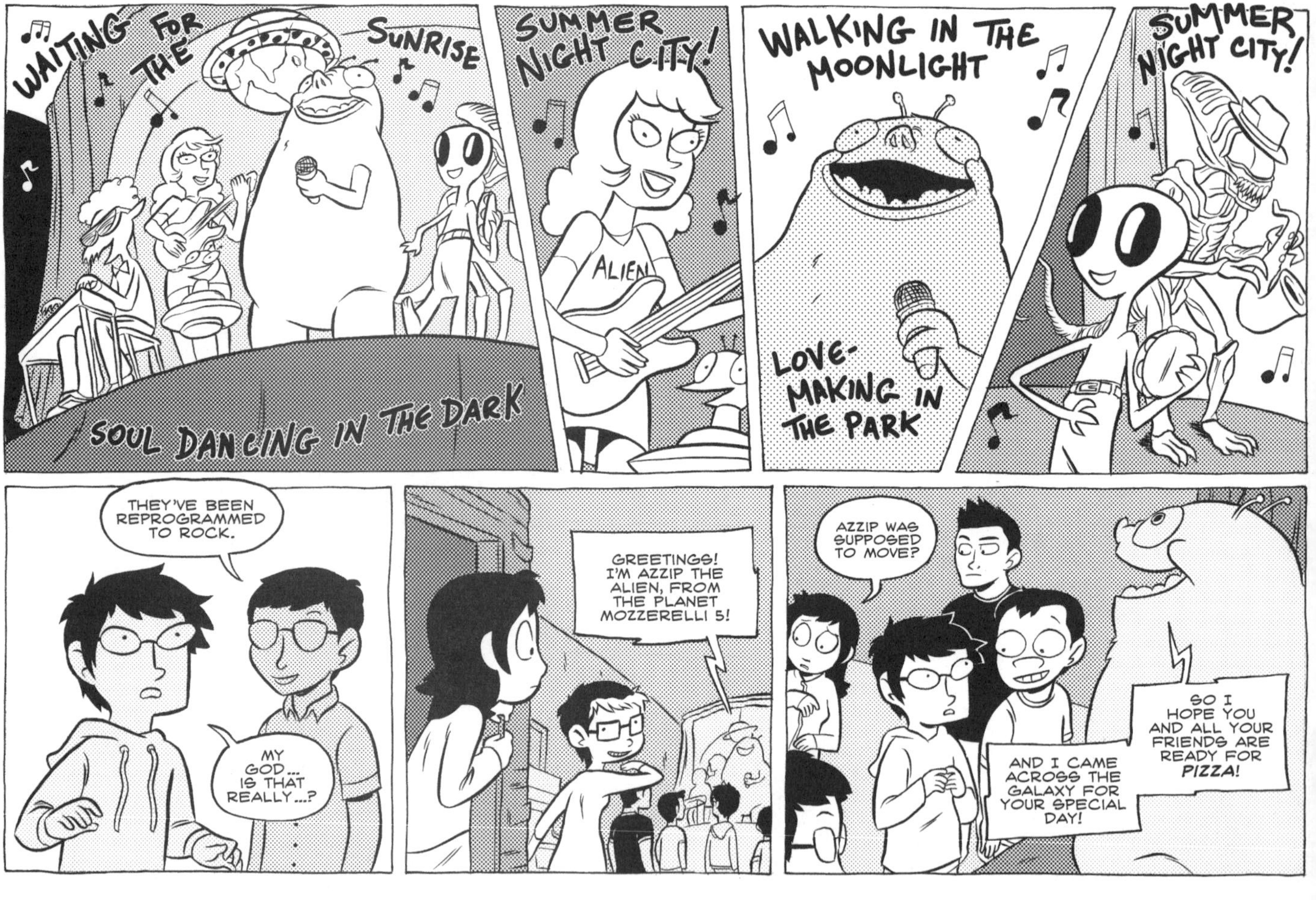
WAITING FOR THE
SUNRISE
SOUL DANCING IN THE DARK
SUMMER NIGHT CITY!
ALIEN
WALKING IN THE MOONLIGHT
LOVE-MAKING IN THE PARK
SUMMER NIGHT CITY!
THEY'VE BEEN REPROGRAMMED TO ROCK.
MY GOD... IS THAT REALLY...?
GREETINGS! I'M AZZIP THE ALIEN, FROM THE PLANET MOZZERELLI 5!
AZZIP WAS SUPPOSED TO MOVE?
AND I CAME ACROSS THE GALAXY FOR YOUR SPECIAL DAY!
SO I HOPE YOU AND ALL YOUR FRIENDS ARE READY FOR PIZZA!

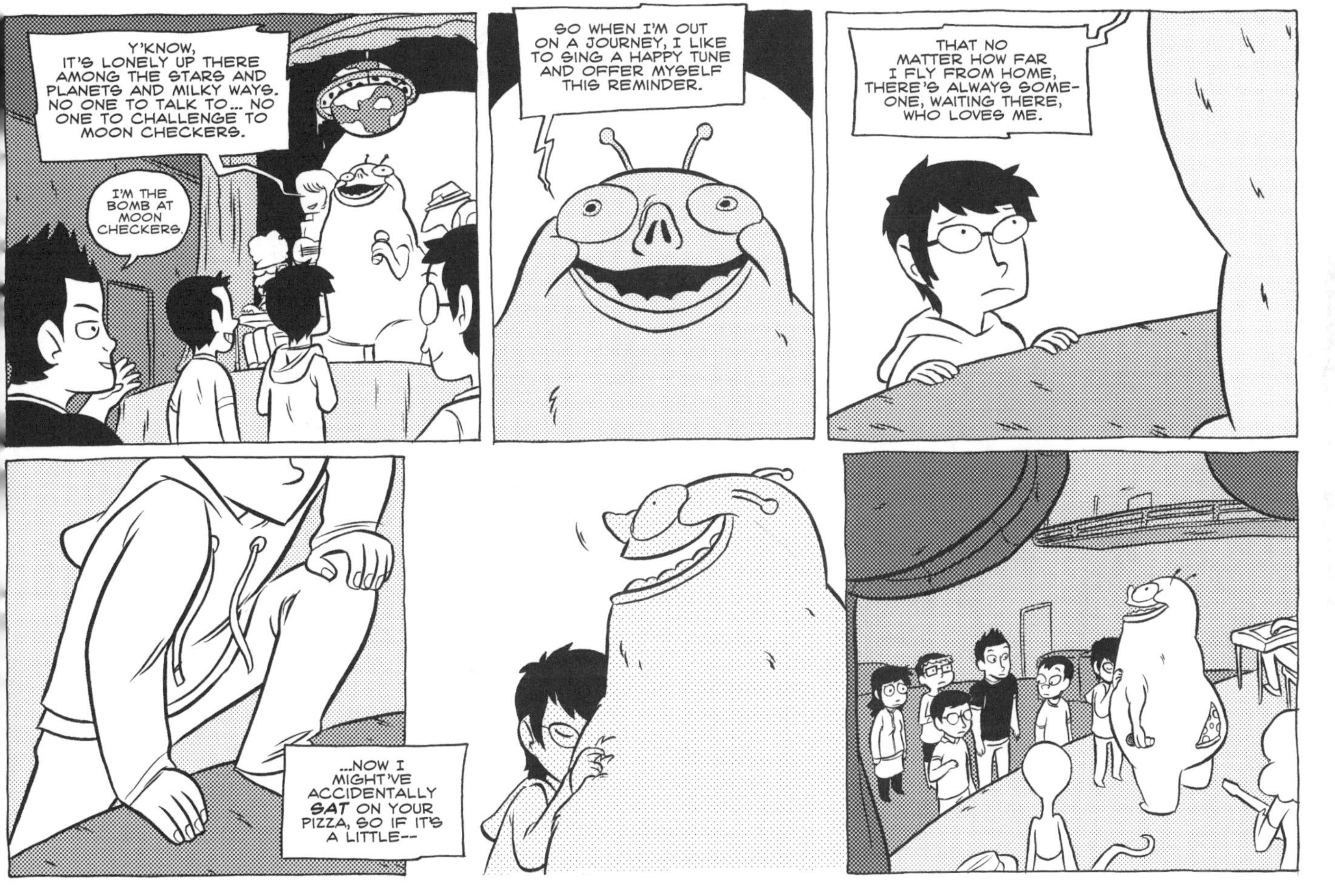
Y'KNOW, IT'S LONELY UP THERE AMONG THE STARS AND PLANETS AND MILKY WAYS. NO ONE TO TALK TO... NO ONE TO CHALLENGE TO MOON CHECKERS.
I'M THE BOMB AT MOON CHECKERS.
SO WHEN I'M OUT ON A JOURNEY, I LIKE TO SING A HAPPY TUNE AND OFFER MYSELF THIS REMINDER.
THAT NO MATTER HOW FAR I FLY FROM HOME, THERE'S ALWAYS SOME-ONE, WAITING THERE, WHO LOVES ME.
...NOW I MIGHT'VE ACCIDENTALLY SAT ON YOUR PIZZA, SO IF IT'S A LITTLE--

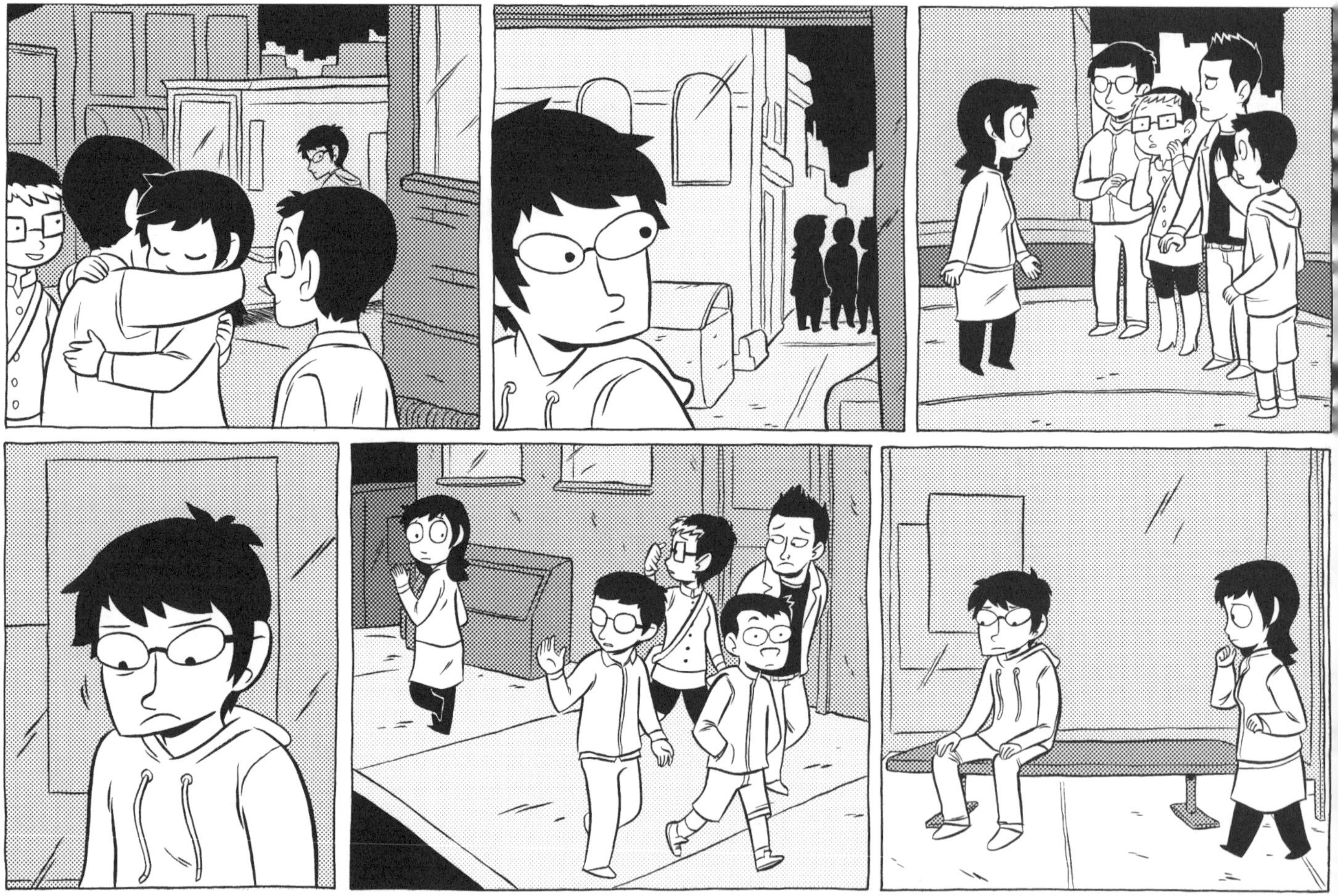

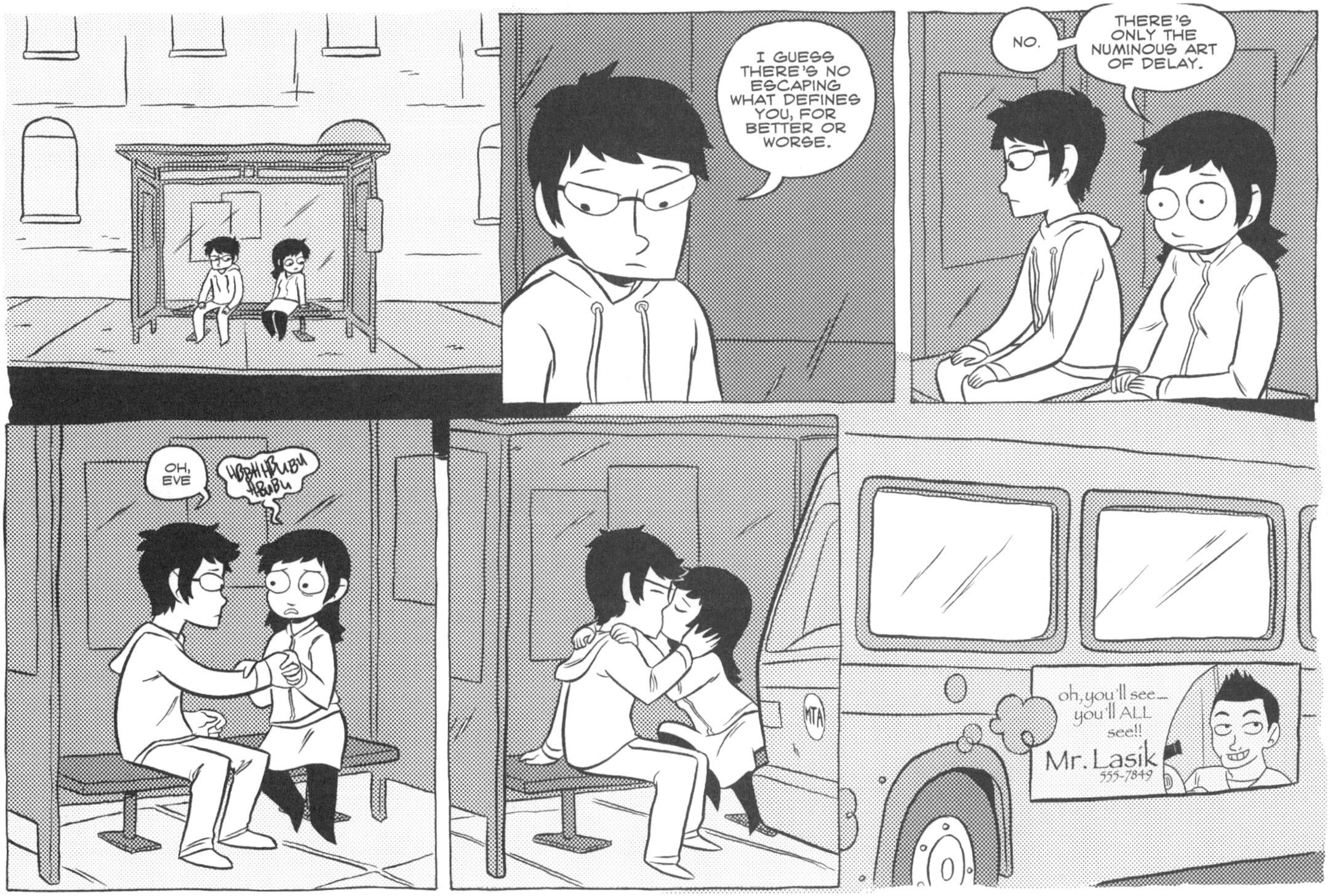
I GUESS THERE'S NO ESCAPING WHAT DEFINES YOU, FOR BETTER OR WORSE.
NO.
THERE'S ONLY THE NUMINOUS ART OF DELAY.
OH, EVE
MTA
oh, you'll see... you'll ALL see!!
Mr. Lasik
555-7849

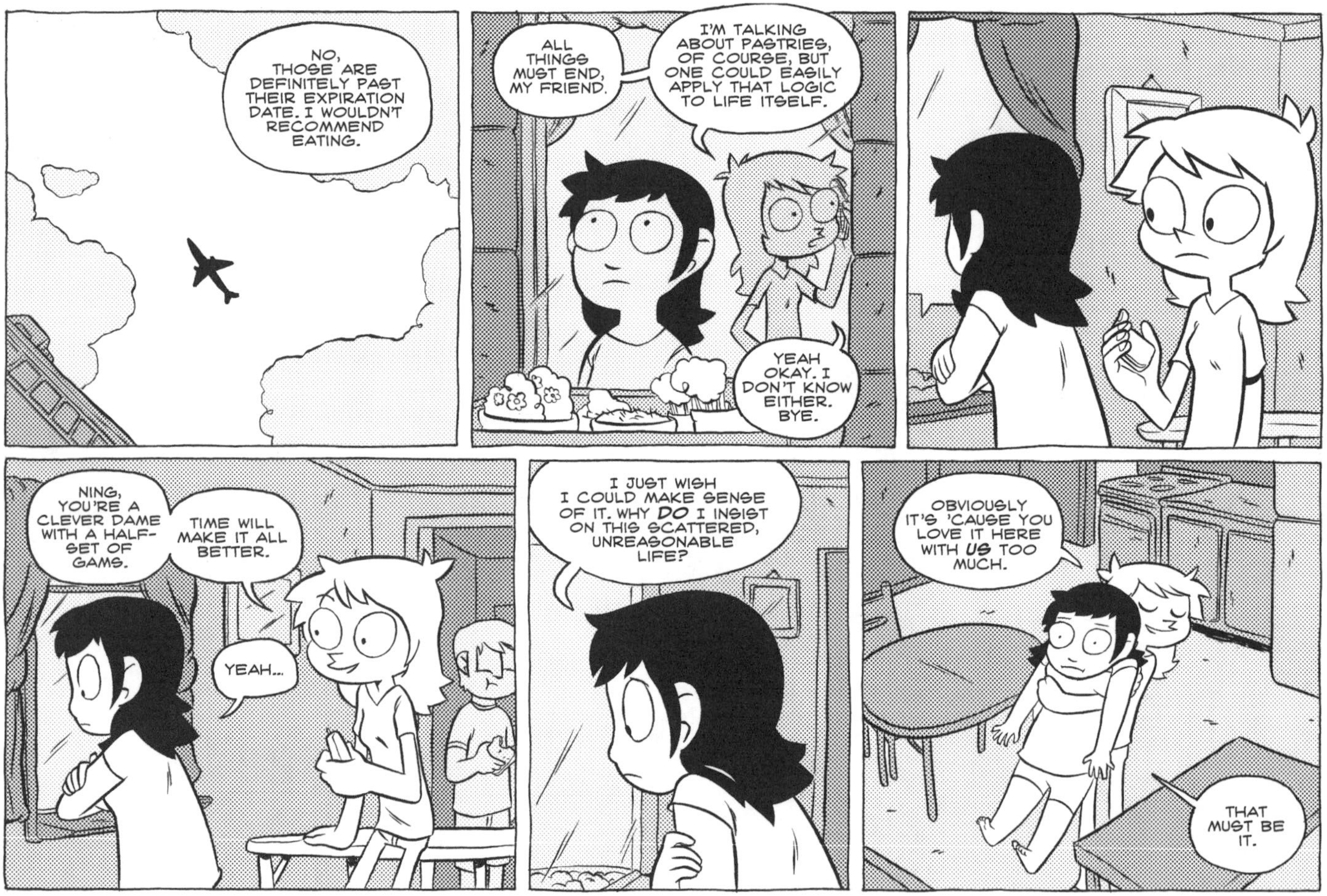
NO, THOSE ARE DEFINITELY PAST THEIR EXPIRATION DATE. I WOULDN'T RECOMMEND EATING.
ALL THINGS MUST END, MY FRIEND.
I'M TALKING ABOUT PASTRIES, OF COURSE, BUT ONE COULD EASILY APPLY THAT LOGIC TO LIFE ITSELF.
YEAH OKAY. I DON'T KNOW EITHER. BYE.
NING, YOU'RE A CLEVER DAME WITH A HALF-SET OF GAMS.
TIME WILL MAKE IT ALL BETTER.
YEAH...
I JUST WISH I COULD MAKE SENSE OF IT. WHY DO I INSIST ON THIS SCATTERED, UNREASONABLE LIFE?
OBVIOUSLY IT'S 'CAUSE YOU LOVE IT HERE WITH US TOO MUCH.
THAT MUST BE IT.

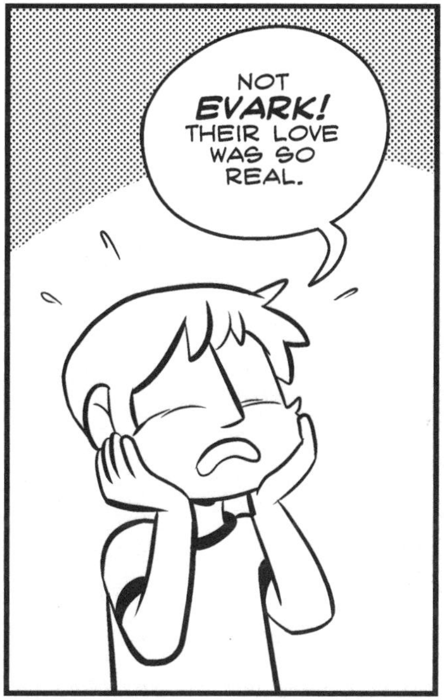
NOT **EVARK!** THEIR LOVE WAS SO REAL.

Meredith Gran barely brought enough carrots for herself,
so she's not sure why she even needs to apologize.

She currently resides in Brooklyn, New York with her dog Heidi.